Language Depı
Deaf Mental Healtn

MW00845091

Language Deprivation and Deaf Mental Health explores the impact of the language deprivation that some deaf individuals experience by not being provided fully accessible language exposure during childhood. Leading experts in Deaf mental health care discuss the implications of language deprivation for a person's development, communication, cognitive abilities, behavior, and mental health. Beginning with a groundbreaking discussion of language deprivation syndrome, the chapters address the challenges of psychotherapy, interpreting, communication and forensic assessment, language and communication development with language-deprived persons, as well as whether cochlear implantation means deaf children should not receive rich sign language exposure. The book concludes with a discussion of the most effective advocacy strategies to prevent language deprivation. These issues, which draw on both cultural and disability perspectives, are central to the emerging clinical specialty of Deaf mental health.

Neil S. Glickman, PhD, is a former unit director and psychologist with the Deaf Unit at Westborough State Hospital and a former psychologist with Advocates Deaf Services in Framingham, Massachusetts. He is currently on the faculty of the University of Massachusetts Medical School and has a private psychotherapy practice. He teaches and consults about Deaf mental health and applications of cognitive behavioral therapy for persons with language and learning challenges.

Wyatte C. Hall, PhD, is an alumnus of the Rochester Institute of Technology and Gallaudet University. After completing a clinical fellowship at University of Massachusetts Medical School, he became a postdoctoral fellow in the University of Rochester Medical Center. His postdoctoral and future faculty-level research focuses on deaf population disparities and the relationship between childhood language experiences and lifelong health outcomes in particular.

"This is the go-to blueprint for anyone providing services to language-challenged individuals who are deaf. In this groundbreaking book, Glickman and Hall, together with a stellar list of contributors, bring you face to face with the ubiquitous nature of language deprivation and show you how it affects the lives of Deaf children and adults. The sage advice and guidance they provide can only enhance the quality of your work with this unique population, whatever your specialization."

Irene W. Leigh, PhD, professor emerita,
Department of Psychology, Gallaudet University

"Language deprivation is a worldwide occurrence with catastrophic consequences for Deaf people. Moreover, it is arguably the most controversial and misunderstood clinical syndrome that could be eradicated with better understanding of its origin and by creating smart public policy. *Language Deprivation and Deaf Mental Health* and its contributors raise numerous crucial issues to address this preventable syndrome and offer many innovative strategies to utilize in mental health, educational, and legal settings."

John Gournaris, PhD, director, Mental Health Program,
Minnesota Department of Human Services,
Deaf and Hard of Hearing Services Division

"*Language Deprivation and Deaf Mental Health* addresses the serious consequences for Deaf people who were not exposed to or could not acquire language fluency. It includes a wealth of clinical information and research findings along with cultural and social justice perspectives. Furthermore, this discussion is set thoughtfully in the current rendition of the oralist-manualist debate: should children with a cochlear implant use sign language? This is a must read for anyone working with Deaf people."

Patrick J. Brice, PhD, professor of psychology,
Gallaudet University

"*Language Deprivation and Deaf Mental Health* pulls together cutting-edge work in the burgeoning field of language deprivation and presents a groundbreaking reframing of the primary issues Deaf people face: Access to language—not sound—is fundamental to healthy development."

Naomi K. Caselli, PhD, assistant professor,
Programs in Deaf Studies, Wheelock College of Education and
Human Development, Boston University

"Drs. Glickman and Hall, nationally recognized pioneers in advancing the mental health care of Deaf people, have assembled a powerful, diverse group of experts to advance our understanding of the birth-to-adulthood nuances and implications of language deprivation syndrome among so many Deaf individuals. This book is essential reading for Deaf leaders, parents of Deaf children, educators, rehabilitation, and mental health professional in the service of Deaf people."

William P. McCrone, EdD, JD, professor emeritus of counseling,
Gallaudet University

Language Deprivation and Deaf Mental Health

Edited by Neil S. Glickman and
Wyatte C. Hall

Routledge
Taylor & Francis Group

NEW YORK AND LONDON

First published 2019
by Routledge
711 Third Avenue, New York, NY 10017

and by Routledge
2 Park Square, Milton Park, Abingdon, Oxon, OX14 4RN

Routledge is an imprint of the Taylor & Francis Group, an informa business

Library of Congress Cataloging-in-Publication Data
Names: Glickman, Neil S., editor. | Hall, Wyatte C., editor.
Title: Language deprivation and deaf mental health /
edited by Neil S. Glickman, Wyatte C. Hall.
Description: New York: Routledge, 2019. |
Includes bibliographical references and index.
Identifiers: LCCN 2018013417 | ISBN 9781138735385
(hardcover: alk. paper) | ISBN 9781138735392 (pbk.: alk. paper) |
ISBN 9781315166728 (e-book)
Subjects: | MESH: Persons With Hearing Impairments—psychology |
Language Development Disorders—psychology | Deafness—
complications | Mental Disorders—therapy | Communication
Barriers | Communication Disorders—etiology | Sign Language
Classification: LCC HV2380 | NLM WA 305 | DDC 362.4/2—dc23
LC record available at https://lccn.loc.gov/2018013417

ISBN: 978-1-138-73538-5 (hbk)
ISBN: 978-1-138-73539-2 (pbk)
ISBN: 978-1-315-16672-8 (ebk)

Typeset in Minion Pro
by codeMantra

This book is dedicated to all the people who have worked, are working, and will work against language deprivation by promoting the human right of deaf people to their natural sign languages.

Books by Neil S. Glickman and Colleagues on Deaf Mental Health

Glickman, N. & Harvey, M. (Eds.) (1996). *Culturally Affirmative Psychotherapy with Deaf Persons*

Glickman, N. & Gulati, S. (Eds.) (2003). *Mental Health Care of Deaf People: A Culturally Affirmative Approach*

Glickman, N. (2009). *Cognitive-Behavioral Therapy for Deaf and Hearing Persons with Language and Learning Challenges*

Glickman, N. (Ed.) (2013). *Deaf Mental Health Care*

Glickman, N. (2017). *Preparing Deaf and Hearing Persons with Language and Learning Challenges for CBT: A Pre-Therapy Workbook*

Glickman, N. & Hall, W. (2018). *Language Deprivation and Deaf Mental Health*

Contents

List of Figures

Foreword[1]

CORINNA HILL

With the publication of this book, the clinical specialty of Deaf mental health returns to the oldest and most salient issue of the Deaf community: access to sign language. Within the past few decades, language deprivation, and all its consequences, has emerged as a controversial topic within disciplines included in this book, such as mental health assessment and treatment, Deaf education, communication assessment and interventions, and interpreting, but it has always been a central topic in Deaf history. Years before this book or even any formal publications recognizing "language deprivation syndrome," the Deaf community recognized the reality and profound costs for deaf children of being denied exposure to immersive, native sign language environments. As Henry B. Camp wrote in 1848, the mass of deaf people living without language was devastating because they have "thoughts and feelings, and hopes and fears, and joys and sorrows, as others, but [they] cannot express them" (212). Yet after Deaf Americans claimed sign language as their choice of language in the nineteenth century, Oralist educators actively worked to deny deaf children access to it, which created a fierce debate over language that continues today.

This brief overview of the battles over sign language in Deaf education puts the current discussion of language deprivation in its historical context. This history tracks the clash between two pedagogical methods, Manualism and Oralism. While these groups are distinguished by their beliefs—the Manualists supported sign language and English while the Oralists believed in exclusive articulation—we cannot draw an explicit fault line in this nuanced history. There was a spectrum of opinions within each group and they shared one basic similarity: Manualists and Oralists both believed that deaf people were entitled to education, while strongly differing on the method of instruction.

Manualists and Oralists, along with deaf and hearing people, have all contributed to the historical discourse over language, which raises several important questions. Who were the Manualists and Oralists? What attitudes contributed to the rise of the two pedagogical methods? How was sign language perceived within and outside the Deaf community in the nineteenth and twentieth centuries? Perhaps the most poignant question is this: since deaf Americans and their advocates had already long argued against the "baseless and wholly erroneous assumption" that spoken language was the best method of communication, why were a great majority of deaf children educated in the oral method in the beginning of the twentieth century? (Stone, 1869, 106).

The battle over sign language begins with the decision made by deaf Frenchman Laurent Clerc to board a ship destined for New York with Thomas Hopkins Gallaudet in 1816. This trip is a watershed moment in Deaf history because Clerc carried over Parisian Sign Language and the French system of manual education. Passed down through generations, Parisian Sign Language blended with home signs—which are gesturally-based signs used at individual homes by deaf children—and Martha's Vineyard Sign Language to form American Sign Language. In 1817, Gallaudet and Clerc adopted sign language as the primary mode of communication when they founded the oldest-living residential school for the deaf in Connecticut.

Before Clerc and Gallaudet established the Connecticut Asylum for the Education and Instruction of Deaf and Dumb Persons, now known as the American School for the Deaf, there were "thousands of deaf-mute children yet uneducated" across America, as exposure to language typically varied by class (Peet, 1855, 4). Wealthy Americans often opted to send their deaf child abroad, usually to oral schools in Britain, while poor deaf children were limited to home signs and rudimentary language (Edwards, 2012, 11–12). While there were several small private schools educating deaf children, there was no state-sponsored school intended for deaf education prior to 1817.

As the American School began enrollment, it unprecedentedly assembled together deaf children and exposed them to sign language. Within the first week, the number of students at the American School rose from three to seven, to 32 students within a year (Turner, 1870, 16). Around 60 years later, 2,100 students had walked the school's grounds (Edwards, 2012, 52). Influenced by Clerc, the American School adopted the French combination method, which, along with writing and fingerspelling, was a combination of natural signs and methodical signs (Edwards, 2012, 38). Natural signs, or "the sign language," is an older form of American Sign Language. Methodical signs refer to artificially developed English signing systems that were limited to classroom instruction. The combination method was endorsed because of the prevalent belief that methodical signs helped students develop fluency in English. Deaf people chose to leave methodical signs in the classrooms, using only natural signs for social events and everyday use.

The American School set in motion the Manualist valuation of sign language and English. Manualism was not strictly limited to teaching sign language as the Manualist advocates encouraged the acquisition of both sign language and English literacy. After the success of the American School, other states such as Kentucky, New York, Pennsylvania, and Ohio followed suit with their own institutions.

Deaf people are one of the few cultural groups, perhaps the only one, where *language* is primarily passed from peer to peer; for this reason, residential schools were instrumental in the development of American Sign Language and the formation of the Deaf community (Baynton, 1996, 4). The growth of residential schools in the nineteenth century benefited white deaf Americans and increased their access to language, but a clear majority of deaf children of color remained isolated. While some northern schools, like American and New York, were racially integrated from their early days, southern states segregated students in separate residential schools. Several southern states withheld funding for "colored" schools well into the twentieth century. West Virginia finally funded a school in 1926 and Louisiana in 1938. Those schools for Black deaf students were often inadequately funded and staffed. Historian Susan Burch identifies a poignant comparison in Mississippi. White deaf students graduated from the Mississippi School in large numbers, but only six Black deaf students graduated from the Mississippi School for the Negro Deaf between 1873 and 1943 (Burch, 2002, 37). Adhering to the Manualist model of instruction, deaf students of color were educated in sign language, but scholars have recognized that students in segregated schools developed their own variation of sign language—colloquially known as Black ASL (Woodward, 1976, 211).

Sign language flourished in the religious climate of Antebellum America. The nineteenth-century Manualists were predominantly Protestants who believed sign language was a divine gift (Baynton, 1996, 124). Those Manualists were influenced by the evangelical message of the Second Great Awakening. The declining belief in Calvinist predestination, the idea that people had no choice in their salvation as it was already divinely planned, inspired masses of men and women to go out and do their part in connecting different groups to God. The evangelical revivalism spread the message that salvation was attainable for populations such as the Native Americans, African Americans, and deaf Americans. Religious reformers, including Thomas Hopkins Gallaudet, considered the lack of language for deaf people morally alarming because they could not access the Christian community or develop a personal connection with God (Baynton, 1996, 17). Many Manualists, therefore, embraced sign language as the best conduit between the deaf and God.

Thomas Hopkins Gallaudet was a minster who graduated from Yale University in 1805, and dozens of Yale graduates followed him to the American School. Those early educators were greatly influenced by the Yale University president, Timothy Dwight, and his message that education contributed to a successful and informed citizenry (Edwards, 2012, 18). Manualists were inspired by the Yale romanticism of art and classicism as they revered natural signs, or the "language of pantomime," as morally and artistically superior to articulation (Baynton, 1996, 86). American Sign Language was not formally recognized as a language by society at large until William Stokoe and colleagues's study in 1960, so natural signs were understood as sophisticated pantomime or gestures. Manualists believed that natural signs were more beautiful and practical for deaf people, rather than having them rely on imperfect vocal cords. They thought the language beautiful because of the romanticized belief that sign language could be traced to antiquity and "was similar to painting" (Baynton, 1996, 87). They also realized it was practical because oralism and lip-reading was ineffective with the "movement of the vocal organs [being] rapid and scarcely perceptible" (Stone, 1869, 106).

Deaf Americans happily claimed sign language because it was the most efficient way to communicate and develop proficiency in English. They grasped that a visual language erected the necessary foundation for language development, including the development of written English literacy. The United States was developing into a connected and industrial nation, and deaf people knew that literacy skills were crucial. Growing innovations in land and water transportation improved speed of communication, which led to booming growth for publications and print media, making Americans increasingly literate in the years leading up to the Civil War. According to the 1840 census, more than 90% of adult white Americans self-reported as literate (Howe, 2007, 455). Deaf Americans realized that fluency in English would allow them to participate successfully in the hearing world, so they encouraged each other to learn how to "write excellent like the speaking people" (Edwards, 2012, 80).

Sixteen years after the opening of the American school, New York decisively broke from the combination method of instruction with the decision to educate students in what historian Rebecca Edwards identifies as a "bilingual-bicultural method" of education (2012, 44). The bilingual-bicultural Manualists educated their students in natural signs only, eschewing the use of methodical signs. The school dropped methodical signs because its leaders felt that artificially coded signing systems were cumbersome, and the method prevented the natural acquisition of language. Not all Manualists endorsed this decision, as some believed the combined method was necessary for deaf education because it exposed students to the "English word order" (Edwards, 2012, 5). We also cannot assume all deaf people affirmed this bilingual-bicultural approach as John Carlin, the nineteenth-century Deaf poet and artist, was "so strongly opposed to the language of signs" in classroom education, favoring instead methodical signs and fingerspelling (Carlin, 1842, 7). Within this polyvocal debate, historians have recognized that support for methodical signs opened the door for Oralism because it could be argued that speaking was the next logical step after signing in the English word order (Edwards, 2012, 6).

The Oralist movement has historically (and contemporarily) consisted of hearing leaders, such as Horace Mann, a well-known education reformer who fought for public education, arguing on behalf of deaf children. He was passionate about public schooling because he believed that inadequate education was the "foundation of the greatest social inequalities" (Mann, 1844, 256). While American residential schools offered accessible education, he disagreed with those institutions because they used a different language than that of the majority and because, in his eyes, they secluded deaf students from the mainstream community. The use of sign language supposedly erected a wall between deaf and hearing people and allowed deaf people to sequester themselves in their own community.

Mann addressed the Massachusetts Board of Education in 1844 and his report has been identified as an important foundation for future Oralist arguments (Edwards, 2012, 149). He argued that sign language was an impractical mode of communication because few hearing people would have the "time, means, or inclination to hold written communication" with the non-speaking deaf (Mann, 1844, 252). Working from what we can now recognize to be a "hearing perspective," he believed sign language prevented deaf Americans from developing as citizens because they didn't learn to converse in the common language of the nation. Deaf people protested against this view. They argued that they could write in English, but Mann believed that was not enough. He insisted that deaf people needed to be able to *speak* (Edwards, 2012, 149), despite conceding that sign language was "a great blessing to a deaf mute" (Mann, 1844, 245). He firmly believed that only the "power of uttering articulate sounds — of speaking as other speak — alone restores him to society" (Mann, 1844, 245).

Mann fostered the growth of American Oralism with his idea that speech alone was "humanizing" and restoring (Edwards, 2012, 158). This idea of "restoration" was attractive to the anxious nation, as the growing prominence of the Oralist movement paralleled with changing cultural attitudes. At the end of the nineteenth century and in the early twentieth century, the landscape of America changed as people moved west, immigrants arrived, cities swelled, factories opened, and wars were fought. Fueled by reform concerns, white middle-class Americans during the Progressive Era sought to reorient America towards progress, making sign language an important battleground. As Historian Douglas Baynton has argued, the Progressive Oralists, who hoped to advance the national community, slowly replaced the generation of Manualist educators concerned with expanding the Christian community (Baynton, 1996, 9).

Charles Darwin's publication, *Origin of Species*, in 1859 impacted how people perceived the origins of the world and ultimately sign language (Baynton, 1996, 36). Darwin advanced the idea that humans are evolving through natural selection. Replacing the creationist theory, his biological view of humanity grew in favor. Darwin's theory contributed to an important shift in perspective as people began to link sign language with savagery. Instead of being seen as a divine gift, sign language came to be perceived as a throwback to a more primitive stage in human development. Oralists rebranded sign language as crude and animalistic, and the grimacing face and waving hands that accompanied the language were perceived as uncivilized (Baynton, 1996, 40).

Inspired by successful policies assimilating Native Americans and immigrants, Oralists argued that deaf children could also be assimilated with the refined method of articulation. By the turn of the twentieth century, oral pedagogy gained the backing of reformers, educators, parents, doctors, and scientists. Those supporters presented oral programs as the optimal method of instruction because they integrated the deaf child within the community under one common language. Samuel Gridley Howe, the famed educational reformer who worked with Mann, argued against residential schools because their concentrations of deaf children communicating in sign language "intensify their peculiarities, and this is bad" (Edwards, 2012, 185).

Oralist policy reached its zenith between 1870 and 1940, with the establishment of over a hundred private and public schools with pure oral programs across the nation (Burch, 2012, 14). As oral institutions flourished, educated hearing women enthusiastically filled vacant teaching positions. Residential schools lagged behind in accepting female teachers, but they were eagerly welcomed by oral programs with their "family-like" philosophy (Burch, 2002, 20). Many of those hearing women equated "voice" with empowerment, so they were motivated by the desire to "liberate" deaf children to speak for themselves (Baynton, 1996, 75). The high number of women teachers at oral programs was not necessarily a beacon of gender equality. They were desirable teachers because they were cheap, as their salary was approximately half of a male teacher's salary (Baynton, 196, 59). Gender stereotypes of women as nurturing and patient reinforced their status as excellent models for young, impressionable deaf children. Oral programs used their large pool of female educators to market themselves to hearing parents as the best option for their deaf child. Not only did their programs teach the child the same language of the parents, it provided them a homelike environment. The growing number of female Oralist educators correlated with the decline of Deaf signing educators, which reduced deaf children's access to natural signing models (Burch, 2012, 20).

In the twentieth century, residential schools strained under the weight of oralist assault. In 1911, the state of Nebraska mandated that all deaf students receive education in the oral method, forcing the Nebraska School to practice Oralism (Burch, 2012, 26). The school in Virginia adopted a similar Oralist policy in 1925, and four years later, New Jersey followed suit. In sum, before the Civil War, a great majority of deaf children had access to sign language in residential schools, but by the end of the Great War, almost all American deaf students (about 80%) were educated in the oral method (Baynton, 1996, 5).

Deaf people were aware of all this, and they were never passive. They proclaimed in 1870 that a deaf person without sign language became an "unfortunate subject of the deprivation [who] must pass through the world shorn of [their] birthright in intellectual and spiritual light" (Angus, 1870, 153–154). The Deaf community knew that sign language was their "birthright," so they actively fought for their language and endeavored to preserve their community. They initiated letter-writing campaigns to educate hearing people, disseminated information in publications, and created film projects to protect sign language. Even at oral programs where sign language was forbidden, deaf students would covertly share the language with each other despite the very real likelihood of punishment, such as getting their hands rapped with rulers or having their hands restrained behind their backs (McCullough & Duchesneau Sharon, 2016, 724). Faced with efforts to eradicate their language, the Deaf community steadfastly replied: "We would like to whisper gently into their ears: RESTORE THE SIGN LANGUAGE" (Buchanan, 1993, 192).

Deaf people have proudly endorsed sign language and written English as the most efficient language and communication options, which is supported by findings showing that "bilinguals are associated with better cognitive outcomes when compared to monolinguals," yet resistance against sign language remains prevalent today (Hall, 2017). In 2016, Meredith Sugar, president of the staunchly pro-Oralist Alexander Graham Bell Association for the Deaf and Hard of Hearing, issued a public statement that continued the Oralist tradition of framing sign language as isolating and inferior. Evoking Horace Mann, Sugar recognized that "ASL exists as a communication option for deaf children," but claimed that the use of the language is "declining" and that spoken language alone leads to "desired outcomes" (Sugar, 2016). She argued that when today's parents are told that their deaf children should or must learn ASL as part of a Deaf culture, they increasingly respond that their children actually are part of a hearing culture, that of their families, friends and the world at large (Sugar, 2016). Sugar was continuing the work started by the nineteenth- and twentieth-century Oralists with her attempt to classify sign language as separatist.

The long-standing bias against sign language continues to be perpetuated by Oralists using biased research methodology. A 2017 study purporting to look at the influence of sign language exposure on the cochlear implant outcomes of 97 children was published in *Pediatrics*, the official journal of the American Academy of Pediatrics and widely read by clinicians, and claimed that "children exposed to sign language performed more poorly on auditory-only speech recognition, speech intelligibility, spoken language, and reading outcomes" (Geers et al., 2017).

Deaf and hearing scientists immediately rebutted the study, classifying it as harmful and misleading (Caselli, Hall, W.C., & Lillo-Martin, 2017; Dye, Kushalnagar, & Henner, 2017; Hall, M.L., Schönström, & Spellun, 2017; Martin, Napoli, & Smith, 2017; St. John, Clark, & Nutt, 2017, among others). They explained how the study's definition of sign language conflated American Sign Language, a natural language with its own unique grammar, with artificial signing systems, such as signing exact English and simultaneous communication (SimCom), which do not carry the same neurodevelopmental benefits as natural languages. Not only does this degrade ASL's legitimacy as a language, it is intentionally misleading, as the reader could reasonably assume that "sign language" means ASL, which will lead them to naturally conclude that ASL harms English acquisition. The study was criticized for many other aspects of its methodology, including, but not limited to, drawing large-scale conclusions from a small pool of children, using non-randomized correlational methodology to assert cause-and-effect, and the existence of clinically significant differences among children at baseline that may influence results. They also pointed to the troubling conclusion of the study, which revealed that poor results in spoken language outcomes were still seen in non-signing implanted children of elementary school age, something about which the authors expressed no concern.

Community news outlets picked up the article as various members and organizations publicly and strongly called on the journal to retract the article (Daily Moth, DTV). Geers (2017) responded to the backlash by stating that manual signs served as a needless "distraction" for deaf children. She argued that time spent learning ASL was time taken away from stimulating and reinforcing spoken language development and claimed that her findings were supported by the research of a renowned sign language linguist, Karen Emmorey. Dr. Emmorey responded to this miscitation, asserting that "nothing in the cited work remotely supports such a conclusion." (Emmorey, 2017). Geers and her cohorts were carrying on the Oralist tradition of placing the responsibility for communication on deaf children and failing to acknowledge that asking deaf children to speak is a "long and arduous process," often with limited chances for success.

What also should not be overlooked is the fact that Dr. Karl White, director of the National Center for Hearing Assessment and Management and a leader of the Early Hearing Detection & Intervention system, and Dr. Louis Cooper, a former president of the American Academy of Pediatrics, coauthored a commentary supporting the Geers et al. publication and calling it an "excellent example of how well-designed research can provide credible and useful information" (Whit and Cooper, 2017). Their commentary faced similar criticisms and accusations of confirmation bias from deaf and hearing scientists, specifically for their uncritical assessment and unquestioning support of Geers et al.'s results and conclusions (Caselli, Hall, & Hall, 2017; Flaherty, Henner, & Spellun, 2017; Hecht, 2017; Martin, Napoli & Humphries, 2017; Mathur, Kushalnagar, & Humphries, 2017; Rathmann, Coppola, & Lieberman, 2017), including one entitled "Vouching for a flawed study is harmful to deaf children" (Hauser, Kartheiser, & Stone, 2017).

This reflects yet another skirmish in the 200-year-old argument. The flawed criticism against sign language remains as unfair, untrue, and oppressive today as it was when it begun. Geers and her colleagues reveal how current attitudes and arguments are deeply rooted in this centuries-old conversation, one in which spoken communication is prioritized at all expenses, as Oralists continue to speak *for* deaf people and not with them.

Language Deprivation and Deaf Mental Health connects the historical background and contemporary conversations of language deprivation—the denial of quality, natural sign language exposure for deaf children—to this newly conceptualized clinical specialty of Deaf mental health. The discussion of language deprivation, as we have seen, is not new (although the terminology might be to many), nor are the arguments by medical and educational professionals about the alleged dangers of exposing deaf children to sign language. What is new, though, is an appreciation of how the unfortunate continuation of this oppressive philosophy and practice of withholding sign language from deaf children creates a disability, language deprivation, which now must be the focus of a wide range of evaluation and remediation efforts.

How does this fact of language deprivation impact cognitive and psychosocial development? What does a quality language and communication assessment look like? Can language deprivation contribute to the development of a unique clinical syndrome, a "language deprivation syndrome"? If so, what is the optimal clinical and, if necessary, legal response to persons with such a condition? Are there emerging best practices for developing language and communication skills *after* the critical period for language acquisition has passed? Interpreting involves moving from one language world to another, but how can one interpret for persons whose language skills are so poorly developed that, perhaps, they do not really have a fully created language world? How does one provide counseling and therapy, the "talking cure," for persons unpracticed in the use of dialogue for self-expression and problem-solving? Language deprivation appears to be becoming recognized as a widespread phenomenon among deaf people who interact with the various clinical systems to the point where we need a new clinical specialty, Deaf mental health, to develop a multifaceted response to persons with this condition.

There is no inevitable associate between language deprivation and deafness. Language deprivation is a social problem, a result of the multi-century experience of dismissing deaf people. In essence, the "ignorance" of deaf people has developed because they were "cut off from all that mass of traditional knowledge of which language is the great store-house" (Peet, 1855, 10). Peet realized that hearing loss was never what deprived a person, that the problem was the lack of language. While this realization is growing, deaf people still are fighting for this to be recognized in society at large. Throughout this history, there has been one constant undercurrent: deaf people have always known what was best for themselves, and that was and still is sign language.

Note

1 We will use "sign language" to preserve how it was historically understood during the nineteenth and twentieth centuries. The language has evolved throughout the years and we recognize it today as American Sign Language.

References

Angus, W. W. (1870). Marginalia. *American Annals of the Deaf and Dumb, 15*(3), 149–160.

Buchanan, R. (1993). The silent worker newspaper and the building of a deaf community, 1890–1929. In J. V. Van Cleave (Ed.), *Deaf history unveiled: Interpretations from the new scholarship* (pp. 172–197). Washington, DC: Gallaudet University Press.

Baynton, D. C. (1996). *Forbidden signs: American culture and the campaign against sign language*. Chicago: University of Chicago Press.

Burch, S. (2002). *Signs of resistance: American deaf cultural history, 1900 to 1942*. New York: New York University Press.

Carlin J. (1842). Written conversation with William Henry Seward and Frances Miller Seward, Auburn, NY. William Henry Seward Papers, Department of Rare Books, Special Collections and Preservation, River Campus Libraries, University of Rochester.

Caselli, N. K., Hall, W. C., & Lillo-Martin, D. (2017, June 19). Operationalization and Measurement of Sign Language. RE: Early Sign Language Exposure and Cochlear Implantation Benefits. Retrieved from http://pediatrics.aappublications.org/content/early/2017/06/08/peds.2016-3489.comments

Caselli, N. K., Hall, W. C., & Hall, M. L. (2017, June 23). From "Communication Options" to Global-Language Proficiency. RE: Opportunities and Shared Decision-Making to Help Children Who Are Deaf to Communicate. Retrieved from http://pediatrics.aappublications.org/content/early/2017/06/08/peds.2017-1287.comments

Camp, H. B. (1848). Claims of the deaf and dumb upon public sympathy and aid. *American Annals of the Deaf and Dumb, 1*(4), 210–215.

Dye, M. W., Kushalnagar, P., & Henner, J. (2017, June 19). Concerns with Data Analysis and Interpretation. RE: Early Sign Language Exposure and Cochlear Implantation Benefits. Retrieved from http://pediatrics.aappublications.org/content/early/2017/06/08/peds.2016-3489. comments

Edwards, R. A. R. (2012). *Words made flesh: Nineteenth century deaf education and the growth of deaf culture*. New York: New York University Press.

Emmorey, K. (2017, July 13). Evidence That Use of Sign Language Is NOT Distracting. RE: Early Sign Language Exposure and Cochlear Implantation Benefits. Retrieved from http://pediatrics. aappublications.org/content/early/2017/06/08/peds.2016-3489.comments

Flaherty, M., Henner, J., & Spellun, A. (2017, June 23). Key Considerations in Studying Multimodal Bilingualism. RE: Opportunities and Shared Decision-Making to Help Children Who Are Deaf to Communicate. Retrieved from http://pediatrics.aappublications.org/content/early/2017/06/08/peds.2017-1287.comments

Geers A. E., Mitchell C. M., Warner-Czyz A., et al. (2017). Early sign language exposure and cochlear implantation benefits. *Pediatrics, 140*(1), 1–9.

Geers A. E., Mitchell C. M., Warner-Czyz A., et al. (2017, July 11). RE: Early Sign Language Exposure and Cochlear Implantation Benefits. Retrieved from http://pediatrics.aappublications.org/content/early/2017/06/08/peds.2016-3489.comments

Hall, M. L., Schönström, K., & Spellun, A. (2017, June 19). Failure to Distinguish Among Competing Hypotheses. RE: Early Sign Language Exposure and Cochlear Implantation Benefits. Retrieved from http://pediatrics.aappublications.org/content/early/2017/06/08/peds.2016-3489.comments

Hall, W. C. (2017). What you don't know can hurt you: The risk of language deprivation by impairing sign language development in deaf children. *Maternal and Child Health Journal, 21*(5), 961–965.

Hauser, P. C., Kartheiser, G., & Stone, A. (2017, June 23). Vouching for A Flawed Study is Harmful to Deaf Children. RE: Opportunities and Shared Decision-Making to Help Children Who Are Deaf to Communicate. Retrieved from http://pediatrics.aappublications.org/content/early/2017/06/08/peds.2017-1287.comments

Hecht, J. (2017, June 25). Risks of Exclusive Oralism. RE: Opportunities and Shared Decision Making to Help Children Who Are Deaf to Communicate. Retrieved from http://pediatrics. aappublications.org/content/early/2017/06/08/peds.2017-1287.comments

Howe, D. W. (2007). *What hath God wrought: The transformation of America, 1815–1848*. New York: Oxford University Press.

Mann, H. (1891). *Annual reports of the Secretary of the Board of Education of Massachusetts for the years 1839–1844*. Boston: Lee and Shepard Publishers.

Martin, A. J., Napoli, D. J., & Smith, S. R. (2017, June 18). Methodological Concerns Suspend Interpretations. RE: Early Sign Language Exposure and Cochlear Implantation Benefits. Retrieved from http://pediatrics.aappublications.org/content/early/2017/06/08/peds.2016-3489. comments

Mathur, G., Kushalnagar, P., & Humphries, T. (2017, June 23). Still Conflating Communication Modes with Language. RE: Opportunities and Shared Decision-Making to Help Children Who Are Deaf to Communicate. Retrieved from http://pediatrics.aappublications.org/content/early/2017/06/08/peds.2017-1287.comments

McCullough, C. A., & Duchesneau Sharon M. (2016). Oralism, psychological effects of. In G. Gertz & P. Boudreault (Eds.), *The SAGE Deaf Studies Encyclopedia* (pp. 724–728). US: Sage Publications Inc.

Napoli, D. J., Martin, A. J., & Humphries, T. (2017, June 23). Confirmation Bias. RE: Opportunities and Shared Decision-Making to Help Children Who Are Deaf to Communicate. Retrieved from http://pediatrics.aappublications.org/content/early/2017/06/08/peds.2017-1287. comments

Peet, H. P. (1855). Notions of the deaf and dumb before instruction, especially in regard to religious subjects. *American Annals of the Deaf and Dumb, 8*(1), 1–44.

Rathmann, C., Coppola, M., & Lieberman, A. (2017, June 23). Children Need Early Access to Language. RE: Opportunities and Shared Decision-Making to Help Children Who Are Deaf to Communicate. Retrieved from http://pediatrics.aappublications.org/content/early/2017/06/08/peds.2017-1287.comments

St. John, R., Clark, T. A., & Nutt, R. C. (2017, June 18). To The Editor: Concerns With Correlative Data. RE: Early Sign Language Exposure and Cochlear Implantation Benefits. Retrieved from http://pediatrics.aappublications.org/content/early/2017/06/08/peds.2016-3489.comments

Stone, C. (1869). Address upon the history and methods of deaf mute instruction. *American Annals of the Deaf and Dumb, 14*(2), 95–120.

Sugar, M. (2016). *Response to Washington post article about Nyle DiMarco: Dispelling myths about deafness.* Retrieved from www.agbell.org/in-the-news/response-nyle-dimarco/

Turner, W. W. (1870). Laurent Clerc. *American Annals of the Deaf and Dumb, 15*(1), 14–25.

White, K. R., & Cooper, L. Z. (2017, June 12). Opportunities and shared decision-making to help children who are deaf to communicate. *Pediatrics, 140*(1), 1–2.

Woodward Jr., J. C. (1976). Black southern signing. *Language in Society, 5*(2), 211–218.

Acknowledgments

First from Neil:

I see this book, and the others I have written or edited with colleagues, as gathering and hopefully advancing the state of knowledge about our ability to serve diverse deaf people in mental health care. I am always aware that, at best, I can reflect and crystalize the excellent work that a community of people is performing. I am also aware that, as a hearing person, I have the additional responsibility of striving to work with humility, knowing this isn't my culture, and knowing the history of hearing mistreatment of deaf people. All hearing people who work with deaf people, just like any member of a dominant culture working with disadvantaged or oppressed people, need to strive for what psychologist Robert Q. Pollard, Jr. calls *cross-cultural legitimacy*. One way to do that is always seeking partnerships with the members of the community and unceasingly recognizing their words, signs, thoughts, and perspectives. That project has additional layers of complexity when considering the impact of language deprivation on the ability of some deaf persons to articulate their ideas. Nevertheless, the subject of language deprivation and language can't be done well without the active involvement of deaf people. Indeed, as Wyatte and I discuss in our introduction, there is no place in Deaf mental health that humility is more called for, especially from hearing people, than when discussing language deprivation and apparent language dysfluency in some deaf people. Thus, the importance of acknowledgments. My first acknowledgement then, is to all the deaf people who are bringing this issue to the forefront of Deaf mental health. The issue can be academic for hearing people, but it is lived by many deaf people.

The idea for this book came from my coeditor and colleague Wyatte C. Hall, and I felt much more confident taking it on knowing that I had in him an astute Deaf partner. Wyatte brought to this project a perspective as a new Deaf psychologist that I, as an "old timer," lacked, plus lots of fresh energy. I appreciate his willingness to challenge me. I think the book is enriched by the dialogue we have had in which we didn't always agree, but persevered.

Wyatte also brought to this book several wonderful colleagues whom I did not yet know. One of those colleagues is Corinna Hill, a Deaf historian, who nicely situates the current concern with language deprivation in its' historical context. Thank you, Corinna, for starting us off so well.

In my previous books, I've provided pages of acknowledgments of the teachers, colleagues, clients, and friends who have influenced me over several decades of work in Deaf mental health. Here I want to acknowledge Michael Harvey, Julia Ball, Melissa Anderson, and Wyatte C. Hall, as well as my coauthors for Chapter 2, Wendy Heines and Melissa Watson, who offered constructive criticism of that chapter and, in the case of Wendy and Melissa, shared some of the work done in their awesome agency PAHrtners Deaf Services in Glenside, Pennsylvania. I want to acknowledge also my decades-long collaboration with Sanjay Gulati, our countless discussions—many of which were at the Red Barn coffee shop in Southborough, Massachusetts—about what we now call, following his lead, *language deprivation syndrome*, and his willingness to allow me to contribute an appendix to his brilliant chapter. I believe Sanjay's chapter on language deprivation syndrome alone will change forever how we understand and work with persons with language deprivation. We've finally got an appropriate name and description for the phenomena that everyone who does this work has long striven to understand.

I was thrilled that a long-term colleague, Joan Wattman, who is an undisputed star in the interpreting world in Massachusetts, brought in a whole community of master interpreters to help her develop her chapter on the applications of the Integrated Model of Interpreting (IMI), and I was especially happy to include this because of the pivotal influence that Betty Colonomos, the developer of IMI, had on me way back in the early 1980s when I was her student at then Gallaudet College and was just forming my thoughts on deaf and hearing people.

I've long been a fan of the communication assessment work done by Charlene J. Crump and Roger C. Williams. I'm convinced that the best measure of excellence in Deaf mental health is the sophistication with which practitioners approach communication assessment, and thus having their chapter, as well as the chapter on formal sign language assessment by Jonathan Henner, Jeanne Reis, and Robert Hoffmeister, advances the cutting edge of our specialty. Basic questions—what interpreting, therapy, or educational resources are needed to work with this person; and, can we diagnose this person as having language deprivation syndrome; and how do we demonstrate that there has been a significant change in this person's language and communication abilities; and, with whom can this *staff* person work effectively without interpreting assistance—all depend on appropriate use of such sign language assessment tools.

I am grateful to Wendy Heines and Melissa Watson for helping me develop my pre-therapy approach at PAHrtners Deaf Services. I'm impressed and thrilled with the work Melissa Anderson and Kelly Wolf Craig are doing to create what will likely be the first full evidenced-based mental health practice with deaf people, including those with language deprivation.

The work that Judy Kegl, Romy Spitz, and their colleagues have done in Nicaragua is groundbreaking in many ways, and I don't know anyone else who could better address the topic of advancing communication and language skills in language-deprived persons; yet everyone who does this work struggles with that challenge. The presence of a community of language-deprived deaf adults in Nicaragua, who were finally brought together and then interacted with linguists and educators, provided a natural laboratory for exploration of the question of what are the best methods for developing language and communication abilities in persons who first learn language after the critical language acquisition period. The field of Deaf mental health must draw on the insights from this fantastic learning opportunity, and we have here two of the key players, sharing their observations and pedagogical methods.

The contributions of Amy Szarkowski and Sanjay Gulati allowed the book to address the biggest elephant in the room when the subject of language development in deaf children is addressed: the question of what cochlear implantation can and cannot accomplish. I don't think a book on the topic of language deprivation would have been honest or helpful without tackling that thorny issue, and I am grateful to both of them for the clarity of their thinking and practice on this topic.

Everything Robert Q. Pollard, Jr. writes is groundbreaking, insightful, and because he is a masterful writer, super clear. McCay Vernon had previously elucidated the condition he called "primitive personality disorder," which Sanjay Gulati updates here with the much better label of "language deprivation syndrome." Vernon was especially forthright in describing the forensic implications associated with language deprivation, especially the issue of incompetence to stand trial for linguistic reasons. Robert Q. Pollard, Jr. has taken the ball from Vernon and moved it much further down the field, presenting in much more detail the strategies needed to do a competent forensic assessment of language-deprived deaf persons. Thus, it is a great honor to have some of his important work included in this book. Wyatte and I are also grateful to Deaf artist Brian Berlinski whose helpful drawings are showcased in Chapter 4 and presented separately in the appendices of that chapter, so they can be copied and use by interested parties. When I'm writing and editing, I'm always thinking about what information I have needed as a Deaf mental health practitioner. On the Westborough State Hospital Deaf Unit, we could have really used those drawings; indeed, we could have really used that chapter!

Obtaining the insights of National Association of the Deaf attorney, and Gallaudet University professor, Tawny Holmes was true icing on the cake. I don't believe we have a more expert person on the subject of advocacy strategies to help deaf children receive fully accessible language and education. I always value especially the insights of people, like Tawny, who have been working on the front lines of their discipline, as both practitioners and educators.

All this is my way of saying how grateful I am to all the contributors of this book. I know that many chapters went through quite a few drafts and required a willingness to hang in there through a sometimes-challenging practice of rewriting. They have all heard me pontificate on how writing is rewriting, that very few of us can produce a publication-ready book chapter without going through numerous drafts, and this requires patience, tenacity, and a willingness to consider constructive criticism. Both Wyatte and I will forever be grateful that you allowed us to showcase your contributions to this new field.

It was a real coup for us to get renowned Deaf artist Nancy Rourke to allow us to use one of her paintings on the front cover of this book and then to find a painting of hers which is so *on target* to the themes of this book. Her agreement to allow that made our month, at least! Thank you, Nancy.

This is my sixth book with the Taylor and Francis world, and my fourth book with their Routledge division. This is my third time having the pleasure to work with Senior Editor Anna Moore, and my first time with Senior Editorial Assistant Nina Guttapalle, both of whom quickly and fully supported our vision for the book and were endlessly helpful with the production process.

Last for me is again acknowledging the steady support of my husband Steven Riel, who is also a writer, and who knows that one doesn't produce a book without making a serious commitment of time and energy, often at the cost of other worthy activities.

Joining me in this appreciation of our colleagues is my coeditor Wyatte C. Hall, who wanted to add these thoughts:

Wyatte:

I would like to thank my wife, Kat, for her ongoing support and making me comfort food during long editing sessions. Thank you to Marlene Elliott for being a sounding board and someone to bounce ideas off. Thank you to all the authors who dedicated time and energy to make this book what it is. This would not be possible without your collective expertise. Finally, I want to thank Neil, my coeditor, for the opportunity to do this project and always working together to push through to a place of agreement when necessary.

Several of the book contributors also wanted to offer acknowledgements so these follow now, in their words:

Melissa Anderson and Kelly Wolf Craig:

We would like to acknowledge the invaluable contributions of the members of this team: Amanda Sortwell, Sue Jones, Gregg Spera, Gloria Farr, Sheri Hostovsky, Wyatte C. Hall, Marlene Elliott, Windell Smith, Jr., Stephanie Hakulin, Raylene Lotz, Fernando Silverstre, Mikey Krajnak, and Ayisha Knight-Shaw.

Sanjay Gulati:

Sanjay Gulati's work ["Deaf Service: a Peek in the Mirror," 2012] was supported by NIH Research Grant # P60 MDO 02261, and specifically by the National Institute on Minority Health and Health Disparities, a project of the Center for Multicultural Mental Health Research within the Cambridge Health Alliance.

Jonathan Henner, Jeanne Reis, and Robert Hoffmeister:

We would like to acknowledge Rachel Benedict, Patrick Rosenburg, and Sarah Fish for their many years of work for the Center for the Study of Communication and the Deaf, and Danielle Kehoe for her work at the Center for Research and Training. We also wish to acknowledge The Learning Center for the Deaf for their involvement in the research and their commitment to a bilingual education for deaf students.

Corinna Hill:

I would like to thank Wyatte C. Hall for his thoughtful suggestions and for reading my numerous revisions. I would also like to thank Professor Thomas Slaughter for his unwavering support and guidance.

Tawny Holmes:

I would like to acknowledge the National Association of the Deaf for its key support for my advocacy and policy efforts over the years, to express gratitude to my lifetime partner, Stephen Hlibok for his constant encouragement in completing her chapter, and finally, to appreciate the coeditors Neil S. Glickman and Wyatte C. Hall for their resilience and leadership in putting this vital book together.

Amy Szarkowski:

I wish to extend my gratitude to three individuals whose insights helped to significantly strengthen this chapter. Drs. Glickman and Hall, editors of this book, provided gentle guidance throughout the process. Dr. Gulati shared his expertise as a wordsmith and was generous with his sage wisdom. I appreciate and respect you, Sanjay.

Romy Spitz and Judy Kegl:

The authors would like to thank the deaf people in the US and Nicaragua for the experiences and research on which this chapter is based. We would also like to thank James Kegl, the Deaf teachers of Nicaragua, and the Nicaraguan Sign Language Project for its efforts to establish Deaf-operated language-learning focused educational programs. This chapter was supported by the Deaf Services Contract ADS-16–4722 awarded to Mobius Inc. by Maine Department of Health and Human Services, Office of Aging and Disability Services and by the Linguistics Department at the University of Southern Maine.

Joan Wattman:

This work was developed in collaboration with Janis Cole and Kelly Decker. Special thanks to Cat Dvar, Alice Harrigan, Michael Labadie-Mendes, and Nathan Fowler. I want to acknowledge Neil S. Glickman, Wyatte C. Hall, and Sanjay Gulati for their editing and comments that challenged my thinking and deepened my analysis. Also, I appreciate the Etna Project in New Hampshire 2016–2017 for taking a session to review the chapter and discuss its implications.

To say I am indebted to Betty Colonomos for her work on the Integrated Model of Interpreting would be an understatement. Relatively early in my career, I took an interpreting workshop for a week from Betty Colonomos and MJ Bienvenu in the woods of North Amherst in 1986. Betty & MJ designed the Teaching Interpreting program at Western Maryland College (now McDaniel College) where I got my Master's in 1991. Betty offered a nine-weekend program called "The Master's Class" at Northeastern University September 1996–May 1997 from which a group of us who attended started a Collective Dialogue group that continues to the present, analyzing our work, presenting at conferences, and encouraging others to form Collective Dialogue groups. The Etna Project, under the auspices of Betty's Bilingual Mediation Center, has been meeting four to five times a year in New Hampshire and Maryland and I have attended every session since its inception in 2002. Betty teaches a series of weekend workshops called Foundations of Interpreting I-VIII, all of which I have attended (some several times), including assisting her with several workshops. Betty continues to be a major force in sign language interpreter education, including the training of legal interpreters, and her IMI approach continues to grow in depth and influence throughout the interpreting world.

About the Contributors

Melissa L. Anderson, Ph.D., MSCI is Assistant Professor, psychologist, and clinical researcher in the University of Massachusetts (UMass) Medical School Department of Psychiatry. She completed her graduate work at Gallaudet University, where she studied intimate partner violence and trauma in the Deaf community. At UMass, Melissa provides individual therapy to deaf clients recovering from trauma and addiction and conducts research on best approaches for working with deaf clients. She is the recipient of a Clinical Research Scholar Award (KL2) administered by the UMass Center for Clinical & Translational Science, with which she and a team of deaf and hearing clinicians and community members are developing and testing a digital American Sign Language therapy manual for treating trauma and addiction.

Charlene J. Crump is the State Coordinator for Interpreting Services with the Alabama Department of Mental Health. In this capacity, she has developed and runs the Mental Health Interpreter Training Project and a supervised mental health practicum program. She established certification standards codified into state law. Alabama is the only state in the nation to certify interpreters as qualified to work in mental health. Her work earned her recognition as employee of the year for the state of Alabama. Additionally, she has been recognized as Interpreter of the year from COSDA 2002 and SERID 2004, Lifetime Achievement Award 2012 from ALRID, Outstanding Alabama Citizen from Alabama Association of the Deaf, and Lifetime Achievement Award form COSDA 2015. In addition to her efforts in mental health, she serves as an executive board member of ADARA, an advisory member of the state's ITP, RID CMP Administrator, and SLPI coordinator. She has served on several national expert focus groups on mental health interpreting.

Meghan L. Fox, PsyD, LMHC is a postdoctoral fellow at the University of Rochester Medical Center Department of Psychiatry and the Rochester Prevention Research Center: National Center for Deaf Health Research. Her research is focused on suicide prevention with deaf and hard of hearing people. She completed her predoctoral internship in the URMC Department of Psychiatry's Deaf Wellness Center track. Dr. Fox is also a licensed mental health counselor (LMHC) and LMHC supervisor. She has provided clinical services and developed community-based programs with deaf and hard of hearing individuals and their families since 2009. Dr. Fox has consulted on legal cases involving deaf persons since 2015.

Neil S. Glickman, Ph.D., is a licensed psychologist in Massachusetts. He was cofounder of the Mental Health Unit for Deaf Persons, a Deaf psychiatric inpatient unit at Westborough State Hospital in Massachusetts, where he worked for 17 years, 14 as unit psychologist and director. He is the author of *Cognitive*

Behavioral Therapy for Deaf and Hearing persons with Language and Learning Challenges (Routledge, 2009) and *Preparing Deaf and Hearing Persons with Language and Learning Challenges for CBT: A Pre-Therapy Workbook* (Routledge, 2017). He is also editor of *Deaf Mental Health Care* (Routledge, 2013) and coeditor (with Michael Harvey) of *Culturally Affirmative Psychotherapy with Deaf Persons* (Lawrence Erlbaum, 1996) and (with Sanjay Gulati) of *Mental Health Care of Deaf Persons: A Culturally Affirmative Approach* (Lawrence Erlbaum, 2003). Neil is on the editorial board for the Journal of Deaf Studies and Deaf Education. He is also on the faculty of the University of Massachusetts Medical School and has a private psychotherapy practice. He teaches and consults on the subjects of Deaf mental health and cognitive behavioral psychotherapy.

Wyatte C. Hall, Ph.D., is a research postdoctoral fellow in the University of Rochester Medical Center. He completed his doctorate in Clinical Psychology at Gallaudet University and a clinical postdoctoral fellowship at the University of Massachusetts Medical School. He researches the early childhood language experiences of deaf people and its associations with lifespan health outcomes within the deaf population. With a special focus on language deprivation and deaf health disparities, he is especially interested in translating empirical evidence to clinical practice to ensure healthy development of deaf children.

Sanjay Gulati, M.D., is staff psychiatrist in the Deaf & Hard of Hearing Service at the Cambridge Health Alliance and in the Deaf & Hard of Hearing Program at Children's Hospital, Boston. He is Assistant Professor of Psychiatry at Harvard Medical School and consults to Deaf schools and mental health programs nationally. He is also coeditor with Neil S. Glickman of *Mental Health Care of Deaf People: A Culturally Affirmative Approach.*

Jonathan Henner, Ed.D., is an assistant professor at University of North Carolina: Greensboro. He is also a consultant in the Center for Research and Technology. He received his doctorate in Developmental Studies from Boston University. There his research focused on factors that scaffold the development of language based analogical reasoning skills in deaf children. Since 2011, Jon has worked on the American Sign Language Assessment Instrument, an American Sign Language based test battery. Since 2013, he has worked with the American Sign Language Concept Learning Resource research team, which is dedicated to creating a sign language based science, technology, engineering, and mathematics web application for deaf children. Jon's current research interests include measurement and assessment of deaf children, test development, and studying how different background characteristics impact the acquisition of American Sign Language and related skills in deaf children.

Wendy Heines, MSW, LCSW, is the Chief Executive Officer for Salisbury Behavioral Health, which she joined in 2003 as the Director of the newly formed Deaf Services Center, now known as PAHrtners Deaf Services. Under her leadership, the staff has grown from 12 to more than 160 employees, and programs include: interpreting, outpatient, case management, community living arrangements for individuals who are deaf with co-occurring developmental disabilities, and a residential treatment facility for adolescents who are Deaf. The program offers services in the greater Philadelphia area and now the greater Pittsburgh area as well. Ms. Heines is a 1991 graduate of Rutgers University with a Master's in Social Work. She has over 25 years of experience establishing and operating behavioral health care programs for Deaf person in New Jersey and Pennsylvania.

Corinna Hill is a PhD student in the history department at the University of Rochester. She holds a BA degree in history from Gallaudet University and a MA degree in history from the University of Rochester. She studies disability, deafness, and gender in the United States in the nineteenth and twentieth centuries.

Robert Hoffmeister, PhD, Founder and Director Emeritus of the Research and Training Center at the Learning Center for Deaf Children and associate professor emeritus of Boston University. At BU, he is currently principal investigator of the ASL Clear project. Bob is originator of the American Sign Language Assessment Instrument (ASLAI), which has since been administered to over 1,700 deaf and hard of hearing children in the country. Cofounder of the program in Deaf Studies at BU, Bob has published over 100 book chapters, research articles, and working papers and has presented internationally on Deaf Education. He has a PhD in Psycholinguistics and Education from the University of Minnesota, an MEd from the University of Arizona, and a BS from the University of Connecticut. Bob is the son of Deaf parents and a heritage signer of ASL.

Tawny Holmes, Esq., is the Education Policy Counsel at the National Association of the Deaf (NAD). She is also a well-known national presenter and expert on language rights and advocacy for deaf children. Before she graduated from the University of Baltimore School of Law, focusing on family law and education policy, she earned a Master of Arts in Family Centered Early Education from Gallaudet University focusing on the ASL/English bilingual approach. Ms. Holmes has four years of teaching experience with deaf and hard of hearing children at all grades at two different schools including as a family educator. She is currently the coordinator of the Education Advocates program as well as chair of the Education Strategy Team and the Language Deprivation Taskforce for the NAD. As of August 2017, Ms. Holmes is also an Assistant Professor in the ASL/Deaf Studies Department at Gallaudet University focusing on early language advocacy and rights.

Judy Kegl, Ph.D., is a linguist and certified ASL/English interpreter. She is currently teaching linguistics in the linguistics department at the University of Southern Maine, where she also directs the Signed Language Research

Laboratory and coordinates the ASL/English Interpreting Concentration in the linguistics major. She has been a principal investigator on numerous grants from the National Institutes of Health and the National Science Foundation and has published extensively on ASL as well as Nicaraguan Sign Language and English. Her specialty areas are theoretical linguistics and neurolinguistics. She is best known for her discovery and documentation of the emergence of a new signed language from non-language origins in Nicaragua.

Robert Q. Pollard, Jr., Ph.D., is Professor and Associate Dean of Research at the National Technical Institute for the Deaf in Rochester, NY. He also is a Clinical Professor of Psychiatry at the University of Rochester School of Medicine where he founded the Deaf Wellness Center, a clinical service, research, and training program. Dr. Pollard has particular expertise regarding deaf persons and mental health, sign language interpreting, and deaf population public health matters. He has served as an expert witness in more than 90 criminal and civil cases involving deaf persons. He has made hundreds of invited addresses throughout the US and abroad. He has been principal investigator on dozens of grants totaling over $6M, authored or coauthored over 100 publications, and produced 15 films in American Sign Language.

Jeanne Reis, MEd, CIT, and CT, is the director of the Center for Research and Training (CRT) and the ASL Clear Project at the Learning Center for the Deaf in Framingham, Massachusetts. The CRT supports culturally and linguistically accessible education for deaf and hard of hearing students by consulting with schools, districts, and states on effective dual language instructional practices in ASL and English. As the ASL Clear project director, Jeanne leads a team of STEM content experts, technical staff, and university students in development of academic content and delivery in ASL. She also provides professional development workshops on using ASL Clear for instruction and interpretation, and collaborates with researchers interested in ASL Clear's innovations in both ASL-first design and ASL STEM content delivery. Jeanne oversees CRT's standardized test translation work and served as an ASL and Math content expert for the Guidelines for Accessible Assessments Project, an 18-state, multiyear research and coalition effort funded by the US Department of Education. She holds an MEd from Boston University, a BA in Linguistics from University of Southern Maine, and a Master Mentor Certificate from University of Colorado Boulder. Jeanne is the daughter of Deaf parents and a heritage signer of ASL.

Romy V. Spitz, Ph.D., is a subject matter specialist for the State of Maine Office of Aging and Disability Services on issues involving deafness, hearing loss, and linguistically challenged individuals. She teaches neurolinguistics in the Linguistics department at the University of Southern Maine. With an interest in communication assessment and habilitation for adults who face language and learning challenges, she has worked with many states who seek to establish innovative deaf services for nontraditional communicators within the mental health, intellectual disability, and vocational rehabilitation service systems.

Amy Szarkowski, Ph.D., is a psychologist who specializes in working with deaf and hard of hearing individuals and their families. Dr. Szarkowski holds an academic appointment as Instructor in the Department of Psychiatry at Harvard Medical School. She serves as a staff psychologist in the Deaf and Hard of Hearing Program at Boston Children's Hospital, where she conducts developmental and psychological assessments, provides counseling and support for young people with reduced hearing and their families, and offers guidance to families considering cochlear implantation. Dr. Szarkowski is a core faculty member for the LEND (Leadership and Education in Neurodevelopmental Disabilities) program at Boston Children's, which trains early career professionals in the health sciences on issues related to working with children with disabilities. Dr. Szarkowski also teaches an adjunct instructor in the Deaf and Hard of Hearing Infants, Toddlers and Families (ITF) Collaboration and Leadership program at Gallaudet University.

Melissa Watson, Ph.D., LPC, BMCBA, obtained her social work degree from Bloomsburg University. She holds two master's degrees—mental health counseling from Gallaudet University, and applied behavior analysis from Florida Institute of Technology. She has a Ph.D. from Capella University in public services leadership specializing in multidisciplinary human services. Melissa has worked with children, adolescents, and adults with behavioral challenges for over 20 years. After spending many of her professional years in Florida, she returned to her home state of Pennsylvania, to work at PAHrtners running the Residential Treatment Facility and Outpatient Programs. Recently Melissa was promoted to Vice President of the Residential Programs at PAHrtners Deaf Services

Joan Wattman, M.S., CSC, CI, CT, SC:L, received her BA in ASL linguistics from Hampshire College and her MS from the Teaching Interpreting Program at Western Maryland College (now McDaniel College). Joan interprets throughout New England, mostly in court and mental health settings, and leads interpreting workshops. For 15 years, Joan has been part of an intensive endeavor studying the Integrated Model of Interpreting (IMI) at the Etna Project/NH along with interpreters and interpreter-educators from all over the United States.

Roger C. Williams, M.S.W., is currently employed by the South Carolina Department of Mental Health as the Director of Services for the Deaf and Hard of Hearing. He was previously employed as the Program Manager for Deaf Services at the Piedmont Center for Mental Health Services. Roger is a South Carolina Licensed Master Social Worker and holds an RID Certificate of Transliteration and an SCAD/NAD IAP Level 5 Interpreting Certificate. In

2009, he was appointed as the United States Representative to the International Institute for Mental Health Leadership's Task Force for the Deaf and Hard of Hearing.

Kelly S. Wolf Craig, Ph.D., is a psychologist and clinical researcher at the University of Massachusetts (UMass) Medical Center. She completed her graduate work at Gallaudet University, where she studied the influence of Deaf identity on body image and eating disorders. At UMass, she provides individual psychotherapy to Deaf and hearing clients who come from all walks of life and are working toward improved mental health and creating their best life! She is one of the recipients of a Pilot Project Program awarded by the UMass Center for Clinical & Translational Science, where she and a team of Deaf and hearing clinicians and community members are developing an American Sign Language translation of the Edinburgh Postnatal Depression Scale.

About the Cover

"How Much Did I Understand?"

Nancy Rourke is an internationally-known Deaf artist and activist. As a full-time professional artist, she is very involved in implementing De'VIA art curriculum for Deaf children. Deaf View/Image Art, also known as De'VIA, is art that examines and expresses the Deaf experience from a cultural, linguistic, and intersectional point of view. She frequently does artist-in-residencies at Deaf schools nationwide where she teaches and makes art in Rourkeism De'VIA. This is a style of De'VIA, modeled after her work, and noteworthy for its use of bold primary colors and Deaf-themes expressing affirmation, resistance, and liberation. Nancy offers the De'VIA retreat, hosting art galleries for Deaf artists, raising awareness of Deaf people through Art. She has a book entitled "Nancy Rourke: Deaf Artist Series."

Nancy writes,

The picture on the book cover—"How much did I understand?"—consists of mirror portraits based on an historical silhouette of Alice Cogswell (who is famously known for being the reason Laurent Clerc came to America and partnered with Thomas Gallaudet to found the American School for the Deaf) reinterpreted through my own personal childhood language experiences.

The left side portrait is painted with oppressively dark colors. The missing puzzle pieces represent my high school experience of language deprivation and limited information access due of the practice of simultaneous communication. Because I was not provided with full language access through American Sign Language, I did not have the complete understanding I needed for rich learning and development of a positive self-image. This is conveyed by the missing puzzle pieces. In addition, the lines coming from the eyes on the left—this view of life—is narrower and more limited compared with the lines coming from the eyes on the right. The one yellow puzzle piece on the left symbolizes the hope in the mist of oppression provided by ASL. The brightly colored portrait on the right is complete without any missing pieces. This communicates the feeling of identity wholeness—a pride in being Deaf nurtured from a life with a complete and beautiful language in ASL.

As a whole, the painting is a commentary on the mental health of Deaf people and the tragic consequences of language deprivation, with the three main themes being Deaf culture and ASL affirmation, language deprivation, and Deaf mental health.

Introduction
Culture and Disability

NEIL S. GLICKMAN AND WYATTE C. HALL

Two Themes

Imagine you are an English-speaking, hearing person who runs a community mental health clinic in a major American city. Chances are that you receive referrals regularly to serve people who do not speak English well. Perhaps you are referred people who are native speakers of Spanish, Portuguese, Russian, Mandarin, or Vietnamese. If you have many such clients, you will probably seek to find clinicians who are fluent in their languages. As a second-best option, you'll draw upon foreign language interpreters. In these situations, you can usually assume something important about your clients. This is something so obvious that you probably don't think about it. You can assume that they are native users of their own languages. Furthermore, you can assume that unless they have suffered some major medical, neurological, or psychiatric challenge, they will be fluent users of their native language. You know, therefore, that you have language barriers to doing effective work. Most likely you realize that the language barriers are among many cross-cultural barriers you face. Hopefully, you also know that it requires various multicultural competencies to handle these language and cross-cultural challenges well (Sue & Sue, 2008).

Now imagine that a Deaf signing person applies for services at your clinic. Are the language, cultural, clinical, and administrative challenges you face similar to those that occur with other people who are not native English speakers? You might well think so, and there are clear similarities. Deaf people are certainly an oppressed minority, and a subgroup of deaf people, those who are culturally Deaf, have a distinct language and culture. Affirmation of this community, culture, and language—what is called a "culturally affirmative" perspective on Deaf people—is taken here as the necessary foundation for any attempt to provide competent and respectful mental health services for deaf people, just as a culturally affirmative perspective would be vital to working

1

with other people with cultures different than one's own (Glickman & Gulati, 2003; Glickman & Harvey, 1996; Leigh, 2010).

The comparison between deaf people and other linguistic and cultural minorities is not, however, a perfect one. Assuming you are knowledgeable about the cultural view of Deaf people, there are still significant ways in which this model does not adequately address the challenges you face when serving deaf people in your educational or treatment setting.

One core difference is the fact that culturally Deaf people, most of whom became deaf early in life, are a relatively small subset of a larger group of people who have hearing loss but experienced it postlingually (i.e., largely as older adults)—thus, the distinction between deaf and Deaf is important to this work.[1] We can talk about culturally Deaf people more positively not by saying they have "hearing loss" but that they have a visual orientation to life, a form of "Deaf gain" (Bauman & Murray, 2014). The larger group of people with post-lingual hearing loss, however, do generally experience this as a loss of hearing and a disability.

An even more important difference is that when working with signing culturally Deaf persons, you cannot assume they are native, fluent users of American Sign Language (ASL). They may well be, but language variation among deaf people is much greater than among hearing people, and "dysfluent language," by which we mean *language that native users would easily recognize to be unclear, poorly developed, and substandard for everyday conversational purposes*, is much more common. This is not the fault of deaf people; nor is it an inevitable consequence of deafness. This dysfluent language develops because most deaf children, even with interventions like cochlear implants, don't learn spoken language effortlessly like hearing children do and are, either intentionally or just due to lack of opportunity, denied opportunities for exposure to rich, natural sign language environments. Even deaf children in "signing environments" often have very poor sign language modeled for them. If, as a child, one cannot easily and naturally receive and practice a *first* language that is modeled by competent native users, one will struggle to learn *that* language as well as other languages. As we will learn in this book, the inability to develop native language skills *in any language* often has devastating consequences for a person's development.

In most of this book, we use the term "language deprivation" to explain this phenomenon of deaf children growing up without quality exposure to any fully accessible language. We use this term knowing that nobody raises a deaf child with the intention of depriving the child of language. We also use the term knowing that some hearing parents try their best to provide their deaf children with quality sign language exposure, including by working hard to learn the language themselves, and that this is easier said than done especially in localities where there are few signing resources to draw upon. We don't wish to do anything but applaud these efforts, nor do we wish to insult or hurt anyone by suggesting they intentionally want to deprive deaf children of language.

Nonetheless, the decision about whether and how to expose deaf children to sign language is bigger than the wishes and intentions of particular parents, physicians, or educators. It extends into the realm of law, educational policy, and social practice. As described by Corinna Hill in the book foreword and Tawny Holmes in the concluding chapter, *sign language deprivation* as educational and public policy—and as standard recommendations from many medical authorities—has persisted over the past three centuries. We use the term "language deprivation" as a way to emphasize that this condition is caused by people and is therefore preventable barring other developmental issues that impact language acquisition.

There are many deaf people who are *not* language deprived. There is nothing fundamental about not being able to hear that means that deaf people must be language deprived. In our opinion, using any phrase other than "language deprivation" risks whitewashing the fundamental fact that nearly all deaf children could be guaranteed a native first language foundation if society was organized and willing to make that happen.

Except in rare cases of extremely isolated or abused hearing children (such as the famous cases of the Wolf Boy and Genie [Lane, 1979]), the language deprivation deaf people may experience is unknown among hearing people. Essentially, for hearing children to experience the same level of everyday language deprivation as deaf children requires extraordinary conditions of abuse and/or neglect. Deaf mental health specialists work regularly with people who have been language deprived, yet clinicians who work only with hearing people (even if they are all users of minority languages) rarely, if ever, encounter anything comparable. They may be aware of language oppression, like the attempts to prevent Native American or Canadian First Nations' people from learning their tribal languages. Even in these horrible circumstances, however, these Native children still grow up with full access to a first language, albeit not their community's native language. In this, we would say they are language oppressed, but they are not language deprived.

Clinicians often do have experience of working with hearing people who are poor language users. This may be due to developmental disorders, head trauma, aphasias, or severe mental illnesses. In these cases, there is a medical basis for the language problem. There are also children raised in impoverished or traumatic environments. All these persons can show dysfluent communication, but unless they have profoundly impaired neurological functioning, they still acquire a native language. Deaf people can experience all these reasons for dysfluent communication, but many have one additional, and enormous, obstacle to language learning. A deaf child can be born with a brain fully prepared to acquire language yet be inadequately exposed to a language the brain can fully perceive and internalize.

It is well known that deaf children raised by native signers acquire language skills comparable to any other child who is exposed to language from birth

(Meadow, 2005). There is no doubt that there are a minority of deaf children who, with interventions like cochlear implantation, do hear enough that they acquire native or near-native spoken language skills (see Chapter 9 by Amy Szarkowski). In between these deaf native signers and speakers, however, are a larger number of deaf people with significantly impaired or dysfluent language skills in sign and spoken language. The extent of dysfluency varies enormously, again much more so than with hearing people, and is largely correlated with the quality of accessible language exposure they received in the first half-decade of their lives. Language deprivation in deaf people can vary from mild to catastrophic. At its extremes, language deprivation is arguably the most profound disability that can exist among human beings given the foundation that language provides for healthy development. It produces some people who are effectively alingual (Schaller, 1991). Even in less severe forms, however, the cognitive, psychological, social, and behavioral implications can be life shattering. In Deaf mental health, we work routinely with people who have these language challenges and we are witness to all the devastating consequences that follow.

Thus, the cultural perspective does not fully capture all the dimensions of Deaf mental health. Working with signing Deaf people often resembles work with minority foreign language speakers, especially when these people are educated and articulate sign language users. If you only work with competent signers, the cultural model for such work has great resonance and appeal. It makes intuitive sense and illuminates well many of the interpersonal dynamics that occur in the therapeutic context.

On the other hand, working with deaf people who have been severely language deprived, and who often have other, accompanying life challenges, resembles more the experience of working with people with developmental disabilities. This is especially true with the need to simplify and concretize communication and counseling strategies. Complicating all this work are additional forms of multicultural identification (e.g., culturally Deaf, culturally Puerto Rican, coming out as a variant of GLBTQ, among many others.) as well additional disabilities (e.g., limited vision developmental trauma, physical health challenges, substance use, etc.) Thus, Deaf mental health counselors find themselves pulled more to either a culturally affirmative or disability perspective, and their need to integrate these sometimes-opposing viewpoints forms the fundamental dialectical tension of this work.

We might summarize this by saying that Deaf mental health is a clinical specialty grounded in both cultural and disability considerations. One cannot do this work well without *both* a deep commitment to culturally affirmative mental health care and an appreciation of the experience of people with disabilities in our culture and society, including the profound disability of language deprivation (see Figure 0.1).

Figure 0.1 Culture and disability as guiding perspectives in Deaf
mental health

Deaf Mental Health

Deaf mental health is the name for this clinical specialty requiring mastery of this complex interplay of cultural and disability considerations. Without special training in Deaf mental health, clinicians make predictable mistakes. Some will be cultural faux pas such as asking culturally Deaf people to use their voice and to speech-read. Others may be serious clinical mistakes, like misdiagnosing Deaf culturally normative behaviors (i.e., highly expressive non-verbal communication) as indicators of psychopathology. We use the term Deaf mental health, as opposed to the older notion of mental health work with deaf people, to highlight that we are describing a distinct clinical specialty where trained clinicians need to have acquired a distinct knowledge base, a variety of specialized skills, and also to have undergone a measure of personal and cultural self-development. This is the second book to take explicitly this frame of reference (Glickman, 2013).

In Deaf mental health, the cultural model of Deaf people is necessary as part of a framework for service delivery. The cultural model emerged in reaction to the long-standing medical-pathological model of deaf people, the conceptualization of deaf people as those with a problem of sensory deprivation. The cultural model, in contrast, focuses upon the Deaf community as a linguistic and cultural minority group (Baker & Cokely, 1980). With growing recognition of sign languages as legitimate natural languages, and a parallel respect for Deaf culture, it was a natural step to argue that mental health services for deaf people should work from a cultural, as opposed to a disability, perspective (Glickman, 1996).

Working from this culturally affirmative perspective, recognizing the sign language abilities of deaf people is very important. Indeed, our developing field needed to do that for half a century before we could have the more nuanced conversation about language problems in some deaf people taking place in this book, and in many places in our field, at present.

Between the 1950s through the 1970s, when organized mental health services for deaf people in the United States began, we had very few properly trained professionals; indeed, the organized discussion of what constitutes proper training to do this work only began with the 1975 Spartanburg Conference on the Functions, Competencies and Training of Psychological Services to the Deaf (Levine, 1977). A half century ago, discussion of "poor language skills" in some deaf people occurred in a context where people equated "language" with spoken language or speech. This is a mistake that, alas, hasn't disappeared, but among Deaf mental health specialists, it is recognized now as uninformed and biased thinking. When ASL was just beginning to be recognized as a fully grammatical language a mere 50 years ago, there were few trained mental health professionals for work with deaf people and fewer places to do this work. Unexamined cultural prejudice in hearing people, what we'd now call "audism" (Lane, 1992), was not named or understood. In the 2010s, at least in some places, we can have a more nuanced discussion about language deprivation and the problems in both sign and spoken language that stem from it. We still need to have this discussion skillfully, because, at least in hearing people, the "pull" to blame these problems on deafness per se, and not examine the social causes, remains powerful. In other words, we need now to make sure that this conversation about language problems is focused on language deprivation, and not deafness.

The Editors' Perspectives on Language Deprivation in Deaf Mental Health

The two editors of this volume, Neil S. Glickman and Wyatte C. Hall, are from different generations. We're both psychologists, but Neil's work in the field began in 1983, after graduation from then Gallaudet College's graduate vocational rehabilitation program. He began work as a rehabilitation counselor with deaf persons and moved into the mental health field in 1986 when he was given the opportunity to cofound a Deaf psychiatric inpatient unit at Westborough State Hospital, in Massachusetts. He went back to school in 1989, became a psychologist in 1993, and returned to the Westborough Deaf Unit in 1996 for 14 more years, then as unit director and psychologist.

Wyatte's work really began with his entry into Gallaudet University's Clinical Psychology Ph.D. program in 2008. His clinical work was primarily with college students throughout his training. Both his internship at the University of Rochester's Deaf Wellness Center and his clinical postdoctoral fellowship at the University of Massachusetts were experiences where he began to explore the mental health implications of language deprivation. Pivoting to research that focuses upon the crucial role of language acquisition in deaf children, he is part of a new generation of Deaf and hearing academics that are attempting to address the language deprivation phenomenon head on.

Neil is hearing, and Wyatte is Deaf. We have a shared interest in the topic of both culturally affirmative mental health care and language deprivation; and we thought we'd both briefly share how these interests developed.

Neil, and colleague Sherry Zitter, established the Westborough State Hospital Deaf Unit as a "culturally affirmative" mental health program for Deaf people at a time when that was a brand new and very radical idea (Glickman & Zitter, 1989). In practice, a culturally affirmative treatment program meant hiring large numbers of deaf staff along with hearing signers, establishing a signing treatment milieu, and adapting treatment methodology so that it was more "Deaf friendly," on top of creating a work environment where cross-cultural conflicts between Deaf and hearing people were handled skillfully. These goals were easier said than done, especially because we had no models of such culturally-affirmative practice, but strong efforts were made to achieve them during the Unit's 23-year history. Westborough State Hospital closed in 2010, and Deaf services moved to the new Worcester (Massachusetts) Recovery Center and Hospital where Wyatte later did some of his postdoctoral psychology training.

In the last decade of the Westborough Deaf Unit's existence, staff conducted research into the communication abilities of the units' deaf patients. We found something that we all knew implicitly but hadn't been able to put our fingers on concretely: more than half of our deaf patients could not be said to possess native language skills in *any* language (Black & Glickman, 2005; Glickman, 2009). Due to language deprivation, and often also to other medical and developmental challenges and psychiatric problems, they were highly *dysfluent* spoken and sign language users.

When the Deaf Unit opened, we naively thought that hiring staff with competent signing abilities and sign language interpreters would overcome the communication challenges. Over time, we developed a deeper appreciation of just how daunting these communication challenges were.

To give one example, we had a day program with treatment groups, but the subjects of who could attend which groups, what resources were needed to lead them, and how to adapt each group were discussed nearly every morning in our daily "rounds." We'd ask, "who can attend Skills Group today?" and "Should we divide it into two or even three groups based on the communication abilities of the current patients?" We'd also discuss each day what adaptations we needed because, most of the time, we didn't have motivated people able to talk well about their lives. Instead, we had clientele who were often—due to language and learning challenges, and fund of information deficits, not to mention the more familiar clinical and behavioral challenges—unprepared to make use of traditional insight-oriented psychotherapy approaches.

As a hearing, second language ASL user, and someone who ran hundreds of skill training groups, I (Neil) was always concerned with whether I had sufficient communication abilities for the clientele in the hospital on any particular day, and if I didn't, who could assist me. I wasn't alone in this. We had Deaf signing staff who were linguistically sophisticated enough to worry about their own communication abilities; and we all worried about how to make our treatment efforts meaningful and relevant.

The highly diverse communication abilities of our clientele also meant that we needed a staff person, a "communication specialist," to assist us with the highly specialized skills of evaluating and matching the communication abilities of patients. As first conceived, we wanted the communication specialist to teach ASL to non-signing staff and guide us in creating a Deaf-friendly space. Over time, we came to appreciate just how many functions a talented communication specialist could assume. You will see that discussion furthered in this book within chapters that deal with language and communication assessment, late language development, and forensic assessment and training related to legal competency. These are all responsibilities that a talented communication specialist could, with the right training, potentially assume. If you administer a Deaf treatment program, you likely appreciate the value of staff that have outstanding communication abilities among other competencies that enable them to perform these duties.

Those of us from the Westborough unit would frequently say variations of "If only everyone here signed in competent ASL! If that were the case, this work would be so much easier!" Turns out, it wasn't the need to provide ASL communication that challenged us the most; it was the need to communicate and treat people who *didn't* use ASL, or any other language, well. When I started work at Westboro in 1986, I was preoccupied with the issue of cultural affirmation; but by the time Westborough closed in 2010, I had become more focused on the issue of how to adapt treatment approaches for persons with "language and learning challenges." I am pleased to see the theme of culturally affirmative mental health care spreading in Deaf services, but I am increasingly aware that this model is insufficient to guide quality work in this specialty.

Years later, while working in a Deaf group home, I was talking to a deaf man in the program about his deaf roommates. All of the residents of this program were deaf from birth and signed. I remember asking this man about a house meeting that was recently held. What did he think about the conversation? He looked at me with some frustration. "I don't understand them," he said, referring to his roommates. I teased him, saying, "but you sign, and they sign." "They have lousy sign language," he replied. "I don't understand them." That moment captured for me the difficulty of serving in one program so many people with widely variant communication abilities, including a majority who were language deprived in childhood.

The clinical director of this program was a native signing, highly competent Deaf professional, and all of her staff were signing Deaf people. She saw the problem of dysfluent sign language as a native signer would. I later attended a staff meeting with them where I was the only hearing person present, and the subject came up of how well we communicated with the residents. I readily acknowledged that I struggled often to communicate well, but as a hearing, second-language ASL user, this didn't surprise anyone. The Deaf clinical director then bravely acknowledged that at times, she understood maybe half of what some of the residents were saying. We then went around the room, and one by one, each staff member acknowledged that they often didn't fully understand the residents. This was very hard for them to admit, because as signing Deaf people, they knew they were hired in part for their communication abilities. It was a relief, however, to be able to acknowledge one "elephant in the room." We all struggled, to varying degrees, with the complex communication challenges of this work, and being Deaf didn't mean one didn't face these communication challenges also.

Thus, my own experience has lead me to believe that cultural affirmation and adaptation of treatment approaches for language-deprived people are the two key themes in Deaf mental health, and I have sought to examine these themes, with colleagues, over the course of my career (Glickman, 2009, 2017, 2013; Glickman & Gulati, 2003; Glickman & Harvey, 1996).

I (Wyatte) grew up in a huge public school with my high school graduating class consisting of approximately 2,000 students. I was fortunate enough that the deaf program in my school was relatively large (approximately 30 students)—although we deaf students were greatly outnumbered. The deaf education program at my school had a deaf classroom where sign language was used and which, for students like me who could keep pace with the public-school curriculum, served as a homeroom and study hall. Other students who couldn't keep up with the public-school curriculum remained in the deaf classroom all day.

Towards the end of middle school, I began to notice something jarring about the deaf classroom and the students who stayed there all day. Looking back now, I can see that my own interests and knowledge base were growing at a reasonable pace parallel to my education; whereas, for other deaf students, their educational progress seemed to remain stuck at a much younger level. I remember wondering why the educational materials in the deaf classroom, such as the reading and math materials, appeared to be at an elementary school level. As time went on and the gap in overall development grew larger, this bothered me, but I did not yet have the context and knowledge to understand it.

Even at the time, however, I had a suspicion that language abilities were at the heart of the matter. When I became an undergraduate, I began to focus on research related to reading abilities of deaf children. This interest continued in my graduate studies, and when it came time to write a dissertation, I looked at the relationship between ASL and English reading skills. Looking back on my education and professional path, seeing my so-called peers steadily fall behind year after year clearly left a lasting mark on me. Why couldn't they read and write as well as I could? Why were their language and conceptual worlds (what we now call "world knowledge" or "fund of information") so far behind everyone else in school? Why was I doing better, and what could be done to help my deaf peers?

It was not until my predoctoral internship year that I received the "words" to describe what I saw growing up and what I could still see affecting many deaf people within the community. My "aha!" moment came while watching an online lecture from Dr. Sanjay Gulati on the subject he discusses in Chapter 1 of this book, the topic that also became the focus of one of my first professional publications (Hall, Levin, & Anderson, 2017) and remains one of my primary research interests. In essence, the condition he called "language deprivation syndrome" seemed to explain much of what I had seen growing up and then later as I began work as a clinical psychologist with deaf people.

Does this mean that I think that my deaf peers growing up had language deprivation syndrome? No, I don't think that's the case. Does it mean they were affected by language deprivation? Absolutely. There is no question that for many of them, their language, maturity, social skills, and understanding of the world were not developing consistently with what one would expect for native users of a language. It's hard for me to be fully confident in these conclusions because as a child I couldn't analyze well what I was seeing, and my memory is imperfect. Were they receiving fluent, native, fully accessible language exposure? No, I don't think they were—neither in school, in their "signing" deaf classroom, and certainly not at home. How much better could they have done if they had a fuller, richer, native sign language experience? Probably quite a lot.

While I cannot assess the language skills and background factors of my deaf peers in retrospect, the idea of language deprivation syndrome made immediate, profound, and intuitive sense to me. It seemed to offer at least a partial explanation for what I had witnessed. This became especially salient for me as I came to the University of Massachusetts Medical School for my clinical postdoctoral year. I worked there alongside Drs. Melissa Anderson and Neil S. Glickman. UMass is unique in that across the street is one of the few, clinical inpatient programs that serves deaf people, and, as Neil mentioned, I did some of my postdoctoral work at this site. This was not the full Deaf program that existed at Westborough State Hospital for 23 years, but it is still an identified Deaf service with a critical mass of deaf patients and does a lot of work with severely language-deprived and dysfluent patients. It was here that I interacted with people even worse off than those I had grown up with. I met deaf people with even more profound levels of language deprivation and with the cognitive and psychosocial aspects of language deprivation syndrome that Dr. Gulati discusses.

As I integrated my childhood and professional experiences, I have become increasingly passionate about the problem of language deprivation. In particular, what drives me now is the fact that this problem is largely preventable. It is caused by either ignorance about the importance of early sign language exposure or, in some cases, the outright bigotry of withholding the language that many Deaf people, over centuries, have considered their birthright. Eventually, I pivoted from clinical work into research because I didn't want to just be a clinician helping people deal with the aftermath of language deprivation. I wanted, through research and intervention development, to change the conditions that fostered the problem.

As I begin to grow a research program, present on the topic, and do projects such as this book focusing on language deprivation, I am often asked something along the lines of "So why are you so lucky? What was different about your upbringing that you avoided consequences many others experience?" Well, I think I'd have to acknowledge that, compared to most of my deaf peers, I didn't experience the same kind of profound language deprivation. This is probably mostly because I was likely hard of hearing as a very young child before losing more hearing in elementary school. I learned to speak on my own, and my parents were not aware of any significant language problems until I entered kindergarten. At that point, teachers told my parents that I was approximately two years behind where I should be for kindergarten-readiness. Those teachers also told my parents that they would use sign communication with me (not ASL, but one of the popular signing systems from the 1970s/1980s that were thought to promote English fluency). They weren't using a natural sign language, but because I was functioning as a hard-of-hearing student, I could benefit from this sign supported speech.

I think I was fortunate because I had just enough hearing to begin acquiring at least some language before going into school. I was fortunate to have teachers who supported visual access to communication and told my parents that this is how it would be, even if they didn't see the need for it at the time. I was also fortunate to have parents who, despite never really picking up any fluency in sign language, gave me every resource and support they could to promote my education, including devoting a great deal of time to reading and doing basic math with me. Eventually, like many deaf people, I found my way to ASL sometime in my young adulthood during college.

Here's the take-home point from my experiences. If normal development is like walking a wide path where there is ample room to fall, scrape one's knees, and get back up, then development without effortless language acquisition is like walking a tight rope without a safety net. I walked this tight rope and somehow got to the other side. Had I been fully deaf from birth, my language development would have been much different. Most deaf children, when having to walk this same tightrope, need the support of a fully accessible language. Without this support, any troublesome wind can knock them off the tightrope. The damage they then experience is more profound than scraped knees. From the safe platform on the other side, with bilingual skills in English and ASL, I look back to see just how thin this tight rope unnecessarily is, how many don't make it, and how easy it is to make things better for deaf children. I was lucky in that I was born with just enough hearing, had parents fully able to commit themselves to my education, and no doubt I'm lucky in other ways I am unaware of. Success for deaf children, however, should not depend on luck. When we ensure that deaf children have rich exposure to natural sign languages, we remove the problems associated with inadequate development of a native language and their developmental path widens, making it far easier for them to reach the other side and seize the full potential every child is born with.

Topics Addressed in This Book

This book assumes the culturally affirmative framework for a multidisciplinary discussion of language deprivation in deaf people. The structure of the book could be conceptualized in two ways. The first is with the picture presented in Figure 0.2, where language deprivation is the hub of a wheel, and the surrounding spokes of the wheel refer to the implications of language deprivation discussed in this book.

The second way to conceptualize the structure of the book is by dividing it into three parts. Part 1 (Chapters 1–4) describes language deprivation syndrome and then presents mental health and forensic interventions. Part 2 (Chapters 5–8) focuses upon communication skill assessment and development and interpreting with language deprived deaf people. Part 3 (Chapters 9 and 10) discusses cochlear implantation, language policy, and advocacy. This is represented by the three parts of a pie, presented in Figure 0.3*

With both structures, it should be clear that we are casting a wide net for the domains of Deaf mental health. Strictly speaking, the more clinical aspects of this work are in the first four chapters. Yet one of the distinguishing

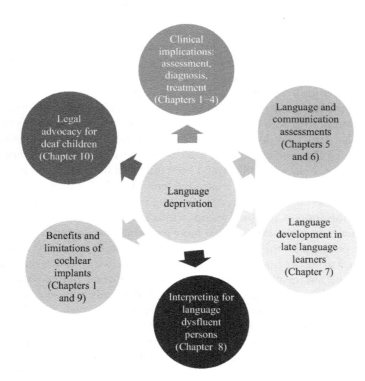

Figure 0.2 Language deprivation and implications discussed in this book

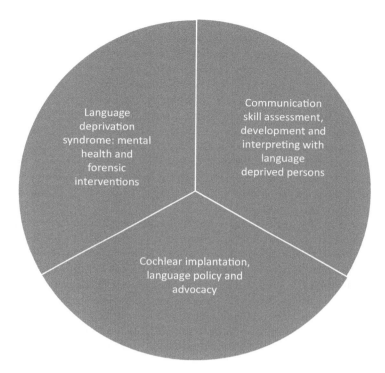

Figure 0.3 The three-part structure of this book

features of this clinical specialty is the need for practitioners to have a broad understanding of language assessment, development, and interpreting. This is because the communication skills and deficits of deaf people vary so much more than those of hearing people, and because all practitioners of this work, deaf and hearing, work regularly and closely with sign language interpreters. It is also because practitioners of this work inevitably find themselves thinking about communication matters such as how to adapt one's language and communication approach and how to develop the communication abilities of one's clientele. Finally, it is because language is inherently a social and political issue. Deaf mental health practitioners, working as we do with at least two languages (and all their variants) and with many language-dysfluent individuals, cannot avoid confrontation with technological, social, and political trends impacting language pedagogy and practice.

A Brief Discussion of This Book's Chapters

Deaf historian Corinna Hill began the book with a foreword placing the theme of language deprivation in its social and historical context. She shows that there is nothing new in having medical, education, and other authorities argue about the alleged dangers of exposing deaf children to sign language. The contemporary warning not to allow deaf children with cochlear implants to sign is just old wine in new bottles. The arguments were misleading, unfounded, and destructive then, and they remain so now.

Following this introduction, the book begins with a chapter by deaf psychiatrist Sanjay Gulati on language deprivation syndrome. Dr. Gulati is, as far as we know, the only Deaf signing psychiatrist in the world, and he is the undisputed authority on this condition. Dr. Gulati describes language deprivation syndrome as, structurally, incomplete neurodevelopment and, functionally, an intellectual disability. He describes the cognitive and psychosocial implications of language deprivation syndrome and common clinical presentations of people with this condition.

The next two chapters address the challenges of psychotherapy when language deprivation is a factor. Glickman and colleagues Wendy Heines and Melissa Watson, from PAHrtners Deaf Services in Glenside, Pennsylvania, present an introduction to his "pre-therapy" model for clinical work with people who lack the language and cognitive abilities needed to make use of conventional "talk" therapy. This pre-therapy model, introduced here through a series of clinical vignettes, is designed primarily to help clinical staff think about and adapt their interventions so that they are both more "Deaf friendly" and also more "language and learning challenged friendly." It is based on adaptations of best practices in the cognitive behavior therapy world and it draws upon what is known about "common factors" that are associated with psychotherapy success, regardless of the treatment model (Duncan, Miller, Wampold, & Hubble, 2010).

In Chapter 3, psychologists Melissa Anderson and Kelly Wolf Craig describe the adaptations Melissa and her team have made to Seeking Safety, an evidenced-based cognitive behavioral treatment for persons with substance abuse and trauma histories. Their adaptation, called Signs of Safety, also draws on what is known about treatment adaptations for deaf persons. Preliminary data indicates this approach holds great promise for therapy-ready deaf persons, including those with moderate levels of language deprivation. It may well become the first evidenced-based therapy practice for this population.

Many people with language deprivation syndrome get in trouble with the law. This problem is discussed in the Appendix to Chapter 1. It falls on forensically trained mental health clinicians to determine whether they are competent to work with their attorneys in a courtroom or whether they could become legally competent with the right assistance. In Chapter 4, psychologists Robert Q. Pollard, Jr. and Meghan L. Fox describes the approach Pollard uses to assess legal competency, including spoken and sign language abilities. They also address the challenges of helping people who are legally incompetent due to language deprivation become competent. Their chapter beautifully illustrates the need for forensically trained mental health clinicians who are both culturally competent and capable of adapting their work for people with language deprivation.

As stated before, the next four chapters are more narrowly focused on communication skill assessment and development and interpreting with language-deprived deaf persons. Because the language and communication skills of deaf people vary so widely, a competent communication/language assessment should occur at the beginning of any treatment program—something rarely done. Indeed, we think it fair to say that the sophistication of any Deaf mental health service is probably reflected foremost in the quality of the communication assessments that are done and the skill to which the findings of these assessments are integrated into intervention efforts. This is the cutting edge of Deaf mental health, a mark of truly expert work.

So why is that type of work so rarely done? This is partially because we have very few validated tools for assessing signing abilities and very few qualified communication assessors. Two chapters on communication assessment are included in this book and are meant to promote this practice. The first, by Roger C. Williams and Charlene J. Crump, who are mental health interpreter educators, describe the current "state of the art" in communication assessment for Deaf mental health as a field. Williams and Crump present their assessment tool, which is available online (See Chapter 5),and discuss how it can be used to further Deaf mental health treatment plans.

As good as this tool is, however, it is not validated by research and therefore cannot be used to compare one person with another. Chapter 6 by Jon Henner, Jeanne Reis, and Robert Hoffmeister, key figures in the development and validation of the American Sign Language Assessment Instrument (ASLAI), is included to present the state of the art in formalized, research-based ASL assessment. Ultimately, assessments must draw on such research-validated instruments but, as Henner et al. describe, this is easier said than done. Their chapter focuses primarily upon tests of receptive ASL skills because it is easier to control for examiner expertise with receptive tests. Both Chapters 5 and 6 also discuss the importance of assuring properly trained communication evaluators.

Working with language-deprived people always presents educators and clinicians with the challenge of helping these people communicate better. Indeed, attention to language development as part of counseling and therapy may well be another hallmark of Deaf mental health, especially when working with deaf children (Bishop, 2013). It is widely recognized that neurodevelopmental capacity for language development is limited after the critical window for language learning closes around five years old. This does not mean, however, that language and communication development cannot still happen, albeit in a more limited form. It clearly can happen, but what would the optimal pedagogical strategies be to facilitate late language development?

A recent historical event, the revolution in Nicaragua in the 1980s, inadvertently produced a natural laboratory in which to study this question. The new government in Nicaragua decided to create the first Deaf schools in the county, and in the process of doing so, they brought deaf people isolated in remote parts of the country together. As there was not yet an indigenous sign language, the expectation was that the deaf children could be taught an established sign language like ASL. Linguists and researchers Judy Kegl and Romy Spitz, among others, were brought in to assist. To everyone's astonishment, the deaf children were not interested in learning a language brought in from outside. Instead, the deaf children spontaneously developed their own sign language. This gave the researchers a front row seat to observe and study the development of a new language. This was a rare and precious opportunity to learn about the human minds' innate capacity for language development (Pinker, 1994).

Kegl, Spitz, and the other linguists involved in this project also had the opportunity to interact with large numbers of essentially alingual deaf adults. These were deaf people who were never educated, never given any language, and who were now well-past the critical period for language acquisition. While these people would never become native language users, the researchers began to explore different pedagogical methods to see whether and how their communication and language skills could be developed. In Chapter 7, Spitz and Kegl discuss what they have learned about language development in these a-lingual deaf persons. They also present their pioneering method, Gramaticas, for helping late language learners. The principles they describe for late language learners have wide applicability in Deaf education and Deaf mental health and should be part of the body of knowledge acquired by anyone in the role of communication specialist with deaf people.

When hearing clinicians are faced with the challenge of serving deaf people for the first time, their go-to intervention is usually to bring in a sign language interpreter. Yet interpreters are professionals trained to translate between competent users of different languages. They are usually not trained to work with people who aren't competent language users. Indeed, the interpreting field is only very recently taking on the challenge of preparing interpreters for work with dysfluent or atypical signers. This topic was probably first addressed by Robyn Dean and Robert Q. Pollard, Jr. through their Demand Control Schema (Dean & Pollard, 2013). Their approach is taught at the yearly mental health interpreter training program sponsored by the Alabama Department of Deaf Services. More recently, the Center for Atypical Language Interpretation (CALI) at the Northeastern University Interpreter Training program has begun a detailed study of "atypical" sign language (a broader category that includes dysfluent signing) and has developed an on-line training program on interpreting atypical sign language. Because much fewer deaf children are being exposed to natural sign languages at residential schools, a generation of deaf children is growing up with even less native signing abilities than usual. The CALI project is in anticipation of the fact that the sign language interpreting world is likely to be increasingly focused on developing interpreting strategies when working with atypical and dysfluent communication.

In a previous volume, we included a chapter on the application of the Demand Control Schema to interpreting and mental health assessment with dysfluent signers (Glickman & Crump, 2017). In this volume, we wanted to expand the conversation by including another interpreting model. In Chapter 8, master interpreter Joan Wattman presents the Integrated Model of Interpreting (IMI), developed by interpreter-educator Betty Colonomos, and describes its applications when interpreting for language-dysfluent people. As Wattman explains, the key idea in IMI is that "to interpret, one must understand." What happens, then, when dysfluent communication interferes with the ability of the interpreters to understand what is being said and to interpret back in a way that the participants can understand? How do interpreters trained in IMI think about this problem, and what interpreting strategies are available to them to promote effective comprehension? Wattman describes the difficult challenges faced by a team of hearing and Deaf legal interpreters when interpreting for a deaf, language dysfluent defendant in a high-stakes legal context.

The final two chapters of the book address cochlear implantation, language policy, and advocacy. In both Chapter 1 by Sanjay Gulati and Chapter 9 by psychologist Amy Szarkowski, there is extensive discussion of cochlear implants and their implications for language development in deaf children. Szarkowksi and Gulati are colleagues who are part of the deaf and hard of hearing program at Boston's Children's Hospital. They work extensively with deaf children and their families, otolaryngologists and other medical personnel, as part of a program that performs cochlear implantation in deaf children, but also strives to be objective and culturally sensitive regarding best practices to promote their language development.

In Gulati's and Szarkowski's chapters, we address another one of the "elephants in the room" in any conversation about language development. Because the proponents of implantation so regularly overstate its benefits—and so regularly advocate against exposing deaf children to a natural sign language—we include this information to provide a realistic and objective account of the benefits and limitations of implantation, and to explain why rich exposure to natural sign languages remains vital for most deaf children before *and* after implantation.

Of course, the best approach to language deprivation is to prevent it in the first place. In a world with a dwindling number of resources for exposing deaf children to rich signing environment, this challenge is becoming increasingly formidable. In Chapter 10, Tawny Holmes, an attorney from the National Association of the Deaf, describes legal and advocacy strategies to ensure that deaf children receive rich, fully accessible language exposure in our current medical, education, and political landscape.

Cultural Insensitivity, Language Deprivation, and Clinical Mistakes

If culture and disability are the two main themes of Deaf mental health, one would expect to see clinicians make clinical mistakes, either because they are insufficiently culturally attuned and skilled, or because they fail to adequately address unique disability considerations, such as the implications of language deprivation, for their interventions.

Failure to consider Deaf people as a cultural and linguistic minority usually entails, for hearing people, failure to appreciate how their being hearing relates to power and privilege, how it shapes one's worldview, attitude, and behavior, just as race, religion, ethnicity, gender, and sexual orientation do (Glickman, 1996; Gournaris & Aubrecht, 2013; Hoffmeister & Harvey, 1996). Hearing people with inadequate cultural self-awareness may also fail to consider how their organization, policies, and procedures contain systematic biases that influence, and perhaps impede, their ability to serve deaf people. One sees this in the all-too-familiar examples of Deaf services administered by culturally uninformed hearing people, where destructive cross-cultural conflicts are omnipresent (Glickman & Heines, 2017). One also sees this in the clinical naiveté of culturally uninformed and unskilled practice. For instance, a hearing clinician in an emergency room who is evaluating a deaf person brought in by the police for psychiatric assessment, might not only not use an interpreter, but also ask a battery of standardized questions in rapid-fire succession, all the while typing on his laptop and barely making eye contact with his deaf patient. This deaf patient, who has been waiting for hours (it is sometimes days), without meaningful communication in a small evaluation room, becomes agitated; and the clinician fails to see how his own behavior, and the communication isolation of the setting, is triggering the patient.

The deaf patient is then psychiatrically hospitalized and sees another hearing clinician who is working for the first time with a deaf person. The unit has obtained an interpreter, at least for this clinical interview (not for most of interactions that happen throughout the day in the unit milieu), but the clinician holds unexamined, unconscious assumptions that psychological problems like depression, anxiety, and poor anger control, perhaps even paranoia and psychosis, must be direct by-products of deafness (he imagines what it would be like for him to be deaf and projects this on to his patient). The clinician can guess that frustration with the poor communication environment of the unit must be making matters worse for the patient, but as the patient doesn't engage, the clinician sees only a deeply disturbed person, and the best the program can offer are medications that target symptoms and behaviors.

In both these situations, the deaf person, triggered by environments where people in power repeat oppressive behaviors, is at high risk for behavioral dysregulation (i.e., "blow-ups"), which could lead to mechanical or chemical restraint, creating layer upon layer of isolation and trauma within the treatment setting. Variations on this theme are common for deaf persons in mental health settings.

There is probably no greater example of the cultural bias of the majority, and their abuse of power, than when medical or educational professionals advise parents of deaf children to prevent their children from having sign language exposure. These behaviors are normative among many medical professionals recommending cochlear implantations. Throughout this book, we argue that it is not strictly the cochlear implantation (which clearly helps some deaf people acquire spoken language skills and others acquire environmental sound awareness), which is problematic but the spoken-language only philosophy that all too often accompanies it. Done with more sensitivity to the needs of deaf children for easily accessible visual communication, cochlear implantation can be part of a multipronged effort to affirm both spoken and sign language and give deaf children optimal exposure to both languages (see Chapter 9).

Another example of such cultural bias of the majority is how assumptions in federal law about "least restrictive educational placements" inevitably privilege the hearing viewpoint that mainstreamed, integrated settings are preferable to specialized Deaf settings. Better language learning opportunities for deaf students require a critical mass of them to be brought together, yet we are seeing these opportunities for deaf peer group interaction and quality sign language exposure disappear, not only as residential Deaf schools close but also as large mainstream programs become rarer (see Chapter 10). This dwindling of specialized Deaf educational resources also means there is a dwindling of appropriately trained teachers and counselors. This creates a negative feedback loop in which the mainstreamed philosophy is bolstered by lack of specialized alternatives, and decreased opportunities for quality sign language exposure further reinforce the apparent inevitability of mainstreaming as the only educational path available.

Between the resurgent Oralist philosophy accompanying the spreading of the cochlear implant industry and the disappearance of quality signing Deaf educational resources, many deaf children today are facing a worsening of the long-standing "language emergency" that Sanjay Gulati says causes language deprivation syndrome. Those of us who have worked in Deaf education and Deaf mental health for decades know how many deaf people have been literally saved by sign language. We shudder to think about the educational and clinical challenges the next generation of providers will face in the absence of specialized Deaf educational and treatment resources, not to mention the tragedy of more deaf people with language deprivation syndrome. We fear that language-deprived and dysfluent deaf signers, with all this implies for psychosocial and cognitive development and functioning, will grow in numbers even as, ironically, increasing numbers of hearing people discover the beauties of natural sign languages like ASL and learn them as second languages at the college level.

The mental health clinicians who work without awareness of the context for the language, cognitive, and psychosocial development problems they encounter will inevitably misattribute all this to deafness. They will have neither the cultural nor the disability perspectives and tools they need to do this work.

How the Conversation about Language Deprivation Goes Wrong

This book advances the discussion of culturally affirmative mental health care for deaf people by highlighting the continuing impact of the disability that is language deprivation. This discussion requires us to examine again the issue of language competencies and deficits in deaf people. For professionals in mental health, education, and interpreting, there is no topic more likely to be mishandled, resulting in new assaults on deaf people, than the complex and highly sensitive issue of language abilities. How can this conversation go wrong? What will the next generation of clinical mistakes look like? We do not think this is hard to predict.

1   To begin with, culturally unaware professionals will continue to confuse language with speech. The acquisition of better speech skills does not equate to the acquisition of language; and focus on speech alone often has the result of neglecting true language and wider cognitive development. No matter our pleas, throughout this book, to consider the problem of dysfluent language in the context of the social cause of language deprivation, that latter point will be lost, and the discussion of language deprivation will just reinforce old incorrect notions about the language problems thought to be inextricably associated with deafness. Indeed, that is our greatest fear in launching this book into the world.

2   Hearing people who are not skilled sign language users will make uninformed judgments and pronouncements about what they presume to be poor sign language skills in deaf people. Indeed, one can "bet the house" that this will happen regularly. Related to this, formal communication assessments will be done by unqualified people. This is one of the major worries described by Williams and Crump in Chapter 5. It is the main reason that the discussion of formal sign language assessment by Henner and colleagues in Chapter 6 is limited to receptive language tests. Communication assessments done by unqualified people already happen, and there is every reason to believe this unfortunate and damaging practice will continue—at great cost to the unfortunate subjects of these evaluations.

3   There is a saying that, "if the only tool you have is a hammer, every problem will look like a nail." The problem of language deprivation syndrome requires new tools. In Chapter 1, Sanjay Gulati offers some suggestions regarding psychopharmacology, but he certainly knows, and writes, that *one can't treat language deprivation with medication.* Nonetheless, wouldn't it be easier for psychiatrists working with language-deprived deaf people to think this syndrome is treated with medication than for systems to provide linguistically and clinically attuned treatment and rehabilitation settings? One of the worst

outcomes we could anticipate would be that a diagnosis of language deprivation syndrome would lead to a treatment plan consisting solely of psychiatric medications.

If you think this can't happen, consider how medical professionals commonly respond to deaf children who have attention, learning, and behavioral problems. What's easier: providing the appropriate educational setting and supports or diagnosing the child with something like Attention Deficit Hyperactivity Disorder or Bipolar Disorder and treating the child with medication? When deaf children have attention, learning, and behavioral problems now, are they more likely to get an alternative educational or treatment setting or service or to receive medication? When deaf adults find themselves in psychiatric crises, how often are they offered anything besides psychiatric medication?

4   The proposed diagnosis of language deprivation syndrome must still be defined with clear diagnostic criteria established through research. The diagnosis explains a lot, but the boundaries of the diagnosis are not yet clear. This means there is a great danger of inappropriate use of the diagnosis, especially considering that milder levels of language dysfluency are extremely common in people born deaf. Predictably, enthusiasm about this new concept could lead to new ways of pathologizing deaf people. The diagnosis of LDS could even be used, in a true upside-down world, to justify further withholding of sign language from deaf children.

5   Proponents of cochlear implants will take great offense to the suggestion that they are somehow promoting language deprivation. Their intention, of course, is to promote language acquisition. The problem of language deprivation will be addressed through more cochlear implantation, not more sign language exposure. Indeed, the whole discussion of language deprivation in this book will be construed as anti-implantation when it is really just pro-sign language.

Deaf mental health clinicians work with many people for whom the high-risk strategy of preventing deaf children from receiving quality sign language exposure creates a bee's nest of psychological, behavioral, and social problems. Oralists who promote this practice never accept long-term accountability for contributing to these poor results. Providing deaf children, implanted or not, quality exposure to natural sign languages is a *no-risk strategy* that doesn't preclude, and likely advances, the acquisition of spoken language abilities.

Conclusion

This discussion about language deprivation and dysfluent sign is a very difficult one to do skillfully and respectfully. It is also a highly political discussion that can't help but be provocative. The problem is akin to discussing poorer academic achievement or lower levels of cognitive and psychosocial functioning when they are found in any group of oppressed and disadvantaged persons. It is just so easy for members of the majority community to presume their own superiority and attribute these poorer performance measures to alleged qualities of the minority people (e.g., lower intelligence, presumed racial or ethnic characteristics, or assumptions about what is psychologically normal and healthy.) To our minds, that is more reason for insisting that this conversation about language deprivation occur in the context of cultural affirmation for Deaf people, and above all in the context of affirmation for natural sign languages.

The tragedy of language deprivation is that it is largely preventable. This condition stems not from the absence of hearing but from the age-old fear of difference. It comes from the inability of the powerful to hear and value what Deaf people, as a group, have always said: not that they shouldn't speak or hear as best they can; but that they *must* sign, and that with rich and full sign language acquisition and expression comes entry into all the world's bounties.

Note

1   Throughout this book, we will follow these conventions for the use of "Deaf" and "deaf." We use the capitalized "Deaf" to refer to Deaf culture, Deaf history, the Deaf community, Deaf interpreters, Deaf schools, Deaf mental health, or explicit references to culturally Deaf or Signing Deaf or Deafblind people. In all other instances, we use the lower case "deaf." When speaking about deaf people in general, the lower case is the default.

References

Baker, C., & Cokely, D. (1980). *American Sign Language: A teacher's resource text on grammar and culture.* Silver Spring, MD: T.J. Publishers.

Bauman, H. -D. L., & Murray, J. J. (Eds.). (2014). *Deaf gain: Raising the stakes for human diversity.* Minneapolis: University of Minnesota Press.

Bishop, K. (2013). Culturally affirmative adaptations to trauma treatment with deaf children in a residential setting. In N. Glickman (Ed.), *Deaf mental health care.* New York, NY: Routledge.

Black, P., & Glickman, N. (2005). Language deprivation in the deaf inpatient population. *JADARA, 39*(1), 1–28.

Dean, R. K., & Pollard, R. Q., Jr. (2013). *The demand-control schema: Interpreting as a practice profession.* North Charleston, SC: Robyn K. Dean and Robert Q. Pollard, Jr.

Duncan, B. L., Miller, S. D., Wampold, B. E., & Hubble, M. (Eds.). (2010). *The heart and soul of change: Delivering what works in therapy* (2nd ed.). Washington, DC: American Psychological Association.

Glickman, N. (1996). What is culturally affirmative psychotherapy? In N. Glickman & M. Harvey (Eds.), *Culturally affirmative psychotherapy with deaf persons.* Mahwah, NJ: Lawrence Earlbaum Associates.

Glickman, N. (2009). *Cognitive behavioral therapy for deaf and hearing persons with language and learning challenges.* New York, NY: Routledge.

Glickman, N. (2017). *Preparing deaf and hearing persons with language and learning challenges for CBT: A pre-therapy workbook.* New York, NY: Routledge.

Glickman, N. (Ed.). (2013). *Deaf mental health care.* New York, NY: Routledge.

Glickman, N., & Crump, C. (2017). Sign language dysfluency in some deaf persons: Implications for interpreters and clinicians working in mental health settings. In N. S. Glickman (Ed.), *Deaf mental health care* (pp. 138–180). New York, NY: Routledge.

Glickman, N., & Gulati, S. (2003). *Mental health care of deaf people: A culturally affirmative approach*. Mahwah, NJ: Lawrence Erlbaum Associates.

Glickman, N., & Harvey, M. (Eds.). (1996). *Culturally affirmative psychotherapy with deaf persons*. Mahway, NJ: Lawrence Erlbaum Associates.

Glickman, N., & Heines, W. (2017). Creating culturally and clinically competent deaf residential treatment programs. In N. Glickman (Ed.), *Deaf mental health care*. New York, NY: Routledge.

Glickman, N., & Zitter, S. (1989). On establishing a culturally affirmative psychiatric unit for deaf people. *JADARA, 23*(2), 46–59.

Gournaris, M. J., & Aubrecht, A. L. (2013). Deaf/hearing cross-cultural conflicts and the creation of culturally competent treatment programs. In N. S. Glickman (Ed.), *Deaf mental health care* (pp. 69–106). New York, NY: Routledge.

Hall, W. C., Levin, L. L., & Anderson, M. I. (2017). Language deprivation syndrome: A possible neurodevelopmental disorder with sociocultural origins. *Social Psychiatry and Psychiatric Epidemiology, 52*(761). doi:10.1007/s00127-017-1351-7

Hoffmeister, R., & Harvey, M. (1996). Is there a psychology of the hearing? In N. Glickman & M. Harvey (Eds.), *Culturally affirmative psychotherapy with deaf persons*. Mahwah, NJ: Lawrence Erlbaum Associates.

Lane, H. (1979). *The wild boy of Aveyron*. Cambridge, MA: Harvard University Press.

Lane, H. (1992). *The mask of benevolence*. New York, NY: Knoff.

Leigh, I. (2010). *Psychotherapy with deaf clients from diverse groups, Second edition*. Washington, DC: Gallaudet University Press.

Levine, E. (1977). *The preparation of psychological service providers to the deaf: A report of the Spartanburg conference on the functions, competencies and training of psychological service providers to the deaf*: PRWAD Monograph No. 4.

Meadow, K. P. (2005). Early manual communication in relation to the deaf child's intellectual, social and communicative functioning. *The Journal of Deaf Studies and Deaf Education, 20*(4, 1), 321–329.

Pinker, S. (1994). *The language instinct: How the mind creates language*. New York: HarperCollins.

Schaller, S. (1991). *A man without words*. Los Angeles: University of California Press.

Sue, D. W., & Sue, D. (2008). *Counseling the culturally different* (5th ed.). Hoboken, NJ: Wiley.

1
Language Deprivation Syndrome

SANJAY GULATI

Introduction

Fifteen years ago, I was asked to evaluate a young deaf man with behavioral problems, labile emotions, and academic difficulties. Nothing in his educational, medical, or psychological testing history seemed to explain his presenting symptoms. He was superficially articulate, charming, and warm—yet his thinking was unusually concrete. He showed gaps in empathy with others and was prone to angrily acting out. Stymied, I speculated that rather than a mental illness, he had "some type of learning disability."

I would now diagnose this patient with "language deprivation syndrome." That is, even though he was educated in programs designed for deaf children, his brain was exposed to insufficient linguistic input in earliest childhood to foster the development of a *truly fluent* first language. Although he later learned a great deal more language, he continued to exhibit deficits in nearly every area of daily functioning, not merely in his language skills. These deficits persisted despite intensive (and expensive) remedial schooling and vocational support.

Perhaps once a century, a child with normal hearing experiences isolation from human contact so profound as to prevent learning a "mother tongue." Among deaf children, by contrast, incomplete language acquisition is epidemic. Acquiring language—any language—is the greatest challenge that deaf children face. Yet the reality and the risks of language deprivation are barely noted in the scientific literature or among the hearing majority. As the example before shows, they are not even readily identified by supposed experts in deafness. Deaf children can be raised in loving homes, treated by medical specialists, fitted with high-tech electronic aids, and provided special education, yet still emerge from childhood with a devastating, permanent, and *preventable* disability.

Early language deprivation seems to cause a recognizable constellation of social, emotional, intellectual, and other consequences. I term this constellation

Language Deprivation *Syndrome* (LDS) to emphasize its internal coherence and its predictability. This name has the advantage of placing responsibility for a child's language and associated outcomes on the surrounding environment. Poor language outcomes, though frequently tolerated, are not "normal" for deaf people. It has the potential disadvantage, however, of exacerbating the pain and guilt that parents, educators, and medical professionals may feel when its seriousness in a particular child's case becomes evident. Language deprivation is often the unintended outcome of well-intentioned efforts to promote a child's language development. Caregivers' intentions, however, cannot substitute for children's actual outcomes. These have all too often been "swept under the rug" in educational and medical research.

Structurally speaking, LDS is incomplete neurodevelopment. Functionally, it is an intellectual disability. Because language mediates and underlies nearly every human activity, those seeking to understand LDS must explore concepts and research from a wide variety of fields. That no single authority takes responsibility for a child's language development may be the main reason the syndrome persists. I delve into some far-flung areas in the following, but as a clinician primarily, I will base this chapter mainly on direct experience with the language-deprived deaf patients whom I have evaluated or treated in various settings. These include my primary work sites at Harvard Medical School, the Deaf & Hard of Hearing Service at Cambridge Hospital, and the Deaf and Hard of Hearing Program at Boston Children's Hospital—as well as past experience at the Mental Health Unit for Deaf Persons at Westborough State Hospital (which was cofounded by this volume's co-editor Neil S. Glickman) and the Deaf schools and programs where I have consulted. Naturally, I owe innumerable patients, their families, and perceptive colleagues for their stories and insights into these complex issues.

Although the phrase "language deprivation syndrome" may be new, the observation, that deficits observed in some deaf people's life skills might be due not to sensory deprivation or to social impoverishment, but specifically to *language* deprivation, is not. Prior to the groundbreaking adoption of sign language into US public education in the nineteenth century, the New York Times described deaf people as existing "in a state of barbarism, unprovided with the most ordinary means of culture" (New York [Daily] Times, Sept 29, 1852). Decades of the successful use of American Sign Language (ASL), disseminated via state schools established nationwide, ended with the rise of "oralism." This philosophy of prioritizing the teaching of speech and lip-reading while banning, and even punishing, the use of sign language led to wholesale language deprivation among deaf people in the twentieth century. "In looking back to the educational methods formerly used with the deaf," said psychologist Edna Levine in 1968, "you would have seen each individual more or less encased in his own little glass tomb" (Rainer & Altshuler, 1968).

As the mental health disciplines emerged, pioneering practitioners published descriptions of LDS (See Altshuler, 1962; Glickman, 2009; Hall, Levin, &

Anderson, 2017; Levine, 1956; Myklebust, 1960; Vernon & Raifman, 1997). The initial understanding was sometimes tinged with condescension based on two assumptions: that deafness must represent a "loss" to the individual and that signed languages must be inferior to spoken. Some early terminology would now be considered pejorative, e.g., *surdophrenia* or *primitive personality disorder,* but a serious effort was begun to describe the lives and experiences of deaf people. In New York, a perceptive observer reviewed three classic descriptions and commented:

> These three sets of results—Myklebust, Altshuler, and Levine—are remarkably consistent. However, the problem of explanation remains: one still doesn't know the etiology of the problems the deaf have. A phenomenological-descriptive model is just a beginning. The actual language of the deaf must be examined in more detail. ...Just how much deprivation exists? At what point do the deaf fail conceptually, and how does this relate (if at all) to their emotional and social problems? Is sign language, which remains the most common means of communication amongst the American deaf, despite the efforts of all education for the deaf in the United States, a language, and does it have limitations? What part do experiential and language deprivation play in creating the condition of the deaf in the United States?
>
> (Kohl, 1966)

Fifty years later, the answers to Kohl's cogent questions have emerged with forceful clarity. The 1960s brought the recognition that sign languages are in fact the linguistic equals of spoken languages. The 1970s saw the rebirth of a confident Deaf culture whose members experience deafness as a valid and satisfying mode of human being. New research vividly demonstrates the brain's time-sensitivity for acquiring language and begins to illuminate the neurological correlates of incomplete acquisition. We can now validate Kohl's intuition that "the single greatest problem" deaf children face is in fact what he called "language disability" (Kohl, 1966).

In 1854, a merchant politely asked a customer to leave his store. When the customer ignored him, the owner tried to shove him out. The customer, who was deaf, later pled guilty to having stabbed the owner. In this unfortunate event, neither person seems fully responsible. A proprietor manhandled a recalcitrant customer. A deaf man defended himself in an unprovoked assault. A misunderstanding between deaf and hearing worlds seems at fault, a theme that can be traced continuously forward in Deaf history all the way to the current debate over "maladaptive cross-modal plasticity" that will be discussed as follows. In a bio-psycho-social-cultural model of mental health, such Deaf-hearing cultural issues loom large. They place a premium on the attitude with which we approach "deaf people's problems" (Glickman, 2013). This chapter is written as this writer's research and clinical work are undertaken: with respect for deaf people's actual lived experiences, and therefore with skepticism toward the narrow view of deafness as mere pathology.

How Does Language Deprivation Happen?

The existence of language deprivation is a corollary to the existence of a critical period for learning one's first language. The most severe cases of deprivation therefore follow a child's not being exposed to consistent and fully elaborated language during the entire critical period, approximately the first five years of life.

Each child's brain and linguistic history is unique; each case of language deprivation is therefore also unique. Broadly speaking, congenitally deaf children are at greatest risk for deprivation while children who become deaf during the critical period are partly protected (examples of the latter include Helen Keller and the strident oral advocate David Wright). Children likely vary in the strength of their "language instinct" (Pinker, 1994)—their inbuilt avidity for language—and the rate and manner in which their critical periods close.

Geography is sometimes decisive: a child born deaf into a remote village may lack for both hearing aids and a local sign language. Such a child may grow up loved and well cared for but without linguistic communication. The ASL interpreter and activist Susan Schaller provided a moving account of one such case in her book, "A Man Without Words" (Schaller, 2012), documenting her passionate efforts to remediate the language deprivation of a man from rural Mexico. Although in countries where the education of deaf children is mandated, language deprivation as profound as that which Schaller describes is rarely seen *clinically,* this does not mean it is rare.

The same factors that impede language acquisition in the first place—geographic isolation, lack of educational opportunities and social services, lack of appreciation that the child (or now, adult) has specialized needs—can result in a language-deprived person's remaining home with family, living homeless, being wrongly placed in an institution for intellectual disability (see Miller, 2016), or being jailed, all without recognition of the person's specific deficits and needs. Such cases can come to light when a legal, medical, or behavioral problem appears or after a long-term support disappears.

Following profound deprivation, the amount of language that can be acquired, even after intensive exposure, is variable. In this regard, Schaller's case was close to the median: "Ildefonso," as she called him, acquired valuable ability to communicate, allowing him to better navigate the world. He did not achieve fluent language. Many such people acquire little language no matter how intense the exposure.

The author has observed only one case of the late acquisition of nearly fluent language. This case is presented with the individual's permission here:

Iromilson, known as "Ro," was born deaf on an island with no indigenous sign language and few services for deaf people. He roamed freely on his bicycle, rarely attending school. He particularly enjoyed the harbor, where he watched fishing boats being built. He communicated via pantomime and "home signing." Home signs are idiosyncratic gestures that arise naturally in each deaf person's environment. Presumably they arise from the brain's "language instinct" (Pinker, 1994) expressing itself in the absence of an actual language to acquire. Unfortunately, even the richest home sign, such as that developed by language-deprived deaf siblings, has never been found to reach the full grammatical power of true language.

Ro's single mother moved her family to the United States in search of education for her son. He wandered Boston at all hours, "stole" a cell phone, and found himself psychiatrically hospitalized. There he vividly gestured the story of his good luck in finding a phone. After failed attempts in local schooling, he was placed in a residential, therapeutic Deaf school.

Ro, now 14, was at first unable to sit still in a classroom, but he had not entirely lost every young child's intense hunger for language and near-magical capacity to absorb its grammatical "machinery." His school was largely staffed, day and night, by fluently signing Deaf people. Over six years of intensive exposure, Ro acquired remarkably fluent ASL. He also mastered some spoken and written English.

Ro still rides his bicycle joyfully but can also engage in team sports. He has friends, and a girlfriend. He has learned a range of carpentry skills and expects to be fully employed. He admires his mother and feels grateful for the sacrifices she made on his behalf—nuanced, empathic thoughts of a type often absent in LDS. He does struggle with residual deficits in world knowledge and associated judgments and would be the first to admit that he can lack common sense. Unfortunately, his success story is vanishingly rare.

Characteristics of Deaf People with Language Deprivation Syndrome

In 1999, the author examined a series of 98 consecutive referrals to the Deaf Service at Cambridge Hospital. Each case was rated for severity of behavioral symptoms and for language fluency. The initial hypothesis was that being unable to solve social and emotional problems with words would lead to "acting out" emotions behaviorally. Despite the coarseness of the categorizations (chosen to ensure high interrater reliability), surprisingly significant correlations emerged: both dangerousness to oneself and dangerousness to others correlated strongly with language dysfluency.[1] *Indeed, nearly half of the variance in these deaf psychiatric patients' aggressive behaviors seemed attributable to problems with language.* Figures 1.1–1.4 describe this dataset.[2]

Note that fewer than half of the patients in this sample demonstrated fluency in American Sign Language. In hindsight, with heightened awareness of the serious consequences of even mild language deficits, the language categories might more accurately be named mild, moderate, and severely dysfluent.

Age of First Language Exposure

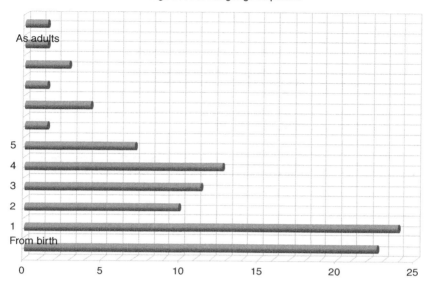

Figure 1.1 Age of first language exposure among 98 Deaf
Service referrals, 1999

Dangerousness to Community

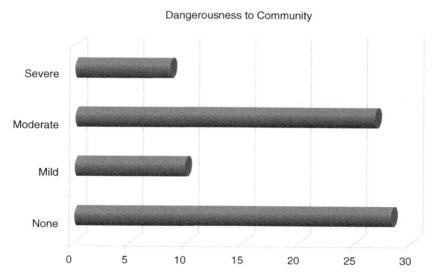

Figure 1.2 Dangerousness to community among 98 Deaf Service referrals

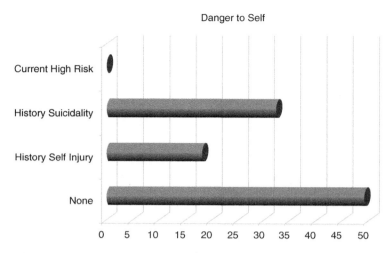

Figure 1.3 Dangerousness to self among 98 Deaf Service referrals

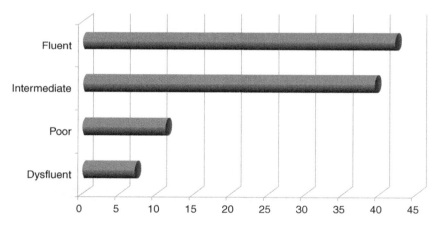

Figure 1.4 Sign Language fluency among 98 Deaf Service referrals

Following the aforementioned pilot work, the author compiled a list of potential descriptors for LDS from published reports and active professionals in the field. The incidence of 53 potential descriptors was then noted in the sample described earlier. The ten outstanding categories of LDS characteristics, presented as follows, paint a picture of LDS as seen in the mental health clinic.

Because data collection and analysis on an ever-expanding sample continue at the time of this writing, the findings here are preliminary. The discriminatory power of individual items relative to other psychiatric diagnoses remains to be determined, as do their independence from one another and prevalence at different degrees of language deprivation.

A Person with LDS May Superficially Appear to Use Sign Language Fluently, But on Closer Examination, Shows Characteristic Linguistic Deficits

Nearly every deaf person who experiences significant language deprivation eventually finds his or her way to some form of sign language, even if educated orally (Gregory, Bishop, & Sheldon, 1995). Late-deafened native users of spoken language, particularly the elderly, are much less likely to seek out sign language, as are mildly and moderately hard of hearing people, who face their own difficulties with social communication but rarely suffer from language deprivation.

To non-signers, the sign language of a person with LDS may be indistinguishable from that of a fluent signer; handshapes and movements can appear natural and impressively fast. Fluent signers (particularly native signers), however, recognize the absence of features and functions of full language, and the more general cognitive and emotional "gestalt" of a person who has experienced language deprivation. In the most severe cases, the language of a deprived person might bear no more relation to fluent ASL than "Me Tarzan, you Jane" does to fluent English.

The characteristic features lacking in the "visual-gestural" language system of those with LDS include tenses, plurals, and standard sentence structures. There is a relative simplification of grammar, so that others must guess at the intended meaning. The nuances involved in this type of guesswork are infinitely intricate and are a primary raison d'être for the specialized field of Certified Deaf Interpreting.[3]

A Person with LDS Struggles with the Concept of Time

A striking and possibly pathognomonic feature of people with language deprivation is difficulty with sequencing and chronology, i.e., an inability to conceptualize time. The patient mentioned in the introduction—the young man with unusual behaviors and mysterious test results—provides a good example of this phenomenon. On psychological testing, his ability to assemble the parts of a static picture into a whole was well above average. By contrast, his ability to order a set of pictures into a meaningful narrative fell below the first percentile. Even the simplest children's story sequences completely eluded him.

The novelist Nancy Huston speculates, "We have no memories of our early childhood because there was not yet an I on which to string fictions" (Huston, 2008). It is possible that the human sense of self arises from the stories—narratives—that we tell ourselves and which are told about us. This observation hints at the vast difficulties with self and agency that those with LDS can experience. A sense of self, after all, is a sense of continuity over time.

Struggles with time, sequencing, and selfhood are not intuitively obvious as consequences of lacking language. They suggest language subtly underlies wide aspects of brain function, including many skills traditionally classified as "nonverbal."

A Person with LDS Struggles with Cause-and-Effect

"The concept of 'why' can only arise from an understanding of time, which is the essential ingredient in narrative. Something happens, then something else happens, then we assign the whole thing a meaning, including our own role in it" (Huston, 2008).

This deficit can have enormous clinical and real-life implications. Difficulty understanding why things happen may lead a person with LDS to experience life as senseless or even traumatic. Patients respond to this powerlessness and confusion in different ways. Some retreat, living quietly within restricted and supportive bounds, e.g., those of a family. Others develop rigid modes of behavior that, although simple and inflexible, at least reliably support a coherent sense of an active self. One long-term patient, for example, rails at the world angrily. She gets her basic needs met by demanding her "rights" as a deaf woman, accusing anyone who crosses her of discrimination. She is unable to turn off her angry approach, however, even when (to others) it appears counterproductive.

To the extent that people with LDS lack an understanding of cause and effect, they are prone to repeating mistakes. To the extent they are unable to discuss cause and effect, they are unable to address their maladaptive patterns.

A Person with LDS Lacks Awareness of a Conversational Partner's Need for Context, and More Generally Lacks "theory of mind"

When fluent language users converse, each builds an image of his or her interlocutor, imagining what the other person knows and how the speaker's words are being "heard." A particularly well-explored area of deficit in those with language deprivation is the inability to construct such an image. The formal name for the skills involved—recognizing that others' minds contain feelings, ideas, and experiences different from our own—is "theory of mind." ("ToM") Patients with the most profound language deprivation appear completely to lack theory of mind (see Morgan and Kegl, 2006; de Villiers and de Villiers, 2012). Patients with the most profound language deprivation appear completely to lack theory of mind ("ToM"). They exist in a solipsistic space where others are not seen as comparable beings or as social equals.

Three European studies on this subject deserve particular mention. In the first, Swedish investigators compared deaf toddlers using auditory approaches (hearing aids, cochlear implants, and spoken language, but no sign language) to matched hearing toddlers. None of the deaf toddlers in this study passed a basic ToM task that posed no difficulty to the hearing toddlers. That is, children, who from an audiological perspective could hear acceptably well, were in fact failing to acquire an age-appropriate and essential skill. The authors commented, "The possession of a theory of mind (ToM) permits us to reason about the mental states of others... A lack of ToM would be a formidable obstacle to all sophisticated forms of human social interaction" (Meristo et al., 2012).

The second study, from Italy, compared the attainment of theory of mind in children from three different schools: one hearing, one deaf bilingual (Italian Sign Language/Italian), and one serving deaf children using a spoken language approach (including cochlear implants, hearing aids, etc.). The primarily signing bilingual children scored highest (ahead of the hearing norm), while the aided, auditory group scored the lowest (Tomasuolo, Valeri, Di Renzo, Pasqualetti, & Volterra, 2013). To linguists, who recognize the benefits of bilingualism, this result is unremarkable. To many in the fields of deaf education and rehabilitation, to whom pursuing two languages might seem to add complication to the already difficult task of teaching one, it may come as a surprise.

Finally, a careful study from the Netherlands examined theory of mind in 72 children who received cochlear implants before age three. One-third had bilateral implants. All had been provided intensive, high-quality spoken language education. The results were troubling: despite early implantation and outward progress in language acquisition, the implanted children failed to achieve theory of mind equal to that of hearing controls (Ketelaar et al., 2012).

Deficits in theory of mind are often evident in conversational style. It is characteristic of those with LDS to utter a phrase or an ungrammatical, confusing sentence followed by, "you know?": [I] LIVE in the TALL BUILDING next to the BROWN BUILDING, YOU KNOW? The hope is that the conversational partner will be able to guess the reference, or somehow magically already knows.

Lacking not only the linguistic tools to express meaning clearly but also the abstract comprehension of the limits of others' knowledge, people with LDS rely on assistance in order to communicate. Such conversation is no longer between equal partners. One must ask clarifying questions, seek corroboration from others, and guess—yet still often give up in frustration. Like story sequencing, theory of mind is a complex, seemingly non-verbal skill whose full development apparently relies on the acquisition of highly fluent language.

A Person with LDS Struggles with Abstract Concepts

The philosopher Ludwig Wittgenstein developed a fertile theory of language acquisition: he suggested we learn language mainly by *using it* in so-called "language games" that we then "play" in all our social interactions (Wittgenstein, 1953). A language game is a language-based mode of social relating and includes every social linguistic interaction from the rote "How are you?"/"I'm fine" to the specific ways in which a doctor might discuss impending death with a patient. Wittgenstein's concept of language game is closer to that of game theory than of, say, a board game. His point is that language does not exist merely for communicating information, but for enabling all forms of social interaction.

Consider an 18-month-old who learns the sign for "I love you." She cannot yet know all the dimensions of the mature ASL or English concepts of love. Yet she can learn to use the sign as a warm expression that will command others' positive feedback and earn her hugs. Her new sign is like a new toy—she stands in her crib, banging the sides to get someone's attention, and then gleefully signs "I love you." Essentially, language creates the possibility of social interactions *that did not previously exist.* Each new sign provides a basis for learning more, as known signs appear in sentences that serve social, emotional, and pragmatic uses. As grammar develops, allowing the meaningful combination of signs, she participates in ever-richer "language games."

Concepts are learned simultaneously with their linguistic symbols. Basic concepts can seem so easy until one tries to explain one to a person who is completely language-deprived. I once spent hours trying fruitlessly to explain to a language-deprived woman that her "husband" was in fact her uncle.

Consider that people with language deprivation do not excel at such seemingly non-verbal (but clearly conceptual) skills as playing chess or doing math (see Blank, 1965). The missing concepts crucially include concepts about oneself and one's place in the world.

As each child develops a complete language, worldly, bodily, and experiential knowledge of many types are simultaneously brought to life. An independent "life of the mind" appears as a child names and reflects on internal states. People with language deprivation can lack this life of the mind. They can struggle to name basic feelings, to recognize the social boundaries that are encoded in words such as "girlfriend," or to reflect on their own experiences. They struggle to see patterns and make generalizations. Lessons learned in one arena are not easily applied to others. The most sophisticated uses of language—poetic description, wordplay, the deepest expressions of one's experience of the world—are often inaccessible. "The limits of my language are the limits of my world," Wittgenstein wrote, an epigram that perfectly captures the challenges of LDS.

The link from learning a word to mastering abstraction may be the essentially metaphorical quality of language—in language, one thing "stands for" another (see Lakoff, 1987). Glickman (personal communication, 2017) tells of working with a language-deprived man on relapse prevention using the conventional ASL sign for "relapse" (literally "slip-and-fall-down"). The patient attended to the ASL phrase "RELAPSE PREVENT" for months before inquiring, "WHO FALL-DOWN?" All of us who have worked in language deprivation can relate to this experience. Similar experiences led Glickman to establish "mindful attention to language and communication" as a guiding principle of his work with language-deprived people (Glickman, 2017).

A Person with LDS Has Difficulty Learning

The mental "desktop" of a person with LDS is typically occupied with a handful of central concerns, leaving little space for new ideas such as feedback from others. Those who know the person well may become familiar with these repeated stories and be able to assist in explaining them (though as with the relapse-prevention story before, some details in an ungrammatical, achronological, and incomplete story may remain mysterious for years).

Since most learning—even learning non-verbal skills such as how to cross a street—occurs via language or linguistically supported experiences, impoverished language contributes directly to difficulty learning. Obviously, this characteristic does not distinguish between intellectual disability and LDS, and reasonably so: LDS is a specific kind of intellectual disability. It does, however, usefully distinguish LDS from such conditions as a depressive or schizophrenic episode in which the patient's ability to learn may vary as the illness varies, but language itself does not form the obstacle to learning.

It is not unusual in a single hour-long meeting for a person with LDS to soak up a dozen new simple signs for objects and to recall and use them easily at the next meeting. It is far more challenging to convey a single abstract noun such as "parenting" or "side effect."

A Person with LDS Struggles with Emotional Regulation

A named feeling serves as a kind of mental container, allowing a person to step back from the feeling, observe it, place it into context, and regulate it. Unable to put feelings into words (which usually requires a cause and effect narrative of events that led to the feeling), people with language deprivation can neither talk themselves through difficulties nor easily avail themselves of emotional support from others. They often appear flooded by feelings, sometimes chronically, a deeply stressful and dysphoric mode of existence.

A Person with LDS Struggles in Relationships

As with healthy emotional regulation, the extent to which language is necessary to healthy human relationships becomes starkly clear when it is absent. In Wittgenstein's model, one might say those with language deprivation have not learned relationship "language games." The games themselves ("going on a date," "getting married") elicit aspects of our personalities, become part of our identities, and provide parameters for socially appropriate behaviors that guide and contain those of us lucky enough to have fluent language.

At the extreme end of "struggling in relationships" lies antisocial behavior. Profound language deprivation along with inadequately structuring early life experiences can result in a victim who makes victims of others, and yet is cognitively incompetent to be held legally or morally accountable. If they result from language deprivation, these behaviors may be thought of as asocial rather than antisocial, but making this distinction may be very difficult in practice. A deaf school principal who offered to rehabilitate a deaf criminal captured the challenge perfectly in 1870:

> The question of the moral responsibility of an uneducated person, born deaf and dumb, is one of the subtlest in metaphysics and in every case in which it comes before the courts is a source of great perplexity. The extremely limited communication possible through any interpreter, however skilled in pantomime, and the utter ignorance of the deaf-mute of the language of the country, united with the absence of all knowledge of either human or divine law, invest the subject with peculiar difficulties… – Isaac Lewis Peet, principal of the NY Institution for the Instruction of the Deaf and Blind.
> (Peet, 1870a, 1870b)

When people with LDS are not competent to stand trial due to language deficits, but are still dangerous, they create a disposition and treatment problem that often has no good solution (O'Rourke, Glickman, & Austin, 2013; See also Chapter 4 and appendix to this chapter). We are scarcely better positioned to manage such cases nowadays than was Principal Peet nearly 150 years ago.

A Person with LDS Has a Reduced Fund of Information, But May Be "street-wise"

The first half of this descriptor overlaps partly with intellectual disability. The second half, however, is often a striking feature of people with LDS with otherwise normal intelligence. Using very limited gesture and language, such a person may learn to navigate the world more adaptively than would be possible for a person with intellectual disability alone. Presumably this is accounted for by the preserved aspects of brain function—those that are not entirely dependent on language. Often street smarts correlate with a strong Deaf identity, which presumably supports self-esteem in social interactions. Street smarts, however, rarely keep people entirely safe. If victimized, additional layers of trauma, confusion, and distrust are added to the patient's psychiatric presentation.

Hall et al. (2017) emphasize the importance of fund of information (FOI) weaknesses in LDS, which also appeared in Glickman's criteria for "language deprivation with deficiencies in behavioral, social and emotional adjustment" (Glickman, 2009, 2013). These were included too in McCay Vernon's conception of "primitive personality disorder" as being due to "cognitive deprivation," i.e., the opportunity to learn facts (Vernon & Rich, 1997). Following Vernon, this author sees deficits in factual knowledge as secondary to deficits in the ability to acquire knowledge, that is, to learn. Those with LDS may lack the abstract structures for imagining that particular knowledge might exist, the skills necessary to access that knowledge, and the introspective abilities required to incorporate new knowledge into more adaptive behaviors. In milder cases of LDS, learning may be more possible, but limited access may restrict FOI. Areas of particular concern include frequent lack of basic knowledge about physical and mental health, sexuality, and healthy relationships. These knowledge deficits profoundly affect quality of life and have obvious clinical implications.

A Person with LDS "acts" Feelings "out"

When humans are unable to communicate needs and feelings, or to look inwards and internally manage them via language, expression of emotion often shifts to behavior. Children with language deprivation can show spectacular levels of such acting-out as they face frustration in identifying and expressing needs, coupled with uncertainty about whether and how their needs can be met.

A four-year-old who was identified as deaf late, and then provided a cochlear implant without remedial support, was adopted and exposed to ASL at age five. His adoptive mother described his behavior when she met him: he hit, bit, and kicked. He "refused to accept authority" and covered her with bruises when she set limits. Lacking language, he was unable to comprehend explanations or predict likely consequences of his behaviors. His tantrums lasted hours and ended only when he was exhausted.

After three years of exposure, he now has enough sign language to communicate everyday needs, but still prefers non-verbal play. "He still doesn't understand the concept of *why*," his mother commented. Yet he is beginning to achieve self-awareness. Imagining a more mature self, and embarrassed by past behaviors, he asked his mother to "throw [my old name] away. I'm [my new name]!"

The Neurobiology of Language Deprivation

The past decade has seen astonishing progress in establishing the functional and anatomical basis for the critical period and therefore for language deprivation. Using functional MRI scanning, Rachel Mayberry and colleagues found that the ability to acquire a first language ("L1") decreases linearly through childhood. Children with later first exposure show slower language processing and make more grammatical errors. Like second-language ("L2") learning, late L1 learning takes further towards the back of the brain. This suggests that kinesthetic and visual qualities of words carry excessive importance in early learning relative to their symbolic meanings and grammatical use. Unlike L2 learning, however, late first language never fully migrates forward into the left hemisphere's dedicated language areas. Wernicke and Broca's areas, and the arcuate fasciculus connecting them, are where reliable and automatic comprehension and production of language occurs (see also Newman et al., 2015).

You cannot choose *not* to read a word or understand a sentence in a language you know fluently. This is the experience of fast, automatic language processing that people with LDS lack. In Mayberry's words, language-deprived people suffer from "…underdeveloped neural language processing that has failed to grow forward in the adult brain due to an absence of language experience during critical moments throughout early brain development" (Mayberry, Chen, Witcher, & Klein, 2011).

Complementing Mayberry's work, Pénicaud and colleagues examined the anatomy of brains exposed to inadequate language. They found reductions in gray matter in the visual association areas of the brain. Native signers had the highest gray matter concentration, hearing people a medium amount, and language deprived people the least. Again, the changes were linear over time. The extent of some of the measured differences was dramatic. Those learning their first language as early teens had 25% to 30% less gray matter in key visual association areas, for example, than native signers. Remarkably, *exposure to language appears to enhance our visual abilities* while exposure to a sign language enhances them further (Pénicaud et al., 2013).

Mayberry's work used functional MRI scans to observe the brain in action. Pénicaud used voxel-based morphometry (VBM) to quantify brain volumes. A third technique, Event-Related Potentials (ERP), measures brain activity as revealed through electrical signals detected through the scalp. ERPs reveal waves of localized electrical activity as the brain processes language. There are characteristic syntactic responses to grammatical and to ungrammatical constructions. As meaning is decoded, semantic ERP responses appear.

Nils Skotora and colleagues in Germany explored these ERP responses in deaf and hearing adults (Skotora et al., 2012). They found that despite processing grammar slowly (and ineffectively), language deprived adults created meaning with normal speed. This electrophysiological result fits the clinical observation that people with language deprivation too easily jump to conclusions, miss subtleties, and feel an unsupported certainty in their beliefs.

The Role of Cochlear Implantation in Language Deprivation

From the early 1990s, when the first children were implanted, the primary criterion for implant success has been the extent to which implanted individuals hear. Measuring from the bottom of the audiogram upwards, any degree of new hearing certainly represents a kind of success. If a deaf child is seen as a potentially fluent user of sign language instead of being defined primarily as a person who cannot hear, however, a different measure of success appears: the maturation of the child's linguistic ability (in any language). From this perspective, a child who is hard of hearing and can produce some understandable speech, but who lacks true fluency and all its attendant skills, will no longer be considered a true "success." On this subject, a vast outcome literature is clear: "Medical professionals are not able to assure that hearing aids and cochlear implants will result in positive language outcomes" (Hall et al., 2017).

Advocates for implantation do not deny the variability and unpredictability of outcomes. However, they too rarely address the actual lived experience of those with negative outcomes. "Only about a third of the sample scored normally on measures of syntax," reported Tobey, Britt, Geers et al. (2012) on testing one group of eight- to nine-year-old children who were implanted at ages two to five. What is life like for the two-thirds who could not process English syntax? Nowhere in their voluminous publications do these well-known researchers describe what we clinicians who work in Deaf mental health can all too easily guess: just as with the "oral failures" of the previous generation, the children who do not acquire spoken language after cochlear implantation become young people who seek out sign language and the Deaf Community and then struggle through life with LDS.

When based on professional advice not to use sign language in order to "force" reliance on sound, LDS can be considered iatrogenic. Imagine a condition in which children are born unable to walk, but able to learn wheelchair use. Now imagine a new "walking implant" which can permit some of these children to walk. However, because the implant does not work reliably, and the children take naturally to wheelchairs, surgeons and physical therapists advise against them. Half or more of the children are rendered unable either to walk or to use a wheelchair with ease, yet academic publications assess only the extent of walking, never the extent of *mobility*. Patients unable to walk satisfactorily seek out wheelchairs and the company of other wheelchair users, but never move as fast or go as far as those permitted wheelchairs from birth.

Such a procedure might be considered unethical, yet it parallels the current situation with cochlear implantation. Caregivers' and parents' desires for their children to walk "normally" might overshadow the more important outcome of being able to ambulate in any mode. The stigma that might attach to the children's use of wheelchairs parallels that of sign language use. This "walking implant" thought experiment arguably underestimates the impact of the unsuccessful "talking implant": communication and thought are more central to our humanity than mere physical mobility.

In any cultural setting, some brain features will be emphasized and others discarded, "depending on biological importance of the feature in the given environment" (Kral, Yusuf, & Land, 2017). "Deaf eyes," the ASL phrase for the special visual acuity of natively deaf people, are in fact different (Codina et al, 2011 & Codina et al, 2017) the neural correlates of enhanced peripheral perception are evident at the retinal level. Whether developing deaf eyes is a good or a bad thing is not a scientific or medical judgment, but a cultural one. In essence, cochlear implantation might be considered a culturally sanctioned cosmetic language procedure.

Parents of a child who was turned down for implantation at Boston Children's Hospital due to her likely having no nerve connection to her cochleae, but who then sought it elsewhere, were advised,

> We're supposed to teach her to hear, as if praising her for hearing is going to make a difference. They [the surgeon and audiologists] stressed it doesn't matter if she wants to wear it — we *have to* keep it on.

These parents chose to ignore this advice, realizing that regardless of how hard they praised her, their daughter's implant provided minimal sound awareness and no access to language, while she communicated naturally and comfortably in ASL.

The hearing research community has recently begun seeking answers to the "enormous variability" (Pisoni, Kronenberger, Roman, & Geers, 2011) long observed in outcome studies of cochlear implantation. "Maladaptive cross-modal plasticity" (MCMP) is the hypothesis that brain areas that can serve specific functions when stimulated by an associated sensory input might be "colonized" by other uses, making them less able to perform their original task (Corina et al., 2017). Thus, visual processing (i.e., sign language) might colonize "auditory" association areas, rendering them inhospitable to auditory stimulation from a cochlear implant. This becomes a justification for restricting access to sign language following implantation.

Yet it is rare that CI recipients achieve 100% word discrimination on hearing alone. Most use their eyes for lip-reading and other contextual visual cues.

Furthermore, nearly all human communication is multimodal. Even as they learn to speak, hearing babies point and gesture. All speakers gesture, interpret body language, process facial cues, and lip-read unconsciously. Reading is cross-modal. It is therefore unclear whether "colonization" of auditory areas with visual skills would be adaptive or maladaptive.

In any case, the MCMP hypothesis is based on a classic sensory-based model of brain organization which is challenged by the newer "Task-Selective Sensory-Independent" (TSSI) model. In TSSI brain modules specialized to various tasks can easily switch to receive input from different sensory channels (Amedi, Hofstetter, Maidenbaum, & Heimler, 2017). In the newer model, (supported by Mitchell, 2017) visual stimulation to "auditory" areas, instead of being problematic, would simply indicate visual input to specific linguistic tasks, independent of modality (spoken or signed). For example, blind people's brains make use of the appropriate task-specific "visual" areas for determining the shape of an object or layout of a room—yet using tactile and auditory rather than visual input.

At the time of this writing, it is not known if very early cochlear implantation prevents the typical cross-modal assignment of auditory areas to visual processing, or the intra-modal organization of vision towards language processing (Glick et al., 2017). To the extent that the imperfect sound delivered by current CIs is inadequate, visual "takeover" might well take place regardless and might be adaptive. Perhaps functional scans will make it possible to triage and track CI patients' brain responses to implantation. Regardless, this author would prefer a focus on "lighting up" the language areas of the brain because so much depends on them. Implant surgeons might better recognize the social, cultural, and linguistic dimensions of the cochlear implant and substitute the goals of overall language, cognitive, and social development for the narrower goals of sound recognition, environmental awareness, and speech.

Consider the case of a young man who asked to share his story here. His parents crossed the world seeking the highest quality cochlear implantation, speech therapy, and oral-based schooling that they could find. By audiological standards alone, he is a cochlear implant success—he "hears" and "speaks," though his clearest communication is in writing. He has LDS, however, to the extent that he cannot manage public schooling. Despite his parents' and providers' commitment to oral approaches, he has sought out sign language himself. Asked why, he wrote, "So I can speke with deaf person who dose not have cochlear implant" [sic]. This small language sample demonstrates the problem of, so to speak, neither walking nor having a wheelchair. The young man's English is inadequate to normal academic or social communication, which leads to rejection from the hearing community, where very high standards for linguistic skill are expected of those who belong.

It was noted earlier that even CI users with apparently strong language skills can show deficits in theory of mind. This may relate to the extraordinary intricacy of normal language processing. Using ERP, a group of Swedish researchers noted a tendency toward "top-down semantic prediction"—in other words, guessing at answers—among implanted children (Kallioinen et al., 2012). Any hard of hearing person is familiar with this difficulty—lacking full information, one guesses and hopes for the best. Guessing makes a precarious foundation on which to build one's life.

Most who seek to "cure" deafness do so not with the evil goal of destroying Deaf culture or depriving deaf people of language, but rather from a belief in the importance of language identical to that of the Deaf community. There is, however, a marked asymmetry of knowledge and power: few oral, auditory-verbal educators or otologists use sign language or count deaf people as friends, whereas most deaf people are acutely aware of the perils of inadequate language. Implant advocates' understanding of the risks of mild language deprivation might well change if they could appreciate both the reality of LDS and Deaf normality firsthand.

None of the aforementioned is intended to deny the potential efficacy of implantation in many cases or the great care that some surgical teams take in selecting and following cases. The concern here is entirely with those for whom implantation and oral/aural approaches unintentionally deny children fluent language.

Making Psychiatric Diagnoses in People with LDS

Accurate psychiatric diagnosis of deaf patients with language difficulties is this author's most challenging and rewarding work. The challenge can be thought of in terms of "seeing" psychiatric illness through the confounding filters of non-fluent language, "communication trauma," cultural mismatch, reduced fund of information, heightened suspicion of caregivers, and/or idiosyncratic beliefs and fears. Some lessons learned over the years follow:

1   Assessment will take more time, often *much* more time. Repeated meetings over weeks or months, or an extended stay in a respite program or inpatient unit, may be necessary to establish a diagnosis that in a hearing person might have been clear within the first hour.
2   Assessment will require more work. Patients are often unable to provide a useable history. Those seeking to assist the patient often have a partial understanding of the patient's experience. The teams in which the author works gather as many sources of current and past information as possible, seeking redundancy in reported symptoms and history, and often engaging in some detective work. We have confirmed cases of language deprivation by contacting relatives in another country or by ascertaining the oral philosophy of a faraway school.

3   The involvement of a Certified Deaf Interpreter and/or a formal communication assessment is frequently essential. When using a Certified Deaf Interpreter, it is important to be mindful that unless one specifically requests phatic attention to language per se, the interpreter may inadvertently conceal language problems in the effort to circumvent them. Skilled CDIs are often highly creative in optimizing visual communication. A time frame, for example, might be established by reference to holidays rather than traditional dates. An empathic repetition of an overwhelmed client's tentative signs might build trust and free expression. The confidence and creativity of the CDI, who is "deaf like me," can reduce the patient's shame or fear of unsuccessful communication. The CDI's presence as a member of the team can model interaction with the perhaps untrusted authority of the clinician. CDI assistance is especially helpful when the patient may know some foreign sign language, when seeking to distinguish psychotic conversation from language deprivation, when physical issues such as cerebral palsy impede clear signing, for deafblind clients, and when there is comorbidity with other diagnoses that affect language, particularly the more severe forms of intellectual disability.

4   Clinicians unfamiliar with deafness should feel free to seek consultation from those who specialize. Specialty team evaluation is often needed in cases of medical comorbidity. Cytomegalovirus (CMV) and congenital rubella infection are leading causes of the combination of intellectual disability and aggressive behavior in deaf patients. Many other forms of pre-, peri-, and post-natal trauma, such as Extracorporeal Membrane Oxygenation (ECMO), can lead to behavioral disturbances later. Frequently, brain damage exacerbates language deprivation and vice versa. A long and growing list of congenital syndromes that include deafness must be ruled out. Families frequently attribute deafness to a fall or other potentially avoidable event and be surprised when genetic testing later shows that the child was in fact likely born deaf.

Two-thirds of the outpatients referred to Cambridge Hospital's Deaf Service show some degree of LDS, a proportion similar to that among inpatients at the Westborough State Hospital's Deaf Unit (Black & Glickman, 2009). LDS eventually appears to be the only diagnosis for fully one-quarter of Deaf Service patients. For patients with both LDS and psychiatric diagnoses, the latter follow the typical profile for a hearing outpatient clinic with two significant exceptions: first, PTSD appears to be far more prevalent, presumably due to a deaf child's vulnerability to abuse and neglect. All too often, deaf patients show severe, chronic, developmental trauma. Second, due to syndromal causes of deafness (e.g., cytomegaloviral infection, an acquired syndrome, or Waardenburg syndrome, a congenital one) intellectual disability and organic brain damage are particularly common.

Treatment

Ro's remarkable late acquisition of ASL did not occur until he was placed in an immersive sign language environment. Such placement is the essential and central remediative treatment strategy for significant LDS. Language exists most richly within a community of language users; contact with that community most effectively transmits it. Even if grammatical skills do not improve, such placement usually strengthens the individual's cultural identity as a Deaf person, a feeling of belonging that seems to be an essential component to most people's happiness. More commonly, there is a flowering of confidence and pride along with improvements in behavior, real world knowledge, emotional regulation, and social skills. As one adult put it,

> All this time my family saw me as broken, as the problem one they had to do everything for. I was sad. I drank. I did not care about myself. But now I understand — I am not broken. I am *Deaf!*

This patient—who had rarely been let out of her parents' sight—subsequently recovered from depression, began dating a deaf adult in another city, became an avid runner, and found meaningful volunteer work despite significant LDS.

Adults with language deprivation have typically endured a lifetime of frustration with communication. They can be flooded with feelings of rage, sadness, and shame. Their unheard and misunderstood stories deserve an attentive audience. Elucidation often requires techniques beyond words: acting scenes out, drawing, or searching for locations, references, or people on the internet. Very frequently, key stories—such as memories of abusive or neglectful experience—are recalled and assembled in small pieces over long periods of time. The reward for this work is frequently a new formulation useful to all who work with the client.

LDS in children is clinically a "language emergency." Very young children even slightly behind in their language milestones deserve intensive intervention. Delays of only a few months may make the difference in whether a child will eventually acquire fluent language. The greatest and most poignant challenge is for the grieving hearing parents of a young child, who may feel that acknowledging a language problem equates to "giving up" on the dream of a child who "hears and speaks normally," to now enter the confusing and politically fraught world of special education. Wrapping one's mind around the concept of a child's risk of lacking language is very difficult even for many well-educated and sophisticated parents. Once an understanding of the child's needs is achieved, accessing the necessary special education services can be an extended process, sometimes filled with dramatic hearings and opposing evaluation reports. Finally, appropriate school placements simply may not be available locally.

Medications can be useful for some LDS symptoms, but *medication alone is never the answer.* Beta-blockers can ease panic and rage. Antidepressants can treat secondary depression. Mood stabilizers are often helpful for aggression. Antipsychotics are sometimes essential for severe behaviors, but given the difficulty that many patients with LDS have in making medical decisions for themselves, a decision to use antipsychotics should be made with the greatest of care and only after obtaining appropriate guardianship. Far too many patients with LDS are treated symptomatically with medications alone to "make the problem go away," rather than being provided the language, educational, vocational, or therapeutic support with which they really need.

Family therapy and education are often crucial, not only with children but with adults. Family members often have a limited understanding of LDS and may believe that observed behaviors result either from deafness alone, mental illness, or from stubbornness or laziness. A full explanation can revise a family's dynamics, increasing compassion and tolerance of the problematic behaviors, and motivating family support for the needed language access and opportunities for independence not available at home.

Specific psychotherapy treatment strategies are described in the Chapters 2 and 3, in this volume, and in Glickman (2009, 2017). Strategies for promoting language and communication abilities are described in Chapter 7. Psychotherapy, "the talking cure," must of course be drastically reconceptualized for such patients. Glickman (2017) developed a model of "pre-therapy" for such persons which emphasizes foundational language, cognitive and psychosocial skills, and the creation of a shared schema or map for "what we do here in the treatment setting," along with strategies intended to make a therapeutic interaction understandable and meaningful. All interventions need to be undertaken with respect for the dignity and autonomy of the individual (see Miller, 2016).

Conclusion

Language deprivation persists in large part because it crosses the boundaries of multiple professional disciplines, none of which is solely responsible for a child's language outcome. Furthermore, LDS straddles the cultural barrier between deaf and hearing worlds, the barrier which creates such misunderstandings as the "assault" of the "rude" customer in 1854. This is a delicate subject that must be addressed: hearing medical "experts" in deafness rarely understand deafness as a lived experience (see Kushalnagar et al., 2010).

The author is aware of no ENT physician in the entire United States, for example, who is a fluent user of American Sign Language. The experiences, expertise, and perspectives of actual deaf people are not easily incorporated into the hearing world systems of medicine and education. Parents naturally want their children to share their language, to be physically "normal," and participate in their own cultural "language games." The concept of language as an entity abstracted from its mode (signed or spoken), and seen as the lynchpin of cognitive and emotional development, is not a simple one.

At the time of this writing, research and advocacy regarding LDS are at an all-time high. A fruitful approach has been to consider fluent language a basic human right (see for example the Nyle DiMarco Foundation and LEAD-K). From this perspective, parents and professionals working with deaf children share an obligation to ensure that language deprivation does not occur. Multiple states have already approved such language-rights legislation. Best strategies for legal advocacy are discussed in Chapter 10.

An obstacle to providing care is the lack of formal diagnostic criteria or reimbursement codes for language deprivation syndrome. Under the DSM-5's classification scheme, LDS would be a "neurodevelopmental disorder." The ICD-10-CM offers code F80.4, "Speech and language development delay due to hearing loss." This reflects the typical view that language is an isolated aspect of brain development rather than foundational one, and the word "delay" is inaccurate. There are two published proposals for formal criteria, by Vernon & Raifman (1997) and Glickman (2009). Hall et al. (2017) provide an overview of past-published research on this condition. Cambridge Hospital criteria are in active development (see Esposito, Gulati, & Prestia, 2012; Gulati, 2014a, 2014b).

Currently a clinical diagnosis, LDS will eventually become a neurological diagnosis, as ever-improving techniques for observing the structure and function of the brain illuminate the mechanisms underlying each symptom. In the meantime, the crucial need is for recognition of the syndrome as an ever-present risk for every deaf child. In developing countries, where high rates of infectious disease and culturally-sanctioned consanguinity quadruple the population rate of deafness, the risk comes mainly from lack of access to appropriate services. In developed countries, the risk most often comes from an overzealous focus on spoken language, from the excessive burden placed on parents to seek out information and resources for their children, and from the tendency to see "language delay," where one might better see "language emergency" and therefore developmental or human emergency.

Language sits at the very core of our humanity. Deafness can create an obstacle to its acquisition but need not create an insuperable one. Awareness and the willingness to take action when needed—even against the local preferred communication mode, the advice of an "expert" in deafness, or parents' fondest wishes for their child—can entirely prevent it. All children deserve to be fluent language users who can lead autonomous and fulfilled lives.

Appendix: Language Deprivation Syndrome, Antisocial Personality, and Criminal Behaviors

Neil S. Glickman

Some adults with LDS display antisocial and even criminal behaviors. They form a small but significant subset of the larger LDS group. These people may present a challenging differential diagnosis between LDS and the spectrum of diagnoses ranging from conduct disorders to antisocial personality disorder to sociopathy. Programs attempting to serve, or manage, these individuals struggle with whether they are seeing primarily a clinical or a criminal matter and with how to combine treatment with limit setting and accountability.

As noted in this chapter, asocial and aggressive behavior is common in LDS and is a typical reason for referral to clinical programs. With children, lack of verbal reasoning, self-regulation, and interpersonal skills can be expected to result in oppositional-defiant behavior and/or conduct disorders. Lack of these self-management skills may inadvertently be reinforced by family or school environments which are either too rigidly based on strict adherence to rules, too lacking in any structure at all, or, as clinicians commonly observe, a random mix of overly restrictive and overly lax parenting and supervision.

By the time these persons reach adulthood, conduct problems and disorders may develop into antisocial personality with a "pervasive pattern of disregard for and violation of the rights of others" (DSM-5). Some of our Westborough State Hospital Deaf Unit patients had multiple involvements with police—or would have, had the police and courts held them legally accountable for their behaviors—but the most common profile was of the person who, as everyone said, "blows up" frequently, evidencing a lack of coping, self-regulation, or distress tolerance skills. These blowups often resulted in a diagnosis of "intermittent explosive disorder," yet intermittent explosive disorder doesn't really describe the clinical picture. If their language and communication deficits contributed to weaknesses in attachment with parental figures, this is likely the first template for a pattern of disturbed relationships. Additionally, there is the issue of pervasive developmental trauma, because language-deprived children are vulnerable to multiple kinds of abuse and neglect, and they have the burden of lack of language structures and communication partners with whom to process these experiences. These different kinds of aversive experiences create a complex portrait diagnostically of people who come to function poorly and behave badly.

Thus, there are multiple pathways through which children with language deprivation can grow into adults with serious asocial or antisocial behaviors, including violent aggression towards others. If there is a distinction in how we think about LDS vs antisocial personality, it is that the violence often seen in clinical samples of persons with LDS appears random, not instrumental. That is, the person "acts out" because they lack language, cognitive, and psychosocial skills to manage their feelings. They also lack the "skills" of theory of mind and empathy, meaning they do not appreciate how their behaviors impact other people. They do not usually seek to harm others, but with such a limited set of skills for intrapsychic and interpersonal challenges, they often find themselves doing so, and then find themselves in conflict with others and with the law.

Consider the deaf adult with LDS who has never had any health or sexuality education he could understand and who lacks the ability to communicate easily with potential friends, not to mention the complex ability of negotiating a sexual encounter, who comes to repeatedly force himself sexually on people, in the process committing an array of sexual assaults. He may come to understand that he is in trouble but may not understand why. He lacks vocabulary and understanding for concepts like "crime," "assault," and "informed consent." He has no understanding of age of consent laws or appreciation that even adults may not be able to give informed consent. Indeed, his knowledge and skill deficits go much deeper. He probably has little understanding of what he feels and no thought through strategies for how to manage his feelings and impulses. Convicted of crimes like indecent assault, he is then required to register as a sexual offender, a concept he also doesn't understand, and to attend a sexual offender treatment program. Even if a program is found that would accept him, usually based on the naïve idea that all they need to do is provide sign language interpreters, it is highly likely he wouldn't understand the treatment. Indeed, it's also highly likely he would not understand even more basic issues such as "what I did wrong," "who are you," "why I am here in this place," "what is supposed to happen here," and how I "get better," whatever that means. When you have someone like this, who may well be sexually dangerous, are labels like "sexual predator" or "sexual offender" warranted?

With conduct and antisocial personality disorder, by contrast, and certainly where there is sociopathy, there is more evidence of organized intention to commit antisocial acts and a reliable pattern of mistreatment of other people for self-serving ends. Purposeful, instrumental violence is not part of our understanding of LDS, but the lines can be blurry in practice. The distinction is very important diagnostically and prognostically and in determining treatment or disposition.

As noted earlier, LDS was previously conceptualized as "primitive personality disorder" (Vernon, Steinberg, & Montoya, 1999) and was considered a matter of extreme under-socialization. The term "primitive personality disorder" is unfairly stigmatizing and masked the fact that this condition is caused almost entirely by preventable social experiences. These are the reasons why I proposed some years ago the alternative diagnosis of "language deprivation with deficiencies in behavioral, emotional and social adjustment" (Glickman, 2009, pp. 331–337.) The new diagnosis of language deprivation syndrome is a more eloquent conceptualization of this condition.

It is not surprising that, where deaf prisoners have been studied, high levels of language deprivation and very poor communication abilities have been found. Research of deaf prisoners in the Texas correctional system, for instance, found that about half of the deaf prisoners demonstrated linguistic incompetence to stand trial (Miller, 2004). Similar findings of high prevalence of language deprivation and a resultant "unfitness to plead" (the UK equivalent of incompetence to stand trial) have been found in Great Britain, which has forensic hospital programs for deaf persons (Young, Howarth, Ridgeway, & Monteiro, 2001). Although Deaf prisoners are usually not grouped together as in these programs, these samples likely represent the population of deaf prisoners fairly. Indeed, a reasonable conclusion is that more deaf people with LDS end up in prison than in psychiatric settings, even though in neither setting is the LDS likely to be recognized.

The differential diagnosis between LDS and antisocial personality or criminality matters because, in practice, people with both conditions will find their way into both treatment and forensic settings. Some of these people who commit crimes simply need appropriate treatment opportunities to develop language, communication, and other skills. They can be helped. On the other hand, some of these people who are in treatment settings really need the firm limits and control that legal and forensic authorities provide. It is no one's intention that the diagnosis of LDS become "a backdoor means for characterizing patterns of criminal behaviors as a new form of psychopathology" (Glickman, 2009), nor to suggest that these individuals be excused from the same expectations for safe social behavior as everyone else. It is our intention, however, to bring a clinical perspective to work with them and to promote the development of desperately needed educational and treatment resources.

Most often, in our experience, individuals with LDS, who have a history of problem behaviors that bring them into conflict with the law, lack the criminal intent that is more characteristic of genuine antisocial personality. On the other hand, it is possible that one can have both LDS and meet criteria for diagnosis on the antisocial spectrum. Given the sympathy that hearing people commonly feel for deaf persons and the terrible plight generally of individuals with LDS, it is quite natural for well-meaning people to seek out treatment resources for them, regardless of the severity of their behavioral challenges, and to assume that these are people who need help, not punishment. This well-intentioned view is sometimes naïve, because people with LDS can be both victims and victimizers. Indeed, Vernon and Vernon (2010) provide a fascinating account of a deaf serial killer who took malicious advantage of the well-intentioned sympathy that many hearing people feel for deaf people (Vernon & Vernon, 2010).

In our experience, successful treatment and management of such individuals *requires* an effective collaboration between specialized Deaf mental health treatment and police, courts, and/or probation. Meaningful interventions would have to include language/communication development, to the extent possible, education and psychosocial skill building, incentives for treatment compliance, and supervision. Someone like a probation officer, who takes their responsibilities of enforcing expectations for safety and participation in treatment seriously, can be enormously helpful. This is especially true in community settings where requirements for supervision and rules like limits on internet access conflict with human rights and may be impossible for mental health providers to enforce.

When the legal system, perhaps because of the difficulties of accommodating the communication needs of the person with LDS, defers entirely to treatment programs, the result can be catastrophic not only the individual but for the treatment program, which needs firm backing from the legal system in order to maintain safety and motivate participation in treatment. Ironically, because legal consequences like jail are more concrete than therapeutic concepts like "relapse prevention," the person might not see a reason to engage in a vague, abstract, and unfamiliar process like therapy unless it is court ordered and there is someone in the "bad cop" role, like a probation officer, enforcing it. Struggles between the mental health and legal establishment over who is responsible and an inflexible either-or mentality that simplifies and distorts a highly complex situation are counterproductive.

Some people with LDS are incarcerated because their rights to due process were violated. Others may avoid legal consequences either because police and courts don't want to deal with them, at least until they engage in very serious crimes, or because they were accurately determined to be legally incompetent (O'Rourke et al., 2013). They may find themselves in a legal and psychiatric limbo where they can't be incarcerated because they are not competent, can't be released because they are dangerous, and can't be treated because their incompetence for linguistic reasons is not something that can be fixed at this stage in their lives. (Remediation for incompetence due to linguistic reasons may sometimes be possible, depending on the severity of language deprivation and the quality of specialized competency training they receive. See Chapter 4 by Pollard and Fox a fuller discussion.)

Without appreciating the need for a complex, systemic response involving Deaf mental health and legal systems, programs that take on the difficult work of serving individuals with LDS may find themselves without legal recourse when attempting to serve some highly dangerous people who happen to be deaf and language deprived. If you have done this work, you know this is not an idle or academic concern.

Notes

1   Note: the word "dysfluent" is usually used in medicine and speech pathology to refer to difficulties with articulation, e.g., stuttering. In Deaf mental health, however, its meaning has come to include the brain-based linguistic difficulties caused by early deprivation.
2   "Deaf Service: a Peek in the Mirror," 2012 was supported by NIH Research Grant # P60 MDO 02261 funded by the National Institute on Minority Health and Health Disparities, a project of the Center for Multicultural Mental Health Research, Cambridge Health Alliance.

3   Williams and Crump, in this volume, describe a communication assessment tool with which qualified examiners can assess fluency in ASL. Tools appropriate for research are described in the chapter by Henner and colleagues. Clinical best practice when there is a question of fluency is formal communication assessment by a qualified and experienced examiner.

References

Altshuler, K. (1962). Psychiatric considerations in the deaf adult. *American Annals of the Deaf, 107,* 560–561.

Amedi, A., Hofstetter, S., Maidenbaum, S., & Heimler, B. (2017). Task selectivity as a comprehensive principle for brain organization. *Trends in Cognitive Sciences, 21*(5), 307–310.

Black, P., & Glickman, N. (2009). Language and learning challenges in the Deaf psychiatric population. In Neil S. Glickman (Ed.), *Cognitive behavioral therapy for deaf and hearing persons with language and learning challenges.* New York: Routledge.

Blank, M. (1965). Use of the deaf in language studies: A reply to Furth. *Psychological Bulletin, 63*(6), 442–444. doi:10.1037/h0022016

Codina, C., Buckley, D., Port, M., & Pascalis, O. (2010). Deaf and hearing children: A comparison of peripheral vision development. *Developmental Science, 14*(4), 725–737. doi:10.1111/j.1467-7687.2010.01017.x

Corina, D. P., Blau, S., LaMarr, T., Lawyer, L. A. (2017). Coffey-Corina Sharon auditory and visual electrophysiology of deaf children with cochlear implants: implications for cross-modal plasticity. *Frontiers in Psychology, 8,* 59. doi:10.3389/fpsyg.2017.00059

Codina, C. J., Pascalis, O., Baseler, H. A., Levine, A. T., & Buckley, D. (2017). Peripheral visual reaction time is faster in deaf adults and British sign language interpreters than in hearing adults. *Frontiers in Psychology, 8,* 50. doi:10.3389/fpsyg.2017.00050

Codina, C., Pascalis, O., Mody, C., Toomey, P., Rose, J., Gummer, L., & Buckley, D. (2011). Peripheral visual reaction time is faster in deaf adults and British sign language interpreters than in hearing adults. *PloS One, 6*(6), e20417.

de Villiers, P. A., & de Villiers, J. G. (2011). Deception dissociates from false belief reasoning in deaf children: Implications for the implicit versus explicit theory of mind distinction. *British Journal of Developmental Psychology, 30*(1), 188–209. doi:10.1111/j.2044-835x.2011.02072.x

Esposito, G., & Prestia, 2012, "The Deaf and Hard of Hearing Service: A Peek in the Mirror." Grand Rounds presentation, Harvard Medical School, March 19, 2012

Glick, H., & Sharma, A., (2017). Cross-modal plasticity in developmental and age-related hearing loss: Clinical implications. *Hearing Research, 343,* 191–201.

Glickman, N. (2009). *Cognitive behavioral therapy for deaf and hearing persons with language and learning challenges.* New York, NY: Routledge.

Glickman, N., ed. (2013). *Deaf mental health care.* New York, NY: Routledge.

Glickman, N. (2017). *Preparing deaf and hearing persons with language and learning challenges for CBT: A pre-therapy workbook.* New York, NY: Routledge.

Gregory, S., Bishop, J., & Sheldon, L. (1995). *Deaf young people and their families.* Cambridge, UK: Cambridge University Press.

Gulati, S. (2014a) Language deprivation syndrome. ASL Lecture Series. www.youtube.com/watch?v=8yy_K6VtHJw, Brown University.

Gulati, S. (2014b) Language deprivation Syndrome. In *September, 2014 Annual Symposium,* Massachusetts Department of Mental Health/Worcester Recovery Center and Hospital, Worcester, MA.

Hall, W. C., Levin, L. L., & Anderson, M. L. (2017). Language deprivation syndrome: A possible neurodevelopmental disorder with sociocultural origins. *Social Psychiatry and Psychiatric Epidemiology, 56*(6), 761–776. doi: 10.1007/s00127-017-1351-7

Huston, N. (2008). *The tale tellers: A short study of humanity.* New York, NY: MacArthur & Co.

Hutchinson, E. D. (2011). A life course perspective. In E. D. Hutchinson (Ed.), *Dimensions of human behavior: The changing life course* (pp. 1–38). Thousand Oaks, CA: Sage Publications.

Kallioinen, P., Olofsson, J., Mentzer, C. N., Lindgren, M., Ors, M., Sahlén, B. S., ... Uhlén, I. (2016). Semantic processing in deaf and hard-of-hearing children: Large N400 mismatch effects in brain responses, despite poor semantic ability. *Frontiers in Psychology, 7.* doi:10.3389/fpsyg.2016.01146

Ketelaar, L., Rieffe, C., Wiefferink, C., Frijns, J. H. N. (2012). Does hearing lead to understanding? Theory of mind in toddlers and preschoolers with cochlear implants. *Journal of Pediatric Psychology, 37*(9), 1041–1050.

Kohl, H. (1966). *Language and education of the deaf.* New York, NY: Center for Urban Education.

Kral, A., Yusuf, P. A., & Land, R. (2017). Higher-order auditory areas in congenital deafness: Top-down interactions and corticocortical decoupling. *Hearing Research, 343,* 50–63. doi:10.1016/j.heares.2016.08.017

Kushalnagar, P., Mathur, G., Moreland, C., Napoli, D. J., Osterling, W., Padden, C., & Rathmann, C. (2010). Infants and children with hearing loss need early language access. *The Journal of Clinical Ethics, 21*(2), 143–54.

Lakoff, G. (1987). *Women, fire, and dangerous things: What categories reveal about the mind.* Chicago, IL: University of Chicago Press.

Levine, E. (1956). *Youth in a soundless world.* New York, NY: New York University Press.

Mayberry, R., Chen, J. -K., Witcher, P., & Klein, D. (2011). Age of acquisition effects on the functional organization of language in the adult brain. *Brain & Language, 119,* 21–69.

Meristo, M., Morgan, G., Geraci, A., Iozzi, L., Hjelmquist, E., Surian, L., & Siegal, M. (2012). Belief attribution in deaf and hearing infants. *Developmental Science, 15*(5), 633–640. doi:10.1111/j.1467-7687.2012.01155.x

Miller, J. (2016). *Wilfred and me.* Kingston, ON: Woodpecker Lane Press.

Miller, K. R. (2004). Linguistic diversity in a deaf prison population: Implications for due process. *Journal of Deaf Studies and Deaf Education, 9*(1), 112–119. doi:10.1093/deafed/enh007

Mitchell, R. E. (2004). When parents are deaf versus hard of hearing: Patterns of sign use and school placement of deaf and hard-of-hearing children. *Journal of Deaf Studies and Deaf Education, 9*(2), 133–152. doi:10.1093/deafed/enh017

Mitchell, T. V. (2017). Category selectivity of the N170 and the role of expertise in deaf signers. **Hearing Research, 343,* 150–161. doi:10.1016

Morgan, G., & Kegl, J. (2006). Nicaraguan sign language and theory of mind: The issue of critical periods and abilities. *Journal of Child Psychology and Psychiatry, 47*(8), 811–819. doi:10.1111/j.1469-7610.2006.01621.x

Myklebust, H. R. (1960). *The psychology of deafness: Sensory deprivation, learning, and adjustment.* Oxford, UK: Grune & Stratton.

Newman A. J., Supalla T., Fernandez N., Newport E. L., & Bavelier D. (2015) Neural systems supporting linguistic structure, linguistic experience, and symbolic communication in sign language and gesture. *Proceedings of the National Academy of Science, 112*(37), 11684–11689. doi:10.1073/pnas.1510527112

New York (Daily) Times. September 29, 1852. "Deaf mutes: The status of the census."

O'Rourke, S., Glickman, N., & Austin, S. (2013). Deaf people in the criminal justice system. In N. Glickman (Ed.), *Deaf mental health care.* New York, NY: Routledge.

Peet, I. L. (1870a). Principal of the NY Institution for the Instruction of the Deaf and Blind (NYT 10/17/1870).

Peet, I. L. (1870b). The Deaf-Mute Murderer Bodine: A letter from Isaac L. Peet (NYT Monday 10/17/1870), 2.

Pénicaud, S., Klein, D., Zatorre, R. J., Chen, J., Witcher, P., Hyde, K., & Mayberry, R. I. (2013). Structural brain changes linked to delayed first language acquisition in congenitally deaf individuals. *NeuroImage, 66,* 42–49. doi:10.1016/j.neuroimage.2012.09.076

Pinker, S. (1994). *The language instinct*. New York, NY: Harper Perennial Modern Classics.

Pisoni, D., Kronenberger, W., Roman, A., & Geers, A. (2011). Article 7: Measures of digit span and verbal rehearsal speed in deaf children following more than 10 years of cochlear implantation. *Ear and Hearing, 32*(1), 60s–74s.

Rainer, J. D., & Altshuler, K., (Eds.). (1968). *Psychiatry and the deaf*. Washington, DC: U.S. Department of Health, Education, and Welfare.

Schaller, S. (2012). *A man without words*. 2nd ed. Berkeley: University of California Press.

Skotara, N., Salden, U, Kügow, M. Hänel-Faulhaber, B. & Röder, B. (2012). *BMC Neuroscience, 13*, 44. www.biomedcentral.com/1471-2202/13/4

Tobey, E. A., Britt, L., Geers, A., Loizou, P., Loy, B., Roland, P., … Wright, C. G. (2012). Cochlear implantation updates: The Dallas Cochlear implant program. *Journal of the American Academy of Audiology, 23*(6), 438–445. doi:10.3766/jaaa.23.6.6

Tomasuolo, E., Valeri, F., Di Renzo, A., Pasqualetti, P., & Volterra, V. (2013). Deaf children attending different school environments: Sign language abilities and theory of mind. *Journal of Deaf Studies and Deaf Education, 18*(1), 12–29.

Wittgenstein, L. (1953). *Philosophical investigations*. Oxford, UK: Blackwell.

Vernon, M., & Raifman, L. J. (1997). Recognizing and handling problems of incompetent deaf defendants charges with serious offenses. *International Journal of Law and Psychiatry, 20*(3). 373–387.

Vernon, M., & Rich, S. (1997). Pedophilia and deafness. *American Annals of the Deaf, 142*(4), 300–311. doi:10.1353/aad.2012.0258

Vernon, M., Steinberg, A. G., & Montoya, L. A. (1999). Deaf murderers: Clinical and forensic issues. *Behavioral Sciences & the Law, 17*(4), 495–516. doi:10.1002/(sici)1099-0798(199910/12)17:4<495::aid-bsl361>3.0.co;2-6

Vernon, M., & Vernon, M. (2010). *Deadly charm: The story of a deaf serial killer*. Washington, DC: Gallaudet University Press.

Young, A., Howarth, P., Ridgeway, S., & Monteiro, B. (2001). Forensic referrals to the three specialist psychiatric units for deaf people in the UK. *Journal of Forensic Psychiatry, 12*(1), 19–35. doi:10.1080/09585180010027842

2

Pre-therapy with Deaf People with Language and Learning Challenges

NEIL S. GLICKMAN, WENDY HEINES,
AND MELISSA WATSON

Introduction

Freud referred to psychoanalysis, the first known form of psychotherapy, as the "talking cure." More than a century later, we have many different forms of psychotherapy, but they almost all depend on language and dialogue. People come to see a therapist, and what they do is communicate with each other in a language. Any language will work, provided they both know it or, as a second-best alternative, use an interpreter. While a therapist can use less verbal activities like play, movement, dance, artistic expression, or pictures, there is still almost always a need to talk about these experiences, and this requires language.

In addition to language abilities, one needs accompanying cognitive skills. These skills are so basic and foundational that they are rarely discussed. They include a well-developed sense of time and the ability to make use of the time and tense structures that one's language provides (e.g., to distinguish clearly what happened before from what is happening now or what may happen, to say what happened first, second, third). Time structures are needed for people to have a sense of cause and effect or to consider possibilities (i.e., if this, then that). Therapists who want their clients to develop insight need these individuals to have the ability to see patterns (e.g., how your father behaved with you is like how you are behaving now; how you think, feel, and react are related to each other and grow out of your early formative experiences). Seeing patterns requires abstract thinking abilities. People who are language deprived commonly struggle with such cognitive abilities.

Perhaps the most basic cognitive ability needed for psychotherapy is the ability to construct a narrative—that is, to tell a story. When someone first starts therapy, the therapist will often ask some version of "what brings you here?" Another way to ask this, which often resonates with Deaf signing people, is, "please tell me your story. What happened to you?" Therapists listen to the stories, ask questions, and comment. They work with these stories to help people explore, understand, and problem solve. Sometimes they may tell stories of their own—for instance, of how people successfully handle challenges. Stories can become metaphors, such as, "this story helps me make sense of my life." Stories take examples and raise them to a more abstract level where people see patterns, make connections, and find meaning.

For therapy to work, therapists and their clients also need to share an understanding of what they are doing. They need a map or schema that they both accept, which guides what they do together. For example, informed consumers seek out therapy with the understanding that this will be a safe and helpful place for them to talk about deeply private matters. If they don't think that is worth doing, or they don't consider the therapist to be a trustworthy, credible helper, or they don't, literally, have the words for talking about their experiences, they will probably not find themselves, at least voluntarily, sitting in a therapist's office.

People seek out psychotherapy with the understanding that talking with a therapist will help them "get better," address a problem, or reach a goal. At a minimum, the person receiving services sees value in the experience of expressing themselves to the therapist. Once the person receiving services has chosen to participate in this process, they can fairly be called a "client." Until then, they are more fairly described as a "person receiving services." The notion of "client" implies informed consent—a decision to be there and use this form of help.

It is well established that for therapy to work, there must be a therapeutic alliance between the client and the therapist (Duncan, Miller, Wampold, & Hubble, 2010). According to a recent study of "how master therapists work," the therapeutic relationship remains the single most important variable in psychotherapy outcome research. Therapeutic alliance is a type of therapeutic relationship that encompasses three factors: "the therapeutic bond between client and therapist, the agreed-on goals of treatment, and an agreement about methods to achieve that goal or goals" (Sperry & Carlson, 2014, pp. 2–3).

These understandings of the preconditions that make therapy possible are quite relevant when working with people who don't want to be in therapy or, more to the point of this chapter, lack a schema for "what is wrong," "how I get better," and "why and how talking to you, a counselor or therapist, is helpful." Indeed, the more that language, educational, and social deprivation have impacted their cognitive abilities—including their ability to make use of a language- and dialogue-based procedure like psychotherapy—the more attention the therapists will need to devote to creating the foundational understanding, skills, and motivation to do this work, a process referred to in this chapter as "pre-therapy."

Pre-therapy as understood here is a process of helping people with language and cognitive deficits develop a useful, understandable schema for what happens in therapy and enough foundational communication and problem-solving skills that they can make use of therapy (Glickman, 2009, 2017). As we will see, this schema is focused on the idea of skills, especially communication skills, but also, later, skills for dealing with what is inside one's body (e.g., feelings, thoughts, impulses, cravings, sensations) and outside one's body (e.g., environmental stressors, other people.) "Learning skills" is a relatively concrete schema for what occurs in psychotherapy, and it is also a schema that provides an entry into the world of cognitive behavioral therapy. The schema of skills can also be easily illustrated with pictures and enacted with concrete procedures like role-playing, two ways it can be adapted further for persons with "language and learning challenges" (Glickman 2009).

In this chapter, we are first going to discuss pre-therapy from the point of view of a clinician sitting with a person who is linguistically, cognitively, and developmentally unprepared to use therapy. We'll use some clinical vignettes based closely on the first author's experience to name and examine some of the challenges of engaging deaf individuals with language and learning challenges in a "talking cure" like psychotherapy. We'll also peer into the therapist's head, examining how they think about these clinical challenges.

In the second part of the chapter, we'll discuss pre-therapy considerations as they played out in a Deaf-centered, mental health treatment agency, PAHrtners Deaf services, in Glenside, Pennsylvania. Pre-therapy efforts usually take a team and work best in therapeutic programs where many staff can reinforce each other's work.

Getting to the Starting Gate of Therapy

Pre-therapy considerations guide the therapist or therapeutic team in thinking about the therapy readiness of the persons they serve, including what clinical and communication skills they need to do this work. The skill set required to work with people who are not developmentally prepared to use therapy is different from that required to work with clients who, with a well-established knowledge base about mental health, call a therapist to ask for help. The difference is comparable to that between the skill set of interpreters who work with fluent users of different languages, who are also educated consumers of the interpreting process, and the skill set of interpreters who work with individuals who don't have native mastery of any language and who also lack understanding of the interpreting process. This would include people who don't understand that the interpreter is conveying information from another person and is not the source of the information herself. It is comparable to the difference between working as a teacher with a well-prepared, motivated student and working with a student who is disruptive in a classroom because he has no reason to think he is capable of learning anything useful in that setting.

In all these cases, the formal educational preparation one received to learn one's discipline does not usually prepare one to work with people who lack the tools to make use of your disciplines' manner of work. It's only very recently, for instance, that interpreting training programs are beginning to discuss the challenges of interpreting dysfluent language (Two examples of this are the yearly Mental Health Interpreter Training program sponsored by the Alabama Office of Deaf Services and the new on-line training offered by the Center for Atypical Language Interpreting at Northeastern University.) As a professional working with these unprepared individuals, more will be asked of you. It takes a much higher level of skill and, indeed, an additional set of skills concerned with engagement strategies, to work with people unprepared to use the services of your discipline.

Put another way, people who *seek therapy* because they have the following beliefs are usually at a good starting point for this process:

"I have a problem"
"I need help."
"I can get help by talking to someone."
"That person is a therapist/counselor. They listen to people and help them."
"Talking about things in therapy is worthwhile."
"I can talk about things."
"The therapist will listen, helping me solve my problems and feel better."
"I can do better. I can learn and improve."
"Therapy will help me learn, grow and feel better. I will become better able to express my feelings and learn other new skills."

The people who are the target subjects of this chapter don't think this way. They don't refer themselves to therapy, even assuming they have some vague idea what therapy means. The problem is not just that no one has ever explained to them what therapy is. The problem is that people unused to, and unskilled in, using language for self-expression (who also have not had many people with whom they could communicate effectively) are not likely to seek out activities centered primarily upon dialogue. They are certainly not likely to seek out dialogue with a person for a purpose as abstract and remote as self-understanding.

When people don't refer themselves to therapy, don't want to be there, or don't understand what therapy is all about, or when the therapist is unprepared to work with individuals with these developmental limitations, there is initial pre-therapy work to do. When clinicians proceed without awareness of these developmental challenges, they will usually quickly conclude that the referred person is a "poor candidate" for therapy. The referred person, in turn, is highly unlikely return, if that is an option for them.

In settings where people are present involuntarily, like hospital or residential treatment, they often resist efforts at therapeutic engagement. They may, for instance, refuse to go to treatment groups or to meet with their assigned clinician. Sometimes they will show their lack of readiness to participate in therapeutic activities through disruptive behaviors. *Other people* may believe they "need therapy." Somewhat more enlightened other people may think, if the individuals are deaf, that "they just need therapy with someone who signs."

There is no question that having signing staff, especially native signing Deaf staff, is enormously helpful, but even that is often insufficient when the patient doesn't understand or know how to make use of this thing called "psychotherapy." Indeed, when the first author of this chapter thinks back on his 17 years of work on a Deaf psychiatric inpatient unit, he realizes that most of what the treatment team was doing was pre-therapy. Our concept of pre-therapy formed there because of how often our deaf patients were unprepared for therapy and how much clinical time was devoted to initial engagement and educational efforts.

Some Relevant Considerations

In the Deaf Community, there are many sophisticated, sign-fluent Deaf people who can easily make use of language-intensive experience like psychotherapy provided that therapists use their language well, or use interpreters, and make other adaptations to fit their learning styles and worldviews (Leigh, 2010). There are also many deaf people who do not use language well. There are many reasons this can be true, but by far the most common reason is language deprivation, the lack of sufficient exposure to a fully accessible language during their critical period for language acquisition. Language problems or *dysfluencies* in language-deprived people range from severe, where the person has almost no formal language, to subtle problems, only visible to native users or highly trained sign communication specialists.

Because psychotherapy, like education, will promote new learning, its success also depends on the person receiving services having learned the most important skill that education produces: the ability to learn. In normally structured education, lesson one in a subject comes before lesson two. If one hasn't mastered lessons one through ten, it will be quite hard to learn lesson eleven. When therapists work with individuals who have been linguistically deprived, it is probably reasonable to assume they are also educationally and informationally deprived. This means more than the fact that they will lack knowledge of the world, something often referred to as "fund of information." It means they are likely missing the foundational structures for learning. They are likely missing not just the content in the lessons, but notions and strategies for learning such as: What is a lesson? How do I learn? How do I change? What is a problem? How do I solve problems? How do I discuss and think about any of this?

The therapeutic efforts in this chapter are focused on deaf people who have, at least, functional communication abilities for everyday needs but who have not mastered enough of any language to be considered native users. Language skills in deaf people vary far more than they do in hearing people, and dysfluent language is more common. Deaf mental health care specialists need not only to be able to sign well, but to be prepared for this language variation. This asks quite a lot of them and is one reason why Deaf mental health care is a distinct clinical specialty.

When people have been so severely language deprived that they lack formal language entirely, even the pre-therapy efforts described here will be insufficient. In some cases, the individuals can be engaged through non-verbal activities like drawing, movement, and play, but the development of language and communication skills, to the extent possible, would have to be the focus of efforts to help them (See Chapter 7 by Spitz and Kegl). If there are therapeutic goals at all, they might be described by the therapist as "the person will use language or some other medium to express themselves safely and therefore have less need to show problem behaviors." Of course, this would be the therapists' goal. The person receiving services would probably not be able to articulate this goal. They might not even know what a "goal" is, much less a "treatment goal." The person receiving services would probably not understand why they are there, who the therapist is, and what is supposed to happen during those meetings. Perhaps they think this is a nice person to talk to who tries to understand them, but that is a far cry from intentional and informed participation in a process called psychotherapy.

The work presented here assumes staff with sophisticated understanding of language and communication diversity in deaf people. It is hard for us to see how this kind of work could be done well outside of a designated Deaf mental health treatment context or, at the very least, by people who are not well trained in Deaf mental health.

Cognitive Behavioral Therapy

When discussing psychotherapy in this chapter, we're working within the broadly defined cognitive behavioral therapy (CBT) world. We work within CBT because the concrete notion of therapy as skill-building (for instance, in the development of skills for coping, dealing with other people, communicating, or problem solving) is discussed mainly within CBT. The CBT tradition referenced here is heavily influenced by the work of Donald Meichenbaum beginning with his early work of self-instructional training (that is, learning to talk to oneself more helpfully) (Meichenbaum, 1977; Meichenbaum & Goodman, 1971), and continuing through his more recent explorations of narrative or constructivist therapy (that is, using metaphor and stories therapeutically) (Meichenbaum, 1994, 2001), as well as his focus on strengths (that is, noticing and building upon what people do well) (Meichenbaum, 2012; Meichenbaum & Biemiller, 1998).

Meichenbaum's CBT work has many applications for pre-therapy. Chief among these is the appeal of centering therapy on the idea of skills, beginning with foundation communication skills. "Learning skills" is a good schema for therapy. In addition, the cognitive dimension of CBT can be approached by working mindfully in therapy through development of the reasonably concrete cognitive skill of "self-talk," and through narrative or storytelling structures. This pre-therapy approach is explored in much more depth in two books by the lead author of this chapter (Glickman, 2009, 2017).

As people become more acculturated into a therapeutic way of thinking and working, formal therapy procedures become more available to them, but these still must be adapted for the language, culture, beliefs, and thinking style of each consumer. This will be demonstrated more fully in the next chapter.

Individual Pre-therapy with Jose

First, let's consider the challenges of pre-therapy conducted by trained Deaf mental health clinician working essentially alone. We'll give two examples, and we'll delve into the mindset of the clinicians as they think about the challenges of their work.

Betty, a hearing therapist in her early 30s, who learned ASL during her college years about ten years ago, is sitting with Jose,[1] an 18-year-old Puerto-Rican deaf man who was first introduced to sign language about six years ago. Betty is a therapist in a psychiatric inpatient treatment program where she is the signing therapist and where interpreters are available. Jose has been hospitalized in this program after a series of incidents in his school of increasingly dangerous behaviors. Most recently, he punched several peers and a teacher's aide in his class room and then ran outside and threw rocks at cars in the parking lot. He was eventually restrained by several staff, two of whom suffered cuts and bruises in the process.

The police brought Jose to a hospital emergency room where he waited several days in a small examination room before being placed on a medical floor of the hospital "for observation." He remained there another week until he could be placed on this psychiatric unit. During most of this time, he had very little communication with hospital staff. They tried to use their video relay interpreting service, but it didn't seem to work with him. Jose's language and cognitive difficulties made it hard for him to understand and be understood by the relay interpreter who knew nothing about his language abilities and wasn't prepared to adapt her communication style for him. The hospital team saw that the interpreter was struggling to understand him, and he her, but they didn't understand where the problem lay. Signing staff from his school visited him several times and explained to him, as best they could, that he couldn't return to the school right now because of his bad "blowup," and that he had to go to another hospital. Jose's response was that he was "sorry" and "fine" and hated staying in this hospital. He didn't understand why he needed to go to another hospital. He said he would not blowup again, and as far as he was concerned, that was the end of the matter.

Betty, the psychiatric inpatient social worker, is generally considered to be a good signer, though sometimes deaf people criticize her signing as "too

English." She has worked for about a decade in Deaf educational and mental health settings. She tries to be "culturally affirmative" in her work. For instance, she understands that deaf people have widely varying language and communication competencies. She respects ASL and works to continuously improve her ASL skills.

Betty knows that even under optimal circumstances, Jose is likely to be challenging to work with. She knows he is oppositional and has conduct problems. He is an angry young man. She's female, not Puerto-Rican or Hispanic, not deaf, and not from his world. He is in a treatment program he doesn't want to be in; nor does he really understand why he is there. His attitude will likely be to say he is fine and to blame other people for his difficulties. These clinical challenges would be enough, but there is an additional challenge that Betty dreads even more. When they start communicating, it quickly becomes apparent that she doesn't understand him much of the time. He's signing in a rapid, disorganized way, and she can't follow his account of what has happened. Similarly, he seems to be struggling to understand her. He looks away a lot. "Why is this?" she wonders. "Is the problem with my signing, his signing, or, in some confusing way, with both of us?" She also wonders whether she is seeing a communication problem, a psychiatric problem, or some combination of the two.

Betty tries to explain to her supervisor about the communication difficulties. This supervisor, who doesn't sign and doesn't understand communication variation among deaf people, is perplexed. Like most hearing people, she has never experienced working with a person with severe language deprivation. She understands about using a different language, like sign language. She thinks it is like using Spanish. She doesn't understand about a person not having native language abilities in some language. Betty's supervisor and other agency leadership hired Betty because she claimed to be a fluent signer. To them, she's a signing therapist, a deafness specialist. They expect her to work well with all deaf clientele. End of story.

Betty is culturally aware enough to question her own communication abilities. Perhaps the communication problems lie with her. She knows she's a second language user of ASL. She welcomes communication assistance when she can get it. She loves working with Deaf interpreters, or Deaf communication specialists, or just a Deaf colleague who signs better than she does, when they are available. When Betty thinks about her competence for this work, she has two competing notions. On the one hand, she can communicate well with many deaf people, and she is generally well regarded in the local Deaf community. She feels good about that. On the other hand, she meets people with whom she feels her communication is poor, and at those times, she doubts herself and considers finding another line of work.

It sometimes feels to Betty that, even though she signs, she lives on a different planet than some of the language-deprived people with whom she has worked. Usually the people she serves have been referred, or pressured, into treatment by someone else. They may have signed a consent to be hospital-ized, but they do not come to the hospital voluntarily. Someone has decided that Jose, and others like him, "need therapy," or, at the least, need psychiatric hospitalization, but Jose doesn't think that. He doesn't even have a conceptual way to make sense of such an idea. Betty's first challenge is to try to bridge this enormous chasm in understanding about why Jose is here and what they are supposed to be doing about it.

In the hearing world, client readiness for therapy has been discussed in sev-eral ways. The most well-known way is through the discussion about "stages of change" (Prochaska & DiClemente, 1992) and a strategy called "motiva-tional interviewing" (Miller & Rollnick, 2002). These concepts refer to an individual's emotional readiness to enter a change-oriented process like psy-chotherapy. They apply to individuals like Jose, who is "pre-contemplation" in his readiness for therapy; but his readiness is compromised further by his language and learning challenges. Jose isn't merely emotionally unprepared for therapy or a process of changing. He is linguistically and cognitively un-prepared for it as well.

In fairness to Jose and people like him, the therapists they are referred to are also, almost always, unprepared to adapt their work to create a better ther-apeutic match with them. Neither are the systems of care, such as the clinics, hospitals, and insurance providers, generally prepared to work with them. They almost always want, for instance, a readily understandable treatment goal very early in the process. That's difficult to do if you don't understand "treatment" and may not even understand "goal" or don't see yourself as hav-ing a psychological problem, whatever that means, that lends itself to therapy or mental health treatment, whatever those mean. It's also difficult to do if you can't really have a clear conversation about the issue.

Maybe the agencies or insurance providers would accept a Motivational Interviewing strategy such as "exploring the pros and cons of maintaining a specific behavior." How would this work, however, with someone who doesn't understand "pro and con" and doesn't understand what it means to have a "problem behavior"? How would it work with individuals who don't have the ability to abstract from their current situation to consider how their behav-iors fall into patterns that cause problems or that alternative behaviors may help solve problems? How would that work with individuals who are unable to clearly tell the story of what has happened to them? Insurance companies, and established theories of psychotherapy, also have no words for such challenges.

Starting the Therapy Conversation

Let's return to Betty, the hearing signing therapist who is trying to engage Jose, recently hospitalized on this psychiatric unit fortunate enough to have a signing therapist and interpreters. Jose has not referred himself and is not seeking therapy or counseling. He's unhappy about everything and angry with everyone. If he has any organized schema for what is happening to him, it's likely to be something like, "people are bad."

Betty knows that *other people* think that Jose has an "anger problem" and that he needs therapy. She also knows that *he* is not likely to think that. It's not that he denies having an "anger problem," but that he doesn't understand the concept. Jose is likely to blame other people for his difficulties. Betty is a good therapist, and she has an idea how to begin work with an angry, hostile young man under typical circumstances. The additional communication challenges, however, make this work more daunting.

Betty starts the meeting with the intent of empathizing with his feelings and point of view. She hopes that by doing this, she'll begin to demonstrate that she is a safe person to talk with. She goes into the room where he is playing a game on his cell phone, introduces herself in sign language, and asks if she can talk with him. Jose shrugs and continues playing with his phone.

"Looks like you are good at that," she signs when he looks up. "What game is it?"

He doesn't answer, but she sees it's a racing game app. She watches for a few minutes, and when Jose looks up again, she asks if she can give it a try. Reluctantly, Jose gives her the phone. She asks him how to play it, putting him in the expert and helper role, and he shows her. This continues for about ten minutes.

"Thank you," she says. "That was fun. Can I talk to you for a few minutes?"

So far, she can manage the communication dynamics. He nods yes to her.

"Well," she says, "I'm a counselor here. I understand you've been having a hard time. People are worried about you. I want to help Can I talk with you? Will you tell me what happened?" She then adds, as an afterthought, "Please tell me your story."

This is a competent beginning. She joined him around an interest of his, empowered him by having him instruct her in the activity, asked his permission to talk, showed a warm smile, expressed concern, and invited him to talk. While this might not always work, it's a good standard approach.

Betty also asked him what has happened to him; she asks him to tell her his story. This is an engaging way to begin with many people, and it establishes right away that they will work with each other though talking about what happens in one's life—that is, through stories. Jose, tentatively at first, starts to respond. He's talking, it seems, about the school, hospital, and different people, but Betty is not getting the full narrative. Betty thinks she is getting the main points. He's angry. He feels his teacher has been mean to him. He thinks the students in his class are jerks. He didn't do anything wrong. If people were nice to him, he wouldn't have to hit anyone.

Betty uses skills at empathic listening. She says back to him what she heard. She tries to reflect his feelings. She checks in about her understanding. She avoids judgments or any statement that Jose could interpret as a reprimand. Because she is a genuinely warm and empathic person, can communicate concern, and has enough signing ability to comprehend, at least, the main points that Jose is saying, he seems to be increasingly willing to talk. She is understanding, she estimates, about 60% of what he says. As part of her skillful interviewing, she asks a lot of structuring questions: the who, what, when, and where questions. Sprinkled through her conversation are questions like, "Who did that? And then what did that person say? Then what did you say? What did you do? Did you notice what you were feeling?" With someone more linguistically competent, she wouldn't need to be so detailed, but Jose needs assistance getting his story out.

A few times, Jose gets impatient with her. "I said that already," he says. Betty wonders, "Did he? I don't think so." Jose's perception appears to be that it is Betty who has the language problem. At one point, he accuses her of having "lousy sign language." She knows to respond non-defensively. "Sometimes I feel I have lousy sign language too," she smiles. "ASL is a beautiful language but it's not an easy language for me. I appreciate your efforts to communicate with me and be patient with me. When I'm not clear, please tell me."

The conversation continues for another 15 minutes. "Not a bad start," Betty thinks, "but how do I raise the concerns we have about his behavior? This is going to be the toughest part. How do I do that without pushing him away?"

She selects an approach she has learned called using a "one-down stance" (Glickman, 2017). That is, she'll treat him as someone who has expert knowledge about himself, and she'll ask him questions from a stance of curiosity, wondering, worrying, or asking for help. She'll avoid telling him what's wrong or giving directives about what he should do. Her initial tactic will be to raise the issue of *other people* being worried about him and see if he's willing to talk about why *they* are worried. This is a bit like playing dumb, but the point is more to engage people by treating them as authorities on their own lives.

"Jose, do you know that your teacher, the school staff, your mom, are all worried about you. I'm worried about you, too. Do you know why people are worried?"

Jose responds concretely. "I'm fine," he says. "Not sick."

Betty clarifies. "Yes, I know you are not sick. You are healthy. That's not why people are worried. Why are people worried?" she asks again.

While there is an ASL sign for WHY, Betty communicates this by role playing school teachers and staff and his mother seeing Jose blowup, looking worried and alarmed, and shrugging their shoulders while signing JOSE WRONG WHAT? The concept of "why" is embedded in that.

He thinks for a minute. "Blowup?" he asks, using a familiar sign.

"Yes, that! Many blowups. People are worried that you are blowing up a lot. If you blowup again and again, what could happen?"

Again, she uses the one-down strategy of inviting him to respond and asking questions. In this way, she puts him in the role of being "the person with the answers." She could tell him why his blowups are a problem, but she knows that ultimately, it would be critical for him to explain that to her.

However, she's asking him a tough question, to consider the possible consequences of his behaviors. It's a natural question for a good therapist to ask, but it assumes a certain level of cognitive development, such as the ability to understand cause and effect.

Jose shrugs. He repeats how other people are mean, the rules are unfair, and life is hard for him. He continues to blame other people and says he didn't blowup, contradicting what he said earlier. He also makes incomplete references to something that happened at a store, a person with the name sign J on the elbow, whom he doesn't otherwise identify, and uses the sign STEAL but without clarifying who steals, or stole, what. It seems like a non sequitur. How is the "stealing" related to the rest of the story? Who is J- and how is that person involved? Several signs seem poorly formed and Betty doesn't recognize them. Jose also fingerspells very quickly and low in the signing space, in a way that makes the fingerspelling difficult to read. Betty suspects that is to cover up that he doesn't really know the English words he is spelling, then he says he kicked a car. Does he not connect kicking a car with the sign BLOW-UP? Betty is starting to feel confused and lost.

"Yes, you are angry. You think the teacher is mean. You don't like the rules. You don't like the other students. But mother, teacher staff are worried? Why are they worried about your blowups? If you blow-up a lot… (she corrects herself),…if you kick the cars, if you steal…what happens to you?"

Betty realizes she just used a conditional sentence: if this, then that. Does Jose understand that structure? Many people with language deprivation seem to struggle with it. Also, she isn't sure he acknowledged stealing anything. Is she confusing him with too many questions? Is she being too abstract?

"School, kick-me-out. I don't care." He replies. (Betty notices he is not referencing time or using tense. Is he talking about what did happen to him or what might happen to him again?)

"You did (FINISH) get kicked out of school," she says, using the FINISH sign to stress past tense. "Can you go back to the school? We don't know. If you are kicked out, no school, what will you do?"

Betty is aware she is again asking a conditional sentence, what would he do *if* he is kicked out of school, and she wonders whether he understands the question. "This is so hard to do without using 'if, then' sentences," she thinks.

"Don't care."

"You don't care. Other people care." (The sign for "care" also means "cherish" and is stronger than the English word "care.") "Who cares? Mother care? Teacher care?" Betty realizes she may have just signed, "who cares for you?" or "Who cherishes you?" She is feeling inarticulate and clumsy in her signing.

Jose looks down and resumes his game. He's indicating the conversation is over. Betty wonders why he wants to stop now. Does he expect her to scold him? Is he embarrassed? Does he think no one cares for him? Or is it something more basic, like not understanding the question or not having the means of articulating his feelings? Betty also doubts herself. Was her signing "too English"? Were her questions too abstract? She wonders whether the hospital will support her asking for help from a Deaf interpreter.

"Thank you for talking with me," Betty signs. "Can I say one positive thing before I go?"

He looks puzzled.

"One thing good. I want to compliment you." (The hand clapping sign for COMPLiMENT is very clear.)

"What?" he shrugs.

"In this meeting, right now, you and me talking, did you kick me?"

"No!" Jose seems alarmed.

"Right, you didn't kick me. You didn't hit me. You didn't yell at me. You didn't blowup. Right?"

Jose nods yes tentatively.

"Right, you talked to me, but you were safe. You didn't blowup. That's great! What did you do instead?" Betty wonders again whether this line of questioning is too abstract for Jose.

Jose shrugs.

"You played on your phone. That's one skill you have. You taught me the game. You have a teaching skill. Then you talked about what happened. You told me a story. You were safe. You didn't blowup. You got angry with me for having lousy sign language, but you didn't blowup and you kept talking. You have some good skills. Thank you for talking with me today."

What is Betty doing? She's doing some things that good therapists would do with any person: meet Jose in his world; communicate empathically; avoid judgments, as best she can. She's also working intentionally with his language and learning challenges. She's assessing whether he has very basic language and cognitive structures, like tense, time sequencing, "if this, then that" sentences. She asks questions that she knows assume some cognitive development, like asking him what other people may think, and then she observes whether he can answer the question. She's being as mindful as she can be about the signs she uses, especially when they are abstract or when the English and ASL don't closely correspond. She's certainly hoping he has these cognitive structures because her work will be so much more difficult if he doesn't.

Betty also knows that in therapy with people at all levels, one talks about what is happening in one's life. If you think of these accounts as stories, then it's easier to help create a structure. Stories have a beginning, a middle, and an end. There are a defined set of people or "characters" in the story. There is a narrative about something happening, and it proceeds through time in a logical way. Stories have a structure.

Betty is pulling for Jose to tell his story, and as he communicates, she reflects his comments and feelings back with paraphrasing, empathizing, questioning, clarifying, and other listening skills. She relies heavily upon questions because they engage people better than statements and because questions pull for him to use more language, think, evaluate, and problem-solve. She's also planting some therapeutic seeds. She's trying to help him discover that he has the ability, the skills, to talk about his life in a safe and meaningful way. She's trying to help him experience how talking with her can be helpful, how he has the ability within him to address problems through language rather than behavior. In the back of her mind, she's also formulating a treatment goal like "Jose will use therapy to talk about his feelings safely," but that is way down the road—if it happens at all.

This would be a huge therapeutic challenge for Betty even if Jose were a fluent user of a sign or spoken language. Jose's language and learning challenges raise the therapeutic difficulty exponentially. Betty signs well, but does she sign well enough to work with Jose? Even with the help of a Deaf interpreter, if one is available, will they be able to establish a meaningful therapeutic process?

Pulling for Stories

How do we bring people with significant language deprivation into a procedure like verbal-based psychotherapy? Jose is an example of a person who has difficulty organizing his experience into a narrative structure that has a set of people or characters who are acting in the world, over time, and experiencing reactions from other people. Jose's inability to organize this information into a clear narrative is one reason he has a poor understanding of cause and effect and how his behavior impacts other people.

When mental health clinicians can't easily communicate with a person, they will tend to rely more heavily on what they can do. They can give medicine, and this means there is a danger that Jose is already overmedicated. They can also do behavioral programming, setting up an environment that rewards, and perhaps punishes, behaviors. This means it is probable that Jose has not had much experience sitting with a therapist who was interested in knowing how he felt, thought, and experienced the world. When he has been exposed to counselors, they have mostly told him about rules and been very directive. Perhaps they didn't sign well or at all. This means that Jose may have very good reasons for not wanting to talk with staff. Betty suspects all of this, and she knows she is going to have to work on fundamentals with Jose. First, she'll have to establish that talking to her, just that, can be helpful. She'll try to distinguish herself from staff who may have come before by showing genuine interest in communicating with him and seeing what he has to say.

Betty wants to engage him in this process of self-improvement though conversation. She'll draw upon the natural human interest in telling and hearing stories. She'll listen as actively to his stories as he'll permit, drawing him out both emotionally and, to the extent possible, linguistically. As he does this, she'll help him notice what skills he is using. He's using language. He's telling stories. He's not hurting himself or other people. He's expressing himself safely and well. He can do this, and she wants to hear more of what he has to say.

She'll start at a developmentally early place. Whatever Jose can communicate, she'll comment positively on his communication abilities and identify skills he used. She may say that he stayed in the room for five minutes and talked to her, that he was interesting, and that she wants to hear more. If he can communicate with her and remain safe, she'll help him discover that he used skills such as "taking turns communicating," "listening, not interrupting," "nodding your head to show understanding," "leaning forward in your chair to show listening," and above all, "communicating safely" or "expressing feelings safely." She'll look for ways to point out how well he is doing (i.e., what skills he is using), and then she'll invite him to say more. She'll use variants of the phrase, "please tell me the story." She'll also ask questions that pull more story out of him.

As she helps him express himself, safely telling his stories, she'll be careful to frame what he is doing in terms of skills. That framing is important to establish a schema around "what we do here." It's a way of addressing his information deficit not only about counseling and therapy, but about using language to express oneself and solve problems. She wants him to realize that, "when we meet, we dialogue, we use communication skills. You tell me what happened, the story, and I ask questions, and the two of us, together, figure out what to do." She uses the sign SKILL as much as possible, especially when referring to communication skills, because she wants to establish the schema that communicating involves skills, that together they work on skills, and that he already has some good skills. If she can establish this schema, she may not only hook him into the process of meeting with her, but also lead him into a world where other skills can be learned. That world, of course, is cognitive behavioral therapy where there are skills for working on most life challenges.

Pre-therapy with Doug

Let's consider another client and therapist. We focus upon Doug, a person seen in an outpatient therapy program where there is a Deaf signing counselor named Sam. Doug is a little further along in therapy than Jose in that he already understands that therapy (the sign for "counseling" is used) is to "express feelings." Doug wants to express his feelings, and not having many people in his life with whom he can sign, he values sitting with Sam to do that. Even though Doug struggles to communicate, from his point of view, his communication with Sam is far better than with anyone in his life, so he eagerly comes to the counseling center to see him. Doug is like many deaf people with language deprivation. He is not a sophisticated user of psychotherapy, but he values communicating with someone who signs who seems interested in him. The challenge for his therapist Sam is to shape his interest in communication, and his natural tendency to strive to tell his story, into a process that serves larger therapeutic purposes. It often seems to Sam like they "just talk," a process that Doug values, but which is hard to justify to insurance as constituting psychotherapy.

Doug is 25 years old and didn't begin to sign until he gained access to a signing classroom and interpreters when he began high school. He took to signing immediately, eagerly working to learn it as fast as he could, but he was well past the critical period of early childhood where learning a native language comes effortlessly. As a late language learner, he struggles to understand and express complex ideas. He could fairly be labeled a "functional signer" because he can communicate about familiar things in sign.

Doug's signing, though, is halting, and he regularly leaves out key parts of speech. He has difficulty conveying clearly who did what to whom, when and how it happened, and what followed (i.e., the element of a story). His knowledge of spoken, written, or signed English is even weaker. He has difficulty understanding what he calls "high sign language" which can mean anything from sophisticated usage of ASL, to English-oriented signing, to any signing about a complicated topic. When he is upset, his language skills worsen, and even Deaf skilled signers like Sam have difficulty understanding him. Although Doug's speech is intelligible to a trained listener, he shows his interest in sign and his developing Deaf identity by not vocalizing while signing.

Doug has an extensive history of abuse and neglect which he doesn't yet have the language ability to process. For now, Sam is just working to help him tell stories and experience him as a sympathetic listener. He's using a procedure the developmental psychologist Lev Vygotsky and narrative therapist Michael White call "scaffolding" (Vygotsky, 1978; White, 2007). That is, he's asking structuring questions to help Doug articulate his story. Planting seeds for future work, he also references the idea of "skill" as often as he can.

Doug is trying to describe an incident that happened at work. Doug washes dishes in a local restaurant. He refers to a supervisor yelling at him, and himself becoming mad; and then he jumps into a series of disorganized complaints about his supervisor, boss, and coworkers. It isn't clear to Sam when this happened or, indeed, if Doug is talking about something he is afraid might happen in the future. Sam also isn't clear about who all the people Doug mentions are and why some are being mentioned. Sam does understand that Doug either thought a supervisor yelled at him, thinks that it might happen, or both, and that he feels angry or fearful about this situation.

Sam shows interest and asks scaffolding or structuring questions.

"When did this happen? Yesterday? Last week? A year ago?" Sam is ready to take out a calendar if it will help.

"Who was the supervisor? Who were the other workers? What were their names?"

"What happened first, second, next"

"How did he feel? How did other people feel? What did he and other people do?"

It takes an hour but Sam *co-constructs* with him the story and says it back to him. He continuously checks his understanding, using the Deaf-friendly and respectful technique of putting the responsibility for comprehension on himself. He says, "I don't understand," "Am I clear?" "Is this correct?" and continuously asks for help with statements like, "I think you are saying x. Is that right? Do I understand you right?"

Sam summarizes, adding structure that Doug omitted. He models what a more coherent narrative would look like. "Last week, on Wednesday, you were at work washing dishes, and your supervisor James came over. James seemed angry. He had an angry face. He said some dishes you washed were still dirty. You felt embarrassed. Other workers were watching James scold you. You think he should have talked to you in private. You became angry. You banged on the sink and then you made a fist. James called the boss. They told you to go home. Maybe you will lose your job. It was a bad day. Did I understand you right?"

Sam also draws on props to help him and Doug construct this story. He has a portable whiteboard that they use to draw who was sitting where. Sam also has a set of dominoes which he sets up, one by one, as the elements of the story become clearer. That was their 50-minute session. It took that long to get that story, and there were still parts that were unclear to Sam, but what was accomplished? Remembering that language and communication are difficult for Doug, Sam helped him tell a story. He also helped set up the schema of "expressing self safely." Sam ended by saying to Doug,

"Nice job telling me this story. Do you know what skill you just used?"

Doug has heard this before. He responds with what he has learned. "Express feeling safe."

"Yes, you did a really good job of that. You used signs and drawing and dominoes to express your feelings. You told me what happened and what you felt. Did you bang on the table?"

"No, no, no." Doug laughs

"Did you hit me or threaten me?"

"No!" Doug smiles.

"So here is a hard question for you. Are you ready?"

"What?" Doug asks.

"Remember before, at work, you pounded on the sink. You threw your brush. You screamed and pushed your supervisor. Remember? Now, you are sitting and talking to me. You are not screaming, throwing things, pushing. You are expressing your feelings safely. Which one, now or before, showed more skill?"

"This one!"

Sam now draws this out of Doug. "This one, yes? Why? What did you do this time that showed more skill?

"Listen. Talk. Take turns. No blowup."

Remember that Doug is 25 years old. Does this sound like the kind of conversation one would have with a 25-year-old with normal intelligence? Obviously, it is more like the conversation one would have with a child. Sam isn't being patronizing. He is working in a developmentally simple level to establish the idea, for Doug, that one talks about feelings in a safe way. He uses scaffolding questions to help Doug with this process. He establishes the idea that doing well involves skills. He asks questions that lead Doug to conclude, on his own, that one set of behaviors is more skillful than another. Sam intentionally uses a great deal of repetition. He does his best to avoid a limit setting or controlling attitude with Doug because he wants Doug to gain the experience of thinking for himself, not just complying with rules.

On the treatment plan, Sam writes down the goal that "Doug will express himself safely through language, drawing, or other means. With increasing confidence in his ability to use language, and more practical communication skills, he will show decreased incidences of aggressive behavior."

There are practical limits to this work, no matter how expertly done. The more language-impaired the person is, the more he or she needs to be working with a team of expert communicators including native signers. Sam is a near-native signer, and he does well with most signing Deaf people; but even he struggles, more often than he'd care to admit, to understand some of the deaf clients with severe language deprivation he serves. The difficulty of referring Doug or Jose to a program with just one signer is that, even if that signer has superb communication abilities, the persons receiving services need to be immersed in an environment with accessible language. Without this immersion in a signing environment, one cannot know what residual capacities for language development they may have. Talking to a signing therapist once a week is no substitute for such language immersion.

In addition, one signing therapist, no matter how skillful, cannot meet the communication needs of every language deprived person; and the communication and clinical burden on this one therapist can be overwhelming, especially when no one else in the agency comprehends the nature and extent of the clinical and communication challenges. Signing therapists who are the only "deafness specialists" in their agency often complain about having to repeatedly educate their supervisors about deaf people, including the complex communication and language issues. They also struggle when they are given the same case load responsibilities as clinicians who work with much more linguistically competent and therapy-ready persons. They find that everything they do with language-deprived persons takes much longer, and almost always involves a lot of "collateral" work with other people. Even having one other colleague who "gets it" can help one survive doing this difficult work. Productivity expectations that take these special challenges into account help them avoid burnout.

Pre-therapy Components in a Treatment Program

The scenarios presented earlier illustrate how a Deaf mental health therapist, working individually with a person with mild to moderate levels of language deprivation, might think about helping these people prepare linguistically, cognitively, and emotionally for a conversation-based enterprise like counseling or psychotherapy. The therapist pays close attention to language and cognitive structures, and to fund of information, to build the persons understanding, capacity, and motivation to make use of therapy.

In most cases, however, this pre-therapy is best done by a treatment team. The model is most appropriate for treatment settings where there are staff teams and therapeutic milieu, and where this group of persons can work together to engage the people they serve in a formal, therapeutic process. The greater the person's language and cognitive impairments, the more likely a team is going to be needed. As conceptualized by the first author, pre-therapy work in these treatment settings has four main components or strategies:

First, there is the process of establishing the schema of skill-building. That is, the providers help the person develop the idea that one manages life problems with skills, and "what we do here" in the treatment setting is "learn skills." The primary way to do this is through the strength-based strategy of noticing and labeling skills that people already have. Staff are trained to notice and label very developmentally simple skills, like coping through playing a game or petting an animal, and staff initiate discussions about the skills needed to handle different stressors that are occurring. "Skill talk" becomes the schema for "what we do here."

Second, staff are taught to work empathically and from a "one-down" stance. That is, staff strive to convey understanding, not exert control. They use a style of questioning designed to elicit thinking, problem-solving, and other psychosocial skills. Once people show these skills, staff ask "What did you just do? What skill did you use?" to help people discover that they can be change agents in their own lives. The attention to the skills a person is already using, but doesn't yet have names for, is strength-based work. Naming for people what they do well (skills they already have, even if they are embryonic) engages much more powerfully than the usual approach of telling people what they do wrong.

Third, staff use very simple cognitive therapy strategies, the kinds one uses with children, to help the people they serve talk to themselves more constructively. Developing self-awareness about cognitive processes is particularly challenging for persons with delayed or impaired language; but if achieved, it opens a world of opportunities for personal and social development. Cognitive therapy techniques that require evaluation of thinking patterns or academic exercises like "examining the evidence" are often beyond this clientele but learning simple self-talk may not be.

Fourth, staff pay close attention to the communication process and use Deaf-friendly teaching and counseling strategies. These include role play, visual aids, stories, and use of Deaf culture references to assist with psychosocial skill building (O'Hearn & Pollard, 2008; Pollard, Dean, O'Hearn, & Haynes, 2009).

Pre-therapy in a Community-Based Mental Health Program

We can illustrate pre-therapy in an agency by discussing how these concepts have been implemented at PAHrtners Deaf Services in Glenside, Pennsylvania.

PAHrtners is a culturally-affirmative provider of services for deaf and hard of hearing individuals, from children through seniors, in the greater Philadelphia area. The services at PAHrtners are aimed at deaf persons who have complex behavioral health challenges and/or intellectual disabilities. These services include a comprehensive day treatment program, case management, psychiatry, outpatient therapy, and specialized mental health interpreting for those who reside in our group homes or in the community (in their family homes or other residential settings). PAHrtners Deaf Services only hires individuals who are fluent in American Sign Language and are sensitive to the range of communication and cultural needs presented by consumers with hearing loss. The agency is administered and staffed by deaf people and hearing allies who strive for the highest levels of cultural affirmation, communication, and clinical competence.

PAHrtners serves many individuals with language and learning challenges stemming from language deprivation and other causes. The communication skills of the clientele fall along a continuum. At one extreme are individuals with almost no language. At the other extreme are Deaf individuals with fluent ASL and good English literacy. The majority fall in the mid-ranges with language dysfluencies, cognitive delays, poor psychosocial skills, and significant behavioral health challenges. Nearly all the individuals that PAHrtners serves either never received behavioral health treatment or received treatment from hearing providers without any knowledge of deaf people. Thus, staff work to engage people who have never had adequate mental health or rehabilitation treatment. Far from being experienced mental health clients, almost all of them are at beginning stages of understanding what a path towards "recovery" or "getting better" looks like.

An example of a common problem PAHrtners staff face *with* clients is their desire for greater independence but their lack of preparedness for the skills and responsibilities that independence requires. Most of PAHrtners clientele were raised in families where things were done for them. They had poor communication with parents and other authorities and other family dynamics that interfered with them becoming independent problem solvers. Some have neurological compromises, which also impact language and cognition. People often said to them that they will be independent later, but for now they needed to accept direction. As a result, they developed a concrete understanding of independence. That is, independence for them means "I decide myself because I'm old enough." By the time of referral to PAHrtners, most had reached adulthood, but still lacked the skills needed for taking care of oneself and one's environment safely. They lacked appreciation that independence requires not just reaching a certain age but having these skills.

Without training, most staff will tell the people they serve what they think they are doing right or wrong. They will explain to them how to become independent and criticize them when they don't act appropriately. When people do not behave as they should, staff will want to impose negative consequences. They will ask, "how can they learn if they don't face consequences?"

The natural tendency of teachers or counselors faced with the challenge of helping such developmentally unprepared people is to become more directive, to tell them what to do. The pre-therapy model presented here combats such directive tendencies, helping therapy providers stay attuned and collaborative. The therapy providers are helped to use communication and relationship strategies, like empathic communication, an attitude of inquiry and curiosity referred to here as a "one-down" stance, and skillful questioning. These are strategies that engage most people, regardless of education or language abilities, and help them develop thinking and problem-solving skills. The tendency of staff in these situations to become authoritarian and overly directive is counterproductive to the primary goals of eliciting informed engagement, turning "people receiving services" into clients, and teaching thinking skills.

The four pre-therapy components described before have been helpful to guide both clinical interventions and staff development. Staff trainings focused on: (1) developing staff ability at empathic communication; (2) developing a shared vocabulary around psychosocial skills; (3) working in a strength-based manner to note and enhance skills already present; and (4) working "one-down" so as to minimize power struggles, decrease violence, and involve individuals in the process of developing their own problem-solving abilities.

All these pre-therapy practices hinge on the first one, the ability of staff to communicate empathically with the people we serve. Empathic communication engages people. It breaks down walls of resistance. Empathic communication also enables staff to shift to a more "one-down" stance where they are partners with the people we serve, not their bosses.

Without empathy, people report feeling that staff members don't listen or understand them, that staff are just bossing them around. When our clientele feel emotionally "heard," they become receptive to the skill-building work we want to make the cornerstone of our program.

Empathic Communication Skills

Empathic communication is often the most difficult skill for staff to master. This skill is associated with listening, reflecting, and being present without judgment. Without training, when faced with a member showing behavior problems, staff tend to skip the step of empathic communication and jump right into problem-solving. For instance, they will omit a statement like "you seem angry," and move into a simplistic strategy like "just ignore him" or "use your coping skills." Perhaps staff feel ineffective or unskilled "just listening." Empathic communication depends on fully linguistically accessible environments, and many PAHrtners staff were raised without experiencing a lot of clear and empathic communication themselves. They were raised in environments where people in authority did things to or for them; and this is often the model they have for "helping." Thus, it isn't surprising that many tend to jump into questions about "what can you do?" and why overly simplistic interventions like "use your coping skills" have appeal. It is also why the pre-therapy model for engaging clientele must attend not just to skills but also to relationship-building strategies like empathic communication.

PAHrtners leadership found they had to spend considerable time teaching the concept and practice of empathy, and this involved demonstrating empathic communication themselves with each other. The bottom line, staff learned over time, was that members would not work with them to learn skills if they did not feel understood and supported. One such example occurred with Dolly, a Deaf young woman with functional signing abilities. Staff wanted to work with her on coping and social skills, but they learned they could not do this without first attending to their relationship with her.

Dolly is an individual with poor self-esteem who frequently assumes that people do not like her and will retaliate against her. She grew up highly dependent upon very controlling adults and was given little opportunity to make decisions for herself.

Dolly loves coffee, but it gives her severe stomachaches. With the staff, Dolly worked out a plan to help her decrease coffee intake, but Dolly wasn't fully on board with this plan. One morning, she was drinking coffee, and she noticed a staff person looking at her. He said nothing to her, but she became upset because she feared he would tell her primary therapist, and she would be in trouble. When she entered the group therapy room, she was visibly upset so the supervisor pulled her aside to speak privately. After ascertaining that her concern was that she was in trouble for drinking coffee, the supervisor surprised her by empathizing with her. "Yes," she said. "Coffee in the morning is so good. I love it also. Trying to give up coffee is hard. You really love coffee, but it gives you stomach pain. Seems you also are afraid that your therapist will be mad at you. Is that right?"

This empathic response disarmed and calmed Dolly and created an opening for the therapeutic conversation pertaining to skills. Without the intentional practice of empathic communication, the supervisor might have jumped into a focus on her behavior, initiating a discuss of how she handles distress or functions in a group. Dolly would likely have felt unheard and disrespected, and the stage would have been set for a possible power struggle. Before we attended to empathic communication skill development in staff, this kind of dynamic was common. It contributed to the ubiquitous problem in Deaf services of clients who "blowup" often, resulting in high levels of violence in the programs.

The supervisor, instead, remembered to "lead (begin) with empathy." That is, before she tried to get Dolly to behave differently, she worked on demonstrating empathic communication. She showed she understood Dolly's feelings, that they made sense to her, and then assured her that she was not in trouble. Her therapist would not be angry, but maybe she would be concerned. She then asked questions from a "one-down" stance, assuming Dolly, not the therapist, had the answers. What did Dolly think her therapist might be worried about? Was Dolly worried about her coffee drinking too? Dolly obviously knew about the abdominal pain that coffee causes her and replied that the therapist would be worried about her stomachache. The supervisor agreed. "Yes, I agree. She might be worried about that. She cares about you and doesn't want to see you in pain."

Having empathized successfully, the supervisor could then venture into problem-solving. She asked Dolly, "what do you think you should do? Do you want to talk to your therapist about this? Maybe the two of you can figure out a plan." Dolly replied "no," but later she did tell her therapist the story of what happened that morning. Her therapist was also ready with empathy and validation. ("Wow. It must be hard for you to stop having coffee in the morning. You love coffee, but you get stomachaches from it. I wonder, were you afraid that if I found out you drank coffee, that I'd be mad with you? Were you afraid to tell me what happened?")

The therapist moved then from empathy and validation to a strength-based attention to skills. ("But look at the skill you just used..."), referring to the skills Dolly used in noticing the problem and communicating about it safely with the therapist. The intentional practice of empathic communication set the stage for discussions about skills. The key learning for staff is this: *Without this attention to empathy, we find we often don't get to discussing skills.*

Noticing and Labeling Skills Already Present

The pre-therapy strategy of labelling preexisting skills was one of the first tools we learned and implemented as a program. This strategy is important because it established in the program a shared schema for "how I improve" and "what we do here." The challenge for staff members was to learn to be very specific in naming skills. For example, they needed help moving from an abstraction like "coping skills" to specific concrete skills like "walk away skill" or "notice my anger level skill." The more concrete and specific skill names are generally more useful to our clientele who tend to be concrete thinkers such as Sharon, for example.

Sharon is a deaf woman with an explosive temper. When angry, she slams doors. Program staff have been trying to help her find alternative, more skillful, ways to express herself.

One day, Sharon was frustrated with something, and a therapist noticed she was getting ready to slam a door but stopped herself. The therapist knew this moment of "not doing a problem behavior" could point the way to discovering a coping skill. The therapist responded empathically, "seems you feel angry" and then commented (using a "one-down" stance), "Wow, I noticed you stopped yourself from slamming the door. That's amazing. How did you do that?"

Sharon replied, "I didn't want to bother you." Her therapist knew this could mean Sharon was trying to understand how her therapist felt. It was, perhaps, a kernel of empathy from her. Her therapist gave her the benefit of the doubt and replied, "You mean, even though you felt frustrated and angry, you thought about me. You didn't want to bother me. You thought about how I feel, and then you told yourself not to bother me?" Sharon didn't realize she did all this, but she accepted the compliment, nodding yes. Her therapist continued to use questions to pull thinking skills out of Sharon. "So then you told yourself not to bother me. Awesome. What could you do now instead of slamming the door?" Sharon thought for a bit and replied, "I could use my 'go outside and walk fast' skill."

What just happened? Using empathic, skillful questions and naming of specific skills, Sharon has been helped to think for herself. She's also, already, having conversations about skills—the kind of conversations that one needs to have in cognitive behavioral therapy. As this schema gets established, and as Sharon comes to understand herself as someone capable of using skills to address problems, the territory for meaningful therapy begins to expand.

Strength-Based Work

It is often difficult for staff members to see skills in people who function and behave badly. Staff need to be helped to name developmentally simple skills (e.g., "play with ball skill"), and staff need to be trained where to look for the skills. As with the example before, staff members can often find the skills if they use the strength-based framework of asking why problem behaviors did *not* happen or did not happen as badly as previously. Staff members used this strength-based strategy to help Saul, a deaf male group home resident described as follows, discover some skills he used:

Saul is a young, deaf male with a history of language deprivation and severe mental illness. Saul often exhibits extreme paranoia. The combination of poor language and cognitive abilities and a mental illness that leads him to mis-perceive the intentions of others means he is often aggressive, and at his worst, we have had to hospitalize him. One day, after a psychiatric hospital discharge, Saul was talking with a staff member about his anger with Joe, a peer. Saul was complaining, and even though his complaints were unreasonable, he was not hitting anyone. Trained to seize upon the lack of a problem behavior (aggression) as evidence of a skill, the staff person commented to Saul: "Amazing, you are mad at Joe but you did not punch him…What helped you walk away?" Saul signed, "NO JAIL DON'T-WANT HOSPITAL AGAIN NO."

The staff person's comment had several purposes: to recognize Saul's achievement of remaining safe, help him to analyze and become aware of exactly what skills he used to stay safe, and then open up possibilities for new kinds of skill training. What skills was Saul using? He was thinking about consequences, a very important thinking skill that staff clearly want to build upon. He was also using self-talk. He was saying to himself, "if I hit people, I will go to jail or the hospital. I don't want that. I need to control myself." Staff certainly want to encourage this kind of intentional, helpful self-talk.

The staff person then helped Saul see this more clearly by role-playing Saul talking to himself. In essence, he was modeling the process of thinking out-loud. He was also "externalizing" the thinking process so Saul could see, and follow, a kind of script for self-talk. In this way, the very abstract process of changing thoughts became much more concrete. Saul is praised for thinking so skillfully, and for talking to himself in this way, and he's invited to do more of it. In time, staff hope to help him embellish this helpful script.Thus, strength-based interventions like this can actually introduce more focused skill training. This is cognitive behavioral therapy adapted in many ways for a deaf person with both language deprivation and severe mental illness.

Working One-Down

Most of the individuals PAHrtners serves have come to expect from their experiences in life that they will be scolded for wrongdoing. They expect, in other words, that authorities will treat them with a "one-up" stance, telling them what they did right or wrong, rewarding or punishing them. Therefore, they have learned to obey or to rebel, but not to think. The pre-therapy strategy of using a one-down stance is designed to move them from people who react, usually unskillfully, to people who engage, hopefully more skillfully. It is designed to pull people into the process of collaborative problem-solving (Greene & Ablon, 2006).

Some common one-down responses are asking permission to discuss something, asking for the individual's help, expressing a worry or concern, showing curiosity about how a person did so well, and asking for their opinion or thoughts. One-down responses often move from empathy to curiosity or worry to questions like "what do we do?"

It has taken some time for our staff to learn this new way of behaving. Some are better at it than others. It also takes time for individuals receiving services, many of whom have never been asked before about what they think and want, to realize that they are being treated differently and can respond differently. They may not initially appreciate this, but as they do, their defensiveness and explosiveness usually lessen. The staff and client interactions move away from power struggles into the realm of collaborative problem-solving where therapeutic programs want to be:

Cindy is a young adult who joined PAHrtners after years of struggles and frustrations with her hearing family. She suffered from depression, and she coped unskillfully by sending emails and social media posts with lots of negative comments and swearing. Naturally she had been punished and scolded for this over the years. She had been told not to behave this way, but she didn't have skills to behave differently. The more limits were set with her, the more she pushed back aggressively; and a familiar, unproductive power struggle repeated itself. Although she was in a treatment program, she wasn't "in therapy." She was pre-therapy and had to be helped to discover that there was another path, one where staff work with her to learn the life skills she needs to handle depression and other negative emotions.

One day, Cindy made another inappropriate posting and got in trouble with the person she had written about. Staff members knew to approach her about this one-down. After empathizing with her embarrassment and frustration with being misunderstood again, staff members expressed concern and asked her permission to discuss the issue. "I'm a little worried right now. Can I talk to you about that? Is now a good time?"

When Cindy agreed, the staff person engaged her in a role play where staff sent to her an angry, hostile email and then asked her how she felt receiving it. Cindy said she felt angry. Staff then role-played posting a negative story about her on Facebook and having her read it, and asked her how she felt. Cindy said she felt embarrassed and angry. The staff person then expressed her worry that Cindy was making people upset with her, making enemies, and it was just making her life worse. Expressing worry is a one-down way to raise a problem for consideration. The staff asked Cindy, "are you worried too? Do you want to make enemies? Do you want people to be mad at you?"

Cindy said she didn't want people mad at her, and the staff person then moved into the "what do we do?" discussion. This required many sessions, but eventually the desired shift happened. Cindy began to consider alternatives and try different behaviors, like "expressing myself safe way" and "asking for help." As she began to demonstrate problem-solving abilities, staff noticed and commented, with statements and questions like, "What skill did you just used? You are thinking! You are using your brain! Awesome!" Her movement from being someone acted upon and reacting to someone who worked with staff members to develop skills for living was essentially her movement from pre-therapy into therapy.

At PAHrtners, the more staff members use these pre-therapy strategies and see for themselves their effectiveness to de-escalate conflicts and engage persons in their own growth and development, the more motivated they become to do more of this. Like the people staff members serve, they need to discover for themselves that a specific set of skills helps them function better and that they can make good things happen.

In an interesting parallel, PAHrtners managers are using these same techniques in working with staff. They are using more empathic communication, discussing staff problems in terms of the skills needed to address them, naming specific skills staff use, and engaging them in collaborative problem-solving from a one-down stance. This results in positive staff interactions, better labor relations, and enhanced work performance.

Another important result is that since staff are all implementing these same strategies, they now have a shared language or schema for communicating what skills are needed. For example, if someone notices that a one-down approach would be effective for a situation, they can simply say, "use one down" and everyone knows what to do.

Limitations of the Pre-therapy Approach at PAHrtners

As discussed earlier, this pre-therapy approach, while aiming at people with language and learning challenges, still assumes some foundation in language. For persons at the extreme ends of language deprivation or impaired cognitive functioning, even this very simplified adaptation of CBT skill-building is well beyond them.

These strategies also don't necessarily work when someone is actively psychotic. Someone like Saul who has a paranoid disorder needs more than psychosocial skill training. They usually also need psychiatric medication, and they may not be accessible to skill training until their thought disorder is stabilized.

PAHrtners has also treated a small number of more sociopathic persons who, in fact, do have the skills they need, but are driven by antisocial motivations. They may also be persons whose behavior is so dangerous that an alliance with police and courts, who can properly take a "one-up stance," is needed (see Appendix to Chapter 1 for discussion of this challenge).

Conclusions

The pre-therapy model presented here has much overlap with known best practices in psychotherapy. For instance, the importance given to empathic listening is shared with virtually all psychotherapies. The use of skillful questions, what Meichenbaum calls, "the art of questioning" (Meichenbaum, 1994, 2001), creates a Socratic dialogue long known to engage persons in active learning. The emphasis upon simple skill-building strategies and the eventual focus upon what Meichenbaum calls "self-instructional training" or self-talk are established procedures within his school of CBT. The "one-down" stance is actually an adaptation of what Meichenbaum referred to as "Columbo" work, based on the television detective who often "played dumb" to get people to tell him what they knew. In addition, the emphasis upon helping program staff and other helpers engage persons in a process of collaborative problem-solving was well described by Greene and associates (Greene & Ablon, 2006) though it is embellished further here to better match the challenges of language and information deprivation.

In both this pre-therapy and much contemporary narrative psychotherapy (White, 1995, 2007; White & Epston, 1990), therapists work through stories or narratives. They build communication competencies through stories. They teach core therapeutic concepts and skills through stories. Sometimes the stories are told or observed. Very often they are enacted in role play. One difference is that stories may be used in pre-therapy for more foundational communication skill-building. That is, stories can be the vehicle through which communication and language skills are developed (See Chapters 3 and 7 for more on this). When working with people who have more extreme levels of language deprivation or impairment, it may well be that a shared focus on language and communication development through the co-construction of stories is all that can be accomplished. Certainly, when working with deaf children experiencing language deprivation, the goal of language skill development is inseparable from whatever therapeutic goals the therapist has in mind (Bishop, 2013).

The main difference between pre-therapy and therapy has to do with the readiness of the person to engage in therapy. Pre-therapy is all about meeting people where they are and moving them towards the starting gate of therapy. Much of this entails learning a practical schema for the process of therapy, buying into the process, and appreciating that dialogue, sharing one's story with a sympathetic listener, is a way to "get better."

Once people are "on board" with the idea that "I can learn skills that will help me do better by talking to this counselor," the world of CBT opens for them, although it still needs to be adapted for deaf individuals with special attention paid to the language and communication challenges. In recent years, we've seen Deaf-friendly adaptations of dialectical behavior therapy modules (O'Hearn & Pollard, 2008), cognitive behavioral therapy (Glickman, 2009), and now a CBT approach for trauma and addiction, *Seeking Safety*, described in the next chapter.

As we come to appreciate all the developmental correlates of language deprivation, we'll have greater understanding for components of pre-therapy. Perhaps we will learn at some later point, following the lead of Spitz and Kegl in Chapter 7 in this book (in particular, their discussion of *Grammaticas*), a variety of strategies for fostering language, communication, and cognitive development after the critical period for language acquisition has passed. Whatever strategies we then learn will likely improve the efficacy of teaching and counseling for many people with language and learning challenges. For while it is mainly just deaf people who suffer extreme language deprivation because of a lack of opportunities for natural sign language exposure, we have a world of clientele with poor language and learning abilities. Our established psychotherapies do not work well with people developmentally and culturally unprepared for them. Deaf mental health explorations of how to reach deaf people with language deprivation may then yield unexpected benefits for other groups of specialized populations, expanding the reach of whom we serve and the nature of how we work.

Note

1 All the names and identifying information of the persons presented in this chapter have been changed to protect confidentiality.

References

Bishop, K. (2013). Culturally affirmative adaptations to trauma treatment with deaf children in a residential setting. In N. Glickman (Ed.), *Deaf mental health care.* New York, NY: Routledge.

Duncan, B. L., Miller, S. D., Wampold, B. E., & Hubble, M. A. (Eds.). (2010). *The heart and soul of change: Delivering what works in therapy* (2nd ed.). Washington, DC: American Psychological Association.

Glickman, N. (2009). *Cognitive behavioral therapy for deaf and hearing persons with language and learning challenges.* New York, NY: Routledge.

Glickman, N. (2017). *Preparing deaf and hearing persons with language and learning challenges for CBT: A pre-therapy workbook.* New York, NY: Routledge.

Greene, R. W., & Ablon, J. S. (2006). *Treating explosive kids: The collaborative problem-solving approach.* London, UK: Guilford Press.

Leigh, I. (2010). *Psychotherapy with deaf clients from diverse groups, Second edition.* Washington, D.C: Gallaudet University Press.

Meichenbaum, D. (1977). *Cognitive-behavioral modification: An integrative approach.* New York, NY: Plenum Press.

Meichenbaum, D. (1994). *A clinical handbook/practical therapist manual for assessing and treating adults with post-traumatic stress disorder.* Waterloo, ON: Institute Press.

Meichenbaum, D. (2001). *Treatment of individuals with anger-control problems and aggressive behaviors: A clinical handbook.* Clearwater, FL: Institute Press.

Meichenbaum, D. (2012). *Roadmap to resilience: A guide for military, trauma victims and their families.* Clearwater, FL: Institute Press.

Meichenbaum, D., & Biemiller, A. (1998). *Nurturing independent learners: Helping students take charge of their learning.* Newton, MA: Brookline Books.

Meichenbaum, D., & Goodman, J. (1971). Training impulsive children to talk to themselves: A means of developing self-control. *Journal of Abnormal Psychology, 77,* 115–126.

Miller, W. R., & Rollnick, S. (2002). *Motivational interviewing: Preparing people for change* (2nd ed.). New York, NY: Guilford Press.

O'Hearn, A., & Pollard, R. Q., Jr. (2008). Modifying dialectical behavior therapy for deaf individuals. *Cognitive and Behavioral Practice, 15,* 400–414.

Pollard, R. Q., Dean, R. K., O'Hearn, A., & Haynes, S. L. (2009). Adapting health education materials for deaf audiences. *Rehabilitaiton Psychology, 54*(2), 232–238.

Prochaska, J. O., & DiClemente, C. C. (1992). Stages of change in the modification of problem behaviors. In M. Hersen, R. M. Eisler, & P. M. Miller (Eds.), *Progress in behavior modification* (Vol. 28, pp. 183–218). Sycamore, IL: Sycamore Publishing Co.

Sperry, L., & Carlson, J. (2014). *How master therapists work: Effecting change from the first through the last session and beyond.* New York, NY: Routledge.

Vygotsky, L. (1978). *Mind in society: The development of higher psychological processes.* Cambridge, MA: Harvard University Press.

White, M. (1995). *Reauthoring lives: Interviews and essays.* Adelaide, SA: Dulwich Centre Publications.

White, M. (2007). *Maps of narrative practice.* New York, NY: W.W. Norton and Company.

White, M., & Epston, D. (1990). *Narrative means to therapeutic ends.* New York, NY: W.W. Norton and Co.

3

Developing Therapy Approaches for Deaf Clients Impacted by Language Deprivation

MELISSA L. ANDERSON AND KELLY S. WOLF CRAIG

In Chapter 2 of this book, Glickman, Heines, and Watson discussed strategies for preparing deaf people impacted by language deprivation for therapy. By applying the strategies that they propose, these individuals become more acculturated into a therapeutic way of thinking and working and, as such, traditional therapy approaches become more available to them. Despite this increased readiness for treatment, available therapies must still be adapted for deaf client's culture, beliefs, thinking style, and language needs.

The current chapter briefly reviews available evidence-based therapies and general guidelines for adapting evidence-based therapies for deaf clients. We then illustrate one therapy approach, *Seeking Safety,* for which Deaf-accessible tools have been developed—the *Signs of Safety* toolkit—that been used effectively with deaf individuals impacted by language deprivation. As the reader will see, this form of cognitive behavioral therapy (CBT) shares many components with the pre-therapy strategies described in the previous chapter. Finally, we will explore remaining limitations of the *Seeking Safety + Signs of Safety* model when used with deaf individuals who exhibit severe language dysfluency and propose next steps for the Deaf behavioral health research agenda.

Evidence-Based Therapies

Hearing individuals seeking help for mental health or addiction concerns have many treatment options. They can select from private practitioners or behavioral health agencies who have access to dozens of evidence-based therapies—i.e., therapy approaches that have been formally researched and found to lead to positive clinical outcome in the general population (APA Presidential Task Force on Evidence-Based Practice, 2006; SAMHSA, 2013). In the past decade, there has been a significant shift toward using evidence-based therapies throughout the behavioral health system. Factors contributing to this shift include an overarching intent to provide treatments that have been proven effective, and the insurance industry's support of certain evidence-based practices via increased reimbursement rates, among others.

Some well-known evidence-based therapy models include, but are not limited to, Acceptance and Commitment Therapy (ACT), Dialectical Behavior Therapy (DBT), Illness Management and Recovery (IMR), Motivational Interviewing (MI)/Motivational Enhancement Therapy (MET), Prolonged Exposure (PE) Therapy, and Trauma-Focused Cognitive Behavioral Therapy (TF-CBT)—a veritable alphabet soup of options! Despite the large number of evidence-based treatments available for the general population, there are *no* evidence-based treatments that have been developed for or evaluated for use with deaf persons (Glickman & Pollard, 2013; NASMHPD, 2012). Currently-available evidence-based therapies fail to meet the unique linguistic and cultural needs of deaf clients (Glickman & Pollard, 2013), for reasons described in the next section.

Adapting Evidence-Based Therapies for Deaf Clients

The majority of evidence-based treatments combine traditional talk therapy with workbooks or handouts. Many of the workbooks or handouts contain sophisticated means for tracking mood, behavior, and thoughts, and use psychological jargon throughout. Deaf people's median reading level falls at the fourth grade (Gallaudet Research Institute, 2003), and many present with low health literacy due to reduced incidental learning throughout the lifespan—e.g., inability to communicate with hearing parents, hearing healthcare providers, or understand spoken health information on TV/radio/public service announcements (Pollard & Barnett, 2009; Pollard, Dean, O'Hearn, & Haynes, 2009). In order to be used with deaf clients, written English treatment materials, therefore, require plain text revisions or translations into American Sign Language (Glickman, 2009a). No evidence-based treatment manuals are currently commercially available that convey information through plain English principles or in American Sign Language. For example, Glickman (2017) has created a training manual for staff of Deaf mental health care programs which draws on evidence-based CBT practices, but it has not yet been evaluated using standardized research methodology.

Equally important are treatment materials that increase clinician cultural competence and enhance client engagement by being inclusive of Deaf values and social norms, acknowledging their history of oppression, and embracing Deaf people's identity as a cultural—not disability—group (Glickman, 2009a; Ladd, 2003; Pollard et al., 2009). Without making this important acknowledgement, mental health professionals run the risk of reinforcing deaf people's history of oppression and/or reenacting communication difficulties which may have contributed to the deaf person's mental health concerns in the first place.

Given these barriers, there are a number of linguistic and cultural adaptations needed to make available evidence-based therapy approaches more accessible, impactful, and efficacious for signing, culturally Deaf clients, especially those affected by language deprivation. Without access to evidence-based therapy tools appropriate for use with signing, culturally Deaf clients, mental health providers of these Deaf individuals must adapt treatment materials themselves (Barnett, McKee, Smith, & Pearson, 2011; National Association of the Deaf, 2003), resulting in various levels of success and presenting a significant challenge to those clinicians attempting to match the needs of clients with language dysfluency.

Attempts to modify traditional therapy approaches for deaf clients have generally followed these principles of Deaf-friendly mental health treatment (Glickman, 2013; Pollard et al., 2009), many of which were reviewed in the previous chapter on pre-therapy:

1 **Adaptations for language**, including careful attention to and matching communication abilities of consumers, simplification and avoidance of English language-based materials, and use of visual and pictorial aids.
2 Attention to fund of information deficits.
3 Reliance upon storytelling and visual metaphors.
4 Teaching concepts through **examples**.
5 The use of active treatment strategies, like **role playing and therapeutic activities**, as a basis for generating discussions and insights.
6 Creative uses of **technology**.
7 Leveraging **peer-to-peer education**, drawing on the desire of Deaf community members to help and teach each other.

Without such adaptations, therapy approaches developed for the general population often fail to engage and retain signing Deaf clients in treatment. However, the truly *critical* adaptations listed before (i.e., mindfully matching communication abilities, avoidance of English, use of visual aids, attention to fund of information deficits) are in direct response to the high prevalence of language deprivation and the resulting language dysfluency that we observe among deaf mental health consumers.

Even when such adaptations are made, many traditional talk therapies rely on the client's ability to formulate a detailed narrative—whether for the purpose of problem-solving, identifying repeating patterns in one's behavior, or intentionally exposing oneself to distressing, trauma-related content. As discussed in other chapters, due to lack of early language exposure and poor educational experiences, many deaf adults enter treatment unable to formulate a narrative or report a coherent timeline of events (Glickman, 2009a, 2009b). This interferes with the use of verbal problem-solving and cognitive processing strategies that many evidence-based therapies require (Glickman, 2017).

Developing *Seeking Safety* + *Signs of Safety*: A Deaf-Accessible Therapy Toolkit for Trauma and Addiction

Here, we illustrate the application of Pollard's and Glickman's principles of Deaf-friendly therapy to the development of a Deaf-accessible approach to treating trauma and addiction among deaf clients—*Seeking Safety* + *Signs of Safety*.

Selection of Clinical Focus

In reviewing the Deaf mental health literature and areas of identified need in clinical settings, the first author of this chapter selected trauma and addiction as critical first problems to address via Deaf-accessible psychotherapy development. Deaf and hard-of-hearing individuals report nearly three times the rate of lifetime problem drinking compared to the general population—33.0% versus 12.3%—and are more likely to be regular marijuana users than their hearing counterparts—35.8% versus 26.7% (Anderson, Chang, & Kini, 2018). Communication barriers and lack of access to appropriate treatment compound the daunting task of addressing addiction.

High rates of comorbid trauma complicate the treatment course for this population (Najavits et al., 2008), with deaf people twice as likely to experience lifetime and past-year trauma exposure compared to individuals in the general population (Anderson & Leigh, 2011; Anderson, Leigh, & Samar, 2011; Black & Glickman, 2006; Porter & Williams, 2011; Schild & Dalenberg, 2012). While 25% of hearing women report lifetime prevalence of domestic violence, this figure surpasses 50% among deaf women (Anderson & Leigh, 2011; Anderson et al., 2011; Pollard, Sutter, & Cerulli, 2014; Porter & Williams, 2011). This disparity has also been documented for rates of sexual assault, sexual harassment, and child abuse (Barber, Wills, & Smith, 2010; Francavillo, 2009; Sebald, 2008).

In addition to these disparities in addiction and trauma, some deaf people have little understanding of recovery concepts—e.g., *substance, relapse, trigger* (Anderson, Glickman, Mistler, & Gonzalez, 2015)—and are unaware that being hit, choked, or coerced into sex is *abuse* (Anderson & Kobek Pezzarossi, 2012). Such health literacy gaps are caused by lack of health education available in ASL and lack of communication access to health professionals and one's own parents (Pollard & Barnett, 2009; Pollard et al., 2009). Compounding these health literacy gaps, there are also a variety of signs for key concepts, such as *hangover* and *blackout*, that can contribute to frustration and confusion (Csiernik & Brideau, 2013).

Given that most deaf people who enter behavioral health treatment have trauma histories and 74% of deaf people in addiction treatment have experienced abuse (Titus, Schiller, & Guthmann, 2008), it was logical to design an integrated trauma and addiction intervention for this population, especially an intervention that would focus on psychoeducation and development of simple coping skills that simultaneously target trauma and addiction.

Selection of Base Intervention—Seeking Safety

To address the behavioral health disparities described earlier, the first author of this chapter assembled a team of Deaf and hearing researchers, clinicians, filmmakers, actors, artists, and deaf people in recovery to develop "Signs of Safety." Signs of Safety is a Deaf-accessible toolkit to be used with an existing, effective, and widely-adopted (Allen, Crawford, & Kudler, 2016) protocol for trauma and addiction—Seeking Safety (Najavits, 2002).

Seeking Safety is a manualized, cognitive behavioral therapy (CBT) model that prioritizes clients' personal safety, including making life changes such as sobriety, addressing suicidal ideation and self-harm, lowering risk of HIV exposure, and leaving dangerous relationships (Najavits, 2002). Seeking Safety includes 25 present-focused treatment topics, each engaging clients in themes relevant to trauma and addiction and helping them to learn a specific CBT skill to target symptoms of both disorders (e.g., "Coping with Triggers," "Honesty," "Recovery Thinking," "Asking for Help"). The skills are divided into four content areas: behavioral, cognitive, interpersonal, and case management.

Seeking Safety has been used successfully with diverse populations, translated into 12 foreign languages, and aligns with many recommended practices for Deaf-friendly treatment—i.e., skill-building and psychoeducation, structured sessions, case management, focus on here-and-now, strength-based work, working "one-down," use of stories, and visual aids (Glickman, 2017, 2013). More importantly, among available evidence-based psychotherapy protocols for trauma and addiction, Seeking Safety is the only appropriate option to adapt for deaf persons impacted by language deprivation given its present-focus (i.e., no need to retell the trauma narrative) and reliance on simple coping skills that simultaneously target trauma and addiction. The coping skills are relatively concrete and easy to understand, and most can be represented with pictures and illustrated with filmed stories depicting Deaf actors using ASL and/or modeling of behavior and self-talk.

Each Seeking Safety session follows the same four-part structure, as outlined in Figure 3.1 as follows: (1) a five-minute check-in; (2) discussion of an inspirational quote related to the current topic; (3) discussion and active practice of content focused on teaching a safe coping skill; and (4) a check out review about what was learned, whether the client had any problems with the session, and their coping skills "commitment" until the next session.

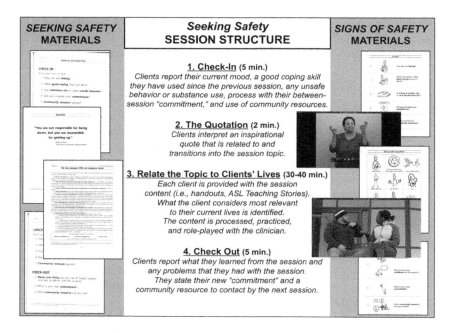

Figure 3.1 Seeking Safety session structure, *Seeking Safety* client materials, and *Signs of Safety* client materials

Development of Deaf-Accessible Therapy Toolkit—Signs of Safety

Despite positive results among hearing individuals, *Seeking Safety*'s client materials, as can be seen in Figure 3.1, rely on written English, assume literacy, and, therefore, fail to meet the unique needs of many signing Deaf clients (Anderson et al., 2015; Glickman & Pollard, 2013). The *Signs of Safety* toolkit attempts to overcome these barriers through the use of a therapist companion guide and Deaf-accessible client materials.

To develop these toolkit materials, our multidisciplinary Deaf and hearing team reviewed the therapist guide and client materials for each of *Seeking Safety*'s 25 topics. The team then identified the "key learning points" that clients, at a minimum, should learn and retain following the review of each topic. To achieve this goal, we followed National Institute on Drug Abuse (NIDA) behavioral therapy development approaches (Rounsaville, Carroll, & Onken, 2001) and Glickman's recommended principles for creating Deaf-accessible interventions (Glickman, 2017, 2013) to develop the following Deaf-accessible **client materials:**

- **ASL teaching stories** on digital video for all 25 *Seeking Safety* topics, which present key learning points portrayed by culturally Deaf actors. Throughout the course of their treatment, clients watch vignettes from this "psychoeducational soap opera," observing the struggles and successes of four recurring characters. The script/ASL storyboard for each teaching story was designed to include dialogue between characters, as well as nonlinguistic modeling of coping skill use.

- A select number of **visual handouts**, which present information using plain English text and visual aids created by Deaf artist, Michael Krajnak. To improve ease of understanding, most English text is presented in ASL word order (i.e., ASL gloss) and many of the visual aids include 2-D representations of ASL vocabulary.

Our team also developed a **therapist companion guide**, which supports clinicians to adapt *Seeking Safety* for Deaf persons, including helpful tips for working with deaf persons, ASL translations of key *Seeking Safety* vocabulary, how issues raised by each *Seeking Safety* topic interact with the Deaf experience, and deaf-related examples of difficult cases.

Target Population

Given the heterogeneity of the Deaf community, *Signs of Safety* was designed to be accessible to a wide range of deaf people. Throughout the therapist companion guide, information and clinical guidance is included that is applicable to individuals who are culturally Deaf, Hard of Hearing, late-deafened, and DeafBlind. The materials in the client toolkit are intended to be easily understood by deaf people with various cognitive and linguistic skill levels. For example, the visual handouts are comprised of highly simplified English text with visual aids, with the goal that clients can rely on English only, pictures only, or a combination of both. Additionally, the handouts are designed with a minimalist approach in high-contrast black and white, appropriate for use with low vision and DeafBlind individuals. The ASL teaching stories include a mix of ASL dialogue between characters to demonstrate interpersonal coping skills, ASL self-dialogue (i.e., "self-talk") to demonstrate cognitive coping skills, and gestural "role plays," which attempt to demonstrate behavioral coping skills without any reliance on language.

Utilizing various modes and levels of language to teach *Seeking Safety* content may bridge the gap for deaf persons with minimal-to-moderate levels of language dysfluency, providing the scaffolding needed for full comprehension of the material. Individuals with severe language dysfluency, however, may only be able to comprehend content delivered via visual aids and gestural demonstration of behavioral coping skills. Even with *Signs of Safety*'s linguistic adaptations, both the visual handouts and ASL teaching stories contain linguistic content that may not be understood by those with severe language dysfluency. Therefore, treatment for these individuals may be most effective if focused on primarily learning behavioral coping skills (e.g., physical grounding, self-care), rather than interpersonal or cognitive skills, which are inherently language-based.

It should also be noted that *Seeking Safety* and *Signs of Safety* are merely clinical tools—these tools are only as good as the clinicians who utilize them. For clients impacted by language deprivation, the success of any therapy approach is highly dependent on the ability of the clinician to match their communication skills and cognitive level. The success of manualized treatments is similarly dependent upon the clinician's ability to further individualize treatment materials to match the client's skill level through modeling, role play, gesture, drawing, and other creative techniques.

For clients with severe language dysfluency, the level of necessary adaption will be extensive. The therapeutic treatment process with severe language dysfluent deaf clients will likely require more sessions than a language-fluent deaf client. The amount of scaffolding and rehearsal necessary to ensure common language, bidirectional understanding, and effective treatment is a critical component for treatment. Additionally, there is more time spent not only on discussing treatment, addiction, and survivor language, but discussing specific signs for each concept and the variations of each sign that may be used and accepted in the person's general community.

Case Example: Using Seeking Safety + Signs of Safety with a Deaf Client Impacted by Language Deprivation

As noted before, *Seeking Safety* presents safe coping skills from four general content areas: *behavioral, cognitive, interpersonal,* and *case management.* Naturally, the behavioral and case management skills are more easily applied to deaf clients impacted by language deprivation, whereas the interpersonal and cognitive skills are a greater challenge. As such, we will focus on a behavioral topic for the current case illustration—working with Stephanie (*pseudonym*), a deaf client with moderate language dysfluency, on "Taking Good Care of Yourself."

The seventh *Seeking Safety* topic—"Taking Good Care of Yourself"—guides clients to explore how well they take care of themselves by using a questionnaire listing specific self-care behaviors (Najavits, 2002). These behaviors range from basic activities of daily living (e.g., "Do you keep up with daily hygiene: clean clothes, showers, brushing teeth, etc.?") to more complex self-care behaviors (e.g., "Do you have at least 10 hours per week of structured time?", "Do you have at least three recreational activities that you enjoy; e.g., sports, hobbies—but not substance use?"). Clients are also guided to explore how problems in self-care may be rooted in experiences of trauma or addiction; for instance, neglect by caretakers throughout childhood may have become internalized as self-neglect. By the end of the session, clients are asked to take immediate action to improve at least one self-care problem (Najavits, 2002).

After completing the **Check-In** *process with Stephanie, Ashley, the therapist, shows Stephanie today's video* **Quotation**—*an ASL interpretation of this quote: "A Deaf person's soul, mind, and body should be their own to mold and cultivate—one way to do it is by starting to believe in yourself." Ashley asks,*

"What does this quote mean to you?" Although Stephanie initially appears confused and did not seem to comprehend most of the quote, even signed clearly in ASL, she did understand the message to *"believe in yourself"* and was able to repeat this back to Ashley. Ashley validates Stephanie's answer and then links her answer to today's treatment topic: *"Yes! Nice job! Believing in ourselves, loving ourselves, and taking care of ourselves are important ways to improve how we feel. Today, we are going to be learning about self-care."* Ashley then checks in with Stephanie about whether she knows the sign for S-E-L-F C-A-R-E, Stephanie shows Ashley one of a few accepted signs for the concept, and Stephanie's preferred vocabulary is used throughout the remainder of the session.

Next, Ashley shows Stephanie today's **ASL Teaching Story**, which shows two vignettes of Deaf individuals discussing their problems with self-care, making action plans to fix one self-care problem immediately, and then practicing self-care skills. Because this teaching story relies more on dialogue than role play or gesture, Ashley and Stephanie pause the video at multiple points to clarify unclear or unfamiliar language. These clarifications require Ashley to be a more active therapist than with most hearing persons or Deaf sign-fluent persons—getting out of her chair to act and mime, draw on the office whiteboard, or search the internet for images and videos that illustrate the intended concept. After the ten-minute video is complete, Ashley and Stephanie then review the Signs of Safety Self-Care Questionnaire, a **Visual Handout** which includes a picture of each queried self-care behavior. Some examples of self-care behaviors are illustrated with Figures 3.2–3.4.

Again, Ashley and Stephanie review each item on the questionnaire, with role play and additional visual aids used as needed to explain any unclear self-care behaviors.

Figure 3.2 "Do you currently have at least two drug-free friendships?"

Figure 3.3 "Do you have at least one hour of free time for yourself each day?"

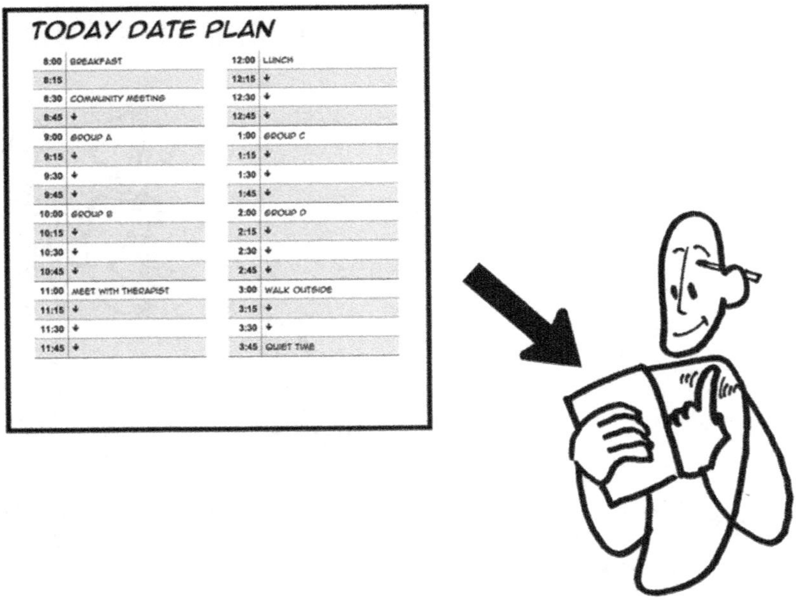

Figure 3.4 "Do you have a daily schedule and 'to do' list to help you stay organized?"

After completing the questionnaire, Stephanie identifies two self-care problems that she is most concerned about—eating a healthful diet and getting adequate exercise. Ashley and Stephanie discuss why these are problems and, with simple, careful questioning, Ashley can ascertain that Stephanie is fearful of leaving her apartment to go to the grocery store or to the gym. She is afraid of being attacked by a stranger from behind, similar to her trauma experience. Ashley validates this fear, explaining that Stephanie's feelings are a normal reaction to an abnormal situation (i.e., the trauma experience) and they work on a concrete action plan to help her overcome her present fears. Together Ashley and Stephanie are able identify a safe, supportive friend who can act as a "buddy" and accompany Stephanie to the food store and the gym. They then write a "script/ASL story board" for how Stephanie can ask her friend to serve in this role, and then they role play the conversation.

Before wrapping up the session, Ashley identifies one additional self-care problem—not taking all medications as prescribed—and expresses her concern (but not disappointment or frustration) that Stephanie often skips psychiatric medication for many days at a time. (Note that expressing concern—"I'm worried"—is a "one-down" intervention which still leaves Stephanie in the decision-maker role (Glickman, 2017)). Stephanie denies skipping her medications on purpose, but rather reports that, with her unstructured schedule, she often forgets to take them. Ashley and Stephanie go to the whiteboard and write down her medication schedule. Ashley then asks Stephanie to get out her iPhone (which she always has with her), shows Stephanie the alarm function of the phone, and together they input multiple daily alarms for each of her medications. At their next session, Ashley will check in with Stephanie about whether this tool worked or if another strategy is needed.

It is then time to **Check-Out**, during which Stephanie follows the visual check-out handout and responds directly to Ashley. She reports that during today's session she "learned about self-care," indicates that she did not have any problems with or feedback for today's session, and then makes a "commitment" (i.e., short-term goal or homework) to ask her friend to accompany her to the grocery store. She completes the Signs of Safety Commitment handout to remind herself of this goal—for Stephanie, this is best communicated by writing her friend's first name and then drawing a picture of an apple and a banana.

As you can see, Ashley used Signs of Safety materials as a Deaf-friendly tool to guide the structure and content of the therapy session. With a different person with different language abilities, this same self-care session would look quite different. The content of the discussion would be influenced by that individual's present self-care struggles. The strategies used to teach and practice the self-care skills might be more reliant on higher-level linguistic or cognitive skills. Due to her language dysfluency, Stephanie did not fully understand the ASL or English content included in these treatment materials. However, what she could understand was leveraged by the therapist, who applied an array of other active teaching strategies to practice the material in more depth. Again, for clients impacted by language dysfluency, the success of any therapy approach is highly dependent on the ability of the clinician to match the communication skills and cognitive level of the person. Manualized therapies are merely a *tool* for therapists to improve the quality of their clinical work. Like all tools, they need to be well used.

Preliminary Findings

The coauthors are currently leading a single-arm pilot study (current $n = 14$) of the prototype version of *Signs of Safety*, in which research participants receive *Seeking Safety* plus *Signs of Safety* client materials. Data are being collected on feasibility (e.g., attendance, retention, rate of enrollment, fidelity, and assessment procedures); participant satisfaction; and clinical outcomes (e.g., PTSD symptoms, substance use disorder symptoms, and coping efficacy).

As of September 2017, participants have reported high levels of satisfaction, supported by our 78% retention rate (11/14), higher than the average rate of 73% observed in addiction longitudinal studies with hearing participants (Kleschinsky, Bosworth, Nelson, Walsh, & Shaffer, 2009). Reported reasons for attrition included lack of interest, readiness, or motivation to engage in the study protocol. Pilot participants have also provided vital feedback about how to produce an improved and even more Deaf-friendly version of the *Signs of Safety* toolkit.

Displayed in Figures 3.5 and 3.6 as follows, preliminary results show reductions in PTSD severity and alcohol use frequency from baseline to immediate

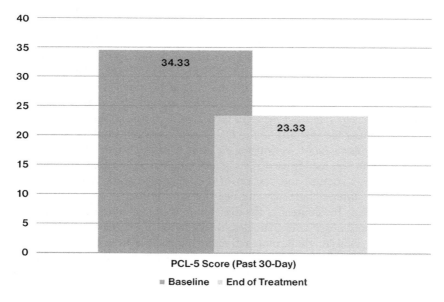

Figure 3.5 PTSD Symptoms from baseline to end of treatment

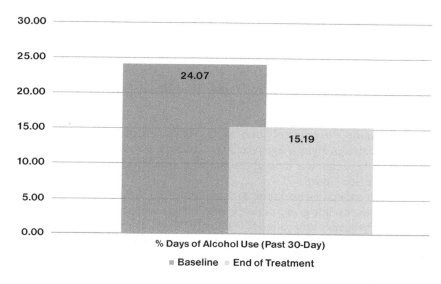

Figure 3.6 Alcohol use frequency from baseline to end of treatment

posttreatment. Inferential statistics are not reported due to small sample size and subsequent insufficient power to detect a large effect size. However, participants exhibited an 11-point mean reduction on the *PTSD Checklist for DSM-5 (PCL-5)*, a clinically meaningful improvement on this measure (Weathers et al., 2013). Additionally, 45% of the sample evidenced clinically meaningful reduction in percent days of alcohol use—i.e., Reliable Change Index >1.96 (Jacobson, Follette, & Revenstorf, 1984; Ogles, Lunnen, & Bonesteel, 2001)— five of whom attained abstinence by end of treatment.

Next Steps

These encouraging preliminary results suggest that further exploration of this line of research is warranted. Future research efforts, which include randomized clinical trials, will be informed by the rich participant feedback received regarding strategies to further improve *Signs of Safety* materials for a professional-quality final version. This research would allow comparison of the efficacy of *Signs of Safety* between subgroups of deaf people—for example, comparing the success of this approach with Deaf sign-fluent versus Deaf language-dysfluent individuals. Once evidence of efficacy is well-established and *Seeking Safety* + *Signs of Safety* is determined to be an evidence-based therapy for deaf individuals, the goal is to disseminate *Signs of Safety* free-of-charge to any interested Deaf mental health clinicians.

More broadly, we hope that the development of *Signs of Safety* will serve as a model for how clinical researchers can successfully conduct randomized clinical trials within the Deaf community using a participatory approach, setting the stage for investigators to develop additional evidence-based therapies for, and more importantly, *with* Deaf people.

Limitations of *Signs of Safety* and Other Traditional "talk therapies"

As noted in the "Target Population" section of this chapter, despite our team's attempts to design *Signs of Safety* to be accessible to a wide variety of deaf persons, we believe that it is most appropriate for a somewhat restricted range of deaf people (see Figure 3.7).

Based on our experiences thus far, *Seeking Safety* + *Signs of Safety* seems best tailored to the middle group of deaf clients—those with minimal-to-moderate language dysfluency and concrete thinking abilities. For the rightmost group, especially individuals whose abstract thinking abilities are quite advanced and who show high levels of insight, *Seeking Safety* + *Signs of Safety* may initially appear too simple. However, it is then the responsibility of the clinician to deepen the level of dialogue and increase the level of nuance in role plays as they apply to each safe coping skill that is presented. The materials serve as a foundation or starting point for more in-depth exploration and application to the client's life and current problems.

With these two groups covered, this means that there is a subgroup of the deaf population for whom *Seeking Safety* + *Signs of Safety* is likely not an appropriate match—individuals with severe levels of language dysfluency. We are encountering an increasing number of deaf people, especially in inpatient psychiatric settings, whose first accessible language exposure occurred in their teens, 20s, or even later in life. With appropriate language exposure, these individuals may eventually acquire some basic sign language communication; yet, their overall language and cognitive skills will typically remain in a much more limited range of functioning (see Chapter 7 by Spitz and Kegl in this volume). For example, they may be able to think and communicate about only those objects that are present "here and now," but will struggle to use any form of symbolism or abstract representation, grasp the meaning of abstract concepts, or talk about the past and future in any in-depth way.

This unique clinical population presents a challenge for therapists who are trained in traditional talk therapies, whether cognitive behavioral, psychodynamic, or otherwise oriented. To work with deaf people with severe language

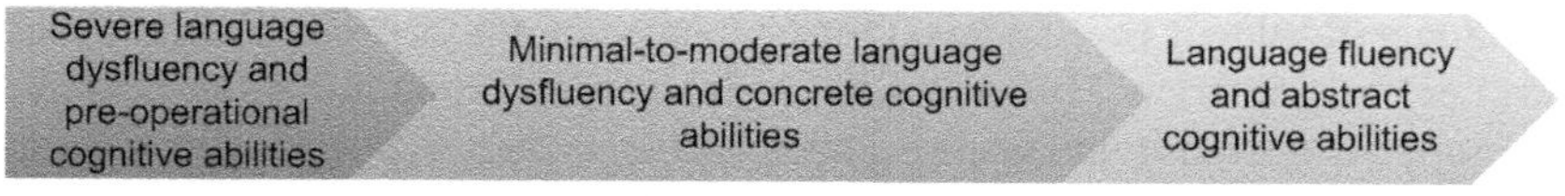

| Severe language dysfluency and pre-operational cognitive abilities | Minimal-to-moderate language dysfluency and concrete cognitive abilities | Language fluency and abstract cognitive abilities |

Figure 3.7 Spectrum of language and cognitive abilities observed among deaf clients in behavioral health treatment settings

dysfluency requires that clinicians think outside the box and step outside of our comfort zone—in essence, letting go of our reliance on language. The *Signs of Safety* toolkit does include client materials that attempt to reduce reliance on any language *and Seeking Safety* does possess some behaviorally-oriented topics that are relatively easy to present through gesture and other nonlinguistic visual approached—for example, the topics of "Grounding," "Taking Good Care of Yourself," and "Self-Nurturing." Yet, *Seeking Safety* + *Signs of Safety* still requires moderate language competence in order to be delivered in full, as do most other evidence-based psychotherapy approaches. With regard to the subset of very language-deprived individuals, it is probably more appropriate to focus on pre-therapy goals, such as the ability to express oneself in something approaching a linear narrative.

Proposed Future Directions for Deaf Behavioral Health Research

Given that available evidence-based psychotherapies are designed for language-fluent populations, we must broaden our schema of "treatment" in order to avoid excluding the population of deaf persons who have been impacted by severe forms of language deprivation. Traditionally, this challenging subpopulation has been managed through the inappropriate prescribing of psychiatric medications or controlling, behavior modification strategies (Glickman, 2007). In other words, if talk therapy is not a feasible option—even in its most behavioral, concrete form—then the only remaining tools to manage mood instability or behavior concerns are pills and perhaps token economies. This historical approach to treating deaf, severely language-dysfluent individuals is too narrow in scope and does these people a significant disservice. Rather, a number of alternative behavioral health treatments are becoming available and generating evidence of efficacy.

One innovative means for engaging deaf individuals with language dysfluency in psychotherapy is through their senses. Sensory-movement-based interventions are minimally dependent on language and frequently used among clinicians who work with deaf people impacted by language deprivation (Trikakis, Curci, & Strom, 2003). Without the use of language, sensory-movement-based interventions allow anxious patients to feel calm, and depressed, lethargic patients to feel more alert after appropriate intervention.

For example, therapists can provide individuals they serve with sensory items such as essential oils (e.g., lavender oil for treating anxiety, peppermint oil for treating depression and lethargy) and food items (e.g., orange for anxiety, fireball candy for depression) or engage them in movement activities (e.g., stretching for anxiety, push-ups for depression). The sensory input provides the physiological satisfaction needed to alleviate emotional dysregulation, which can be particularly useful for those who struggle to use language to regulate their feelings of distress. The use of such sensory-based treatment interventions was a major component of the treatment model on the

Westborough State Hospital Deaf Unit and was responsible for much of the improvement seen in patient behaviors and unit safety (Trikakis et al., 2003).

Another option in the sensory-movement-based realm, Trauma Center Trauma Sensitive Yoga (TC-TSY) attempts to address core clinical issues of safety, trust, self-efficacy, empowerment, and mind-body awareness (i.e., introspection) via a structured, predictable, non-process-oriented trauma-sensitive yoga class (van der Kolk et al., 2014). One can easily imagine how non-process-oriented yoga could be used to treat deaf people with severe language dysfluency—by relying on facilitator and peer modeling of yoga forms, incorporating visual aids and yoga flashcards to reinforce this modeling, and even using video materials as needed. In fact, the Advocates Deaf services program in Framingham, Massachusetts, offered yoga classes by a Deaf Kripalu-certified instructor for about two years. These classes were very popular, even with some severely language-dysfluent persons. Unfortunately, as with so many such innovative treatment efforts, the clinical team did not collect outcome data to evaluate their program.

Although the developers of TC-TSY conceptualize the model as an adjunctive treatment to be used alongside more traditional psychotherapy approaches (van der Kolk et al., 2014), it does present an interesting opportunity to explore whether such body-based treatments on their own can provide behavioral health symptom relief for deaf people with severe language dysfluency. Other alternative treatment options that do not necessarily require language fluency include, but are not limited to, art therapy, dance/movement therapy, meditation, and wellness/self-care-oriented approaches.

Conclusion

Once deaf clients are acculturated into a therapeutic way of thinking and are ready to receive treatment, there are no Deaf-accessible evidence-based therapies currently available to them. We anticipate that *Seeking Safety* + *Signs of Safety* will become the first such evidence-based therapy for therapy-ready deaf people, including those impacted by moderate levels of language deprivation. Additional adaptations of evidence-based talk therapies for deaf clients are desperately needed, especially for the subpopulation of deaf language-dysfluent individuals, who are significantly more underserved and at-risk than those who possess a sufficient first language foundation.

References

Allen, J. P., Crawford, E. F., & Kudler, H. (2016). Nature and treatment of comorbid alcohol problems and post traumatic stress disorder among American military personnel and veterans. *Alcohol Research, 38*(1), 133–140.

Anderson, M. L., & Kobek Pezzarossi, C. M. (2012). Is it abuse? Deaf female undergraduates' labeling of partner violence. *Journal of Deaf Studies and Deaf Education, 17*(2), 273–286. doi:10.1093/deafed/enr048

Anderson, M. L., & Leigh, I. W. (2011). Intimate partner violence against deaf female college students. *Violence Against Women, 17*(7), 822–834. doi:10.1177/1077801211412544

Anderson, M. L., Chang, B., & Kini, N. (2018. Alcohol and drug use among deaf and hard-of-hearing individuals: A secondary analysis of NHANES 2013–2014. *Substance abuse, 16*, 1–8. doi: 10.1080/08897077.2018.1442383

Anderson, M. L., Glickman, N. S., Mistler, L. A., & Gonzalez, M. (2015). Working therapeutically with deaf people recovering from trauma and addiction. *Psychiatric Rehabilitation Journal.* doi:10.1037/prj0000146

Anderson, M. L., Leigh, I. W., & Samar, V. (2011). Intimate partner violence against deaf women: a review. *Aggression and Violent Behavior: A Review Journal, 16*(3), 200–206. doi:10.1016/j.avb.2011.02.006

APA Presidential Task Force on Evidence-Based Practice. (2006). Evidence-based practice in psychology. *American Psychologist, 61*, 271–285.

Barber, S., Wills, D., & Smith, M. J. (2010). Deaf survivors of sexual assault. In I. W. Leigh (Ed.), *Psychotherapy with deaf clients from diverse groups* (2nd ed., pp. 320–340). Washington, DC: Gallaudet University Press.

Barnett, S., McKee, M., Smith, S. R., & Pearson, T. A. (2011). Deaf sign language users, health inequities, and public health: Opportunity for social justice. *Preventing Chronic Disease, 8*(2), A45.

Black, P. A., & Glickman, N. S. (2006). Demographics, psychiatric diagnoses, and other characteristics of North American deaf and hard-of-hearing inpatients. *Journal of Deaf Studies and Deaf Education, 11*(3), 303–321. doi:10.1093/deafed/enj042

Csiernik, R., & Brideau, M. (2013). Examining the intersection of addiction and issues of ability in Canada. *Journal of Social Work Practice in the Addictions, 13*(2), 163–178.

Francavillo, G. S. R. (2009). *Sexuality education, sexual communication, rape myth acceptance, and sexual assault experience among deaf and hard of hearing college students* (Unpublished doctoral dissertation). University of Maryland, College Park, MD.

Gallaudet Research Institute. (2003). *Literacy and deaf students.* Retrieved from http://gri.gallaudet.edu/Literacy/ - reading

Glickman, N. S. (2007). Do you hear voices? Problems in assessment of mental status in deaf persons with severe language deprivation. *Journal of Deaf Studies and Deaf Education, 12*(2), 127–147. doi:10.1093/deafed/enm001

Glickman, N. S. (2009a). Adapting best practices in CBT for deaf and hearing persons with language and learning challenges. *Journal of Psychotherapy Integration, 19*(4), 354–384.

Glickman, N. S. (Ed.) (2009b). *Cognitive-behavioral therapy for deaf and hearing persons with language and learning challenges.* New York, NY: Routledge.

Glickman, N. S. (Ed.) (2013). *Deaf mental health care.* New York, NY: Routledge.

Glickman, N. S. (2017). *Preparing deaf and hearing persons with language and learning challenges for CBT: A pre-therapy workbook.* New York, NY: Routledge.

Glickman, N. S., & Pollard, R. Q. (2013). Deaf mental health research: Where we've been and where we hope to go. In N. S. Glickman (Ed.), *Deaf mental health care* (pp. 358–388). New York, NY: Routledge.

Jacobson, N. S., Follette, W. C., & Revenstorf, D. (1984). Psychotherapy outcome research: Methods for reporting variability and evaluating clinical significance. *Behavior Therapy, 15*, 336–352.

Kleschinsky, J. H., Bosworth, L. B., Nelson, S. E., Walsh, E. K., & Shaffer, H. J. (2009). Persistence pays off: Follow-up methods for difficult-to-track longitudinal samples. *Journal of Studies on Alcohol and Drugs, 70*(5), 751–761.

Ladd, P. (2003). *Understanding deaf culture: In search of deafhood.* Tonawanda, NY: Multilingual Matters.

Najavits, L. M. (2002). *Seeking safety: A treatment manual for PTSD and substance abuse.* New York, NY: Guilford Press.

Najavits, L. M., Ryngala, D., Back, S. E., Bolston, E., Mueser, K. T., & Brady, K. T. (2008). Treatment for PTSD and comorbid disorders: A review of the literature. In E. B. Foa, T. M.

Keane, M. J. Friedman, & J. A. Cohen (Eds.), *Effective treatments for PTSD: Practice guidelines from the International Society for Traumatic Stress Studies* (2nd ed., pp. 508–535). New York, NY: Guilford Press.

NASMHPD. (2012). *Proceedings from NASMHPD Deaf Mental Health Research Priority-Consensus Planning Conference: Final list of 34 research priorities.* Retrieved from www.nasmhpd.org/docs/NCMHDI/NASMHPDDeaf_Mental_Health_Research_Priority_Consensus_Planning_Conference_34 Priorities.pdf

National Association of the Deaf. (2003). *Position statement on mental health services for people who are deaf and hard of hearing.* Retrieved from National Association of the Deaf website at http://nad.org/issues/health-care/mental-health-services/position-statement

Ogles, B. M., Lunnen, K. M., & Bonesteel, K. (2001). Clinical significance: History, application, and current practice. *Clinical Psychology Review, 21*(3), 421–446.

Pollard, R. Q., & Barnett, S. (2009). Health-related vocabulary knowledge among deaf adults. *Rehabilitation Psychology, 54*(2), 182–185. doi:10.1037/a0015771

Pollard, R. Q., Dean, R. K., O'Hearn, A., & Haynes, S. L. (2009). Adapting health education material for deaf audiences. *Rehabilitation Psychology, 54*(2), 232–238. doi:10.1037/a0015772

Pollard, R. Q., Sutter, E., & Cerulli, C. (2014). Intimate partner violence reported by two samples of deaf adults via a computerized American sign language survey. *Journal of Interpers Violence, 29*(5), 948–965. doi:10.1177/0886260513505703

Porter, J. L., & Williams, L. M. (2011). Auditory status and experiences of abuse among college students. *Violence Vict, 26*(6), 788–798. doi:10.1891/0886-6708.26.6.788

Rounsaville, B. J., Carroll, K. M., & Onken, L. S. (2001). A stage model of behavioral therapies research: Getting started and moving on from stage I. *Clinical Psychology: Science and Practice, 8*(2), 133–142.

SAMHSA. (2013). *National registry of evidence-based programs and practices.* Retrieved from www.samhsa.gov/nrepp

Schild, S., & Dalenberg, C. J. (2012). Trauma exposure and traumatic symptoms in deaf adults. *Psychological Trauma: Theory, Research, Practice, and Policy, 4*(1), 117–127. doi:10.1037/a0021578

Sebald, A. M. (2008). Child abuse and deafness: An overview. *American Annals of the Deaf, 153*(4), 376–383. doi:10.1353/aad.0.0059

Titus, J. C., Schiller, J. A., & Guthmann, D. (2008). Characteristics of youths with hearing loss admitted to substance abuse treatment. *Journal of Deaf Studies and Deaf Education, 13*(3), 336–350. doi:10.1093/deafed/enm068

Trikakis, D., Curci, N. D., & Strom, H. (2003). Sensory strategies for self-regulation: Non-linguistic body-based treatment for deaf psychiatric patients. In N. S. Glickman & S. Gulati (Eds.), *Mental health care of deaf people: A culturally affirmative approach.* Mahwah, NJ: Lawrence Erlbaum Associates.

van der Kolk, B. A., Stone, L., West, J., Rhodes, A., Emerson, D., Suvak, M., & Spinazzola, J. (2014). Yoga as an adjunctive treatment for posttraumatic stress disorder: A randomized controlled trial. *Journal of Clinical Psychiatry, 75*(6), e559–565. doi:10.4088/JCP.13m08561

Weathers, F. W., Litz, B. T., Keane, T. M., Palmieri, P. A., Marx, B. P., & Schnurr, P. P. (2013). *The PTSD Checklist for DSM-5 (PCL-5).* Retrieved from the National Center for PTSD at www.ptsd.va.gov/

4

Forensic Evaluation of Deaf Adults with Language Deprivation

ROBERT Q. POLLARD, JR. AND MEGHAN L. FOX

The involvement of deaf people who have significant language deprivation in the complex legal system presents numerous challenges. How can such people's legal rights be protected if the Miranda Warning (aka "police caution" in the UK) is incomprehensible? How can accused people adequately collaborate with their defense attorneys if they cannot express themselves or comprehend legal advice due to language deprivation? How do such individuals fare in prisons when guard directives or public address announcements cannot be understood (even if an interpreter is present, which is rare)? Can language-deprived deaf individuals adequately convey needs or complaints such as illness symptoms or harassment to legal authorities through gesture/mime alone? How can they establish relations with other prison inmates which may be key to protection from exploitation? How can they participate in educational or rehabilitation opportunities which might improve their chances for parole or benefit them after release? These questions are particularly poignant in light of a recent decision by the Supreme Court of Texas (Beeman v Livingston, 2015), which held that Texas prisons are not "public facilities" as defined by applicable laws that would otherwise require prisons to provide reasonable accommodations for persons with disabilities. Thus, deaf inmates in Texas are not legally entitled to reasonable communication accommodations such as sign language interpreters or videophones with which to communicate with persons (including family and attorneys) outside prison.

The presence of deaf people with language deprivation in the legal system is not an infrequent occurrence nor a situation that is easily addressed, even with the assistance of skilled, certified deaf interpreters (CDIs). Oswaldo Martinez, a Salvadoran immigrant with severe language deprivation, was charged with capital murder but has languished in the Virginia legal system since 2005 (Dugan, 2017). According to this *Washington Post* story:

> Unable to read, write or enunciate more than a few small words, Martinez communicates mainly through pantomime, grunts and crude drawings. As

a result, even though experts say he is not psychotic or severely intellectually impaired, he remains legally incompetent to stand trial because he cannot assist in his defense or understand what is happening in a courtroom.

This is a situation that I (Pollard) have encountered over a dozen times in my
work as an expert examiner.[1] Almost always, the deaf individuals with whom I
conduct competency evaluations have demonstrated a degree of language deprivation that was apparent to their attorneys (sometimes via consultation from an
interpreter), leading to the evaluation request. Relatively few of my competency
evaluation requests stemmed from suspicion of mental disorder *alone*, which is
the *usual* reason that hearing persons are referred for competency evaluations.

The main purpose of this chapter is to provide specific recommendations
and advice regarding the conduct of competency evaluations with deaf persons who present with language deprivation. Contextual information also is
presented regarding legal competency and language deprivation issues in forensic settings generally.

What Is legal Competence?

In a landmark 1960 ruling, the US Supreme Court recognized that a defendant must be judged competent to stand trial for such legal proceedings to
take place (Dusky v. United States, 1960). The Dusky ruling and related state
statutes often merely cite the need for defendants to have the capacity to understand the proceedings against them and possess the ability to collaborate
with their attorney(s). In practice, however, competency to stand trial (aka,
adjudicative competence, competency to proceed, fitness to plea, fitness for
trial) requires knowledge in six specific areas: (1) the crime(s) one has been
charged with, (2) the potential punishments associated with each charge,
(3) the attorneys involved in the case and their adversarial roles,[2] (4) the nature of pleas, plea options, and "plea bargains," (5) the key personnel involved
in a trial and their respective roles,[3] and (6) the key steps involved in a trial.[4]
As noted, beyond this knowledge, defendants must have the linguistic and
cognitive abilities to collaborate effectively with their attorney(s).

In my experience with deaf defendants referred for competency evaluations, limitations in "fund of information" regarding legal issues alone are
significant enough that education is virtually always needed in one or more of
the aforementioned topic areas for the individual to reach minimal standards
of competency (Pollard, 1998b; Pollard, 2014; Pollard & Berlinski, 2017). If
the individual is language deprived as well, that challenge is all the greater.
Table 4.1 depicts the rank order of requisite legal knowledge that I observe
among deaf defendants, starting from the topics that are easiest to understand
and progressing through those that are increasingly difficult to understand.
Over the many competency evaluations I have conducted, this rank order has
remained remarkably consistent.

Table 4.1 Competency knowledge rank order typical of deaf defendants, from easiest to most difficult

---

1. One's own story regarding the legal problem
2. The attorneys involved in the case and their respective roles (i.e., PD/defense attorney, DA)
3. Identifying trial personnel (i.e., PD/defense attorney, DA, judge, witnesses, jury)
4. Understanding trial personnel roles (i.e., PD/defense attorney, DA, judge, witnesses, jury)
5. Key steps that take place in a trial (e.g., testimony, jury deliberation, decision, judgement)
6. The crimes one has been charged with and how they may differ from one's "story"
7. The potential punishments associated with each charge
8. What a pretrial plea is and how it differs from a posttrial judgement of guilt or innocence
9. Plea bargains

Source: ©2017 *Journal of Social Work in Disability and Rehabilitation*. Used with permission.

Relevant Literature on Language Deprivation in Forensic Settings

The presence of severe language deprivation among a subset of the deaf population, and the frequent co-occurrence of cognitive and psychosocial difficulties, has long been recognized (Grinker, 1969; Rainer, Altshuler, Kallmann, & Demin, 1963). This constellation of symptoms was first termed "primitive personality disorder" by Altshuler and Rainer (1963) and later championed by McCay Vernon in his publications advocating justice for deaf defendants. Later, this constellation of symptoms was termed "surdophrenia" by Norwegian psychiatrist Basilier (1964). More recently, Glickman (2009) proposed the term "language deprivation with deficiencies in behavioral, emotional and social adjustment" to capture this set of characteristics with a less pejorative label while Hall, Levin, and Anderson (2017) and Gulati (Chapter 1, this volume) propose the diagnostic term "language deprivation syndrome" to highlight the social cause of the condition.

It should not be surprising that the knowledge and judgment problems that often are associated with language deprivation can lead to behaviors that result in encounters with law enforcement. In addition to lacking requisite competency knowledge and, usually, the ability to collaborate effectively with defense attorneys, deaf defendants with language deprivation are vulnerable and disempowered (Bramley, 2007; Miller & Vernon, 2002). They may mistakenly confess to offenses, make poor witnesses, and their conduct may inadvertently generate the impression that they lack remorse for their actions (McAlister, 1994; Miller, 2004; Miller & Vernon, 2001; Vernon, Raifman, & Greenberg, 1996).

While severe language deprivation is a rather low-incidence affliction among the general deaf population, it is frequently observed among deaf persons accused of crimes. Vernon, Steinberg, and Montoya (1999) studied the cases of 28 deaf murderers, 13 of whom (46%) were functionally illiterate with no sign language or speech ability. Miller, Vernon, and Capella (2005) reported that 20.2% of "violent" deaf offenders in a prison population study possessed what they termed "minimal language skills" (another term sometimes used to refer to language deprivation) severe enough that the authors suspected these persons should have been deemed incompetent to stand trial. A British study of over 200 deaf persons in forensic settings found that 41.2% manifested "communication difficulties" (Young, Howarth, Ridgeway, & Monteiro, 2001). Miller (2004) gathered data on the "entire prison population in the state of Texas" and reported that 50% of these inmates had limited reading and other language abilities severe enough to lead Miller to doubt whether they had received due process during arrest and adjudication.

Beyond research studies, case law has recognized the presence and legal significance of language deprivation. In the case of People v. Lang (1979), the defendant, who was raised at home without any formal education and had no language system, was found incompetent to stand trial (Vernon, 1996). Miller and Vernon (2001) offer two other examples. In the case of Wilson v. North Carolina, the defendant was originally deemed incompetent to stand trial due to mental retardation (now termed "intellectual disability"). However, it was later determined that he was not intellectually disabled but, instead, used an obscure North Carolina sign language known as the Raleigh Dialect, a mixture of American Sign Language (ASL) and North American Indian Sign Language (NAISL). Similarly, these authors note, in Wisconsin v. Hindsley (2000), lawyers for that defendant, who also used a combination of ASL and NAISL, successfully motioned for the suppression of statements Hindsley made to police.

LaVigne and Vernon (2003) describe other legal cases where language deprivation was a prominent issue. In Jackson v. Indiana (1972), the deaf defendant could not read, write, or otherwise communicate. He was found incompetent to stand trial based, in part, on language deprivation although he was intellectually disabled as well. In Shook v. Mississippi (2000), the deaf defendant was found incompetent to stand trial due to language deprivation alone. In Holmes v. State (1986), the Florida Court of Appeals determined that a deaf defendant with limited language skills should have been deemed incompetent when it was discovered that he was not able to communicate on the witness stand, including the inability to answer questions essential to his defense. In State v. Smith (1985), the Louisiana Court of Appeals explicitly excluded any claim that a deaf defendant must be mentally ill or mentally retarded to be deemed incompetent to stand trial; that is, language deprivation alone was judged a sufficient cause for a finding of incompetence. The Wisconsin Court of Appeals reached a similar conclusion in the case of State v. Haskins (1987).

Unfortunately, there is a dearth of published literature regarding *how* forensic evaluations of deaf persons with language deprivation should be conducted. LaVigne and Vernon (2003) provide valuable though somewhat general guidance. While not addressing potential forensic evaluators per se, Miller and Vernon (2002) gathered data from 46 sign language interpreters, many of whom had worked with language-deprived deaf defendants or inmates, which yielded relevant evaluation information. Further guidance for or about interpreters in forensic situations has been provided by Miller and Vernon (2001), Vernon and Miller (2001), Brunson (2007), and in a particularly detailed publication by Tuck (2010). Even literature regarding the conduct of forensic evaluations with deaf persons who *do* have language proficiency is rather limited (e.g., Davidson, Kovacevic, Cave, Hart, & Dark, 2015; Harry, 1986; O'Rourke & Grewer, 2005; Pollard, 2014; Pollard & Berlinski, 2017).

As noted, the main purpose of this chapter is to present specific recommendations and related advice regarding the conduct of competency evaluations with deaf persons who manifest language deprivation. This information can, of course, also be useful in conducting competency evaluations with deaf individuals who have competent language skills (see Pollard & Berlinski, 2017) and conducting evaluations with language-deprived deaf persons outside the realm of forensics.

Conducting Competency Evaluations in Light of Language Deprivation

Preparation

In my (Pollard's) view, competency must be evaluated within a broader context of one's basic cognitive abilities, language abilities (signed, written, and spoken), and fund of information. These capacities relate to the requisite competency topics noted before and, furthermore, apply to the *specific* circumstances of the defendant. Such circumstances include the narrative (story) of the individual's alleged criminal behavior, the specific charges they are facing, the associated potential penalties, the attorneys (defense and prosecution) involved in the case, and potential witnesses, among other topics.

I first request this legally-relevant case information from the attorneys who engage me. Competency statues applicable to the state in question also must be obtained and studied. I then request as much background information as may be available regarding the defendant, including his or her social, educational, medical, psychiatric, and legal history. When language deprivation is suspected, I also often request photos of the defendant, his or her family, any victims of the alleged crime, and other relevant parties, including the defense attorney(s) because such photos can be helpful when communicating with the defendant.

I always bring maps to evaluations of language-deprived individuals, to stimulate conversation about their place or country of origin (some of the defendants I've worked with have been immigrants) or simply their travels in the United States, their knowledge of where they are presently being held, and where I live and have traveled to meet them. I find using maps to be an excellent "ice breaker," helping to establish rapport and, importantly, allowing me to observe individuals' communication abilities and adjust my communication approach accordingly.

Finally, I never evaluate a deaf individual—language deprived or otherwise—without access to a whiteboard or a large pad of easel paper (~2′ × 2.5′, available at office supply stores) that I can write/draw on and affix the sheets to walls. (It's helpful to obtain the kind of easel paper with sticky backing at the top. Masking tape will suffice but requires more time and effort and may damage paint.) I ask attorneys to provide me with these easel pads at the evaluation location since bringing them on an airplane is difficult. If I am using a whiteboard rather than easel pads, I take photos of the writing/images produced during the evaluation. (The easel pages can simply be brought home.) Prisons may not allow cell phones, in which case I'll request to bring a standard camera if using a whiteboard and not an easel pad.

About Collaborating with Certified Deaf Interpreters (CDIs)

Working with Certified Deaf Interpreters (CDIs) is a relatively new approach to clinical work with deaf people in various settings. CDIs can bring tremendous value to the process given their native sign language fluency, ability to foster communication through a variety of visual and/or gestural methods, and cultural world knowledge. Skilled CDIs also tend to foster increased trust when working with a deaf client while improving information exchange and, accordingly, service outcomes.

Actually, though, I rarely work with CDIs during my forensic evaluations of language-deprived individuals. This has more to do with the context surrounding these evaluations, especially time limitations, than a presumption that my signing skills are native-like (they are not) or not appreciating the value that CDIs can offer in many clinical settings. I have been conducting forensic evaluations for over 30 years, long before CDI training became available. Clinicians with less experience and non-fluent sign language skills absolutely should work in collaboration with a qualified CDI when evaluating language-deprived deaf people.

Interpreters, deaf or hearing, are generally trained to facilitate communication between parties regardless of the quality of the deaf individual's sign language skills. When deaf individuals present with language deprivation or other forms of dysfluency (Andreasen, 1980; Pollard, 1998b), interpreters typically strive to "make sense of" the individual's signing, as best they can. This is especially the case when CDIs are brought into a situation after a hearing interpreter has struggled to understand a deaf client. This pressure to make sense out of very challenging language is even greater for a CDI in such situations.

Given the frequent co-occurrence of language deprivation and mental disorder (whether of psychiatric or neurological origin) among deaf people in forensic settings, it often is unclear whether their dysfluency has arisen from mental disorder and/or insufficient exposure to sign language (aka, "social origin dysfluency"). This differential diagnostic challenge is obfuscated if interpreters presume, or assert via their translations, logic or meaning in the deaf person's language that is not actually present, which can be very problematic both diagnostically and legally. Strategies for interpreting in language-dysfluent situations exist (Pollard, 1998a) but require special training. Deaf or hearing interpreters who work in psychiatric or forensic settings should take advantage of such educational opportunities. The weeklong mental health interpreter training hosted by the Alabama Department of Mental Health (www.mhit.org) is particularly recommended.

Let me explain why I usually conduct forensic evaluations alone but also offer advice on how evaluators and interpreters (both deaf and hearing) can work together most effectively.

1   My competency evaluations are conducted within strict time limitations since I am always doing so during an out-of-town trip. (I've never had such a case in my hometown.) If I were working with a CDI, the typical approach would call for me to convey to the CDI (in ASL) what I wished to communicate to the client and then the CDI would communicate with the client using a variety of methods and then provide input back to me (in ASL). This back-and-forth process would greatly extend the time involved compared with communicating directly with the client myself.

2   It also would be time-consuming for me to guide the CDI regarding the multi-method communication approaches that forensic evaluations with language-deprived individuals require (Pollard & Berlinski, 2017)—"Here's what I'm trying to achieve right now...let's try it this way." It would be rare for a CDI to be familiar with the specific methods that I have learned are optimally effective in these situations. Providing such guidance would take up valuable time.

3   Direct engagement with a deaf client facilitates my own rapport with that person—rapport that otherwise might be formed with the CDI instead. The importance of this rapport cannot be understated for gaining maximum cooperation and information disclosure from the client, in part because the client and I are in a 1:1 relationship rather than in a triadic relationship with an interpreter.

4   Evaluations frequently require me to be quite assertive in directing, and redirecting, the conversation to essential points. It is common for clients to take up valuable time retelling "their story" of the alleged crime or otherwise addressing irrelevant topics. Redirection is much more effective when I am in the forefront of communication and have a direct relationship with the client.

5   Finally, in my evaluation reports and court testimony, it is *far more* influential to state that the communication between myself and the defendant occurred directly and was not mediated by a third party unrecognized by the court as an evaluation expert. As the engagement of CDIs in legal situations grows, the courts may well learn to recognize their expertise and utility in such situations.

While non-fluent signers absolutely should collaborate with a CDI during forensic evaluations, even sign-proficient evaluators are advised to engage a CDI as a "communication monitor." The CDI can observe the interactions between the evaluator and client, take over communication when prudent, and provide observations about the client's language abilities during or after the evaluation. This approach would circumvent many of the concerns I just listed and would lend an "extra set of eyes" to enhance and reinforce an evaluator's methodology and conclusions.

It is important to approach working with deaf and/or hearing interpreters as a partnership. This requires meeting with the interpreter(s) ahead of time and explaining and agreeing on the goals and methods of the evaluation, such as when communication will shift from the examiner to the interpreter(s). In my experience, freelance interpreters are much less likely to be engaged in the multi-method communication approach discussed herein than are staff interpreters who work regularly in psychiatric or forensic settings. This multi-method approach is far more "liberal" (Dean & Pollard, 2005) than interpreters' typical view of their role—which is often perceived as restricted to translating and producing language utterances alone—but is more in keeping with the linkage between role *and* responsibility common to other practice professions (Dean & Pollard, 2013). This underscores the necessity to encourage interpreters to use any means of communication that may facilitate engagement and comprehension with a language-deprived person (e.g., drawings, role play, and other visual aids). This should take the form of an ongoing dialogue with the interpreter(s) *throughout* the evaluation, so it is understood what the evaluator's communication objective is *at that specific moment,* allowing the interpreter(s) to determine or advise what communication strategies will work best to achieve that objective.

Initial Evaluation Stage

Upon meeting language-deprived evaluation subjects, I'll spend a short time in casual interaction (linguistic and behavioral), often employing maps and attempting to gauge and adjust to their communication abilities and preferences. In my experience, deaf defendants are extremely pleased and cooperative when meeting an evaluator (or anyone else) who can sign, due to their infrequent encounters with sign-fluent persons involved in their case. The downside of this is that defendants often want to discuss all sorts of topics that are not relevant to the evaluator's goals, especially given the limited amount of time allotted for evaluation appointment(s). I've already mentioned the re-direction that is necessary in this regard. I dress neatly but casually for these evaluations, never with a tie (which may be dangerous in forensic settings) or other formal attire that might underscore my role as an authority in an unhelpful manner. In addition, I need to dress comfortably, given the amount of movement I must engage in when doing role plays, affixing poster papers to walls, and frequently walking back and forth between them and/or a white-board while engaging in the evaluation conversation.

Assessing Cognitive Functions

As noted, a thorough competency evaluation must address factors beyond the subject's knowledge of the legal topics listed in Table 4.1. The requisite ability to confer effectively with one's attorney(s) requires a number of intact cognitive functions, including attention, concentration, language, short and long-term memory, and adequate intelligence and critical reasoning skills. I therefore assess a range of cognitive abilities, albeit usually at a screening level, before turning my attention to the legal knowledge topics pertaining to competency. If screening procedures reveal significant cognitive ability defi-cits, then further assessment is called for. Any forensic evaluation should in-clude a formal mental status exam (MSE). I will not describe MSE procedures here. See Pollard (1998b) for thorough coverage of MSE procedures with deaf individuals.

Many authors have provided guidance on psychological testing with deaf individuals (e.g., Brauer, Braden, Pollard, & Hardy-Braz, 1998; Elliott, Glass, & Evans, 1987; Zieziula, 1982). I will not address this topic here, though I recommend that readers be familiar with my five-step process for evaluating the appropriateness of a given evaluation tool for use with deaf individuals (Pollard, 2002). Otherwise, the measures and procedures described as follows are those I tend to use most often when evaluating cognitive and language functions with deaf adults (especially when time is limited). These methods and procedures are not intended to be an exhaustive or exclusive listing of po-tentially useful evaluation tools. Valuable measures and procedures are sure to emerge in the future through continuing research in Deaf mental health and related fields.

Attention and Concentration

I like to use Knox's Cubes Test (Stone & Wright, 1980) for this purpose be-cause it's highly visual and the instructions can be easily "acted out" if neces-sary. The test consists of a small board with four wooden blocks arranged in parallel. The examinee must watch the examiner demonstrate patterns of taps on the blocks and then repeat the patterns. The patterns become increasingly lengthy, from three taps to seven or more. Age norms are provided up to an expected maximum performance of an 18-year-old, which should be applicable to adults who are not elderly. "Unexpected" errors early in one's performance or unexpected successes toward the ceiling of one's performance suggest inconsistencies in concentration, beyond the age-equivalent attention score the test generates.

This test, as with several others I recommend in the following, does not have, nor would it benefit from having, deaf norms. See Pollard (2002) for a discussion of when norming a psychological test with deaf persons is beneficial or detrimental.

The Rey-Osterrieth Complex Figure Test

I find this test (Meyers & Meyers, 1995a, 1995b) very useful on a variety of levels. It involves copying a complex pattern of interwoven geometric shapes from a "stimulus page" onto another piece of paper. Conveying this simple instruction is easy, even to persons with language deprivation. The task requires concentration, visual perception, gross and fine motor skills, visual-motor integration skills, and the ability to plan and execute a successful approach to making the complex drawing, thus providing evidence regarding a number of cognitive functions that can be pursed further with other tests, if desired, when an individual's performance is poor. Deaf norms don't exist and are not needed for this test.

Memory

After copying the Rey-Osterrieth Complex Figure, the examinee is asked to reproduce the drawing about 20 minutes later from memory alone, providing evidence regarding visual memory. Regarding the assessment of verbal (signed) memory, most language-deprived persons I've evaluated would not be able to respond well to the Signed Paired Associates Test (Pollard, Rediess, & DeMatteo, 2005), primarily because the instructions are more complicated than the test items themselves, but it may be worth considering for persons with less severe language deprivation. The ASL Stories Test (Pollard, DeMatteo, Lentz, & Rediess, 2007) is usually out of the question for this population, as it requires good receptive and expressive ASL skills.

Instead, I use a brief, unpublished screening method of verbal (signed) memory, referred to as the "Store, Dog, Black, Train" test, which I learned while working at the University of California San Francisco's Research and Training Center on Deafness and Mental Health. The examinee is instructed (via sign, gesture, etc.) that you want them to remember four signs. I always "index" the four signs by pointing to four outstretched fingers on my hand, in succession, as I show the examinee each sign. The signs are: *store, dog, black,* and *train*. You can even draw these four concepts, or write the words, on a paper or white board. Many, but not all, language-deprived person will know these common signs. The examiner repeats the four-sign sequence as many times as necessary until the examinee can recall all four signs over *two* consecutive immediate recall attempts. The vast majority of persons will require only one or two presentations before being able to recall all four signs. (They don't have to be recalled in order.) Failure to recall all four signs after two learning trials is suggestive of a learning difficulty that may have its source in attention, concentration, short-term memory, or a number of other potential cognitive deficit areas.

The examiner then tells the person that they'll be asked to recall the four signs (about 20 minutes) later. For this recall trial, it is helpful to once again index the four previously referenced fingers of your hand as you prompt the examinee to recall the fours signs. I even "fold down" the corresponding finger when the examinee correctly recalls that particular sign. Most examinees will recall all four signs. Failure to recall more than two, provided the immediate recall trial(s) were successful, is suggestive of a verbal memory problem. If they do not recall one or more of the four signs, there are two "levels" of hints that can be provided. The first is a bit abstract and may not be successful with some language-deprived persons. The examiner provides the following hint(s) for any sign(s) that the examinee failed to recall: for *store*—"It's a kind of building"; for *dog*—"It's an animal"; for *black*—"It's a color"; and for *train*—"It's something you can ride in." If these hints are understood but the person still does not recall the sign(s), it is further evidence of a verbal memory problem. Finally, one can offer three multiple choice options for any signs that are not recalled (e.g., for *black*, offer three colors to choose from, including black). Again, if these second-level hints are understood but the person still does not recall the sign(s), it is still further evidence of a verbal memory problem. There are no deaf norms for this procedure, although my experience in using it a great many times is described earlier.

Non-Verbal Intelligence

I tend to use the Raven's Progressive Matrices Test for this purpose (Raven, Raven, & Court, 2000). It requires the examinee to view a series of increasingly complex visual patterns, some which portray very abstract relationships, and select the proper "missing piece" from among a number of choices. Deaf norms don't exist and are not needed for this test. In addition to yielding a non-verbal IQ score, there is a method for assessing the validity of the test administration based on the examinee's pattern of correct and incorrect answers. It also is quite easy to convey the instructions for this test non-verbally. To accomplish this, I photocopied the possible answer choices for the first two test items (which are six images about one square inch each) and cut them apart, saving them in an envelope for reuse. I lay out the cut-out answer choices for the first item over the top of the corresponding answer choices shown in the test booklet. It is then a simple matter to point to the "missing piece" in the stimulus image, then physically put several (wrong-answer) cut-out choices onto the missing piece area and "act out" the concepts of "no, not right" and "almost right" (one answer choice is almost, but not completely right) and then encourage the examinee to put the correct cut-out piece in place. I then do the same with the second test item. Subsequently, examinees learn to simply point at their preferred answer in the test booklet, negating any further need for using cut-out answer choices. I've *never* seen this method of conveying the test instructions fail. This is important, because conveying the instructions to other so-called "non-verbal" IQ tests is more complicated and often hard to accomplish with a person who is language deprived.

Language Evaluation

One cannot take for granted any aspect of a language-deprived individual's communication abilities, even if they sign "decently." A proper evaluation should take into consideration a number of specific sign language abilities: fingerspelling (expressive and receptive), sign production fundamentals (handshape, location, palm orientation, and movement), sign vocabulary, and sign language grammar and syntax.

I am not aware of useful, standardized tools for gauging these abilities in language-deprived deaf persons. Rather, I attend to these issues, based on my knowledge of ASL linguistics, while communicating with the examinee, and document my observations about the subject's linguistic abilities in my report. Examiners who not well-versed in ASL linguistics, even if they are skilled signers, should work with interpreters who are capable of providing this linguistic information via their observations and interactions with the examinee. The chapters on communication assessment by Charlene J. Crump and Roger C. Williams, and also by Jon Henner, Jeanne Reis, and Robert Hoffmeister reflect the state of the art of this important and developing area of expertise.

English language abilities (at least in the US and Canada) also must be documented. These include: alphabet and number knowledge, written vocabulary comprehension, written sentence comprehension, and expressive writing abilities (vocabulary, spelling, grammar, syntax, and even punctuation and capitalization). While sign language abilities usually are a greater strength than English abilities in language-deprived deaf individuals, it is nevertheless imperative to examine and document English language abilities because they are crucial regarding competency issues such as one's ability to read documents, understand handwritten notes, etc. Some of the available instruments are described below. The judgement of any evaluation tool's appropriateness for use with deaf individuals should be subject to the five-step test cited earlier (Pollard, 2002). Some language-deprived individuals hail from other countries and/or the language of their home is not English. In such cases, information regarding their proficiency in the non-English language(s) to which they may have been exposed should be provided whenever possible. Information from records or from family members may be helpful in this regard.

Finally, a deaf individual's ability to speak should not be overlooked. In my experience, some evaluators—in particular those in the deaf field—dismiss speech ability as either irrelevant to a primary sign language user or "politically incorrect" to address in an evaluation. I disagree; *any* means that a deaf individual can use to communicate, especially a person with language deprivation, should be assessed and documented. Accordingly, I always ask evaluation subjects to offer me a sample of their speech, if they are not already in the habit of vocalizing when signing. If they can do so in English, I can assess the intelligibility of their voice myself. Deaf or hard-of-hearing evaluators can do the same via input from a hearing individual—preferably one who is familiar with "deaf voice" characteristics such as a sign language interpreter. If the examinee can only vocalize in another language, where possible, I will observe them speaking to a family member or someone proficient in that language and ask their opinion of the deaf person's speech intelligibility.

Fingerspelling

Usually, my first approach to a language evaluation is to write the 26 letters of the English alphabet, out of order (to minimize the influence of "overlearning" based on alphabetical order), on a whiteboard or poster paper. I then ask the examinee to show me the fingerspelled equivalent of each letter, as I point to it, documenting whether their response is correct, incorrect, or partially correct (e.g., wrong palm orientation).[5] It is quite common for language-deprived deaf individuals to perform this task with less than 100% accuracy. If so, that is a more fundamental problem than limited ability to fingerspell <u>words</u> per se. Palm orientation may be erroneous (especially involving the letters "P" vs. "K" and "G" vs. "Q" which involve similar handshapes but different palm orientations) or other fingerspelled alphabet proficiency gaps may be noted. The consequences of deficits in fingerspelling ability are significant in terms of both expressive and receptive communication competency, including one's ability to learn English vocabulary relevant to legal settings, and therefore are crucial to document for attorneys, competency trainers, and the interpreters who work with them.

To evaluate signed number concepts, I write (on a whiteboard or poster paper) the numbers 1 through 10, in order, followed by three ellipses (...) as well as some numbers above 10, including some in the hundreds and thousands. I always include 20, 25, 30, 50, 100, 1,000, and 5,000 as well as variants of these numbers (e.g., 44, 360, 1,540, etc.). I do so because, in my experience, language-deprived individuals often present numbers above 10 as individual digits (e.g., 120 is signed as "1" then "2" then "0" rather than the ASL sign for 120). Regarding my use of the ellipses after the written number 10, I invite examinees to "keep going" (via gesture) to see how far they can go in their ability to sign numbers. The inability to use the proper ASL signs for the numbers 1–10 (versus simply showing fingers) would be a significant language deprivation finding. Further deficits or oddities in expression or comprehension of numbers should be documented because they may have significance regarding the individual's legal situation and related communication.

Sign Language

Since, by definition, language-deprived deaf individuals lack significant sign (and other) language abilities, evaluation and documentation of their sign skills is a difficult matter—in particular, in relation to how their communication abilities, or lack thereof, are best explained to legal authorities, who may have limited or no knowledge regarding sign language and its complex linguistic features. As noted before, my evaluation of an individual's sign skills is primarily derived from my direct experience in communicating with them, not through the use of formal evaluation tools. However, I do recommend review of the two communication assessment chapters in this volume and consideration of the recommendations contained therein.

My reports describe the individual's sign communication abilities in *functional* rather than in formal, academic, linguistic terms. By "functional," I mean that my reports endeavor to describe, in terms understandable to persons unfamiliar with sign language, what the individual communication strengths and weaknesses are, especially in regard to his or her legal situation or circumstances. Can they competently articulate the "story" leading to their legal involvement? In what way(s) is their narrative lacking in linguistic clarity (e.g., use of "home signs" or other idiosyncratic vocabulary, gestures, poverty regarding time references, cause-effect logic/clarity, actor-referent clarity, or other key linguistic problems commonly noted among language-deprived persons)? To what degree might deficits in fund of information or other nonlinguistic features of their communication abilities (e.g., superstitions, thought disorder) be affecting their sign communication? While too numerous and complex to elucidate here, *anticipating* and then responding to questions such as these is essential for producing a comprehensive and effective evaluation report.

I sometimes use the California Picture Vocabulary Test (Layton & Holmes, 1985) as a rough gauge of receptive sign vocabulary, even though it was normed on deaf children and includes English-based signs on some items and iconic signs on others that detract somewhat from its usefulness. Nevertheless, it has value in eliciting receptive sign vocabulary data if one is cautious in how such data are reported.

English

The Rhode Island Test of Language Structure (RITLS; Engen & Engen, 1983) is a great tool for evaluating deaf persons' English *syntax* knowledge because it keeps the sign vocabulary of the items quite simple while varying the syntactic difficulty of the 100 sentences presented. The sentences are presented in Manually Coded English and may be too difficult for more severely language-deprived subjects (plus it takes a long time to administer). The test's norms provide interesting opportunities to compare a subject's overall performance, not only to other deaf individuals (up to age 18), but also to norms regarding the types of English syntax that tend to be easier versus harder for deaf individuals to comprehend. I have evaluated two deaf subjects in forensic situations who could not comprehend *any* of the five RITLS sentences that include a negation concept (e.g., "not" or "can't"), which had crucial implications for these individuals' ability to comprehend legal questions. That is, they only could respond to questions presented in the affirmative; they could not comprehend or accurately respond to questions or assertions that involved a negation ("not") concept.

Regarding reading comprehension, I tend to use the Peabody Individual Achievement Test – Revised (PIAT-R) reading comprehension subtest as a start (Markwardt, 1989). It first presents a written English sentence and the examinee then must choose from among four response pictures the one that best matches the meaning of the sentence. In my experience, few severely language-deprived persons correctly respond to the test's practice items, much less the first few (easiest) actual test items. Still, it's a useful tool to document reading ability or lack thereof. Norms provide ("hearing") grade equivalent scores, which I find more comprehensible and relevant to persons in the legal system than standard scores or percentiles.

It is extremely common for deaf individuals' response patterns on this reading comprehension subtest to include "early" errors—below the average grade-equivalent level they eventually earn on the test, while also *successfully* responding to some items that are beyond their average grade-equivalent score. This happens when people do not acquire English vocabulary, grammar, and syntax knowledge in a smooth, grade-level progression—a common situation for deaf persons or anyone for whom English was not acquired as a primary language. For such persons, English language learning is a more erratic process, influenced greatly by their unique life experience exposure to various words and sentence types.

I also like the reading subtest of the Kaufman Functional Academic Skills Test (Kaufman & Kaufman, 1994), which presents "real life" reading tasks involving common public signs/placards, newspaper ads, product labels, recipes, etc. This measure, as well, often is too difficult for severely language-deprived persons, especially because they must comprehend questions posed by the examiner while viewing the reading stimuli. When feasible, the "real life" value of the data obtained can be influential in legal settings.

Regarding English vocabulary, the Peabody Picture Vocabulary Test (PPVT; Dunn & Dunn, 2007) and the Expressive One-Word Picture Vocabulary Test (EOWPVT; Martin & Brownell, 2010) are two that I have employed, but doing so requires considerable deviation from the normal administration procedures.[6] The PPVT is intended for administration to hearing persons, where the examiner pronounces the vocabulary word in question and the respondent selects from among four pictures the one they believe depicts that vocabulary term. When using this tool, I do so as a reading test—showing the deaf individual the stimulus word on a typewritten sheet I've made before asking them to select the pictorial answer. Of course, I cannot use the test's norms to gauge the subject's performance, but it often is quite useful to be able to document words that the subject was or was not able to associate with the response picture, especially when erroneous answers (e.g., "close" ones) shed further light on their attempts at word recognition. This same type of error analysis is valuable when administering the PIAT-R reading comprehension subtest described earlier.

Regarding expressive, written English proficiency, again, there are many standardized measures available, but none, to my knowledge, are useful with language-deprived deaf individuals. I use a tool known as the "Cookie Theft Picture," a task from the Boston Diagnostic Aphasia Examination (Goodglass, Kaplan, & Barresi, 2000), to elicit a sample of the individual's written English. It depicts a "busy" kitchen scene where a mother is overlooking an overflowing sink, a boy is almost falling off a stool while stealing cookies from a jar high on a shelf, a girl is reaching up to him, and other things. The examinee is simply asked to write down what they observe in the picture, hopefully a few sentences. While many language-deprived persons respond with just a few words or limited sentence attempts, I find the ability to quote their verbatim responses to this picture quite powerful in my evaluation reports.

Evaluating Competency Knowledge

Exploring the competency topics listed in Table 4.1 certainly is a challenge with language-deprived individuals, since the primary means of obtaining the relevant data must emerge through conversation. Previously, I have described the multimodal approach to communication that I recommend for competency evaluations. The use of multiple, flexible communication methods is particularly important in gathering competency knowledge data because one cannot use psychological tests to obtain such information. However, a set of visual communication tools developed for me by deaf art therapist Brain Berlinksi has proven invaluable—the seven illustrations depicted in Figure 4.1. In our recent publication (Pollard & Berlinski, 2017) we address how these illustrations can be used to elicit competency knowledge data, especially from individuals with limited language fluency.

One will note that the artwork is "minimalist" in style, avoiding obvious depictions of race and gender so that subjects might more readily "see themselves" or others involved in their legal situation in the images. Other aspects of the artwork, referred to as "key props," are both creative and effective, such as the flag behind the judge in the first image, the finger poised on the juror's

Figure 4.1 Brian Berlinski's competency topic illustrations
Source: ©2017 Journal of Social Work in Disability and Rehabilitation.
Used with permission.

chin in the fifth image, conveying that that he or she is deep in thought, and the sixth image where jurors are depicted in a variety of calm and argumentative poses during deliberation.

Though highly effective in stimulating competency-related conversation, the utility of these images is limited to eliciting information regarding competency topics 2–5 from Table 4.1. They cannot be used to elicit conversation about topics 1 and 6–9, although other illustrations Mr. Berlinski has made for *specific cases* I was engaged in have proven just as useful in addressing these other matters (see Pollard & Berlinski, 2017 for an example). Still, the ability to evaluate an individual's knowledge regarding competency topics 2–5 is significant, especially when language deprivation makes conversation in the absence of visual stimuli challenging.

Competency Training

Oswaldo Martinez, mentioned at the beginning of this chapter, like some other language-deprived deaf defendants I've evaluated, underwent years of sign language training in efforts to "restore" him to competency (a term misapplied to persons who *never had* the requisite language skills to be considered competent, unlike mentally ill hearing defendants who, with appropriate psychiatric treatment, may well be "restored" to competency).

Sign language training in such circumstances is usually focused on specific vocabulary and concepts relevant to competency, not on a broader approach to improving one's sign language fluency. That is, the individual receives instruction on competency topics per se along with the introduction of sign (and English) vocabulary necessary only for discussions of competency topics. A popular competency curriculum I've seen employed with both deaf and hearing defendants was developed by the Florida State Hospital (2011). In a recent case I was involved in, the persons responsible for instructing a language-deprived deaf defendant on competency issues told me that the average hearing person successfully completes the Florida curriculum in three months or less. The deaf individual they had been working with had been receiving competency instruction for over *four years.*

Can competency training for severely language-deprived deaf individuals ever be successful? The answer depends not only on the individual's degree of language deprivation but on many other factors such as IQ, other cognitive abilities and deficits, language learning opportunities, and especially the fiscal and other resources and personnel allocated to work with such individuals.

Across the numerous competency cases I've been engaged in, I've offered a variety of opinions and recommendations in response to this question, ranging from "this person cannot ever be brought to competency regardless of the length or nature of intervention efforts that are reasonably possible" to "this person is competent" (usually only after needed education that took place during my evaluation) to "this person could become competent if the following recommendations for educational and other interventions are followed." Sometimes, at the request of legal authorities, I provide detailed opinions regarding the methods, time, and estimated costs associated with competency training goals that I predict could be reasonably successful. In some cases, I am asked to reevaluate the individual's competency after such interventions have taken place, in which case I will document the progress the individual has made toward competency and make or adjust recommendations for further training if competency standards have not yet been reached.

Closing

While employing the competency evaluation methods described before and adhering to recommendations for follow-up intervention that emerge from expert evaluation is the ideal, the reality for most language deprived-deaf people in the legal system is far more dire (Miller, 2001; Vernon, 1996; Vernon et al., 1999). It is common for deaf defendants with severe language deprivation to be incarcerated in prisons or forensic psychiatric facilities for years on end, even though they may not have a mental disorder, while efforts to teach them sign language and requisite competency information drag on unproductively. Defense attorneys may argue that such efforts are hopeless (if they have expert opinions to assert this) and that continued incarceration/confinement is a violation of their client's civil rights because they have not been, and cannot be, adjudicated. Some court rulings have recognized this. For example, in 2013, a judge declared Mr. Martinez "unrestorably incompetent," convinced by mounds of expert reports that his language deprivation was intractable due to not having had language stimulation during the critical period of language development. A similar ruling finally was made in 2017, in a case I was engaged in since first declaring the defendant unrestorably incompetent in 2011, and again so after each of three subsequent reevaluations.

Why do such rulings remain rare and so much time, expense, and other resources get consumed in attempts to bring the most serious cases of language-deprived defendants to competency? There are several reasons. First and foremost, severe language deprivation (in the absence of an obvious psychiatric or neurological cause) is a phenomenon unique to certain deaf individuals and therefore unfamiliar to most persons in the legal and mental health professions; social origin language dysfluency simply does not happen to hearing people. Unsurprisingly then, the typical course of competency "restoration" that hearing defendants undergo, perhaps supplemented via sign language interpreters, often is relentlessly pursued because it *is* successful for the vast majority of hearing defendants.

Second, the assumption that "we'll just teach him/her enough sign language so that we can communicate about competency topics" is rampant, especially when the deaf individual otherwise presents with "normal" human characteristics, such as having been employed or raised a family. This assumption is grounded in ignorance regarding the complexity of sign language, the challenges of adult language learning, and especially lack of recognition that learning sign vocabulary is just a tiny step toward understanding the complex, unfamiliar, and sometimes abstract concepts required to demonstrate competence. The three analogies presented in the appendix to this chapter were drawn from evaluation reports wherein I was attempting to convey to the reader how intractable *legal* incompetence can coexist with many areas of competence within a single individual. Attorneys and judges have found these analogies educational.

A third reason that competency training can be so doggedly pursued, despite expert opinions to the contrary, is because terminating competency training may result in the release of the accused (unless they are mentally ill and considered a danger to themselves or others), which is not an outcome that some attorneys and judges, especially those whose employment depends on reelection, want to have "on their record." What to do with defendants who are judged intractably incompetent yet still potentially dangerous (but not to a degree that reaches the threshold necessary for involuntary commitment to a psychiatric facility) is a thorny dilemma that plagues not only judges and attorneys but professionals in the deaf services fields who often end up with responsibilities regarding the treatment or oversight of such persons. To quote character Will McAvoy from the American television series *The Newsroom*, "The first step in solving a problem is recognizing there is one" and, to engage an African proverb in this context, "it takes a village," or *will* take a village, of multidisciplinary efforts to address this thorny problem. More on such collaborative recommendations appears as follows.

A fourth reason that effective competency evaluation and training recommendations are less available than desired is due to the dearth of experts able and willing to perform the types of competency evaluations described herein. While psychologists have been interested in deaf people since the late 1800s (Pollard, 1993), the modern era of psychological investigation and service provision by sign-fluent professionals (including those who are themselves deaf) who are truly qualified in this discipline is still young (Pollard, 1996). While the number of such individuals is growing, especially the number of deaf professionals, many hesitate to engage in forensic work for a variety of reasons.

> Some find the prospect intimidating because they lack experience in this area, are apprehensive regarding the prospect of cross-examination, or prefer to avoid the stress that can be associated with an expert's role in litigation generally, especially in high-stakes legal cases.
>
> (Pollard & Berlinski, 2017, p. 2)

It is hoped that this chapter will inspire qualified psychologists and other professionals in the deaf field to become more involved in forensic work—the need is desperate.

More specifically, we call for the development of specialized training programs and other initiatives that will increase the number, competency, and confidence of otherwise-prepared (e.g., sign-fluent, deaf-savvy) persons to practice in forensic settings. Relevant strategies could include developing a network of experienced professionals who can provide mentored guidance via online consultation and supervision groups, establishing training and advocacy committees within prominent organizations (e.g., the National Association of the Deaf, the American Psychological Association, and the American Deafness and Rehabilitation Association), and including forensic practice topics in educational settings that already are preparing the next generation of deaf mental health professionals.

What should attorneys, judges, and other personnel within the legal system take away as the major learning points from this chapter? First, bear in mind that this chapter (and indeed this entire volume) focuses on a small though not insignificant subset of the deaf population. Most deaf individuals either already are competent to stand trail or can become competent via instruction in some key, legally relevant fund of information issues. That being said, as noted before, deaf individuals with language deprivation are very much over-represented in the criminal justice and mental health systems and, accordingly, can be *expected* to be encountered therein.

Toward this end, the legal system needs to work closely with deaf-savvy experts in the fields of law (there are a growing number of deaf lawyers), law enforcement, corrections, psychology, and interpreting to expand and improve knowledge and resources that can be brought to bear in preserving language-deprived deaf persons' (and all deaf persons') legal rights and access to effective competency training in the pursuit of justice.

Appendix A: Three Useful Analogies[7]

The Alien Planet Analogy

You are born on another planet where communication is by voice, but almost entirely within a frequency range that is outside the normal range of human hearing—let's say at the high frequency range a dog can hear but humans cannot. People attempt to communicate with you in this way, but you can only hear an occasional glimpse of a sound that happens to fall in your human range of hearing. Remember, you are an infant. You are given no special treatment or apparatus to allow you to perceive 95% of these high-frequency speech sounds that people use around you. But your brain is otherwise healthy. You can see; you can observe; you can even reason to a degree limited only by your lack of exposure to language and education (and your innate intelligence). You can feel emotion and desires. You can try to convey things to others through your behavior—such as acting out or miming—and they can do the same with you. But you receive no education, other than a life of watching things happen around you and interacting with people and your environment without communication and without formal education. Despite your constraining circumstances, you learn to cook, sew, play simple games, even engage in a vocation such as gardening or carpentry simply by "figuring them out" visually, especially if you benefit from the assistance of a patient (though noncommunicating, other than gesture) parent or mentor. Remember, in this analogy, you have no language ability and you do not "think in words"—you just see, do, and learn visually, with your otherwise healthy brain.

Now, further imagine that this planet has rules, laws, etc., that are completely unlike those of Earth. (Not that you'd know anything about Earth laws either, having grown up in this isolated way on this planet.) Perhaps this planet's moral/legal system is similar to some ancient, geographically-isolated indigenous island society that pre-existed Roman times here on Earth or it contains elements of "extreme" Jewish, Islamic, or Christian rules of behavior that would be wholly unfamiliar to you, having grown up in communicative isolation and without formal education. Now, imagine that you somehow happen to run afoul of this planet's laws. You did something that has caused you to be incarcerated. Recognizing your communication limitations, the authorities have determined that you must be evaluated for competency to stand trial. Let's say the criteria for competency are the same on this planet as are those in the US.

By now, you've figured out that you are in some kind of trouble or at least that you have been forcefully moved and confined to this place where all sorts of rules are restricting your former freedom. You may or may not know what specific thing you did that got you placed here. Even if you did understand that, let's consider the steps necessary to bring you to a state of legal competency in this society. You cannot communicate (and thus cooperate) with your "attorney"— if you even had any idea what an attorney *was* in this society, whose laws, we already noted, are completely unfamiliar to you. It is crucially important to recognize that there would be no way that the concept of an "attorney" would even exist in your mind. Your prior life experience wouldn't have exposed you to such a person or concept, at least not in any way you could understand, even if your uncle who you saw occasionally (and couldn't communicate with) was an attorney. You also don't know other fundamental aspects of competency knowledge—the meaning and role of judges and juries, the adversarial (or other) nature of this planet's legal system, charges (versus a specific behavior you are accused of doing, which are very different things), sentences, plea bargaining, etc. Remember, you don't have prior knowledge of these legal constructs; maybe this society uses these legal constructs, maybe not. Maybe it uses legal constructs that are completely different from these—you don't know.

Recognizing this challenge, someone in that legal system who is familiar with your "condition" recognizes that the high-frequency speech sounds people use on this planet will not be effective for communicating with you. Fortunately, there exists other people on this planet who are like you (although you don't know many), as well as some persons who not only use the high-frequency language, they also have skill in making low-frequency speech sounds in the range you are capable of hearing. A person is found who not only knows how to use this low-frequency language but also is qualified to conduct competency evaluations in this society.

So, your special evaluator arrives to interview you. You are skilled in "acting things out," as is he—having worked with persons like you before. His attempts at using the low-frequency language with you reveal that you are not at all skilled in understanding or producing that language, even though you can "hear" it. This low-frequency language is not the same as "acting things out"—it truly is a language, to which your brain has not been sufficiently exposed. Just because you can hear these sounds does not mean you can understand or respond to them, just like visiting a foreign country on Earth does not automatically make you fluent in that country's language, even though you can hear it "perfectly."

Suppose I am this evaluator, charged with judging your competency to stand trial. Without a shared language system, leaving us only to use gesture, drawings, and perhaps a few words I can teach you, or words that you might have picked up from others like yourself, how far can we go in accomplishing my task? If I show you pictures of a judge or jury, how will I convey to you their role to the necessary level of comprehension? (You certainly can't convey these things to me; your experience has never brought you into contact with such topics.) How would I explain what an attorney is, much less a prosecutor versus a defense attorney? How would I explain that this thing you did (let's say you recognize what behavior got you into trouble) could be associated with a number of different legal "charges" (an abstract concept you'd have no comprehension of), much less discuss with you the advantages and disadvantages of pleas and plea bargains? All you can do is simply tell me, and retell me (via acting out and a few words), your version of this behavioral incident that got you into trouble. Maybe you admit to doing something the law considers wrong; maybe you don't. It doesn't matter. I cannot give you the language or the knowledge to discuss this matter with me at the level, or with the competency focus I need, to accomplish my mission.

So, let's imagine that the authorities now decide that you are presently incompetent to stand trial but since this low-frequency language exists, you should be taught to use this language and thus eventually be brought to competency. Even if I had thousands of hours with you, this task would be herculean. With your brain long-past the fertile period of language learning, I would endeavor to teach you a language with which you are almost completely unfamiliar (although physically capable of using). This would be 1:1 instruction—not immersion in a social environment where this language is used by many people, which would enhance your learning curve, over time. Sure, you could learn nouns and verbs in this way, through pictures, etc. But knowledge of "words" (especially words that are limited to things you can observe rather than abstract and other linguistic-function words such as prepositions and "wh" question words) does not imply that you can understand or produce *sentences* of any complexity. In addition to certain words that are essential for sentence formation, there is grammar, syntax, and other elements of language you would have to acquire in order to communicate at the most basic level. How am I to teach you to understand *and use* these other elements of language and, furthermore, give you the knowledge necessary to attain legal competency? It is a practical impossibility given your age and the lifetime of language and learning impoverishment that you have been subjected to.

The Library Analogy

Imagine that the minimal criteria for legal competency is akin to a bookshelf with ten books on it. (These ten books contain the necessary information and "abilities," such as intelligence and language, to achieve competency.) Given the biological, language, and educational impoverishment that has stunted his cognitive development, Mr. Defendant's mental bookshelf has *room* for only five books. Furthermore, his limited language, education, and life experience to date has only allowed two books to be placed on those shelves. Through *intensive* language and other educational interventions, we might be able to increase the size of his mental library from two books to its limit of five books. But virtually all of these books would be of a simplicity relegated to the children's section of his mental library. His lifelong language and learning impoverishment would not only preclude the inclusion of the vast majority of "adult" books (except perhaps a few on topics with which he's particularly, visually familiar, such as janitorial tasks), but at his age, his mental library is limited in "growth capacity" and cannot be expanded to house the requisite ten books needed to achieve legal competency.

The Football Analogy

Let's compare the minimum cognitive, language, and knowledge capacities needed for competency to the goal line of a football field. The conclusions of my first evaluation report suggest that, at that time, the defendant was at about the 10-yard line (with 90 yards to go) on the path toward competency. Since then, he has been served at a forensic psychiatric facility, undergoing competency evaluation training in group and 1:1 sessions with sign language interpreters. He has made some additional progress, comparable to being on the 25-yard line (again, only in the areas of certain, *concrete* legal knowledge and related vocabulary). With more time at this facility, based on the education methods currently being used, I'd speculate that he might make it to the 35-yard line in the next year. If the instructional methods at this facility were substantially improved (in accordance with the recommendations in this chapter) I'd speculate he could make it to the 45-yard line in a years' time. However, there would be no chance—regardless of the excellence of instructional methods used—of advancing him to the goal line at the end of the field because his cognitive and language deficits constitute a finite limit on how far he can progress. Education alone cannot overcome those limitations and they cannot be repaired via psychiatric or medical treatment.

Appendix B: Brian Berlinski's Competency Topic Illustrations Enlarged

We reproduce here, one figure per page, in the landscape mode in which they were drawn, the seven images from Figure 4.1. These figures can be copied and used by readers. We thank Robert Q. Pollard, Jr., Meghan L. Fox, and Brian Berlinski for making these drawings available, and we again acknowledge the permission granted by the Journal of Social Work in Disability and Rehabilitation (Figures 4.2–4.8).

Figure 4.2 Judge

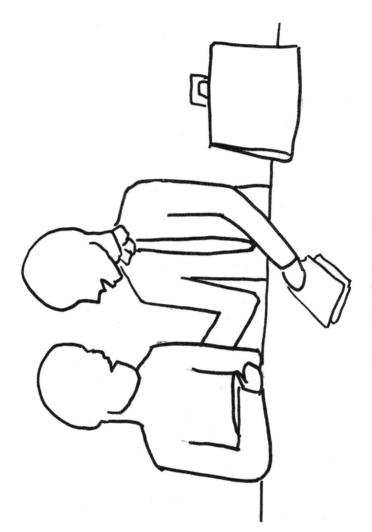

Figure 4.3 Defendant and attorney

Figure 4.4 Prosecution and defense

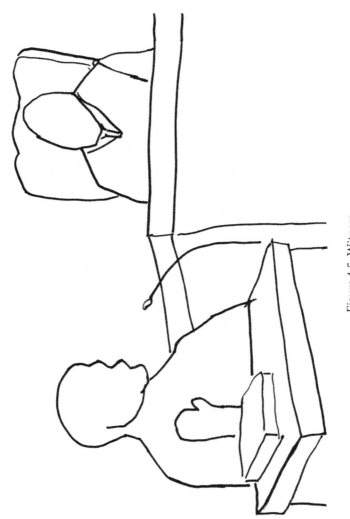

Figure 4.5 Witness

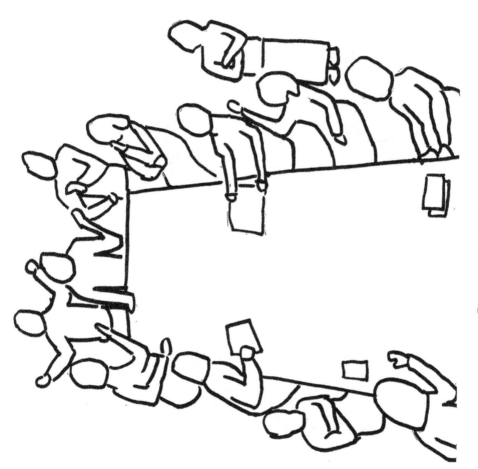

Figure 4.6 Jury deliberating

Figure 4.7 Jury watching and listening

Figure 4.8 Outcome

Notes

1   I am a clinical psychologist and fluent in American Sign Language. I am not deaf. However, I have worked exclusively in the deaf field for over 30 years. The majority of my clinical practice is devoted to forensic cases, ranging from evaluations of competency and criminal responsibility to Americans with Disabilities Act litigation and other topics where my experience with deaf persons, deaf-related scholarship, and/or general training as a psychologist bear relevance.
2   The defense attorney, often a public defender, and the prosecuting, district attorney.
3   Including the key attorneys, the judge, potential witnesses, and the jury.
4   Plea, testimony, jury deliberation, the jury's decision, and judgement/sentencing. Also, that a plea of guilty precludes a trial.
5   One could also do the opposite—present the fingerspelled letter of the alphabet and ask the evaluation subject to point to the corresponding letter.
6   This does not mean that a given tool should not be employed in an evaluation if it is not perfectly designed for the person or situation at hand. I compare an assessment tool to a mechanical tool, like a wrench or hammer. One might use the tool in an unconventional way to try and achieve a certain result. As long as an evaluator explains how the tool may have been used in an unconventional manner, and how norms, etc., might not apply, there still can be value in the data obtained, provided it is reported honestly and interpreted carefully.
7   These three analogies were written about specific deaf individuals I (Pollard) evaluated; they are not intended to be representative of any subgroup of deaf individuals. That being said, these three individuals had several characteristics in common: they immigrated to the US as adults from countries where there was little or no deaf education, their families did not sign, and they had cognitive impairments beyond language deprivation alone.

References

Altshuler, K. Z., & Rainer, J. D. (1963). Distribution and diagnosis of patients in New York State mental hospitals. In J. D. Rainer, K. Z. Altshuler, F. J. Kallman, et al. (Eds.), *Family and mental health problems in a deaf population* (pp. 195–203). New York, NY: Columbia University Press.

Andreasen, N. C. (1980). *Scale for the assessment of thought, language, and communication (TLC)* (Unpublished manuscript). University of Iowa, Department of Psychiatry.

Basilier, T. (1964). Surdophrenia. *Acta Psychiatrica Scandinavica, 39*, 363–372. doi:10.1111/j.1600-0447.1964.tb04948.x

Beeman v. Livingston, 468 S.W.3d 534 (Tex. 2015).

Bramley, S. (2007). Working with deaf people who have committed sexual offences against children: The need for an increased awareness. *Journal of Sexual Aggression, 13*(1), 59–69. doi:10.1080/13552600701365530

Brauer, B. A., Braden, J. P., Pollard, R. Q., & Hardy-Braz, S. T. (1998). Deaf and hard-of-hearing people. In J. H. Sandoval, C. L. Frisby, K. F. Geisinger, J. Ramos-Grenier, & J. Dowd-Scheuneman (Eds.), *Test interpretation and diversity: Achieving equity in assessment* (pp. 297–315). Washington, DC: American Psychological Association.

Brunson, J. L. (2007). Your case will now be heard: Sign language interpreters as problematic accommodations in legal interactions. *Journal of Deaf Studies and Deaf Education, 13*(1), 77–91. doi:10.1093/deafed/enm032

Davidson, F., Kovacevic, V., Cave, M., Hart, K., & Dark, F. (2015). Assessing fitness for trial of deaf defendants. *Psychiatry, Psychology and Law, 22*(1), 145–156. doi:10.1080/13218719.2014.919690

Dean, R. K., & Pollard, R. Q. (2005). Consumers and service effectiveness in interpreting work: A practice profession perspective. In M. Marschark, R. Peterson, & E. Winston (Eds.),

Interpreting and interpreter education: Directions for research and practice (pp. 259–282). New York, NY: Oxford University Press.

Dean, R. K., & Pollard, R. Q. (2013). *The demand control schema: Interpreting as a practice profession*. North Charleston, SC: CreateSpace Independent Publishing Platform.

Dugan, P. (2017, March 13). Deaf, mute and accused of murder, an undocumented immigrant has been in legal limbo for 12 years. *The Washington Post*. Retrieved March 15, 2017 from www.washingtonpost.com/local/social-issues/deaf-mute-and-accused-of-murder-an-undocumented-immigrant-has-been-in-legal-limbo-for-12-years/2017/03/13/6f53c29c-fe8d-11e6-99b4-9e613afeb09f_story.html?hpid=hp_rhp-top-table-main_deaf-830pm%3Ahomepage%2Fstory&utm_term=.60c0ad67df2d

Dunn, L. M., & Dunn, D. M. (2007). *Peabody picture vocabulary test manual* (4th ed). Bloomington, MN: Pearson.

Dusky v. United States, 362 U.S. 402 (1960).

Elliott, H., Glass, L., & Evans, J. W. (Eds.). (1987). *Mental health assessment of deaf clients*. Boston, MA: Little, Brown.

Engen, E., & Engen, T. (1983). *Rhode island test of language structure*. Baltimore, MD: University Park Press.

Florida State Hospital (2011, August revision). *CompKit: Competency to stand trial training resources. A comprehensive approach to competency restoration for criminal defendants.* Available from Florida State Hospital, P.O. Box 1000, Chattahoochee, FL 32324.

Glickman, N. (2009). *Cognitive-behavioral therapy for deaf and hearing persons with language and learning challenges*. New York, NY: Routledge.

Goodglass, H., Kaplan, E., & Barresi, B. (2000). *The Boston diagnostic aphasia examination manual* (3rd ed). Bloomington, MN: Pearson.

Grinker, R. R. (1969), *Psychiatric diagnosis, therapy and research on the psychotic deaf*. Washington DC: Social Rehabilitation Service, Department of Health, Education and Welfare.

Hall, W. C., Levin, L. L., & Anderson, M. L. (2017). Language deprivation syndrome: A possible neurodevelopmental disorder with sociocultural origins. *Social Psychiatry and Psychiatric Epidemiology*. doi:10.1007/s00127-017-1351-7

Harry, B. (1986). Interview, diagnostic, and legal aspects in the forensic psychiatric assessments of deaf persons. *The Bulletin of the American Academy of Psychiatry and the Law, 14*(2), 147–162.

Holmes v. State, 494 So.2d 230 (Fl. Ct. App. 1986).

Illinois v. Lang, 391 N.E.2d 350 (Ill. 2d. 1979).

Jackson v. Indiana, 406 U.S. 715 (1972).

Kaufman, A. S., & Kaufman, N. L. (1994). *Kaufman functional academic skills test manual*. Circle Pines, MN. American Guidance Service, Inc.

LaVigne, M., & Vernon, M. (2003). An interpreter isn't enough: Deafness, language, and due process. *Wisconsin Law Review, 5*, 844–936.

Layton, T. L., & Holmes, D. W. (1985). *Carolina picture vocabulary test (for deaf and hearing impaired) manual*. Austin, TX: Pro-Ed.

Markwardt, F. C. (1998). *Peabody individual achievement test – Revised manual*. Minneapolis, MN: Pearson, Inc.

Martin, N. A., & Brownell, R. (2010). *Expressive one-word picture vocabulary test manual* (4th ed.). Austin, TX: PRO-ED, Inc.

McAlister, J. (1994). Deaf and hard of hearing criminal defendants: How you gonna get justice if you can't talk to the judge? *Arizona State Law Journal, 26*, 162–200.

Meyers, J. E., & Meyers, K. R. (1995a). *Rey complex figure test and recognition trial*. Lutz, FL: PAR.

Meyers, J. E., & Meyers, K. R. (1995b). Rey complex figure test under four different administration procedures. *The Clinical Neuropsychologist, 9*(1), 63–67.

Miller, K. R. (2001). Forensic issues of deaf offenders (Doctoral dissertation). Lamar University, Beaumont, TX.

Miller, K. R. (2004). Linguistic diversity in a deaf prison population: Implications for due process. *Journal of Deaf Studies and Deaf Education*, 9(1), 112–119. doi:10.1093/deafed/enh007

Miller, K. R., & Vernon, M. (2001). Linguistic diversity in deaf defendants and due process rights. *Journal of Deaf Studies and Deaf Education*, 6(3), 226–234. doi:10.1093/deafed/6.3.226

Miller, K. R., & Vernon, M. (2002). Assessing linguistic diversity in deaf criminal suspects. *Sign Language Studies*, 2(4), 380–390. doi:10.1353/sls.2002.0021

Miller, K. R., Vernon, M., & Capella, M. E. (2005). Violent offenders in a deaf prison population. *Journal of Deaf Studies and Deaf Education*, 10(4), 417–425. doi:10.1093/deafed/eni039

O'Rourke, S., & Grewer, G. (2005). Assessment of deaf people in forensic mental health settings: A risky business! *Journal of Forensic Psychiatry & Psychology*, 16(4), 671–684. doi:10.1080/14789940500279877

Pollard, R. Q. (1993). 100 years in psychology and deafness: A centennial retrospective. *Journal of the American Deafness and Rehabilitation Association*, 26(3), 32–46.

Pollard, R. Q. (1996). Professional psychology and deaf people: The emergence of a discipline. *American Psychologist*, 51(4), 389–396.

Pollard, R. Q. (1998a). *Mental health interpreting: A mentored curriculum*. Rochester, NY: University of Rochester.

Pollard, R. Q. (1998b). Psychopathology. In M. Marschark & D. Clark (Eds.), *Psychological perspectives on deafness* (Vol. 2, pp. 171–197). Mahwah, NJ: Lawrence Erlbaum, Inc.

Pollard, R. Q. (2002). Ethical conduct in research involving deaf people. In V. A. Gutman (Ed.), *Ethics in mental health and deafness* (pp. 162–178). Washington, DC: Gallaudet University Press.

Pollard. R. Q., Jr. (2014, October 2). What if your client is deaf? *Atrium Experts Monthly Newsletter*, 9(4). Available at www.atriumexperts.com/blogs/view/case-consulting-what-if-your-client-is-deaf

Pollard, R. Q., Jr., & Berlinski, B. (2017). Forensic evaluation of deaf individuals: Challenges and strategies. *Journal of Social Work in Disability and Rehabilitation*, 16(3), 261–275.

Pollard, R. Q., DeMatteo, A., Lentz, E., & Rediess, S. (2007). A prose recall test using stories in American Sign Language. *Rehabilitation Psychology*, (52)1, 11–24. doi: 10.1037/0090-5550.52.1.11

Pollard, R. Q., Rediess, S., & DeMatteo, A. (2005). Development and validation of the Signed Paired Associates Test. *Rehabilitation Psychology*, 50(3), 258–265. doi:10.1037/0090-5550.50.3.258

Rainer, J. D., Altshuler, K. Z., & Kallmann, F. J. (Eds.). (1963). *Family and mental health problems in the deaf population*. New York, NY: Department of Medical Genetics, New York Psychiatric Institute, Columbia University.

Raven, J. C., Raven J., & Court, J. H. (2000). *Raven manual*. Oxford, UK: Oxford Psychologists Press.

Shook v. Mississippi. No. 2:93CV118-D-B, 2000 WL 877008 (N.D. Miss. June 8, 2000).

State v. Haskins, 407 N.W.2d 309 (Wis. Ct. App. 1987).

State v. Smith, 471 So. 2d 954 (La. Ct. App. 1985).

Stone, M. H., & Wright, B. D. (1980). *Knox's Cube Test*. Wood Dale, IL. Stoelting Company.

Tuck, B. M. (2010). Preserving facts, form, and function when a deaf witness with minimal language skills testifies in court. *University of Pennsylvania Law Review*, 158, 905–955.

Vernon, M. (1996). Deaf people and the criminal justice system. *Deaf American Monograph*, 46, 149–153.

Vernon, M., & Miller, K. (2001). Linguistic incompetence to stand trial: A unique condition in some deaf defendants. *Journal of Interpretation, Millennial Edition*, 99–120.

Vernon, M., Raifman, L. J., & Greenberg, S. F. (1996). The Miranda warnings and the deaf suspect. *Behavioral Sciences and the Law*, 14, 121–135. doi:10.1002/(SICI)1099-0798(199624)14:13.0.CO;2-R

Vernon, M., Steinberg, A. G., & Montoya, L. A. (1999). Deaf murderers: Clinical and forensic issues. *Behavioral Sciences & the Law, 17*(4), 495–516. doi:10.1002/(SICI)1099-0798(199910/12) 17:43.0.CO;2-6

Wilson v. North Carolina. 1996 US Dist LEXIS 16221 (1996).

Wisconsin v. Hindsley. 99-1374-CR; 2000 Wisc. App. LEXIS 437 (2000).

Young, A., Howarth, P., Ridgeway, S., & Monteiro, B. (2001). Forensic referrals to the three specialist psychiatric units for deaf people in the UK. *Journal of Forensic Psychiatry, 12*(1), 19–35. doi:10.1080/09585180122591

Zieziula, F. R. (Ed.). (1982). *Assessment of hearing-impaired people: A guide for selecting psychological, educational, and vocational tests.* Washington, DC: Gallaudet College Press.

5

Communication Skills Assessment for Individuals Who Are Deaf in Mental Health Settings

ROGER C. WILLIAMS AND CHARLENE J. CRUMP

Introduction

Susan, a deaf 53-year-old woman, was hospitalized several times at a variety of public and private hospitals. Communication access ranged from virtually none to interpreters and staff fluent in American Sign Language (ASL). Each hospitalization found the respective treatment teams (including the interpreters) spending up to a week determining the best way to communicate with her. Even with these efforts, she was usually discharged without clear communication having ever been established. However, when she was admitted to a hospital program which had Deaf treatment services, she received a careful communication assessment. Among the findings were that her best means of expressing language differed from her best means of receiving language. When she signed, she tended to use ASL with many grammatical features borrowed from English, giving the false impression that her English language skills were better than they were. The language assessment showed that she had difficulty understanding English grammar-based signing and needed ASL grammar to receive and process information. In addition, she had difficulty with fingerspelling, often being unable to remember the beginning of the word by the time she arrived at the end. She could read words on paper, but she could not process the same words well through fingerspelling. This assessment altered how program staff communicated with her, and this led to a more successful treatment experience.

Most professionals working in the field of Deaf mental health, whether by training or by intuition, work to match the language output of the person with whom they are communicating. However, when, as with Susan, a person's expressive language skills differ from their receptive language skills (a condition known as "asymmetrical" language abilities), staff misjudge how to provide information, and the person receives information in a way they have difficulty processing. This is particularly true when the situation is compounded by language deprivation and/or mental illness.

Each signing professional worked diligently with Susan to provide the best language services they could. From the communication assessment, staff learned, in addition to the fact that she needed language input in ASL, that she couldn't easily remember new words, that signing to her frequently had to be slow and repetitive, and that fingerspelling was usually an unsuccessful communication strategy. They also came to a better awareness that she often "blanked out" when people were communicating with her. It was not a dissociative trauma reaction. It was more likely a language processing problem. When these variables were taken into consideration, this level of communication accessibility shortened her hospitalization and, when used by other hospitals, reduced her length of stay by three days or more.

Susan had this information also, and she could use it to explain and advocate for what she needed to get the most effective treatment. She could, for instance, ask that medication information be written down, not fingerspelled, and that important diagnostic information be repeated in several sessions, with clear ASL interpretation.

Serena, a 58-year-old deaf female, was hired as a mental health technician at a group home that works with individuals who are deaf with mental illness. As part of her employment, she was required to take and pass a Medication Assistant Certified (MAC) Worker examination. This required readings, two days of classroom lecture, a written examination, and a performance examination. Serena is bright, but she struggled with the material. Even with sensitive hearing instructors working in conjunction with highly qualified interpreters, she could not comprehend and retain the required information, and still failed the examination.

On her second attempt, a communication specialist was brought in, and her deaf peers at the group home provided mentoring for her. Serena would seem to grasp the concepts while involved in a mentored task but was unable to transfer that information into the classroom. The same hearing instructors taught the class, but a different interpreter was brought in when one of the original team members was not available. This team interpreter happened to have experience in communication assessments and noted that while Serena's language output was primarily English-based signing, she seemed to respond better to questions that were in ASL. Also, despite being given specific information during the training by instructors through interpreters, in written form, and through mentoring with deaf peers, Serena would sometimes respond as if she had never had any exposure to the information. Although there was some improvement, she failed the second attempt as well.

Eventually, the second interpreter began to recognize that Serena showed some of the language dysfluency patterns associated with congenital rubella syndrome. Serena also seemed to forget new information, fingerspelled exceptionally slowly, and struggled with receptive fingerspelling—often asking others to write the new words down for her, an intuitive survival and self-advocacy skill. Staff observed that Serena occasionally tuned out while watching the interpreters. She asked questions regarding somewhat basic information that she had been repeatedly taught in previous sessions. Noting these linguistic factors, the interpreter asked Serena how she became deaf and was not surprised to find that her hearing loss etiology was congenital rubella.

While Serena was not a consumer for whom a formal communication assessment was required, she still benefited from an analysis of her language skills.

Based on the results of the communication assessment, her interpreters began using ASL (rather than matching Serena's language output), and more closely monitored when Serena was inattentive. When she started to tune out, they switched to a more dialogic interpreting style in which they would ask her what a concept meant and then dialogue with her about it. This required the use of consecutive interpreting and more time. Instead of fingerspelling words, the interpreters wrote them down for her. More time was spent at the group home with Serena performing the activities, rather than discussing them or watching peers. Additionally, a captionist was hired so that the information was provided in written English alongside ASL. With these supports, based on a better understanding of her communication abilities and needs, Serena passed the MAC exam on her third attempt.

The interpreters discussed with Serena what they learned about her communication abilities. This is not a typical task for interpreters but, in this case, it was welcome information. Serena learned how the rubella etiology of her deafness probably affected her language abilities. Serena began crying as the discussion progressed. She admitted that she knew she struggled more than she felt she should in many different environments but had always been told by her parents and teachers that she had an intellectual disability in addition to being deaf. As she has been able to incorporate these changes into her accommodation requests, her ability to succeed academically and vocationally has improved dramatically.

In Alabama and South Carolina, communication assessments are required for any person who is deaf and receives mental health services (Administrative Code, 2010; South Carolina Department of Mental Health, 2014; Williams & Crump, 2013). This chapter will provide a discussion of historical informal attempts to analyze sign language used by deaf persons and why they have not always been effective. We will discuss what information a quality communication assessment can provide and how it can assist in treatment and educational interventions. We then discuss the communication skills assessment developed by the Alabama and South Carolina Departments of Mental Health. This instrument and procedure can be found at www.mentalhealthinterpreting. net/communication-skills-assessment.html. We recommend that readers access this assessment while reading this chapter to provide an easy reference.

History of Communication Assessments in Deaf Service Programs

The need for communication assessments of deaf people with complex or idiosyncratic means of communication is becoming more recognized. This is partly in response to the growing awareness about the highly diverse ways deaf people communicate and more appreciation that "knowledge of sign language" in staff is no indication they are qualified to meet these communication challenges. This interest in communication assessments is also a response to the growing recognition of how language deprivation remains a problem for some deaf people and how this deprivation impacts the development of language, communication, cognitive, and psychosocial skills.

There is good reason to believe that the presence of deaf people with significantly dysfluent language in clinical populations is very high when compared with hearing individuals. Approximately 2%–3% of the general population have a language disorder (Law, Boyle, Harris, Harkness, & Nye, 2000). For the population we service, that proportion is likely higher than the 50%. Black and Glickman (2009) found that 66% of the deaf population seen at the Westborough Massachusetts State Hospital Deaf Unit over a seven-year period had either grossly impaired or functional but non-fluent language skills. Glickman (2009) reviewed all the deaf psychiatric and vocational rehabilitation literature available to date, finding reports of similar communication challenges in most, if not all, Deaf mental health programs. His review found that in virtually every hospital which had a Deaf inpatient program, and reported their findings, staff believed they saw a large subset of deaf patients with significant language and communication challenges as well as an array of behavioral and psychosocial challenges. This was common enough that they presumed they were seeing some new kind of psychiatric disorder and they attempted to name and describe the disorder. In Chapter 1 of this book, Gulati names this condition "language deprivation syndrome" (See also discussions in Glickman, 2009; Gulati, 2014; and Hall, Levin, & Anderson, 2017).

The principal criteria for this proposed syndrome are language deprivation and dysfluency. To reliably make such a diagnosis, we need to improve and standardize communication assessments. The tool we present here is one way to begin that process. This tool is a work in progress and, as noted in the assessment manual, is designed to provide qualitative information about the subject's communication skills. It has not been subject to the rigorous psychometric requirements which would validate comparisons between subjects. The use of communication assessments is still in at an early stage in the clinical specialty of Deaf mental health. Hopefully, additional tools will be developed which will provide that level of rigor. Chapter 6 of this book, by Jonathan Henner, Jeanne Reis, and Robert Hoffmeister, documents progress towards having psychometrically validated ASL assessment tests. Their review emphasizes receptive ASL tests because they worry about bias introduced by unqualified examiners, and receptive tests are less subject to examiner bias. We worry about evaluator bias also (see section that follows on examiner qualifications) but believe that it is crucial to assess expressive skills as well.

Hearing people, listening to other hearing individuals who share the same language speaking with significant dysfluency, would immediately perceive that something is wrong. However, when hearing professionals with no experience serving deaf persons encounter language dysfluency, they frequently assume it is either a normal result of being deaf, a manifestation of cognitive disability, or an indication of mental illness. They may also assume the interpreter, therapist, or language specialist pointing out the dysfluency is not competent. This means that language deprivation and dysfluency may be overlooked as possible reasons for emotional or behavioral challenges the person may show. It may also mean that treatment recommendations do not sufficiently consider how the person needs to receive, process, and express information.

The Alabama Department of Mental Health and South Carolina Department of Mental Health developed similar communication assessment instruments (Crump, 2005; Williams, 2003). They were inspired by, and built upon, the work of Greg Long, who created a communication assessment tool for individuals in employment settings (Long & Alvares, 1995). That tool was designed to improve the match between the communication skills required for successful employment in those settings and the abilities of the deaf worker. A presentation at the 2012 ADARA Breakout conference detailing each respective assessment instrument and procedure inspired the goal of merging the two assessments into one tool that would be employed in both states and made available to other programs. The assessment tool and procedure described here are the result of that collaboration.

Sign language interpreters typically perform an informal communication assessment at the start of an assignment. In the not-to-distant past, individuals were trained to spend a few minutes communicating with the client in the waiting room before a session. This, in theory, allowed the interpreter an opportunity to assess how the Deaf person communicated. Interpreters might ask the deaf person questions such as why they were coming for this appointment. They would observe what words the person fingerspelled and preferred signs for specific concepts. This informal assessment yielded an impression as to whether the person was difficult or easy to understand. This analysis was often shared with other professionals, including therapists, and typically included comments such as, "It's a tough one, they use ASL, but not well," "They have minimal language skills and are difficult to understand," or "They don't understand fingerspelling." While interpreters are usually appreciative of any information that can prepare them for the interpreting assignment, these brief, summary judgments were often overly simplistic, misleading, or wrong. They provided little insight into the specific nature of the person's communication skills and deficits.

These brief assessments also did not provide adequate guidance for the interpreters on how to adjust their interpreting to meet the needs of the client. In some situations, they even interfered with treatment. For example, the interpreter is mistakenly advised that the individual has some "home signs" when the individual is experiencing a psychotic episode and those "home signs" are neologisms, made-up words that are a product of mental illness. An interpreter who chooses to interpret highly dysfluent language into coherent or even articulate spoken English may deprive the therapist of needed clinical information regarding the client's state of mind. Yet, in this same example, an interpreter who glosses, providing a word-for-word transliteration, or simply states that the message doesn't make sense, without providing an analysis of how the message is incoherent, may bias their interpretation in the direction of making the deaf consumer seem even more linguistically and intellectually incompetent.

Interpreters often worry that their interpretation may negatively skew the impression the clinician has of the deaf person. Interpreting the content, register, and emotion of a message is complex and difficult. Any interpretation inevitably alters the message and any difficulties in comprehension can potentially magnify that alteration.

Sometimes interpreters turn to people in the deaf consumer's life to gather more information about that person's communication abilities. This leaves room for misunderstanding. Family members, for instance, often hold inaccurate assumptions about the language abilities of their family members. They may tell clinicians or interpreters "he can't understand that" or "she doesn't know how to sign," statements which may be misleading. Interpreters lacking objective information about the person's language and communication abilities, and depending on inaccurate or incomplete information, expose these clients to risk of misdiagnosis or mistreatment.

Matthew, a hearing sibling of Marcus, who is a 40-year-old deaf male, accompanied Marcus to an appointment with a vocational rehabilitation counselor. Marcus had not been exposed to ASL until he was 15 and as a result showed very dysfluent sign communication. In the appointment, Matthew spoke for Marcus. Matthew told the counselor what job skills Marcus had and what he wanted. When the counselor, with basic conversational sign skills, inquired how Matthew could understand Marcus' language, Matthew replied "I know what he wants." In this situation, the counselor was never able to communicate directly with Marcus, who remained in an infantized and dependent position. A good communication assessment would have guided the counselor on the communication accommodations that Marcus needed not only in their interview but also on the job.

There are many stories like those of Marcus, Serena, or Susan to which professionals working with deaf people can relate. The wide variation in communication abilities of language-deprived deaf people makes it difficult for even a sign fluent therapist or qualified interpreter to communicate well with every deaf consumer. Having an objective communication assessment is one way to explore language abilities and deficits, eliminate ineffective communication approaches, and share what specific gestures or home signs, unique to this person, may mean.

Social and Medical Causes of Language Dysfluency in Deaf People

Human beings can develop language dysfluency because of many medical, psychiatric, and psychological conditions. The term "dysfluency" is used most often to refer to speech articulation difficulties like stuttering. We're using the term differently. Following Pollard (2013), who, in turn, based his definitions on Andreasen's (1986) study of language, thought, and communication disorders in psychiatry, we use the term dysfluency to refer to two phenomena.

The first are specific disruptive errors in language use that are atypical for native users of a language. Examples would be unnecessary repetition of a sign or word or omission of key parts of speech.

The second kind of dysfluent communication refers to a general lack of proficiency that is significant enough to impair communication with someone who is proficient in the language. Thus, dysfluent language can refer to specific errors which may, or may not, be repeated or ongoing patterns. Our interest is primarily in ongoing patterns—that is, errors that are repeated reliably, for at least a period of time. A hearing person who is intoxicated, and who is slurring their speech, would be dysfluent until they sober up, for example. The medical cause, alcohol intoxication, would be widely assumed, especially if the person displays other behaviors we associate with intoxication. A person who has just had a stroke, and who struggles to remember words/signs, and speaks or signs in a slow, hesitant, halting manner, shows another form of dysfluency.

The first discussions of sign language dysfluency in recent Deaf mental health literature referred to well-known psychiatric causes. Alice Thacker was the first person to identify sign language dysfluencies in severely mentally ill deaf people that correspond to dysfluencies seen in hearing people (Thacker, 1994, 1998), and subsequent authors, including Trumbetta, Bonvillian, Siedecki, and Haskins (2001), continued this discussion. Pollard (1998b) has also made important contributions to the identification of sign language dysfluency related to psychiatric problems. Poizner and colleagues (Poizner, Klima, & Belllugi, 1987) studied deaf people who had experienced strokes and identified aphasias in sign language that correspond to aphasias in spoken language. We know also that deaf people with severe levels of autism can engage in behaviors like echolalia (repeating words or phrases) as well as have difficulty with pronouns like "I" or "me." Severe levels of developmental disorder can impair language development in deaf and hearing people alike (Morgan, Herman, & Woll, 2007). Both groups can also have specific language learning disabilities, although diagnosis these in deaf people is far more complicated (Pollard, 1998b). Crump and Hamerdinger (2017) have identified how common causes of hearing loss may impact language development in deaf people.

While the medical and psychiatric reasons for language dysfluency in hearing people may also be causal factors for deaf people and deaf people may have additional medical/neurological bases for language dysfluency associated with the etiologies of deafness, the single greatest factor accounting for poor language skills in deaf people is language deprivation. If one combines the inability to acquire spoken language as a native user with the lack of quality exposure to natural sign languages during the critical period for language development, you are deprived of the language learning experiences that would result in a full, native language. Language deprivation in deaf children, of course, is not inevitable. It is the result of the choices that a society makes, as mediated through medical professionals and parents, about the extent to which deaf children are given the sign language exposure that would enable them to become native signers.

In saying this, we are aware that advocates for cochlear implantation of deaf children often object to the notion that they are depriving deaf children of language exposure. Of course, their intention is the opposite. Many claim that cochlear implantation makes spoken language accessible enough so that hearing impaired children can acquire it as native users. Both Gulati and Szarkowski, in their respective chapters of this book, critically evaluate these claims. It is not our intention to debate this, but to point out the practical reality, reconfirmed continuously in our work, that the language skills of deaf persons vary enormously and that implantation is no guarantee of spoken language acquisition. Some deaf children do well with implantation, but many others do not. If implantation comes with a message that the children should not be exposed to sign language, or if the children don't have sufficient quality ASL exposure, they will probably be poor signers also. Interpreters and clinicians who specialize in Deaf mental health encounter deaf people routinely who, with or without implantation, lack native language abilities in any language. This communication assessment is designed to give a broad picture of their communication abilities and deficits.

One of the most sophisticated and important questions in Deaf mental health care is this: are the language problems we are observing due to a psychiatric or medical condition or are they more likely a result of language deprivation in childhood? Indeed, you can infer how sophisticated someone is about Deaf mental health by their knowing enough to ask this question.

We don't yet have a research-based way to answer this question, though we have an increasing body of skilled observations, by many knowledgeable informants, about particular kinds of dysfluencies that manifest in sign languages. Many people have observed, for instance, that deaf people with severe language deprivation frequently do not reference time clearly, or establish subject, predicate, and object unambiguously, or follow the common topic, comment structure of ASL (Black & Glickman, 2005; Glickman, 2009; Glickman & Harvey, 2008; Witter-Merithew, 2017). They often don't indicate clear transitions or segues from one topic to the next, or they mix relevant and irrelevant information in a way that a more skilled "storyteller" would not. These kinds of language dysfluencies often result in the conversational partner asking a lot of structuring and clarifying questions (i.e., who, what, when, where, how). These language dysfluencies can certainly resemble certain kinds of dysfluencies associated with psychosis. In time, we hope research will enable us to more definitively relate the specific kind of language problem with specific etiologies. We are just beginning to even appreciate the complexity of this diagnostic challenge.

One thing we can say conclusively, however, is that dramatic and quick changes in language abilities, either for the better or worse, occur because of medical changes in the brain. When someone's language problems are due mainly to language deprivation, and the person is now an adult, any improvements because of language and communication learning will be slow and incremental, taking months, if not years.

In Deaf mental health, it is unfortunately common to lack good background information about some of our patients. This is partly because the persons themselves are not good informants and the people around them are not able to judge their language and cognitive abilities. Thus, we have worked with people whom we suspected showed language dysfluencies likely due to mental illness (for example, very loose, tangential, paranoid, or bizarre thinking) and, using this communication evaluation tool, were able to demonstrate dramatic improvement in language and communication following administration of psychiatric medication. We understand we are using some faulty logic here, akin to the observation that if you hit something with a hammer, and it goes into a piece of wood, it must therefore have been a nail. In the real world of psychiatry, especially in Deaf mental health and psychiatry, we are asked to intervene without good information informing our assessment. This communication evaluation provides some crucial data points for intervention and may be especially valuable when clinicians cannot get good history.

Appropriate Referral Questions for a Communication Assessment

Any communication assessment starts with "what do you want to know about the person's language and communication abilities and deficits?" As with all evaluations, communication assessments are done for a reason. Integral to conducting a communication assessment is determining what is the referral question being asked and what information is needed to provide an answer. People who know what questions to ask make the best assessment referrals. While a general question like, "tell me about this person's communication skills and weaknesses?" is acceptable, vague questions will often elicit vague responses. The more precise the question, the more likely one is to get a satisfactory answer. Generally, communication assessments are called for when someone uses an atypical or nonstandard form of communication or when they have difficulty expressing themselves or being understood.

Typical questions which can be addressed by a communication assessment include:

- To what extent does this person use standard American Sign Language?
- Which ASL vocabulary and grammatical structures seem to be used well and which others seem weak or lacking?
- Is there a difference between the best way this person expresses him/herself and how he/she best receives information?

- Is there a variant of sign communication that works best in communicating with this person?
- Can this person benefit from the use of a sign language interpreter in a therapy group or classroom or do their language requirements necessitate a tutor or one-on-one instruction?
- What language competencies or experience would be needed on the interpreting team?
- What kind of communication supports are needed for this person to benefit from a treatment/rehabilitation/educational plan?
- Can you describe the kinds of sign language dysfluencies that you see?
- Can you provide any guidance about what the nature of the language errors the person is making may mean?
- Has there been a change in this person's language and communication abilities over this time period? If so, what is the nature of the change?
- Is fingerspelling an effective way to communicate with this person?
- Does this person understand and use well a contact language like Signing Exact English?
- Can this person follow a conversation when the other individual signs and speaks at the same time?
- How extensive is the vocabulary of this person in English and ASL? Do they use vocabulary from some other sign language?
- Does this person utilize home signs that only a few people know?
- Does this person use standard signs in some idiosyncratic way?
- Are reading and writing effective communication methods for this person?
- Does this person have comprehensible speech? How effective are they at spoken communication?
- Is speech reading an effective communication strategy for this person?

Because the process of obtaining these communication assessments is new, and because our knowledge of how language deprivation impacts specific language abilities is still rudimentary, we would expect that, with time, research, and experience, we will be able to answer additional questions. Given the unique communication challenges in Deaf mental health, it is our belief that the growth of this clinical specialty will be highly correlated with growing understanding about communication assessment, including using these results to guide educational programming, mental health interventions, interpreting, and other interventions with deaf people.

Communication Assessments and Treatment or Remediation Interventions

How can a good communication assessment assist with treatment or remediation interventions? To begin with, the communication assessment guides the team as to how their client needs to receive information. We have seen that knowing that a person "communicates in sign language" is not enough information to guide interventions when the person's sign skills are dysfluent or atypical. Thus, knowing that a person cannot process more English-like variants of sign, even though her own expressive signing tends to be more English-based, is vital information. Knowing that a signing person does not really understand complex ASL grammatical features like classifiers, and needs information presented in short, concrete sign phrases, is also very helpful, provided the team can accommodate those communication needs.

Communication assessments yield information about idiosyncratic ways that a particular consumer communicates, such as the use of home signs, the mixing of signs from American and foreign sign languages, the tendency to mouth some words in a foreign language the person has been exposed to (e.g., a consumer who signed TOMORROW but mouthed "mañana"), or the appearance of what may be sign neologisms (e.g., a consumer who invented a sign for a computer keypad on his nose) or clanging (the repetition of sign parameters like handshape in a way that isn't meaningful semantically), both of which are likely indicators of a psychotic thought process. It can provide guidance for communication with deaf persons who have additional challenges that impact sign communication such as deaf-blindness or cerebral palsy, or motor rigidity related to strokes and other neurological conditions. One deaf patient, for instance, was unable to move the fingers of his nondominant hand. This raised diagnostic questions (it turned out to be due to a stroke) as well as greater challenges in understanding him.

Our new attention to language dysfluency among deaf people has raised the bar considerably about the communication skills needed in providers and teams. It's fair to say that most signing clinicians, even if they are deaf themselves, cannot communicate effectively with every deaf consumer, especially when the person has experienced very severe language deprivation. It's also fair to say that there are some deaf consumers with whom virtually no one can communicate well. It is important to recognize this because signing clinicians are routinely expected to be able to communicate well with every deaf consumer, and their inability to do so, coupled with lack of appreciation by supervisors and administrators of the language deprivation problem, contributes to talented people leaving this field.

As certified Deaf interpreters become more available, teams working with deaf consumers increasingly ask, "do we need a CDI?" This question is hard to answer in the abstract, because the skills of specific CDIs, and specific standard interpreters, vary also. A better question to ask, and one more suited to the goals of a communication assessment, is "what are the communication competencies and deficits of this person, and what are the communication skills that are needed in providers and interpreters who work with this person?" This question inevitably leads one to ask the corollary— "what are the communication skills of our 'signing' staff, and do we need to supplement their communication skills, in some instances?" Communication assessments of staff can help answer these questions.

Thus, as our fields' sophistication about addressing communication diversity in deaf people develops, we will increasingly understand that it takes a team of people to do this work and that at least one member of the team must be a genuine sign communication expert, not merely a person who "knows sign language." As we come to seriously grapple with the implications of language deprivation and dysfluent language, we believe we will come to appreciate that it is unrealistic to expect "sign fluent clinicians," even if deaf themselves, to be able to communicate effectively with every deaf person served by their program.

In addition to providing guidance about necessary communication skills in staff, communication assessments can inform the process of interventions like counseling and teaching. They can advise providers about *how* information is best conveyed. For instance, communication assessments may clarify whether a person needs communication supports beyond the provision of an interpreter such as one-to-one-tutoring, visual aids, hands-on learning, a dialogic style of teaching (i.e., not lecture, but question and answer, with dialogue), and careful "unpacking" of abstract ideas. The communication assessment may specify the importance of interpreting teams working consecutively, not simultaneously, at a pace that follows the needs of the consumer, not the provider. As we learn more about best practices for language and communication skills development in late language learners, we would expect communication evaluations to incorporate these findings (See the pedagogic recommendations in Chapter 7 by Spitz and Shephard).

Communication assessments are not psychological assessments, but they can certainly contribute to a fuller picture of the cognitive abilities of the client. Language and communication skills are strongly related to the "fund of information" that a person has regarding issues like physical and mental health, interpersonal relationships, sexuality, society and the law, and how to work with a counselor or an attorney. A person who is very language deprived is also very likely to be information deprived. This means they don't just need an interpreter. They need staff prepared to help them learn language, communication, and specific content areas.

As Pollard discusses in Chapter 4, language deprivation has a major impact upon whether a person accused of a crime is competent to participate in their own defense. Deaf mental health clinicians who sign well, but lack the expert communication skills required to evaluate very dysfluent consumers, can find that a well done communication assessments informs and complements their own assessment of the client or defendant's cognitive abilities and legal competency. In our appendix, we include a communication assessment that was used as part of a forensic assessment of a deaf defendant, and that was used to support the conclusion that the person was not competent to work with her attorney in her defense.

While the assessments can be shared with Deaf and signing members of a treatment team who would have the necessary cultural background and linguistic understanding to readily make sense of the report, these reports are also written for practitioners involved in medical, mental health, and legal systems, which are primarily made up of people with no background in Deaf mental health. This can guide supervisors and administrators about needed resources, policies, and practices. This might include justifying additional time needed to provide clinical services or supporting the hiring of communication specialists. Hopefully, it will advance the day when naïve administrators no longer get away with assuming that just providing a signer or an interpreter constitutes communication inclusion for every deaf consumer. We hope it will also advance the day when clinicians and interpreters doing this work are given the time and resources needed to adapt their interventions to people with complex communication needs.

As the field of Deaf mental health progresses, one clear indicator of our growing sophistication will be the skillfulness with which programs and personnel respond to this communication diversity among deaf consumers. An effective response to this communication diversity is certainly dependent upon a solid communication assessment.

The Structure of the Communication Assessment

The communication assessment used in Alabama and South Carolina is designed to assess an individual's relative strengths and weaknesses across a continuum of communication modalities. It is also designed to identify an individual's most effective communication strategies. It is structured so to permit those with severe language deficits to demonstrate skills. The definition of competence does not necessarily reflect a high degree of fluency or skill. The assessment was originally developed for use with individuals with significant communication dysfluencies and uses stimulus materials designed for easy comprehension. It does not allow for meaningful comparisons between individuals, nor does it compare one individual to a group norm. Attempts to interpret scores in these ways represent invalid applications of this instrument.

Given the significant heterogeneity of the communication skills and experience of the population, collection of background information is invaluable in understanding how an individual communicates. The assessment looks at the whole person and their communication environment. It looks at their language and communication history, their communication strengths and weaknesses, and the degree of fit between these abilities and weaknesses and the communication demands of the environments they navigate. Data is collected in these domains:

- cause and nature of their hearing loss
- family history

- social background
- psychiatric history
- medical history
- educational background
- familiarity with, and use of, interpreters and adaptive equipment
- visual or motor disabilities that impact language
- other medical issues such as dementia, stroke, cerebral palsy, or traumatic brain injury

The language and communication capabilities examined include speech recognition and production, reading comprehension, writing, expressive and receptive fingerspelling, expressive and receptive manual communication skills, and familiarity with assistive communication devices. In addition, the evaluation attempts to describe and understand the specific kinds of sign language dysfluencies that are present.

Family communication background for each family member includes their age and gender, hearing status (hearing, hard-of-hearing, deaf), and method and quality of communication with the client (American Sign Language; contact languages, such as Pidgin Signed English or Manually Coded English systems; cued speech; speech and lipreading; written notes; home signs; gestures; or other communication strategies). Some family members may use more than one system and will have different levels of fluency in different communication modalities. All applicable modes of communication used by each family member with the client should be indicated. This information should be obtained for each member of the client's household now and during childhood.

As part of our evaluation, we also observe, where possible, the person communicating in their natural social contexts such as with family, friends, and associates. We observe how the person communicates with others with whom they do not share a language or easy means of communication. Among other things, these observations help identify how aware the client is of communication limitations within their environment and how flexible they are in addressing those.

Of course, a person's formal school experiences will have a dramatic impact on the development of their language skills. As much as is possible, either from client report or record review, we attempt to identify the complete trajectory of their school experience. Considerations include the setting in which education occurred—mainstream, residential, contained classroom, among others, and determining the fluency of their language models. This information is essential in trying to determine potential language deprivation, as opposed to dysfluency caused by some process. An individual educated for 12 years within a signing residential school for the deaf in a regular curriculum who uses ASL poorly presents different concerns from someone with a similar lack of ASL fluency who has attended mainstreamed classrooms without an interpreter for the same 12 years.

A thorough communication assessment should include determining the person's familiarity with, and ability to use, a variety of assistive listening devices (e.g., videophones, hearing aids, signaling devices, assistive animals). We typically ask about each in the interview portion. We also ask a variety of questions designed to assess their experience and skill working with standard and deaf interpreters. We frequently find, for instance, basic knowledge gaps such as assuming the interpreter is the person generating the message or having no idea how to obtain an interpreter when they need one.

During the administration of the assessment, the assessor(s) shift between communication methods. These transitions (as between speech recognition and speech or writing and fingerspelling) should be explained to the client. Signing clients may express a lack of enthusiasm for the speech-oriented components of the assessment; and oral deaf clients may express reluctance to shift from the speech-oriented subtest to the subtest assessing signing skills. The purpose of the assessment may need to be explained several times, with repeated efforts made to encourage the client to continue with focused effort on all components. If the client's comprehension permits, the assessor may describe the process of the assessment and inform the client that all areas of communication will be included and specifically mention that speech, speech recognition/lipreading, reading, writing, fingerspelling, and signs will each be used. It is expected that individuals will have relative areas of strengths and weaknesses, and some areas of the assessment will be easier and relatively enjoyable while other areas may present some struggle for the client. Nevertheless, the assessor will make every effort to assist the client as much as possible to complete each component. The sole exception is the assistive communication section, which should only be used if the client uses a device or aid. The assessors note any differences between expressive or receptive communication abilities within specific modalities. For example, it's not at all uncommon to find that a person receives information better in one sign modality than another. We have met persons who consistently demonstrate that they depend on ASL to receive information but whose language output is closer to Signed English. This is one of many reasons the individual is not asked directly for their communication preference, although it is often volunteered during the interview. Our experience has been that individuals will often answer what they think the "right" answer should be. Throughout the interview, the assessor should be looking for examples of dysfluency which are tabulated on a separate section. For instance, we regularly look for common kinds of language weaknesses such as (see the complete assessment for additional examples):

- Poor vocabulary
- Isolated signs/phrases
- Inability to sequence events in time
- Spatial disorganization (space, referents, sign inflection, etc.)
- Sign features formed incorrectly

- Missing syntaxial aspects (topic-comment, subjects, pronouns, verbs, etc.)
- Repeated signs
- Excessive use of gesture and pantomime
- Refers to self in third person
- Inappropriate facial and/or emotional expression

If the client demonstrates these characteristics during the interview, it is noted on the assessment form. Additional dysfluencies not identified may be added, at the assessor's discretion, such as signs from a foreign sign language being used with no recognition that they are not ASL or using signs which were created by an unqualified interpreter.

The scores from each of the areas (speech and speech recognition, reading and writing, fingerspelling, and expressive and receptive ASL) are then tallied and a written report is produced. This report describes the results of the assessment, the demographic and historical data collected, and, perhaps most importantly, recommendations for how information is best provided to the client.

Qualifications of Assessors

One indicator that Deaf mental health care is being done badly is when people assume the attitude that any level of signing competence is "good enough." The idea that all one needs to communicate well with deaf people is a little sign language is not far removed from the assumption that all deaf people can lipread. It took several decades for the awareness of ASL as a language to become widely accepted, something that can still be an ongoing issue. It also took decades for the field of interpreting to adopt formal standards, training, and credentialing process. We need to adopt the same high standards for the new field of communication assessments with deaf people. Not just anyone can do it. Just "signing" does not quality you. Just being Deaf does not qualify you. Just being an interpreter, certified or otherwise, does not qualify you. There is a distinct knowledge base and skill set required to do this work; and even if there aren't many people yet who can do it, an untrained, unqualified person is likely to do more damage than no assessment alone.

We have unfortunately seen situations where assessments are being completed by individuals lacking sufficient training and/or oversight. In these cases, the appearance of a valid communication assessment may give legitimacy to conclusions which are not supported by actual evidence.

Like any assessment, the CSA requires that the assessor(s) be trained and qualified to administer the instrument. This is a test of the client's communication skills across the entire continuum of communication methods. Administration by an assessor who possesses less than native-level skills in the areas tested will not only represent an unethical use of this test and do a great injustice to the client but will also result in an invalid assessment.

In order to responsibly administer this instrument, the assessment team should consist of a native sign language user who is deaf and a sign-fluent hearing person. Sign fluency is defined as a person who possess demonstrated fluency in American Sign Language by attaining a Superior Plus on the Sign Language Proficiency Interview, a Certification from the National Registry of Interpreters for the Deaf, certification from the National Association of the Deaf at Level 4 or higher, Level 4.5 or higher on the Educational Interpreter Proficiency Assessment, A Master or Advanced level from the Texas Board for Evaluation of Interpreters, or an equivalent. This includes the ability to fingerspell fluidly and proficiently, at a rate of about four letters per second or slightly slower than ordinary conversation. Receptive fingerspelling skills must be excellent. In addition, the assessor who is hearing (or at least one member of the assessor team) must be able to hear and understand speech at the level of a quiet conversation or have access to this information through alternative strategies. This also includes being able to speak clearly and fluently, without strong accent or speech impairment, or being able to utilize alternative strategies, such as an interpreter. Depending on the communication competencies of the subject, the assessors should also be proficient in manually coded English systems and visual-gestural communication. She or he must also be familiar with the assistive communication device or aid used by the client, if applicable. Each person would assess within their primary language strengths, but also must be willing to consult with the other member of the team when making determinations regarding language competencies.

The assessor(s) should have a minimum of eight hours of training in the assessment which includes an overview of instrument, an overview of types and patterns of dysfluency, and samples of collected information and written assessments. After completing the training, new assessors should have a review by a qualified assessor of five assessments that include videotaped sample of their assessments, the raw data collected, and the final report. We also recommend ongoing training, on an annual basis, consisting of at least eight hours which may include additional training in assessment tools or in language use and dysfluency.

Assessments should be done by at least two individuals working collaboratively whenever possible. The team should include at least one native signer who is Deaf, particularly when a consumer's language is significantly dysfluent.

As with any new process, caution is important. When individuals who are unqualified, or who work without having supervision/consultation, provide assessments, the misused of this tool and process can result in significant harm to the clientele. One of the problems in the emerging Deaf mental health specialty is that we don't yet have systems in place to assess and certify persons capable of doing this work. Our concern about unqualified individuals performing these assessments is based on too much bad experience.

In psychology, there is something called the Dunning-Kruger effect (Kruger & Dunning, 1999), whereby people believe their abilities are much higher than they really are. When this happens, people can fail to recognize their own biases and limitations, at great cost to the people they serve. If this is true for people in general, it is certainly true in our new clinical specialty where standards and formal training and credentialing processes are rare. As the list of qualifications for communication assessors should make clear, this is highly demanding and specialized work, and an assumption of humility about one's own abilities is good clinical practice. Any review of a communication assessment must include a review of the process and assessor who produced the assessment.

Conclusion

The use of a comprehensive communication assessment can provide many benefits to the organization which uses them. It can provide the treating professionals with guidelines for the most effective use of staffing and other resources in performing their work. Not only does this make treatment more effective, it reduces the potential for wasting valuable resources providing treatment in a manner not accessible to the client. It provides clear evidence of compliance with the standards of The Joint Commission, which provides accreditation for healthcare facilities, as well as documenting the individual assessment of needs required by the Americans with Disabilities Act. It also provides consumers with a better understanding of their own language and gives an avenue for them to better advocate for communication to happen in a way that is effective for them. Our consistent experience has been that the time required to do a communication assessment is paid back tenfold by improvements in service effectiveness and efficiency.

One of the hallmarks of the growing sophistication of Deaf mental health is our increasing ability to respond to the enormously wide range of communication abilities and deficits that we see in deaf people. As a field, we are moving beyond descriptions of clients as "signers" or "ASL users" to much more nuanced and objective appreciation of their language abilities. Hopefully, we are leaving behind the days when people's communication abilities were summarized with statements like "low functioning deaf" or "grass roots deaf." Likewise, with staff, we are also moving beyond the idea that "knowledge of sign language" is an adequate statement of the requirements needed to do this work.

Imagine, for a moment, what Deaf mental health would look like if we routinely performed comprehensive communication assessments on both the individuals receiving services and the staff providing services, and we used these assessments to organize our intervention efforts. Imagine how much more effective and individualized our work would be, not to mention how many errors we would avoid. In time, we believe we will get there, and we will look back on the days when people thought that "he uses sign language" was enough information on which to base one's work as unbelievably naïve. We might then ask ourselves, "How could we have been so simple-minded about this complex and challenging work?"

Appendix: Sample Communication Assessment Report

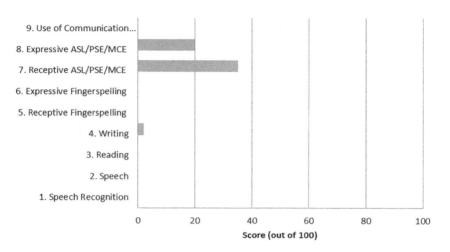

Figure 5.1 Sample communication assessment

Referral Information

Ms. Smith was referred for the Communication Skills Assessment by her attorney, Michelle Jones of the County Public Defender's Office. During an earlier interview with Ms. Jones, the sign language interpreter had raised a concern about her language competence and ability to understand the language needed in a legal situation.

Background Information

Ms. Smith is a 35-year-old white deaf female, who came to the United States as a young adult, with no motor disabilities or vision impairment. She reported no difficulty in seeing or understanding the examiner. Background information was obtained from Ms. Smith and, as will be detailed in the report, she has severe language dysfluency, so some of the collected information is unclear or potentially inaccurate. This was particularly true when trying to get her educational history.

Ms. Smith has a severe congenital sensorineural hearing loss. She reports that she became deaf at six years of age, although she was not sure of the reason. She was unable to provide any information about the etiology of her hearing loss. She is the only deaf person in her family. No one in her family knows sign language and they communicated with her by speech, which she reports she did not understand. She is the second eldest of four children, although her older brother is deceased. Her parents divorced when she was 12 and she remained with her father, who has since passed away.

Ms. Smith attended a small hearing school until age 12 but had no access to the instruction. She could not identify anything she learned during her time in school but did enjoy playing with the other students. She left school when her parents divorced, and her father did not have the funds to pay for continued schooling. In 1995, at age 22, she immigrated to the United States from her birthplace in a foreign country with her new husband and moved to two other locations before moving to her current residence. She lives with her husband, Johnnie, who is also deaf. Her father-in-law lives in the house next door. Her only language instruction has been provided by her husband, who apparently uses an idiosyncratic mixture of her native country's sign language and American Sign Languages.

Ms. Smith had a basic understanding of the role of an interpreter and was aware that she had used one in the past. She did not know how to arrange for an interpreter, stating that her husband had that information. She knew she needed an interpreter for her interactions with her attorney or the court but did not seem to know that it was reasonable to ask for an interpreter for medical appointments or other situations. She does not wear a hearing aid or use an amplified telephone. She states she had a hearing aid for a short time when she was a child but that she was not able to keep the aid. She is unaware of signaling devices and does not have them. She did not know about videophones but her husband has a cellular phone with text capacity. She would like to be able to have a phone but states she does not know how to read or write, which was consistent with this evaluation. She does not have captioning on her television.

Testing Administration

Ms. Smith was interviewed at the County Detention Center in X town. The initial interview and testing instructions were conducted in American Sign Language and gestures. The interview was done by a Qualified Mental Health Interpreter and a Peer Support Specialist and native user of American Sign Language. Ms. Smith appeared to understand the instructions, although multiple repetitions were sometimes necessary. She was unsure of her answers, often stating that she did not know sign language and that she was not able to complete sections which required speech or writing. She was very attentive to the examiner's responses and scoring and was visibly concerned when unable to complete a task. Once Ms. Smith understood the instructions, she was cooperative. Overall, her performance is thought to be a good representation of her communication abilities.

Testing Results

Ms. Smith's profile is consistent with her reports of a complete lack of formal language instruction. She was not exposed to accessible language until age 29, significantly past the critical window for language learning, roughly until age eight. She has had limited opportunity to develop her language skills in either English or American Sign Language. She does not have fluency in any area of communication. She has difficulties across the communication spectrum. For everyday communication and during the test administration, Ms. Smith performed best in American Sign Language with considerable gestures and sign-mime. She has no usable skills in the oral or written communication domains. She does not know fingerspelling as she has no knowledge of the English needed to understand fingerspelling.

Ms. Smith's American Sign Language reflected her limited contact with the Deaf community and ineffective education. She had difficulty with vocabulary and with many of the abstract grammatical structures of ASL. When sentence structure or non-manual markers dictate sentence meaning, she was not able to comprehend the sentence, focusing on the few signs she recognized, rather than understanding the whole sentence.

Similarly, her expressive ASL was lacking in ASL grammar or structure. For example, there was no evidence of eyebrow movement to indicate topic or the use of incorporated numbers in her sentences. She had some nonstandard signs, some signs from her native Sign Language, and at least one which was completely incomprehensible. When understanding ASL, she has difficulty with sentences that use the rhetorical question format or require spatial visualization. She could answer questions about identity and concrete events but could not understand any question which required reference to an abstraction. For example, she could not answer a question such as "What would make you happy?" or "What do you wish for?"

Her signed communication was fraught with dysfluencies, including a lack of vocabulary, incorrect or absent grammar, major gaps in fund of knowledge, and a lack of spatial structure or non-manual markers.

Scoring Grid

The scoring grid provides a quick visual representation of the assessment results. While this individual does not have full fluency in any communication modality, her relative strengths are in expressive and receptive ASL. But, as can be seen, even in those areas, she is experiencing significant challenges.

Conclusions

Ms. Smith is a 35-year-old white female, deaf from birth, of unknown etiology. Her communication strength is in the manual communication arena and this should be used as her primary mode of communication. However, in no communication arena were her communication skills sufficient to understand abstract or complicated information. Her oral and written skills are insufficient for any communication, although someone who knows her very well may be able to identify familiar words from her lip movements. Ms. Smith is aware of her communication limitations and perceives this is the result of intellectual deficiency, although her communication pattern is more consistent with language deprivation. She is likely to nod or respond as she thinks is appropriate without comprehending the interaction.

She is aware of some of the technological devices available such as captioning or text phones. However, her ability to use these devices is impaired by her lack of competence in English.

Ms. Smith would need significant and extensive instruction to improve her knowledge of American Sign Language or to gain a basic understanding of English. It is unlikely that she would ever gain full fluency in any language, but she could improve her language skills. This could include an expansion of vocabulary and an improved ability to identify time sense and perspective (i.e., did the event she is reporting happen in the past or at present and was she an observer or a participant?). The types of errors she made during the interview were fairly consistent and more likely reflect a lack of education and language exposure than a neurological or learning disorder.

As to the specific questions which resulted in Ms. Smith's referral, Ms. Smith's limited communication skills and inability to handle abstract information prevent her from comprehending or expressing the information needed to understand legal proceedings, including her ability to assist her attorney in her defense, understand her legal rights, or make choices about available options. She is able, with an experienced deaf/hearing interpreter team using a combination of Visual-Gestural communication and American Sign Language, to communicate about concrete events and provide information about the events which led to her arrest. However, she lacks sufficient language fluency to understand witnesses in a courtroom during a proceeding, refute testimony or assist her attorney when cross-examining witnesses. She lacks knowledge about the roles of individuals in a courtroom and did not know what a judge did or that there were other attorneys than Ms. Jones.

Outside of legal settings, information provided to Ms. Smith should be provided using examples, demonstration, and visual representation, rather than depending on language to understand needed information. She should also have access to interpreters who are familiar with Visual-Gestural communication, ideally in deaf/hearing teams.

References

Administrative Code Chapter 580-2-9. Community Programs Standards. (2010). Alabama Department of Mental Health.

Andreasen, N. (1986). Scale for the assessment of thought, language and communication. *Schizophrenia Bulletin, 12*(3), 473–482.

Black, P., & Glickman, N. (2005). Language deprivation in the deaf inpatient population. *JADARA*, *39*(1), 1–28.

Black, P., & Glickman, N. (2009). Language and learning challenges in the Deaf psychiatric population. In Neil S. Glickman (Ed.), *Cognitive behavioral therapy for deaf and hearing persons with language and learning challenges*. New York: Routledge.

Crump, C. (2005). *Communication assessment for individuals who are deaf or hard of hearing* (Unpublished instrument).

Crump, C., & Hamerdinger, S. (2017). Understanding etiology of hearing loss as a contributor to language dysfluency and its impact on assessment and treatment of people who are deaf in mental health settings. *Community Mental Health Journal*, *53*(8), 922–928. Springer Publishing. doi:10.1007/s10597-017-0120-0

Glickman, N. (2009). *Cognitive behavioral therapy for deaf and hearing persons with language and learning challenges*. New York, NY: Routledge Publications.

Glickman, N., & Harvey, M. (2008). Psychotherapy with deaf adults: The development of a clinical specialization. *JADARA, 41*(3), 129–186.

Gulati, S. (2014). Language deprivation syndrome. ASL lecture series. www.youtube.com/watch?v=8yy_K6VtHJw

Hall, W. C., Levin, L. L., & Anderson, M. L. (2017). Language deprivation syndrome: A possible neurodevelopmental disorder with sociocultural origins. *Social Psychiatry and Psychiatric Epidemiology*. doi: 10.1007/s00127-017-1351-7

Kruger, J., & Dunning, D. (1999). Unskilled and unaware of it: How difficulties in recognizing one's own incompetence lead to inflated self-assessment. *Journal of Personality and Social Psychology, 77*, 1121–1134.

Law, J., Boyle, J., Harris, F., Harkness, A., & Nye, C. (2000). Prevalence and natural history of primary speech and language delay: Findings from a systematic review of the literature. *International Journal of Language & Communication Disorders*, *35*(2):165–188

Long, G., & Alvares, R. (1995). The development of a communication assessment paradigm for use with traditionally underserved deaf adults. *Journal of the American Deafness and Rehabilitation Association, 29*(1), 1–16

Morgan, G., Herman, R., & Woll, B. (2007). Language impairments in sign language: Breakthroughs and puzzles. *International Journal of Language and Communication Science, 42*(1), 97–105.

Poizner, H., Klima, E. S., & Belllugi, U. (1987). *What the hands reveal about the brain*. Cambridge, MA: The MIT Press.

Pollard, R. (1998a). *Mental health interpreting: A mentored curriculum* [Videotape and users' guide]. Rochester, NY: University of Rochester School of Medicine.

Pollard, R. (1998b). Psychopathology. In M. Marschark and M. D. Clark (Ed.), *Psychological perspectives on deafness* (Vol. 2, pp. 171–197). Mahwah, NJ: Lawrence Erlbaum Associates.

Pollard, R. (2013). *Mental health and deaf individuals: On-line training for clinicians*. Missouri Department of Mental Health. Retrieved from http://dmh.mo.gov/deafsvcs/training.html

South Carolina Department of Mental Health, Services for the Deaf and Hard of Hearing (2014). *Serving clients with Limited English Proficiency*. Columbia, SC.

Thacker, A. (1994). Formal communication disorder: Sign language in deaf people with schizophrenia. *British Journal of Psychiatry, 165*, 818–823.

Thacker, A. (1998). *The manifestation of schizophrenic formal communication disorder in sign language* (Doctoral Dissertation). St. George Hospital Medical School.

Traumatic brain injury: Hope through research. (2002). Office of Communications and Public Liaison. NIH Publication No. 02-2478. National Institute of Neurological Disorders and Stroke, National Institutes of Health. Retrieved from www.ninds.nih.gov/disorders/tbi/detail_tbi.htm

Trumbetta, S. L., Bonvillian, J. D., Siedecki, T. Jr., & Haskins, B. G. (2001). Language-related symptoms in persons with schizophrenia and how deaf persons may manifest these symptoms. *Sign Language Studies, 1*(3), 228–253.

Williams, R. (2003). *Communication skills assessment* (Unpublished instrument).

Williams, R., & Crump, C. (2013). *Communication skills assessment* (Unpublished instrument). Retrieved from www.mentalhealthinterpreting.net/communication-skills-assessment. html

Witter-Merithew, A. (2017). Language analysis team report. Center for Atypical Language Interpreting, Northeastern University. www.northeastern.edu/cali/wp-content/uploads/ 2017/01/CALI-Language-Analysis-Team-Report_PUBLIC.pdf

6

Using Standardized, Receptive ASL Assessments in Deaf Mental Health

JONATHAN HENNER, JEANNE REIS, AND
ROBERT HOFFMEISTER

Introduction

It is difficult for most of us to imagine what life would be like without a continuous stream of language to accompany and narrate the multitude of moment-to-moment experiences. Language is so inherently intertwined with the human experience that Bickerton notes, "Maybe it's the only thing that makes us human" (Bickerton, 2009, p. 3). Even when deprived of language, humans will generate their own language-like systems to communicate with those around them (Goldin-Meadow & Mylander, 1984). Provided a sufficient number of conversation partners, homegrown language-like practices can grow into fully-realized community languages (Senghas, 1995). Our cultural and social identities, and community memberships, are facilitated through language (Hansen & Liu, 1997). Notions of power are enacted within and upon the field of language; we gain power or disempower others by choosing to discourse in one language over another or crafting utterances in particular ways (Cummins, 2000; Dijk, 2001). Speaking a language that is not widely regarded as a "prestige" language (such as African American Vernacular English; AAVE) has powerful implications for education, social ranking, social justice, and legal justice (Cummins, 2000; Rickford & King, 2016).

Given the critical role language holds in building the foundation of our cognitive, mental, and social processes, it is not surprising that language disorders may be an indication of possible psychiatric disorders (Andreasen, 1986; Beitchman, Nair, Clegg, Ferguson, & Patel, 1986). Although there is still much to be learned in this domain, signs of atypical language, such as being limited to two-word sentences, can indicate more serious problems that have the potential to impact every area of an individual's life (Visser-Bochane, Gerrits, Der Schans, Reijneveld, & Luinge, 2017). Language assessments, therefore, are an essential tool for professionals whose daily work revolves around language, such as in the education, medical, and mental health fields.

Language assessments and evaluations are most often administered in print or orally. When either method is used to evaluate deaf people who use a signed language as a primary language, the results are likely to be limited and may even misrepresent the factors being measured. Medical professionals who provide service to signing deaf populations, therefore, must be familiar with the array of signed language assessments currently available and the strengths and limitations of each. The goals of this chapter are twofold: (a) to first examine what sign language features and elements can be measured by signed language assessments, and (b) to provide an overview of the set of receptive ASL assessments currently available to mental health professionals.

Language Assessments in Psychology and Psychiatry

The relationship between language disorders and disability is often fiercely debated (Brown, Aylward, & Keogh, 1996; Sun & Wallach, 2014). Researchers hold varied opinions regarding whether language disorders are disabilities in themselves, and the extent to which such disorders contribute to other forms of disabilities, such as socio-emotional and behavioral disorders. Sun and Wallach (2014) argue that language disorders are a form of learning disability. They point out that diagnoses such as *language delays*, *specific language impairment (SLI)*, and *specific learning disability (SLD)* exist on a spectrum of language disorders. Each diagnosis is based on the results of very different kinds of language assessments. SLDs tend to be diagnosed when children begin struggling to learn how to read and write, whereas SLIs are diagnosed using oral assessments such as the Clinical Evaluation of Language Fundamentals (CELF). The selected language assessment may cause a child with one underlying disability to be diagnosed with several (see Sun & Wallach, 2014). Uncertainty surrounding the diagnosis of language disorders makes intervention and support difficult.

Identifying and delineating language disorders is challenging even for experts. What is not disputed is how serious the impact of impaired language is to the entire human experience, given that language facility is paramount to better emotional functioning, stronger familial and community relationships, increased academic success, and overall quality of life. In what Beitchman et al. (1986) called a "landmark study," Cantwell, Baker, and Mattison (1979) found that in a sample population of 100 language delayed hearing children (mean age = 5;5), over half (*n* = 53) had an existing psychiatric diagnosis. The Cantwell et al. study demonstrates how language can be related to mental well-being.

In a follow-up study, Cantwell and Baker (1980) examined the academic abilities of 106 hearing children (mean age = 8;6) who had a communication disorder diagnosis. Twenty-nine of those children were considered academic failures, defined by failing grades in at least one school subject. Eighty-three percent of the children in the academic failure group had a psychiatric diagnosis, compared to 30% of children in the group who were not considered academic failures. One major finding was that the academic failure group had more struggles with *language* as opposed to *speech*. This study also indirectly highlights that oral language or speech is neither the best nor sole measure of language.

Beitchman et al. (1986) also examined the relationship between speech and language disorder (SLD) diagnosis, and later psychiatric disorder diagnosis. In assessments of a representative sample of English-speaking kindergarteners in Canada, 142 students were identified as having SLD. When compared to a control group without a diagnosed SLD, the 142 children had a significantly increased likelihood of being diagnosed with a psychiatric disorder, including attention deficit and emotional disorders, with girls impacted at a much higher rate than boys. Cantwell et al. (1979), Cantwell and Baker (1980), and Beitchman et al. (1986) were among the earliest researchers to demonstrate the relationship between language, academics, and psychiatric disorder diagnosis.

In a more recent review of the literature on the relationship between language disorders and psychiatric disorder diagnosis, Sundhem and Voeller (2004) write "language disorders and learning disabilities carry a significant risk of comorbid psychiatric disorders that appear in early childhood and can persist into adulthood" (p. 824). They strongly encourage that psychiatrists be trained to recognize learning disabilities (and ergo, language disorders). Thus, language assessment is a crucial part of not only diagnosing possible psychiatric disorders, but also for determining or consulting on intervention options.

Language Disorders in Psychiatry with Deaf People

The key takeaway from the previous section is that language disorders and psychiatric disorders are strongly connected. What, then, is the situation faced by deaf people, who most often are born to hearing parents who do not use sign language (Mitchell & Karchmer, 2005)? Most members of this population have experienced critical developmental years without readily accessible language input—the situation you were asked to imagine at the beginning of this chapter. Those individuals are at great risk for language deprivation related developmental problems (See Chapter 1 by Sanjay Gulati). While many hearing parents now choose assistive hearing technology, such as cochlear implants, for their children with the expectation that doing so will provide access to spoken language, some children do not successfully employ these devices to achieve full language acquisition. Even children whose implants work as intended are shown to have language delays for a variety of reasons (Niparko et al., 2010; See also Chapters 1 and 9 by Gulati and Szarkowski, respectively).

There is evidence that native signers, typically Deaf children who have Deaf parents, may be the only population of deaf people who *do not* suffer from language dysfluency (Braden, 1987). Braden nevertheless acknowledges that even native signers may experience inaccessible and inadequate language environments, such as when teachers and interpreters in signing deaf education programs are not fluent enough signers to provide instruction aligned to school curricula standards. Native signers, therefore, may also be susceptible to language dysfluency if their schooling environments do not support the home language.

Given the high potential for language disorders in deaf people, the need for language assessments specifically designed to evaluate deaf people's facility with a sign language is critical. These tools are essential for professionals who serve deaf populations seeking information on contributing factors, underlying causes, appropriate support services, interventions, and diagnoses related to language disorders. Assessments that consider the principles of signed language are appropriate for evaluating signed language skills, just as assessments that consider the principles of spoken language are appropriate for evaluating spoken language skills. Assessments such as CELF and Peabody Picture Vocabulary Test (PPVT) may, in rare cases, be a sufficient measure of deaf people's spoken language skills, but these tools cannot effectively or reliably evaluate their signed language skills. Simply hiring individuals with generalist skills to translate or interpret oral or written language assessments has also been shown to be an ineffective means of assessing either English or signed language skills (see Haug, 2011; Haug & Mann, 2007; Henner, Hoffmeister, & Reis, 2017 for additional discussion).

Interpreters are not trained in test development. They cannot compose, present, and validate an assessment in another language, especially when they are expected to do this "on the fly." As Hoffmeister and Harvey (1996) explain, many hearing people overestimate their own signing skills, which is a source of significant intercultural conflict and trauma for the signing Deaf community. The body of research in this area suggests that when interpreted or translated by a nonexpert team, an assessment (in the target language) will be a wholly different one than the original assessment (in the source language). In sum, it simply cannot be assumed that an interpreted or translated assessment measures the same constructs as the original. For the most accurate and valid results, it is critical to use sign language assessments developed specifically to assess signed language constructs.

The Current State of Sign Language Assessments

The history of the modern, normed sign language assessment is relatively short. The most successful normed sign language assessment currently in use, The British Sign Language Receptive Skills Test (BSL-RST; Herman, Holmes, & Woll, 1999), is comparatively young. While various sign language assessments were developed and deployed before the BSL-RST was published, and more have been generated in the years since, very few have been normed. Even fewer have been normed using the arguably superior *Rasch* approaches (Magno, 2009).

Rasch approaches are generally considered superior to classical approaches because they: (a) provide item level analysis, by evaluating variability in individual questions and (b) consider how different participant characteristics affect performance on those individual questions. Hearing loss is a low-incidence occurrence; those who are Deaf and signers make up a smaller proportion of the whole, and those who are Deaf and *native* signers are an even smaller proportion (Mitchell, 2006; Mitchell & Karchmer, 2005). Properly norming a signed language assessment, therefore, has been an expensive and time-intensive challenge requiring thoughtful planning and expertise of critical participants—such as Deaf native signers with training in assessment and linguistics.

Over the past 20 years, there have been advancements in computer-based testing (CBT; see Henner et al., 2017) and videoconferencing technology. These advancements have made it possible to norm many new signed language assessments with suitable norming populations. Assessments such as the American Sign Language Proficiency Instrument (ASLPI; Gallaudet, 2014) can be conducted remotely through videoconferencing if proctors and evaluators strictly adhere to established procedures. The American Sign Language Assessment Instrument (ASLAI; Hoffmeister et al., 2013) (which is managed by the Center for Research and Training [CRT] in Framingham, Massachusetts) uses a computer-based interface and real-time interaction with a database to generate rapid results and reporting. The technology of the ASLAI allows for constant adjustments of norms as additional test takers and administrations are added to the database. Some assessments opt for paper-and-video presentation of test items over computer-based approaches, such as the American Sign Language Receptive Skills Test (ASL-RST; Allen & Enns, 2013; Enns & Herman, 2011) adapted from the BSL-RST. These assessments are discussed later in this chapter.

Each proctoring method for signed language assessments—remote, in-person and computer-based—has advantages, disadvantages, and associated costs. The factor of primary importance in all assessments is that each test has been normed on deaf populations, using either classical or item response-based frameworks (e.g., Rasch). Normed tests allow evaluators to predict how well a typical test taker should perform on the whole test or perform on different items in the test given their characteristics (e.g., age, deafness, or sex). It is important to be aware of the norming population as well; one challenge for evaluating adult populations is that most of the modern signed language assessments were normed on children. This is because, in the post-BSL-RST era, researchers were motivated to develop assessments that provided a better understanding of sign language acquisition in deaf children which could lead to the creation of appropriate interventions for those who experience language deprivation. Some signed language assessments did have adult norming populations, including the ASLAI and the American Sign Language Comprehension Task (ASL-CT; Hauser et al., 2016).

Professionals may conduct signed language assessments with deaf people who were not represented in the norming population. Their results will be individual; they must be understood in isolation. Results of non-normed tests must be contextualized for the test taker only, as they cannot demonstrate where the individual's performance stands within a population. Succinctly, the data can only be compared to the same individual's future retakes of the same test. Subsequent results can be used to measure either language improvement or language degradation from the first test instance.

Can Sign Language Assessments Be Used in Psychiatric and Psychological Practice?

Language disorders are found in all populations of children. They are diagnosed among hearing children who have full access to a natural first language and incidental language learning opportunities. Deaf children with hearing parents usually do not have those advantages, putting them at high risk for language disorders and language deprivation syndrome. The significant overlap between language disabilities and mental health problems highlights the complexity of differential diagnostic efforts to tease apart language problems thought to be primarily related to language deprivation, and language problems associated with psychiatric or neurological conditions like schizophrenia or aphasia.

Psychologists and other proctors of mental health assessments have recognized the unique challenges of using assessments with language-deprived deaf people. Glickman (2007) writes that many clinicians may misdiagnose deaf people with psychiatric disorders because their client's spoken or signed language dysfluency resembles that found in disorders such as schizophrenia. As an ethical professional community, we must therefore continue to develop better signed language assessments and fully understand the limitations of existing tools.

What Kind of Information Can Be Provided by Sign Language Assessments?

While the current crop of sign language assessments are technological marvels and phenomenally useful tools, the challenges of developing and norming them relative to spoken and written language assessments are ubiquitous. Morere (2013) points out that signed language assessments are necessarily limited by the existing language variability in deaf populations where very few acquire signed language as a first language. Many deaf people learn to sign at ages where maturational constraints make it challenging to achieve even near-native fluency in the language (see Henner, Caldwell-Harris, Novogrodsky, & Hoffmeister, 2016; Novogrodsky, Henner, Caldwell-Harris, & Hoffmeister, 2017). Establishing norming standards based on native signers means that results of non-native signers will naturally show deficits due to the range of input. Still, native signers provide the clearest language acquisition patterns needed to identify the ages where input can most impact later display of language deprivation.

Morere's concerns about the limited variability in the norming population of signed language assessments are shared by many other researchers (Beal-Alvarez, 2016; Mann, Roy, & Marshall, 2013). Some assessments, like the ASLAI, provide additional norms for non-native signers that do not directly compare them to native signers. Nevertheless, the items were developed and standardized on native signing adults, so this may not fully address Morere's (2013) concerns about variability in non-native signers. There also exist dialectical variations in many signed languages, including ASL. For example, Black ASL is an accepted dialectical variation of ASL with unique lexical and syntactic properties (McCaskill, Lucas, Bayley, & Hill, 2011). As of this writing, no signed language assessments exist which considers a deaf person's possible use of Black ASL. Additionally, Mann et al. recognizes that many assessments do not provide norms for deaf children who may have disabilities, and other subgroups of deaf children.

In spite of the many difficulties, signed language assessments—even at their current state of development—are vital tools for diagnosticians. By selecting an appropriate assessment, a diagnostician will be able to collect critical information about a deaf person's signed language phonological awareness, understanding of morphology, syntax, lexical abilities, and overall language proficiency. The following sections describe each feature listed earlier and provide suggestions for which assessments can be used to gather data related to specific features.

Within this chapter, the assessments discussed will be measures of receptive language rather than expressive ones. At the time of this writing, the available receptive assessments will support a diagnosis of a language disorder and are the best and most practical tools for developing a snapshot of a person's language abilities. Their results cannot, however, independently diagnose any kind of psychiatric disorder and should not be used to do so. We do not recommend expressive assessments because they introduce a host of issues that have been discussed elsewhere (Bochner et al., 2015; Henner et al., 2017). Expressive signed language test items are likely to be scored and evaluated by non-native signers who do not have appropriate expertise and/or training, which can invalidate the results of the assessments (Morford, Grieve-Smith, MacFarlane, Staley, & Waters, 2008; Novogrodsky et al., 2017). In language assessment, native-language judgments are critical to accurate scoring of phonological, morphological, and grammatical elements. Subjectivity is another factor that impacts scoring. As Schaefer (2008) explains, rating production data, even with comprehensive rubrics, is a complicated affair. Medical professionals who use production assessments may inadvertently provide different scores not because of signing abilities, but because of the race and/or gender of the participant. In sum, although production data generally provides good insights into a person's mind and psychological functioning, without methods and assessments that are objective and based on native proficiency, practitioners cannot be assured that fluency and bias do not skew their understanding of test takers' expressive language.

Practitioners seeking to assess signed language abilities should therefore use those available receptive instruments that meet criteria noted in this chapter, as they are much less susceptible to rater fluency and biases. Biases are built into assessments by test developers, which means that variability can be predicted and controlled using norming processes. If practitioners choose to use expressive assessments, they must first understand their own personal limitations in assessing signed languages—a tremendous challenge—as language ideologies are often unconscious and difficult to self-evaluate, especially for those without extensive linguistics training. Practitioners must also evaluate the limitations of current expressive assessments, which is difficult for those who are unfamiliar with psychometrics and assessment.

How do Receptive ASL Assessments Measure ASL Abilities?

Receptive ASL assessments generally measure linguistic abilities using a stimulus-response structure. For example, the general format of the ASLAI follows a consistent theme: a stimulus video is presented followed by four video responses. A multiple-choice structure allows both prompts (questions) and response choices to be offered in ASL, paralleling typical printed test formats in other languages. While the interfaces for assessments noted as follows differ, the user experience for participants does not change greatly.

Typically, a prompt is presented, followed by several response choices. Prompts and responses can be either dynamic events (video clips) or a still frames (pictures). Response choices include one correct answer and a controlled set of distractors. Test developers will usually design distractor choices that provide additional information about the test takers' current knowledge and abilities. For example, an assessment designed to evaluate knowledge of ASL vocabulary may include one distractor answer choice that is phonologically similar to the correct answer and one that is semantically similar to the correct answer.

In the following section, we briefly discuss the parts of ASL that can be assessed by current receptive ASL assessments. Much of the linguistic information has been simplified to make it more accessible to a broader audience. We recommend that practitioners interested in conducting language assessments with deaf clients have—or gain—a more formal and technical understanding of linguistics, particularly in the linguistics of signed languages.

Phonology

Phonology can be examined through receptive assessments. When evaluators discuss production errors in signers, they are most often referring to phonology. Phonemes in all languages, including signed languages, refer to the smallest meaningful units of that language (Van der Hulst & Mills, 1996). Signed languages are typically described as having five parameters, that is, five differential components that can be combined to produce words (somewhat equivalent to the way words are built in spoken languages). They are

(a) handshape/palm orientation,[1] (b) movement, (c) location, and (d) non-manual markers. The meaning of a word in a signed language can be altered by changing a phonological component, such as *handshape;* a similar process in spoken language occurs when the phoneme 's' is added to indicate plural in English.

Handshape/Palm Orientation

Handshape refers to the articulation of the hands and the joints of the fingers. It can be classified according to ease of articulation (Coppola & Brentari, 2014). Various researchers posit that ease of articulation drives much of production choice in signed languages and the age at which the handshapes are acquired (Battison, 1978; Siedlecki & Bonvillian, 1997). Easier-to-produce handshapes are acquired earlier and appear more often in ASL words. Deaf people who use home sign[2] tend to use less complex handshapes. More complex handshapes are noted as a defining feature of formal signed languages (Coppola & Brentari, 2014). Approximately 40 handshapes are used in ASL (McQuarrie, Abbott, & Spady, 2012).

Palm orientation refers to the direction of the palm in the articulatory process (e.g., for the right hand, palm facing left, down, or up). It is often considered a subset of handshape, although it can be shown as a distinct phonological element via testing of minimal pairs, a linguistic method of distinguishing distinct phonological units. In a minimal pair test, if changing a single phoneme creates a new meaning, then the phoneme is considered distinct (e.g., the difference between the C and the B in the English words: *cat* and *bat*).

Movement

Van der Hulst and Mills (1996) describe movement as a "dynamic" notion, with "movements having starting and ending points" (p. 11). The physical structure of a movement with beginning and end points creates a path. Movement within handshapes supports meaning. For example, the simple twisting movement in the sign "BLUE" differs from the arc movement that results in "DARK-BLUE" (Sandler & Lillo-Martin, 2006).

Location

Location can be roughly defined as the place where articulation of a sign begins (Battison, 1978). Battison identified four major locations for signed languages: (a) the head, (b) the trunk, (c) the arm, and (d) the hand. Location currently has expanded to additional components providing more detailed spatial descriptors, such as: ipsilateral, contralateral, proximal, distal, and contact area on the body.

Non-Manual Markers

Non-manual markers, often referred to as super-articulatory arrays, are movements of the face and body which can create or modify meaning in signed language production. Non-manuals are often used to differentiate different types of syntactic categories, including but not limited to: (a) yes/no questions, (b) topicalization, (c) negation, (d) relative clauses, (e) agreement, and (f) conditionals.

Morphology

Inflectional

Morphemes are generally defined as the units of meaning in languages. The study of morphology includes *inflectional* and *derivational* morphology.

Inflectional morphology is the study of morpheme affixes that give words a specific grammatical property or type of meaning. Types of grammatical properties include: (a) aspect, (b) tense, (c) case, (d) voice, (e) number, (f) gender, (g) mood, or (h) agreement. Current signed language assessments tend to focus on aspect, case, and number, which are discussed as follows.

Aspect

Inflection for aspect describes how a verbs' meaning is extended over time. Tense inflection is different, because tense puts an action in a specific timeline (e.g., yesterday/past) (Baker, van den Bogaerde, Pfau, & Schermer, 2016). In signed languages, aspectual inflection tends to be produced by moving a verb in a series of arcs or lines and by extending or shortening the time it takes to complete the movement through the arc or line.

Agreement

In signed languages, agreement presents a complicated picture (Lillo-Martin & Meier, 2011). For this chapter, it is assumed that in ASL, case inflects for first person and third person (everyone else) (Meier, 2002). To "agree," signers typically begin the verb at the point in space representing the agent (sentence subject) and move their hand (path) to the point in space representing the patient (sentence object). Certain verbs, called "backward" verbs (such as INVITE), start at the linguistic patient, or object, and move to the agent, or subject (Meir, 1998). Some signed languages allow for auxiliary agreement, whereby agreement morphology is not embedded in the verb stem (Pfau & Steinbach, 2008; Steinbach, 2011). Rather, a *trace* (pointing moves from X to Y space) done with an index finger establishes agreement between agent/subject and patient/object. Auxiliary agreement is not a feature in ASL; however, practitioners may encounter it with patients who learned the signed languages of other countries. Agreement verbs can also include reciprocal meanings where each hand moves from left to right and right to left simultaneously (e.g., THEY GIVE EACH OTHER/"EXCHANGE"). Agreement verbs require a path of movement (Gee & Kegl, 1982).

Number

Number inflections describe plurality (e.g., is there a single item, several, exactly five?). Signed languages may indicate number through repetition of movement in stamps, or arcs (Hoffmeister, 1978, 1980), or by adding lexical number signs. A stamp usually denotes a specific count of items, whereas an arc describes an unspecified number of items (for example, a signer articulates the sign CHAIR with an arcing movement to indicate that there are many chairs, but the exact number is unknown).

Inflectional morphology does not change grammatical category. For example, an inflectional affix cannot change a noun into a verb. This differs from derivational morphology, which does change the grammatical class of a word.

Derivational Morphology

When an affix turns a noun into a verb, this is a derivational process at work. Compounding, or forming new words by combining two different words, can be considered a form of derivational morphology as well. One of the first kinds of derivational morphology taught in ASL classes is agentive morphology (+ PERSON). Examples of agentive morphology are RUN + PERSON (runner) or PSYCH + PERSON (psychologist). Other types of derivational morphology in ASL are deriving nouns from verbs (FOOD, EATING) and adjectival derivations (BLUE, DARK-BLUE).

Classifiers

Classifiers, which include "depiction verbs," are an integral part of many languages, including signed languages. Classifiers, in linguistics, are morphemes that vary to align with the noun or verb they are associated with (see Allan, 1977 for a discussion on classifier morphemes). They are considered a type of complex predicate, which are polymorphemic (Supalla, 1986), or polycomponential (Morgan & Woll, 2007). In other words, classifiers in signed languages combine with other morphemes to describe motion events, or how objects are arranged in space relative to each other. Because classifiers play a large role in signed languages, the literature on the ontology and acquisition of classifiers is rich (see Emmorey, 2003 for examples). Here we focus only on the overarching categories that contain classifiers: *classifier handshapes, verbs of location,* and *verbs of motion.*

Classifier Handshapes

Classifier handshapes are specific handshapes which have independent morphological meaning (e.g., CL:3, representing a vehicle) but may still have differential meanings in context (e.g. CL:1 representing a person). Supalla (1986) describes a system that includes, but is not limited to, handling classifiers, size and shape classifiers, body classifiers, and body part classifiers.

Verbs of Location

Verbs of location are a way to describe the arrangement of objects in space and their position relative to each other (Supalla, 1986). These verbs have no path morphemes. Classifiers representing objects are inserted into verbs of location to generate sentences specifying the location of an object. Verbs of location may demonstrate plurality via stamping (count numbers) or arcs/lines (indefinite amount, e.g., a number of cars stuck in traffic).

Verbs of Motion

Classifiers representing objects are embedded into verbs of motion to describe *action* or *events*. They generally have path and direction, as well as manner (among other types of verb inflections). The basic structure of a verb of motion is a Path from X (indicating agent/subject) to Y (indicating patient/object) where the classifier handshape is inserted into the initial loci of the path and continues along the path to the loci of the endpoint, for example, THE CAT BOUNDS AWAY (Gee & Kegl, 1982).

Syntax

Assessing signed language syntax is probably among the more difficult feats that non-native signing evaluators are asked to do using checklists and/or analyzing expressive signing. Grammatical judgment abilities for signed languages are not easily acquired in late-, first-, and second-language learners (Boudreault & Mayberry, 2006; Henner et al., 2016; Novogrodsky et al., 2017). Luckily, the majority of available receptive ASL language assessments have a syntax component to them. Syntax is a vital part of language; practitioners should consider having a syntax component to all of their signed language assessments. Here we explore the following syntactic features: word order (topic comment), negation, conditionals, wh-q, rhetorical questions, complement structure, and relative clauses.

Word Order

Word order in ASL is more flexible than in spoken English (Chen Pichler, 2010); this is common in languages that have rich morphology. Lillo-Martin points out that ASL is allowed flexibility because it is a "topic-oriented" language, or rather a "discourse-oriented" language. Discourse-oriented languages have syntactic and morphological elements that allow speakers to understand each other through elements like "topic-chaining" where a topic is assumed to be stable throughout a conversation unless otherwise changed.

A well-known aspect of word order in ASL is "topicalization," or "object fronting." In topicalization, the object is fronted in the sentence "STORE, I GO." Trained ASL instructors are familiar with the tendency for second language learners to generalize the Object-Subject-Verb structure of topicalization. While Object-Subject-Verb seems to be common in ASL, the underlying structure (what happens in the brain) is Subject-Verb-Object, much like English (Chen Pichler, 2010). Therefore, depending on context, I GO-to STORE is just as appropriate as STORE, I GO.

Negation

Understanding negation involves understanding the truth value of a sentence. Negation simply turns a true statement into a false one. For example, the truth of SHOES, I BOUGHT is negated by SHOES, I-did NOT BUY. In ASL, negation can be done both lexically (e.g., NOT) and through non-manual markers (e.g., HEAD-SHAKE).

Conditionals

Conditionals, like negation, are a way of modifying the truth value of a sentence. Conditionals are usually composed of two components, with one component's truth value depending on the other. For example, IF HAVE MONEY, (move head/pause) BUY SHOE. The second clause, BUY SHOE, is only true if HAVE MONEY is also true. Otherwise it is false. Conditionals, in ASL, can be expressed both lexically (IF) or non-manually through raised eyebrows.

Wh-Q

Wh-Q are syntactical structures that deals with sentences containing who, what, where, why, when, and sometimes how. Wh-Q structures are different in ASL than in spoken languages; however, this is beyond the scope of this chapter (Lillo-Martin, 2000). Nevertheless, Wh-Q tends to be placed at the end of the sentence in ASL, but it could also appear in the beginning in select cases. Wh-Q in ASL can be done both lexically and non-manually.

Rhetorical Questions

Rhetorical questions, or Rh-Q, is a structure in which, in English, the speaker asks a question for which no answer is expected. Rh-Q in ASL is a common syntactical structure and the signer is expected to answer their own question. For example, CHOCOLATE DARK BEST, WHY? BECAUSE TASTE BEST. Practitioners should be aware of the common use of Rh-Q structures and learn to recognize it in ASL production.

Complement

Complement structures are a special kind of sentence that has two clauses; one clause is embedded in the other. The embedded clause can also be an argument for the verb in the main clause (Baker et al., 2016). In English sentences, *that* is usually an indication of a complement clause ("She thinks that the dark chocolate is delicious"). Complements are also a vital syntactic structure in ASL. Complement structures in ASL can be used with verbs of communication (X said "Y"), verbs of desire (X wants "Y"), and cognitive verbs (X knows "Y") where Y equals an embedded sentence (Schick, deVilliers, deVilliers, & Hoffmeister, 2007).

Role Shift is a way of using spatial elements to differentiate or focus on constituents, or clauses, within a sentence. It is a discourse element which separates different speakers or topics. Role shift is produced by either tilting shoulders or heads towards left or right spaces relative to the signer to mark separate discourse elements. Role shift is also a vital way of indicating complement structures.

Relative Clauses

Relative clauses are a syntactical structure wherein an embedded clause serves to provide additional information about arguments. For example, MAN, GRAY BEARD, BLUE PANTS, HE GIVE BOOK TO HER. Relative clauses are differentiated through non-manual realization in ASL (Stokoe, 1980).

Vocabulary

Because vocabulary knowledge is widely recognized as both critical and foundational, vocabulary tasks in signed languages are among the more prevalent, accessible, and familiar, particularly for educators of the deaf. Better vocabulary knowledge usually indicates superior academic reading performance (Qian, 1999, 2002). Students who have higher ASL vocabulary knowledge also tend to perform better on tests of English proficiency (Novogrodsky, Caldwell-Harris, Fish, & Hoffmeister, 2014). More generally, people with better vocabulary are believed to be more intelligent than those with more limited vocabulary (Anderson & Freebody, 1985). Moreover, having a limited vocabulary or using familiar vocabulary incorrectly is one of the easiest-to-recognize indicators that an individual has some form of language disorder (Glickman, 2007; Hall, Levin, & Anderson 2017).

Assessing discrete vocabulary in signed languages can be difficult because there is some disagreement on what constitutes a sign/word (Johnston & Schembri, 1999). The fundamental issue is examining the relationship between classifier[3] signs and lexical items. Moreover, some classifier signs "freeze" into words and then stand as single concept representations, although they may still sometimes revert back to classifier-type use (Supalla, 1986). This is a problem also confronted by other languages that rely on complex predicates, such as Turkish or Japanese (Matsumoto, 1996). Johnston and Schembri (1999) describe a hierarchy in signed languages that moves from monomorphemic signs to signs and finally to gestures; the full scale of this discussion, however, is beyond the scope of the chapter. Practitioners will likely need to consider the difference between lexical signs and classifier signs for evaluation purposes. The ASL-CT, for example, claims that each of its items employs classifiers signs (Hauser et al., 2016). Therefore, the extent to which it assesses *vocabulary* may be muddled.

What Are Some of the Available Receptive Sign Language Assessments?

Practitioners interested in acquiring receptive sign language assessments can find additional information at www.signlang-assessment.info. Here, we have created a table (Table 6.1) that lists ASL receptive assessments that practitioners may wish to use in their practice:

Table 6.1 Receptive American Sign Language tests

Assessment Name	Authors	Norming Range	Types of ASL Assessed

American Sign Language Assessment Instrument (ASLAI)	Hoffmeister et al. (2013)	3;6–18;5 (Adult)	• Analogical reasoning
			• Classifiers
			  • Handshapes
			  • Verbs of motion
			  • Verbs of location
			• Literacy
			• Syntax
			  • Agreement
			  • Conditionals
			  • Complement structure
			  • Pronominalization
			  • Negation
			  • Rhetorical questions
			  • Relative clauses
			  • Simple sentences
			  • Wh questions

			• Vocabulary
			  • Antonyms
			  • Synonyms
			  • Definitions
			  • Rare

American Sign Language Receptive Skills Test (ASL-RST)	Enns and Herman (2011)	3;0–13;0	• Classifiers
			  • Handshapes
			    • Size and shape specifiers
			    • Handling
			  • Verbs of location
			    Number/Distribution
			    Spatial verbs
			  • Size and shape specifiers
			• Morpho-syntax
			  • Conditionals
			  • Negation
			  • Noun/Verb distinction
			  • Role-shift

American Sign Language Phonological Awareness Test (ASL-PA)	McQuarrie et al. (2012)	4;0–7;0	• Phonology
			  • Handshape
			  • Location
			  • Movement

American Sign Language Comprehension Test (ASL-CT)	Hauser et al. (2016)	Adults	• Classifiers
			  • Handshape
			  • Verbs of motion
			  • Verbs of location
			• Morpho-Syntax
			  • List Buoys
			  • Role shift

American Sign Language Discrimination Test (ASL-DT)	Bochner et al. (2015)	Adults	• Phonology
			  • Handshape/palm orientation
			  • Movement
			  • Location
			  • Non-manual markers

What Do Scoring Reports Look Like?

Depending on method of administration, summaries and analysis of scores may be provided to detail the results of an ASL language assessment. For the ASLAI, individual score reports are provided as part of a package of services through the Center for Research and Training. Score reports from the ASLAI are designed to help stakeholders easily understand the results of the assessment. The kind of information provided categorizes scores (e.g., Vocabulary or Grammar). The CRT/ASLAI report provides a normed participant score, rather than raw scores. Normed scores compare test takers' performances to their similar aged peers, with a possible range of Significantly Below Average (SBA) to Significantly Above Average (SAA). The ASLAI score report further details results by participant background criteria. For example, if participants have hearing parents, their sub-scores are compared to others with hearing parents, rather than to deaf parents.

Not all receptive assessments require scores be sent through an assessment center. The ASL-RST, for example, provides a score report that practitioners may tabulate themselves.

Conclusion

A variety of receptive signed language assessments are available for profession-als who need to determine if a deaf person with whom they are working has a delay or deficiency in specified sign language skills. Receptive signed language tests are recommended over expressive, production tests because they are less subject to examiner bias, more research-based, and technically feasible at this time. Caveats to using sign language assessments have been noted previously.

Many signed language assessments are limited in the kind of signed lan-guage data they can provide. For example, signed language assessments typi-cally do not provide accurate information on the signed language abilities of signers who may use a minority dialect, such as Black ASL. Additionally, there are few assessments that have norming data for subpopulations of the deaf, such as deaf persons with disabilities or within racial/ethnic groups. As noted, most do not have normative data for adult deaf persons.

Practitioners must also be careful that they are not using signed language assessments to diagnose psychiatric disorders, as many symptoms of psychi-atric disorders overlap with language deprivation disorders. Despite the lim-itations, the data provided by these signed language assessments provide an objective description of a person's receptive ASL abilities as compared with peers, which can inform assessment, diagnosis, interpreting, and interven-tion. They certainly enable one to say more objectively that a deaf person is not a fluent or native sign language user, and they enable examiners to be more precise about the kinds of ASL structures a person understands. They can also be used as measures of language development or progress.

The inclusion of objective sign language measures advances Deaf mental health practice well beyond the superficial observation that the person "uses sign language." Indeed, as several writers in this book comment, a marker of sophisticated work in Deaf mental health may be the extent to which formal language assessment has been done and incorporated into larger assessment, diagnosis, and intervention plans. In spite of the effectiveness of current as-sessments, future assessment development must focus on the variety of signed language use in deaf populations and increase norming standards so that as-sessments are valid for use with diverse deaf people.

The Amazing Deaf Academy of Learning
ID: 099999   DOB: 2002-03-12

Raymond, Bobby

HP Hearing Parents   **15** 14 years, 12 months old

ASLAI
Student Score Report
2016–2017
2017-03-02

Score Summary

Vocabulary									
SVOC Vocabulary: Simple		VOCDA2 Vocabulary: Difficult		VST2 Vocabulary in Sentence		SYN4 Synonym		ANT4 Antonym	
HP	All	HP	All	HP	All	HP	All	HP	All
A	BA	A	BA	A	A	AA	A	AA	A

Grammar and Comprehension									
STXS Syntax: Simple		STXD Syntax: Difficult		CMP4 Comprehension		ANG3 Analogies		ROPLAB Real Objects and Plurals	
HP	All	HP	All	HP	All	HP	All	HP	All
SAA	AA	BA	BA	A	BA	A	A	A	BA

Understanding Your Scores

All scores shown are relative to other students who tested in the same age group. Note that we do not display raw numerical scores because these scores are not weighted and are subject to misinterpretation. The two scores shown for each task represent a) your score relative to the subset of students in your age group who also have **Hearing Parents**, and b) your score relative to all students in your age group.

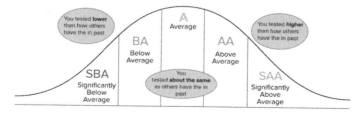

You tested **lower** than how others have the in past

A Average

You tested **higher** than how others have the in past

BA Below Average

AA Above Average

SBA Significantly Below Average

You tested **about the same** as others have the in past

SAA Significantly Above Average

Subconstruct Scores

Syntax: Simple STXS									
STXS Overall		VOM Verbs of Motion		VOL Verbs of Location		PLU Plurals		NEG Negation	
HP	All	HP	All	HP	All	HP	All	HP	All
SAA	AA	AA	A	SAA	SAA	A	BA	A	BA
PRO Pronominalization									
HP	All	HP	All	HP	All	HP	All	HP	All
SAA	SAA	--	--	--	--	--	--	--	--

Syntax: Difficult STXD									
STXD Overall		PLA Plain		TC Topic Comment		WH-Q Wh-Q		NEG Negation	
HP	All	HP	All	HP	All	HP	All	HP	All
BA	BA	SBA	SBA	BA	BA	BA	BA	SAA	SAA
ARG Agreement		COND Conditional		RHQ Rhetorical		RELC Relative Clause		COMP Complement	
HP	All	HP	All	HP	All	HP	All	HP	All
BA	SBA	SBA	SBA	SBA	SBA	AA	A	SAA	A

Comprehension CMP4									
CMP4 Overall		EXP Expository		FIC Fiction		LIT Literal		INF Inferential	
HP	All	HP	All	HP	All	HP	All	HP	All
A	BA	BA	SBA	A	BA	SBA	SBA	SAA	AA

Analogies ANG3									
ANG3 Overall		CAUS Causality		PUR Purpose		NVP Noun-Verb Pairs		WP Whole-Part	
HP	All	HP	All	HP	All	HP	All	HP	All
A	A	BA	BA	SAA	SAA	SAA	AA	SAA	AA
PHO Phonology		ANT Antonym							
HP	All	HP	All	HP	All	HP	All	HP	All
A	A	SBA	SBA	--	--	--	--	--	--

Real Objects and Plurals ROPLAB									
ROPLAB Overall		SP/ALT Spatial:Alternating		SP/ROW Spatial:Rows		BPCL Body Part Classifiers		MRN Mass/Random Nouns	
HP	All	HP	All	HP	All	HP	All	HP	All
A	BA	SAA	SAA	SAA	SAA	SAA	SAA	SAA	SAA

Notes

1 Here we combine handshape and palm orientation into a single component.
2 Home sign is naturally occurring gestures that have become standardized/productive over time. Typically, home sign is developed within homes of Deaf children where hearing parents do not use a Signed Language but allow gestural production to occur. See Goldin Meadow, and Coppola for more details.
3 Here we use classifiers to also mean depiction. We follow that throughout this chapter.

References

Allan, K. (1977). Classifiers. *Language, 53*(2), 285. doi:10.2307/413103
Allen, T. E., & Enns, C. (2013). A psychometric study of the ASL Receptive Skills Test when administered to deaf 3-, 4-, and 5-year-old children. *Sign Language Studies, 14*(1), 58–79. doi:10.1353/sls.2013.0027
Anderson, R. C., & Freebody, P. (1985). Vocabulary knowledge. In H. Singer & R. B. Ruddell (Eds.), *Theoretical models and the processes of reading* (pp. 343–371). Newark, DE: International Reading Association.
Baker, A., van den Bogaerde, B., Pfau, R., & Schermer, T. (2016). *The linguistics of sign languages: An introduction.* John Benjamins Publishing Company. Retrieved from https://market.android.com/details?id=book-IECEDAAAQBAJ
Battison, R. (1978). *Lexical borrwing in American Sign Language.* Silver Spring, MD: Linstok Press.
Beal-Alvarez, J. S. (2016). Longitudinal receptive American Sign Language skills across a diverse deaf student body. *Journal of Deaf Studies and Deaf Education, 21*(2), 200–212. doi.org/10.1093/deafed/enw002
Beitchman, J. H., Nair, R., Clegg, M., Ferguson, B., & Patel, P. G. (1986). Prevalence of psychiatric disorders in children with speech and language disorders. *Journal of the American Academy of Child Psychiatry, 25*(4), 528–535. doi:10.1016/S0002-7138(10)60013-1
Bickerton, D. (2009). *Adam's tongue: How humans made language, how language made humans.* Farrar, Straus and Giroux. Retrieved from https://market.android.com/details?id=book-s7UqXppMR8QC
Bochner, J. H., Samar, V. J., Hauser, P. C., Garrison, W. M., Searls, J. M., & Sanders, C. A. (2015). Validity of the American Sign Language discrimination test. *Language Testing, 33*(4), 473–495. doi:10.1177/0265532215590849
Boudreault, P., & Mayberry, R. I. (2006). Grammatical processing in American Sign Language: Age of first-language acquisition effects in relation to syntactic structure. *Language and Cognitive Processes, 21*(5), 608–635. doi:10.1080/01690960500139363
Braden, J. P. (1987). An explanation of the superior performance IQs of deaf children of deaf parents. *American Annals of the Deaf, 132*(4), 263–266. doi:10.1353/aad.2012.0723
Brown, F. R., III, Aylward, E. H., & Keogh, B. K. (1996). *Diagnosis and management of learning disabilities: An interdisciplinary/lifespan approach* (3rd ed.). San Diego, CA: Singular Publishing Group.
Cantwell, D. P., & Baker, L. (1980). Academic failures in children with communication disorders. *Journal of the American Academy of Child Psychiatry, 19*(4), 579–591. doi:10.1016/S0002-7138(09)60963-8
Cantwell, D. P., Baker, L., & Mattison, R. E. (1979). The prevalence of psychiatric disorder in children with speech and language disorder. An epidemiologic study. *Journal of the American Academy of Child Psychiatry, 18*(3), 450–461. doi:10.1097/00004583-197922000-00004
Chen Pichler, D. (2010). Using early ASL word order to shed light on word order variability in sign language. In M. Anderson, K. Bentzen, & M. Westergaard (Eds.), *Variation in the input, studies in theoretical psycholinguistics* (Vol. 39, pp. 157–177). New York, NY: Springer. doi:10.1007/978-90-481-9207-6

Coppola, M., & Brentari, D. (2014). From iconic handshapes to grammatical contrasts: Longitudinal evidence from a child homesigner. *Frontiers in Psychology, 5,* 1–23. doi:10.3389/fpsyg.2014.00830

Cummins, J. (2000). *Language, power and pedgogy: Bilingual children in the crossfire.* Clevedon, UK: Multilingual Matters.

Dijk, T. van. (2001). Critical discourse analysis. In D. Schiffrin, D. Tannen, & H. Hamilton (Eds.), *The handbook of discourse analysis* (pp. 352–371). Malden, MA: Blackwell Publishers, Ltd.

Emmorey, K. (2003). *Perspectives on classifier constructions in sign languages.* Psychology Press. Retrieved from https://market.android.com/details?id=book-9cB5AgAAQBAJ

Enns, C. J., & Herman, R. C. (2011). Adapting the assessing British Sign Language development: Receptive skills test into American Sign Language. *Journal of Deaf Studies and Deaf Education, 16,* 362–374. doi:10.1093/deafed/enr004

Gallaudet. (2014). American Sign Language Proficiency Interview (ASLPI). Retrieved July 6, 2017, from www.gallaudet.edu/asl-diagnostic-and-evaluation-services/aslpi

Gee, J., & Kegl, J. (1982). Semantic perspicuity and the locative hypothesis: Implications for acquisition, *The Journal of Education, 164*(2), 185–209.

Glickman, N. (2007). Do you hear voices? Problems in assessment of mental status in deaf persons with severe language deprivation. *Journal of Deaf Studies and Deaf Education, 12*(2), 127–147. doi:10.1093/deafed/enm001

Goldin-Meadow, S., & Mylander, C. (1984). Gestural communication in deaf children: The effects and noneffects of parental input on early language development. *Monographs of the Society for Research in Child Development, 49,* 1–151. Retrieved from http://psycnet.apa.org/psycinfo/1985-28434-001

Hall, W. C., Levin, L. L., & Anderson, M. L. (2017). Language deprivation syndrome: A possible neurodevelopmental disorder with sociocultural origins. *Social Psychiatry and Psychiatric Epidemiology,* 1–16. doi:10.1007/s00127-017-1351-7

Hansen, J. G., & Liu, J. (1997). Social identity and language: Theoretical and methodological issues. *TESOL Quarterly, 31,* 567–576. doi:10.2307/3587839.

Haug, T. (2011). Methodological and theoretical issues in the adaptation of sign language tests: An example from the adaptation of a test to German Sign Language. *Language Testing, 29*(2), 181–201. doi:10.1177/0265532211421509

Haug, T., & Mann, W. (2007). Adapting tests of sign language assessment for other sign languages – A review of linguistic, cultural, and psychometric problems. *Journal of Deaf Studies and Deaf Education, 13*(1). doi:10.1093/deafed/enm027

Hauser, P. C., Paludneviciene, R., Riddle, W., Kurz, K. B., Emmorey, K., & Contreras, J. (2016). American Sign Language Comprehension Test: A tool for sign language researchers. *Journal of Deaf Studies and Deaf Education, 21*(1), 64–69. doi:10.1093/deafed/env051

Hauser, P. C., Paludneviciene, R., Supalla, T., & Bavelier, D. (2008). American Sign Language – Sentence reproduction test: Development & implications. In R. M. de Quadros (Ed.), *Sign languages: Spinning and unraveling the past, present and future. TISLR9, forty five papers and three posters from the 9th. Theoretical Issues in Sign Language Research Conference,* (pp. 155–167). Florianopolis, Brazil.

Henner, J., Caldwell-Harris, C. L., Novogrodsky, R., & Hoffmeister, R. J. (2016). American Sign Language syntax and analogical reasoning skills are influenced by early acquisition and age of entry to signing schools for the deaf. *Frontiers in Psychology, 7,* 1982. doi:10.3389/FPSYG.2016.01982

Henner, J., Hoffmeister, R., & Reis, J. (2017). Developing sign language assessments for the deaf and hard of hearing. In S. Cawthon & C. L. Garberoglio (Eds.), *Research methodology in deaf education.* Oxford, UK: Oxford University Press.

Herman, R., Holmes, S., & Woll, B. (1999). *Assessing sign language development.* Coleford, UK: Forest Books.

Hoffmeister, R. (1978). The development of demonstrative pronouns, locatives, and personal pronouns in the acquisition of American Sign Language by deaf children of deaf parents (Unpublished doctoral dissertation), University of Minnesota, Minneapolis.

Hoffmeister, R. (1990). The influential POINT. *Proceedings of the National Symposium on Sign Language and Sign Language Teaching.* National Association of the Deaf.

Hoffmeister, R., Fish, S., Benedict, R., Henner, J., Novogrodsky, R., & Rosenburg, P. (2013). *American Sign Language Assessment Instrument (ASLAI): Revision 4.* Boston University Center for the Study of Communication and the Deaf.

Hoffmeister, R., & Harvey, M. (1996). Is there a psychology of the hearing? In Neil S. Glickman & Michael Harvey (eds.), *Culturally affirmative psychotherapy with Deaf persons.* Mahwah, NJ: Lawrence Earlbaum Associates.

Johnston, T., & Schembri, A. (1999). On defining lexeme in a signed language. *Sign Language and Linguistics, 2*(2), 115–185.

Lillo-Martin, D. (2000). Aspects of syntax and acquisition of WH-questions in American Sign Language. In Karen Emmory and Harlan Lane (eds.), *The Signs of Language Revisited: Anthology in Honor of Ursula Bellugi and Edward Klima* (pp. 401–414). Mahwah, NJ: Lawrence Erlbaum Associates.

Lillo-Martin, D., & Meier, R. P. (2011). On the linguistic status of "agreement" in sign languages. *Theoretical Linguistics, 37*(3/4), 95–141. Retrieved from www.degruyter.com/view/j/thli.2011.37.issue-3-4/thli.2011.009/thli.2011.009.xml

Magno, C. (2009). Demonstrating the difference between Classical Test Theory and Item Response Theory using derived test data. *The International Journal of Educational and Psychological Assessment, 1*(1), 1–11.

Mann, W., Roy, P., & Marshall, C. (2013). A look at the other 90 per cent: Investigating British Sign Language vocabulary knowledge in deaf children from different language learning backgrounds. *Deafness & Education International, 15*(2), 91–116. doi:10.1179/1557069X12Y.0000000017

Matsumoto, Y. (1996). *Complex predicates in Japanese: A syntactic and semantic study of the notion 'word'.* Center for the Study of Language and Information.

McCaskill, C., Lucas, C., Bayley, R., & Hill, J. (2011). *Hidden treasure: The history and structure of Black ASL.* Washington, DC: Gallaudet University Press.

McQuarrie, L., Abbott, M., & Spady, S. (2012). American Sign Language phonological awareness: Test development and design. In *Proceedings of the 10th Annual Hawaii International Conference on Education* (pp. 1–17). Honolulu, Hawaii.

Meier, R. (2002). The acquisition of verb agreement: Pointing out arguments for the linguistic status. In G. Morgan & B. Woll (Eds.), *Directions in sign language acquisition* (p. 115). Amsterdam, The Netherland: John Benjamins Publishing Company.

Meir, I. (1998). Syntactic-semantic interaction in Israeli Sign Language verbs: The case of backwards verbs. *Sign Language &# 38; Linguistics, 9, 1*(1), 3–37. Retrieved from www.ingenta connect.com/content/jbp/sll/1998/00000001/00000001/art00002

Mitchell, R. E. (2006). How many deaf people are there in the United States? Estimates from the Survey of Income and Program Participation. *Journal of Deaf Studies and Deaf Education, 11*(1), 112–119. doi:10.1093/deafed/enj004

Mitchell, R. E., & Karchmer, M. A. (2005). Parental hearing status and signing among deaf and hard of hearing students. *Sign Language Studies, 5*(2), 231–244. Retrieved from http://muse.jhu.edu/journals/sls/summary/v005/5.2mitchell.html

Morere, D. A. (2013). Methodological issues associated with sign-based neuropsychological assessment. *Sign Language Studies, 14*(1), 8–20. doi:10.1353/sls.2013.0021

Morford, J., Grieve-Smith, A. B., MacFarlane, J., Staley, J., & Waters, G. (2008). Effects of language experience on the perception of American Sign Language. *Cognition, 109*(1), 41–53. doi:10.1016/j.cognition.2008.07.016

Morgan, G., & Woll, B. (2007). Understanding sign language classifiers through a polycomponential approach. *Lingua. International Review of General Linguistics. Revue Internationale de Linguistique Generale, 117*(7), 1159–1168. Retrieved from http://linkinghub.elsevier.com/retrieve/pii/S0024384106000209

Niparko, J. K., Tobey, E. A., Thal, D. J., Eisenberg, L. S., Wang, N. Y., Quittner, A. L., & Fink, N. E. (2010). Spoken language development in children following cochlear implantation. *JAMA, 303*(15), 1498–1506.

Novogrodsky, R., Caldwell-Harris, C., Fish, S., & Hoffmeister, R. J. (2014). The development of antonym knowledge in American Sign Language (ASL) and its relationship to reading comprehension in English. *Language Learning, 64*(December), 749–770. doi:10.1111/lang.12078

Novogrodsky, R., Henner, J., Caldwell-Harris, C., & Hoffmeister, R. (2017). The development of sensitivity to grammatical violations in American Sign Language – Native signers versus nonnative. *Language and Learning. 67*(4), 791–818.

Pfau, R., & Steinbach, M. (2008). Agreement auxiliaries and transitivity in sign languages. *Workshop on Transitivity Köln.* Retrieved from http://home.medewerker.uva.nl/r.pfau/bestanden/Koeln 2008 transitivity.pdf

Qian, D. D. (1999). Assessing the roles of depth and breadth of vocabulary knowledge in reading comprehension. *The Canadian Modern Language Review, 56*(2), 282–308.

Qian, D. D. (2002). Investigating the relationship between vocabulary knowledge and academic reading performance: An assessment perspective. *Language Learning, 52*(3), 513–536.

Rickford, J. R., & King, S. (2016). Language and linguistics on trial: Hearing Rachel Jeantel (and other vernacular speakers) in the courtroom and beyond. *Language, 92*(4), 948–988.

Sandler, W., & Lillo-Martin, D. (2006). *Sign language and linguistic universals.* Cambridge, UK: Cambridge University Press.

Schaefer, E. (2008). Rater bias patterns in an EFL writing assessment. *Language Testing, 25*(4), 465–493. doi:10.1177/0265532208094273

Schick, B., deVilliers, P., deVilliers, J., & Hoffmeister, R. (2007). Language and theory of mind: A study of deaf children. *Child Development, 78*(2), 376–396.

Senghas, A. (1995). The development of Nicaraguan Sign Language via the language acquisition process. *Proceedings of the 19th Annual Boston University Conference on Language Development,* (1984), 543–552. Retrieved from www.columbia.edu/~asl038/pdf/Senghas1995a.pdf

Siedlecki, T., & Bonvillian, J. D. (1997). Young children's acquisition of the handshape aspect of American Sign Language signs: Parental report findings. *Applied Psycholinguistics, 18,* 17–40. Retrieved from http://journals.cambridge.org/production/action/cjoGetFulltext?fulltextid=2747400

Steinbach, M. (2011). What do agreement auxiliaries reveal about the grammar of sign language agreement? *Theoretical Linguistics, 37,* 209–211. Retrieved from www.degruyter.com/dg/viewjournalissue.articlelist.resultlinks.fullcontentlink:pdfeventlink/$002fj$002fthli.2011.37.issue-3-4$002fthli.2011.016$002fthli.2011.016.pdf?t:ac=j$002fthli.2011.37.issue-3-4$002fissue-files$002fthli.2011.37.issue-3-4.xml

Stokoe, W. C. (1980). Sign language structure. *Annual Review of Anthropology, 9*(1), 365–390. doi:10.1146/annurev.an.09.100180.002053

Sun, L., & Wallach, G. P. (2014). Language disorders are learning disabilities. *Topics in Language Disorders, 34*(1), 25–38. doi:10.1097/TLD.0000000000000005

Sundhem, S., & Voeller, K. (2004). Psychiatric implications of language disorders and learning disabilities: Risks and management. *Journal of Child Neurology, 19*(10), 814–826.

Supalla, T. (1986). The classifier system in American Sign Language. *Noun Classes and Categorization. Proceedings of a symposium on categorization and noun classification. Eugene,* Oregon, Oct. 1983, Volume 7 of Typological Studies in language. Colette Grinevald Craig (Editor). John Benjamins Publishing, 1986

Van der Hulst, H., & Mills, A. (1996). Issues in sign linguistic: Phonetics, phonology and morpho-syntax. *Lingua. International Review of General Linguistics. Revue Internationale de Linguistique Generale, 98*(1–3), 3–17. Retrieved from www.sciencedirect.com/science/article/pii/0024384195000305

Veinberg, S. C., & Wilbur, R. B. (1990). A linguistic analysis of the negative headshake in American Sign Language. *Sign Language Studies, 68*, 217–243. doi:10.1353/sls.1990.0013

Visser-Bochane, M., Gerrits, E., Der Schans, C., Reijneveld, S., & Luinge, M. (2017). Atypical speech and language development: A consensus study on clinical signs in the Netherlands. *International Journal of Language & Communication Disorders, 52*(1), 10–20.

7

Enhancing Communication Skills in Persons with Severe Language Deprivation

Lessons Learned from the Rise of a Signing Community in Nicaragua

ROMY V. SPITZ AND JUDY KEGL

Introduction

Language is a uniquely human ability that is at the heart of all we do and who we are. The language acquisition process is also unique in that unlike many other developmental skills, language acquisition has a limited window of time in which it must happen. A native, first-language foundation can only be learned if the child has consistent exposure to language models during the period from birth to approximately six or seven years of age. Scientists call this neurodevelopmental window the critical period for language acquisition (Lenneberg, 1967). This concept of a critical period applies to all languages, including both spoken and sign languages (Mayberry, 2010). Certain parts of language, such as the phonology (the sounds of a particular language) and the grammar (the rules determining word and sentence formation), have a specific time period for acquisition. Phonology must be reasonably well mastered within the first few years and grammar by age six or seven, or the person will likely never develop native mastery in this first language (Newport, 2002).

Critical periods are not seen in every aspect of language. The learning of words, for example, can occur at any age. We learn new words daily as we encounter them (e.g., weir) or as they are invented (e.g., humblebrag). Beyond words, however, a person's first or native language cannot be learned in pieces or word-by-word. It cannot be learned with occasional or very short exposure to the language, such as attending a few deaf events throughout the year. The child must have access to and interaction with persons using the grammar of that language on a regular basis. When this doesn't happen, the person is at risk of becoming an adult with lifelong language deprivation, with all the accompanying cognitive and learning challenges (Glickman, 2007). The impact of language deprivation is devastating to the person's overall development as a human being, including the ability to think, recall, and reflect on their own thoughts and actions. It results in deaf adults who are undereducated, underemployed, and overrepresented in social services and correctional facilities (Duggan, 2017; Vernon, Steinberg, & Montoya, 1999).

In our work as professionals who do communication and language assessment in legal, educational, vocational, and social service settings in the United States, we meet language-deprived deaf individuals frequently. For one of us (Spitz), working with language-deprived deaf children and adults is a daily occurrence. Language deprivation is a real and ever-present danger in every country that has deaf people—which is to say, everywhere.

Most efforts to mitigate language deprivation in deaf children focus on prevention. We work with healthcare and early intervention providers to ensure that deaf children receive the language experience and person-to-person interaction they need to acquire a first language before age five. Yet, there will always be groups of deaf children at risk of language deprivation. These groups include immigrants and refugees arriving from other countries where language intervention and education for deaf children was not available, children who grew up in rural areas in the United States who live well beyond reasonable daily commuting distance to the nearest deaf early education program, those who received education in spoken language-only environments but did not develop adequate spoken language skills, and those educated in "total communication" environments where the quality of sign language exposure was poor. Language deprivation in deaf children will continue to be the primary developmental risk for deaf children in the foreseeable future because of the general dearth of natural sign language exposure opportunities.

While prevention measures are the primary intervention, this does not help adults who have already experienced language deprivation. This chapter takes another direction, discussing a method of remediation developed from our work in establishing language programs for deaf individuals in Nicaragua. We focus here on those people who are severely language deprived, especially those who come to us with limited words/signs or who have never encountered sign language before. Yet the application of these methods is not limited to that severely deprived group. The basic methodology can be used to improve the communication of people with milder levels of language deprivation.

Who Can Remediate Language Deprivation?

As language and communication assessors in public schools, we sometimes have the opportunity (if the school will take it) to recommend implementation of these methods through deaf educators and communication therapists. In adult settings such as social service and vocational settings, however, there is no consistent avenue for communication therapy. Some options for paid therapy exist in states that have carved out services such as pre-employment training through Vocational Rehabilitation or communication training through State Medicaid Home and Communication Based Services Waivers (e.g., Maine Medicaid Nontraditional Communication Services) but most states have not created such services.

We need to do a better job of advocating for states to include communication training for any client with language deprivation by highlighting the relevance of communication to the vocational and/or independent living outcomes. In the meantime, we also need to think about how this work can be done in smaller steps, using existing resources. Currently, we assist professionals without communication and language expertise, including case workers, therapists, and direct care staff, to apply our methods to provide an opportunity for the persons they serve to develop more effective communication skills. It would be ideal if such training were included within an expanded curriculum for Deaf service programs.

Within the mental health world, it would seem ideal that signing mental health providers with language-deprived clients include some of our methods for developing communication skills into the kinds of pre-therapy processes described by Glickman (2017 and in Chapter 2 in this volume). It is slower and harder than one might imagine. It takes a willing therapist or communication specialist and a motivated student who are both able to put in the time and the effort. In Nicaragua, these necessary ingredients all came together, providing a laboratory for linguists and educators to experiment with methods to promote language and communication skills development in language-deprived individuals.

Nicaragua 1980–Present

In mid-1980s Nicaragua, we were privileged to witness the birth of a new language, something that human beings—much less linguists—rarely see. Prior to the 1980s, deaf children and adults in Nicaragua largely had no accessible language exposure. There was no indigenous sign language and there were no schools for the deaf (Polich, 2001). Deaf people communicated within their families through a limited gesture system, known as "home-sign" systems (Kegl & Iwata, 1989; Senghas & Coppola, 2005). For the deaf person in the home, that small number of home-sign gestures was sufficient to signal their basic needs and desires to their families. They were sufficient to communicate about events that they and their families had shared such as going to church, cutting grass with a machete, or making tortillas. Yet home-sign systems do not have a fundamental grammar that allows the message to be immediately understood without shared information. They were not sufficient to communicate non-shared events such as the three-legged dog the person saw this morning or the fire that almost burned them last week, and they were not sufficient to communicate with people outside the family. They were also not sufficient for deaf children to go to school and achieve the national expectation of a fourth-grade education.

Government-based deaf educational programs arose in the 1980s, bringing deaf children together, each with their own repertoire of home-sign gestures. Sharing of gestures led to a conventional (shared) vocabulary that allowed them to more easily communicate with each other about shared events, but it did not result in a language. The students had no shared grammar system with rules for how to put the signs together into sentences. The ability to detect and impose rules on what is signed and how it is signed requires a brain with the neurodevelopmental window for language acquisition still open. The original group of students was too old. It was not until the next generation of very young children saw the shared gestures and applied their innate neurological skills to the gestural "data" that the shared gestures became imbued with grammatical rules. Those rules created by the first generation of young children created a brand new language known as Idioma de Señas de Nicaragua (ISN) (Kegl & Iwata, 1989; Kegl & McWhorter, 1997; Kegl, Senghas, & Coppola, 1999).

Once created, ISN became the standard of language acquisition and communication that all students worked toward. The first generation of ISN signing students were the models and their expectation was that everyone would use ISN signs and grammar. The youngest students easily attained this goal simply from exposure and desire to communicate with their older ISN-using peers. Slightly older students, ages 8–10, achieved the signs and some of the grammar, but not full fluency. Those students who were teenagers when ISN was created were already well past the critical period. While they learned the signs, they did not learn the underlying language.

The Nicaraguan Sign Language Projects

During the 1990s, the Nicaragua Sign Language Projects (NSLP) developed as a nonprofit organization committed to studying ISN (www.nicaraguansign languageprojects.org). In 1995, the NSLP changed focus from research to intervention in order for deaf ISN teachers to spread this new language to areas outside of the government-run schools for the deaf on the west coast of Nicaragua. Unlike the Government-based schools, the NSLP created schools were (1) developed intentionally for the purpose of spreading ISN as a language and (2) open to deaf people of all ages. Over our time in Nicaragua, we met and collected communication data from over 400 deaf adults who had spent their lives without exposure to language. Nicaragua allowed us the opportunity that few interveners are ever afforded, a chance to focus on the habilitation of communication and language in an adult population over a long period of time. As part of that journey, we were able to ask questions about the possibility of late-learners acquiring language. We were also able to try out a number of approaches to teaching communication and language that were informed by our background as linguists and developmental psychologists.

Principles for Addressing Language Deprivation

While we present one methodology for increasing communication skills in this chapter, there are principles that should be addressed in any method that purports to address the teaching of language to adults. We review these here.

The Critical Period for Language Acquisition Still Applies

We believe that it is only in the first six years or so that the brain has the neuroplasticity to take in language, through the eyes or ears, as a frozen, unanalyzed chunk, analyze it for parts and rules for how those parts work together, and then use that knowledge to reproduce the language they heard or saw. Our methods do not overcome this barrier when that neurodevelopmental window has shut. Instead we see our goal as comparable to a "Turing Test" used in Artificial Intelligence (Turing, 1952). Turing asked if a computer could be trained to "fake" the capacity for language well enough to fool a human. We ask if a language-deprived person can be trained to learn enough parts of communication so that their messages are more language-like. We don't claim to teach people to have an automatic, internalized linguistic system based on a natural acquisition process. We teach them basic parts of how a specific language works so as to improve their communication abilities. We are interested in the best pedagogical strategies to further that aim. Through use of shared stories, visual representations, and repetition, we work toward helping these people apply enough parts to "pass" as language users. One might say they become functional signers like many deaf people in the United States who receive either late or incomplete exposure to sign language. They communicate, but they never acquire anything like native language abilities. Their language limitations continue to be significant educational and social handicaps for them throughout their lives.

The Language Process Needs to Be Observable

An important part of our process is forcing language to "sit still." Language happens in milliseconds and then it is gone. In normal conversation and even when we model skillful language use, there is no way for the learner to slow down or stop the process in order to see the parts of language. Just as you need to stop a car's engine or take it apart to see the parts and how they work together, any successful method for teaching communication and language must include a way to make language "stop" in the moment for the learner to see and learn the parts and understand how they work together.

A Language User Needs to Identify Core Parts of Language

The language-deprived adult learner can see some parts of language, such as words, that they can connect to concepts they already know. They cannot see other parts, such as the grammar of the language. They can see us formulate a sentence, but there is no meaningful way for them to know which parts of what they see are important to notice. People who do not know ASL cannot "see" the eyebrow raise that marks a yes/no question in ASL until it is pointed out to them. Even then, it may not show up in their own production of signed messages. People who do not have Spanish fluency are not going to be able to identify changes in a word ending that mark a verb for person or tense (e.g., *comprendo* [I understand] versus *comprendí* [I understood]) unless someone points it out and explains it in the person's own language.

This inability to "see" and "hear" what is obvious to any person who already knows the language is why modeling alone is insufficient to teach language. There is no way to identify and explain the parts in the modeling process. For adults with language deprivation, communication abilities must be developed in a much more strategic and intentional manner. Someone who knows the language identifies salient pieces of the grammar and presents it tangibly, one piece at a time, providing many opportunities for practice and mastery. The trick is to draw the language-deprived individual's attention to those salient pieces of grammar and help lead them to discover and try to use them. In sum, simply watching is not enough.

There Must Be Communication Accountability

Communication accountability is the most important tool in any training designed to increase communication. Communication accountability is the idea that a person cannot get what they want (e.g., successfully communicate a message or get something desired) unless they communicate in a way that any communication partner can understand. In other words, the person must meet expectations for what constitutes acceptable language. This does not mean that we do not accept any message unless it is perfect. It means that we have expectations based on what we believe the person can produce. Those expectations may be simple, such as messages must contain some kind of information about "who did what." The expectation can be more complex, such as requiring that messages contain the correct grammatical signals of ASL for "who did what to whom" within the sentence (i.e., verb agreement). Any messages that do not meet the expectation (despite shared knowledge) are responded to as incomplete, and more information is requested until it does meet the expectation. True communication growth occurs when the learner must meet the linguistic expectations of those they are communicating with.

Communication accountability explains why deaf Nicaraguan home-signers don't develop elaborate gesture systems. For the deaf Nicaraguan home-signer who remains with his family, there is no communication accountability. There is no expectation of the deaf person producing clear language and no model inside the family members' head of what a fluently signed message should look like. Instead, families most commonly focus on addressing immediate needs. Rather than expecting the deaf child to provide all the information, the families accept one or two gestures (tortilla) and fill in the blanks to create the message ("I'm hungry" or "Is it lunch time yet?"). The same thing often happens in the home of American deaf children when teachers and parents accept approximations of clear language as "good enough" if they are able to infer the rest of the message. Good early language intervention programs for the deaf are designed to counter that and to provide deaf children and their parents with language models which subsequently hold all involved parties accountable for the child's continued language growth.

Communication accountability depends on two factors—a learner who wants to convey a message and a listener who won't accept minimal signs that don't communicate the message clearly. In Nicaragua, the basic gestures that worked in the home did not work in the school. Deaf students did not know each other's gestures and did not share the life experiences of the person that would make those gestures meaningful. Each student then had to figure out how to communicate with other students if they wanted to be able to communicate in classrooms and on the playground and school bus. They had to change the way they communicated to meet others' expectations; that is, they needed to demonstrate communication accountability. That need to change or repackage signs to make a clearly understood message drove the Nicaraguan students to share each other's signs, providing a richer input that fed the creation of the language. They then passed that language on to future cohorts of students and through them to future generations.

The lesson for those of us working with language-deprived children and adults is clear. If those of us who have language are constantly inferring the person's message based on our shared knowledge and not expecting them to provide a better message, communication growth cannot happen. The attitude that the deaf person's language skills are "good enough" effectively destroys language learning.

Meeting People at Their Communication Level

Another important principle for teaching language and communication is to meet students where they are, understand and match their current communication abilities, and then help them expand these. Part of that requirement is understanding that a language user and a language-deprived person may see and experience the same event but the way they process and express thoughts about it will be very different. Communication skill training begins by understanding the language and communication "baseline" of the student.

For example, one of us worked with Harmon, a deaf, language-deprived adult, at an institution in Maine in the United States. Harmon's family gave him up as a young child due to their inability to cope with his hearing loss. He spent his childhood in institutions for "thrown-away" children. He spent much of his adulthood in institutions for people with mental and cognitive deficits, even though he was neither mentally ill nor intellectually disabled. His exposure to some form of signing happened in adulthood when he was placed in an institution that had grouped all deaf clients, most whom did have intellectual disabilities, into one unit. The residents learned signs from the Institution's vocabulary sign book (Derry, 1985), supplemented by whatever signs the staff knew or learned.

When Harmon was in his 50s, Maine closed its institutions and he was released into a community living environment with hearing housemates. Harmon would spend hours chatting with anyone who would sign with him. He would package his signs and gestures into long strings (e.g., when talking about a dog sitting next to a dog house, he signed "HOUSE, WET, GO-IN, OUTSIDE, SUNLIGHT, ROUND-BOWL, EAT, EAT-WITH-MOUTH, ALL-GONE, GETTING-FATTER"). Harmon loved to chat using the signs he knew as well as gesture, pictures, pointing, or taking you to the location where a relevant event occurred. He was very social and would converse about many topics including Christmas. His personal signs that he used to refer to Christmas could be any of the following: *White (which could also mean old)*, TREE, BOX *(for gifts)*, FAT, OLD/BEARD *(Santa Claus but could also mean his housemate who is older and at some point had a beard)*, *pointing to the roof (often paired with* FAT *or* WHITE *and followed by box)*. Any one of these signs/gestures or combinations of these signs/gestures could be used to have a conversation about Christmas, for example: white, box, fat, roof, box, me ("At Christmas I received a Christmas present."), white, beard, box-points to television ("the older housemate and I watched Christmas shows on television"), happy ("We had a good time"), you-know (yes like always)....you? ("Did you have a good Christmas?").

Harmon's experience of Christmas was probably very close to ours. His concept of Christmas was similar to ours as a day to eat, drink, and be merry and to give and receive gifts, but the way he packaged his signs to form a message about Christmas was very different than ours.

Our words are put together using grammar in order to convey a message that is understood by any other speaker of our language. Harmon's words are put together based on their importance to him and how central they were to his memory of that day. We could teach him the ASL signs for "Christmas," "present," or "Santa Claus," but that would not solve the language packaging problem. We could model the correct way to sign this story until next Christmas and it would not solve the communication problem. In order to help him expand on his communication and make it more easily understood by people who do not know him, we need to understand how he thinks about Christmas. We need to take this story as he signs it now, break it into manageable chunks, and help him learn to *repackage* the signs in a way that others understand.

For our approach to communication habilitation, it does not matter whether the person's communication is very limited, such as Harmon's, or more advanced, such as adults who communicate through contact variety sign (an English-influenced form of signing formerly described as Pidgin Signed English). You can only move the person toward more complete, language-like signing if you begin where they are. The goal is to help them move incrementally towards fuller communication, and perhaps from there to more complex and formal language, by focusing upon a limited number of language features at a time, making them visible and concrete. This process is facilitated by a story protocol.

Using a Story Protocol to Teach Language/Communication

In Nicaragua, all of our teaching methodology builds upon a story protocol, whether we are talking about history, science, or current events. We don't teach language by words and sentences. We teach by presenting a story and using a combination of modeling and retelling with feedback. Rather than trying to teach the sentence word-by-word and then build the story sentence-by-sentence, we start with the story as an event and work our way down—allowing the learner to incrementally build up to a language representation of the story.

This method begins by ensuring that teachers and students see the same story and work, therefore, from the same set of "facts." We do this through sequential pictures or movies. Once we establish the shared event, the story is told in ISN (or in gesture) by a teacher who breaks the story down into segments or episodes, then each of the students retells the story episode by episode using their own signs and gestures. On subsequent retellings, the teacher and the other students in the community of students provide feedback to the person while encouraging the inclusion of details and/or clarifying information.

In recounting the story, each student is held accountable for producing signing that can be understood by the others (communication accountability). When a piece of communication regarding the story cannot be understood from what the student produced (even if it can be inferred in the shared context), the teacher and other students indicate a lack of understanding and probe for more systematic communication until the intended information can be understood solely from the communication produced. The student's signing does not need to follow ISN grammar; it needs to convey the information in the story segment without requiring guesswork or inference on the part of the instructor or group. The student cannot rely on pointing to the picture and they cannot rely on previous knowledge. Instead, they must convey the part of the story they chose to tell by repackaging their signs and gestures. By observing other students and by observing the modeling of the teacher, the student gains a sense of which changes work and which do not.

Let us discuss a simple example using the classic story of *The Three Little Pigs*. In a mixed group where some have only gesture, a teacher will gesture the story. They may present the story several times, inserting signs where appropriate until the students have the full sense of the story that the pictures in the *Three Little Pigs* convey. Each student then recounts the story to the best of their abilities to the group. With each iteration, each student borrows from the others to their own level of ability. On additional days, the same story is presented again by the teacher. Each time the telling of the story is elaborated with more signs and more details and the process begins again. The students pick up more strategies from each other and then attempt to convey more of the story.

At times, the teacher may elaborate a story by using another technique called *story breakdown*. Here, another teacher holds an imaginary remote control that allows the first teacher to freeze or rewind the storyteller at any point and elaborate about grammatical constructions. If the narrator makes a role shift and becomes one of the characters in the story and then shifts the grammar to first person (I, me) reference, the teacher will point to the frozen storyteller and ask, "Who is this?" eliciting from the students that it is no longer the narrator, but, let's say, one of the pigs. In this way, metalinguistic concepts like role shift and person-marking are introduced with students grasping in their own time what they are capable of understanding. Story breakdown can be used at any point and each time reveals another aspect of ISN grammar, such as spatial agreement, pronouns, subject and object marking, or classifiers.

A single story will be repeated numerous times over days or even weeks. Once comprehended, it is also elaborated, and new dimensions of grammar and description are added, always spiraling on a shared event and giving each student the ability to assimilate the story and express it in their own words to the best of their ability.

The same approach used on the *Three Little Pigs* was used to teach the story of Louis Pasteur and the concept of bacteria and pasteurization. It was also used to teach the story of the French revolution, Gandhi's peace initiatives, and the discovery that the earth revolves around the sun rather than vice versa. With creativity and patience, this strategy can be used on any story.

Of course, these stories are more abstract and more challenging than *Three Little Pigs*, but they are approached in the same way, namely establishing the event using pictures, movies, and gestures and then building from there. We start with a hook to the student's current experience base. In the Pasteur story, for example, someone gets sick and it spreads to someone else. We establish the context and build upon it. Someone takes a medicine and gets better. How does that work? Many people get sick, but some don't. Why? Some people got injections and they didn't get sick. How does that work? We use metaphors like injecting little soldiers into a person that fights the disease they have or injecting soldiers who stand at the ready so if an invading illness enters, they are ready to go to battle. We use drawings of a hypodermic needle with little soldiers lined up inside. We use the injected-soldiers metaphor to build the concept of a vaccine. We move from the existing hooks we started with to new hooks we have created to further expansions that establish what is actually happening at the molecular and cell level. The nuances of one story can take literally weeks, even months, to fully unfold. Essentially, the point is that if we know where to start in terms of fund of knowledge, then we can build from there. With more time allowed for the process, more complex concepts can be conveyed.

Why the Story Protocol Method Works

The story protocol works because it begins with a shared event. We all start with an understanding of what we are trying to tell each other. Without that basis, we would spend all of our time doing the kind of communication sleuthing that language-deprived people face every day. We would be trying to find common agreement on what might have happened in the event rather than on guiding the student to clearly communicate about the event. It works because the repeated opportunities to retell the story after seeing countless other retellings allow each student to see options used by others to package that event in language and try them out for themselves within their current level of ability. And it works because of the requirement for accountability.

Sometimes the inclusion of someone else's signs or phrases by the student doesn't successfully work to communicate what happened in the story segment. That "failure" drives the student to experiment with what they gained from observation until they find a repackaging of signs that communicates the segment they chose to sign successfully. That failure provides an opportunity of not-so-gentle nudging for the student to either apply what he has seen work before (the model of the teacher, the successful retelling of other students) or to force him to innovate in how he makes a sign or combines signs to make a clearer message.

Communication Accountability Drives Progress

What drives progress in the story protocol described before? Why would a student innovate, trying out new "hypotheses" of how to communicate, rather than simply memorize the handshapes or key sign vocabulary related to each picture or story segment and then repeat the associated signs when they are cued by the picture or a model? For a young child, the driver of improvement comes from a language-ready brain that can identify and assimilate the dimensions of grammar as they unfold. The "driver" is the same one we see when our own children seem to pick language out of the air. Pinker calls this driver "the Language Instinct" (Pinker, 1994).

For language-deprived adults, however, the driver must be different. They no longer have that innate, instinctual ability to simply soak up languages and figure out their rules. They do, however, have two other drivers that are available to both children and adult learners: (1) motivation to communicate, and (2) response to social pressures or communication accountability.

Most people, even those without language, have a strong desire to communicate their thoughts with others. In our method, that desire to communicate fuels experimentation with different signs and sign combinations, but it does not drive the student to a specific grammar. Simple exposure to the grammar is not enough on its own. It is the response to communication accountability and social pressures that directs the student toward the grammar.

The adult student can see the feedback signals received by other students. They can see the teacher's response to their own messages. They can see the frown when the teacher is struggling to understand what the student signed. It sends the signal to add something or change information around (repackaging) to be understood. They can observe the other person's expression clear and brighten when their repackaging of signs succeeds in transmitting the message. They respond to social pressures that direct them along a path toward a specific grammar. This happens by observing the continued attention someone receives when their message is understood and peers encourage them to tell more of the story, and the loss of attention that happens when communication fails.

Social pressure and communication accountability are powerful drivers to communication improvement. They are easily applied in social settings such as the NSLP classroom. It is more difficult to do here in the US where most of the work with language-deprived persons occurs in a one-to-one setting. How do we take the principles and methods learned in Nicaragua and apply them in one-to-one settings?

Using a Story Protocol to Teach Language/Communication in Noncommunity Situations

As teachers, counselors, and other service providers who work *individually* with clients, there is still a way to accomplish much the same kind of individual progress if we follow the principles of beginning from a shared conceptual structure (a known story) and insisting on communication accountability. The difficult step is replacing that learning component and social pressure that stems from the student observing others retelling the same story. Without having these other peers as language models, there is more dependence on the student's motivation to communication and their desire *and ability* to be innovative with their sign repackaging. It increases the importance of the teacher in identifying specific language parts to be learned and modeling them clearly without including more complex parts of language. It is especially important to keep in mind that we can only work one or two steps above the language skills that the individual student already has.

Let us suppose the student is just beginning to understand the concept of including information on who did or said something. There are multiple ways to do this in signed languages including spatial reference and role shifting. This hypothetical student is currently at a skill level where they understand and use basic spatial referencing. Spatial reference is a grammatical tool that allows a sign language user to indicate who did an action and what person or object was acted upon. Signers do this by establishing locations in space and then moving or orienting a verb, such as TELL-TO or LOOK-AT between locations to signal who was the actor and who was the recipient (who tells whom; who looked at whom). The pairing between the spatial location and the person remains constant as does their relationship to the person signing.

Role shifting is another grammatical tool that accomplishes the task of indicating "who tells whom" by actually taking on the role of one of the characters and then talking from that character's viewpoint ("I (the character) said _____"). Because role shift requires the student to constantly track who is doing the speaking based on details such as body shifting and eye-gaze, and because multiple role shifts are typically involved in the exchange, it is a more difficult aspect of grammar to master for an adult learner.

For a fluent signer, a story like the *Three Little Pigs* would include both spatial referencing ("The big bad wolf stomped up to the house made of bricks") and role shift ("and said to the pig, 'Little Pig, let me come in'"). From the learner's perspective, including role shift in the modeling of the segment adds an additional grammatical feature and thus increases the complexity of the learning task. It's more effective to continue with the spatial referencing before introducing a new grammatical feature, like role shifting.

Expert communication teachers teach one language feature at a time, building incrementally from the baseline language abilities of the person. Inexperienced language teachers, by contrast, will just think that by modeling skilled ASL, the person will copy what they see and learn from that copy. That's several bridges too far for the language-deprived brain.

Staying with the spatial referencing skill, the skilled teacher takes the extra time to maintain the spatial reference by adopting a narrator view which allows them to refer to (rather than act out) the actions and comments of the wolf and the pigs. It would be as if we told the story by saying "then the wolf said he would huff and puff and blow the pig's house down" rather than saying "And the wolf threatened, 'I'll huff and puff and blow your house down.'" The teacher maintains this level of reference until the student shows sufficient mastery that the teacher could take the next step of role shifting and then use the *story breakdown* method described earlier to ensure that the student followed the change in perspective (becoming the wolf) by *freezing* the action and asking "who am I now?"

The question of what constitutes one step beyond the student's current communication strategies does not have an easy one-size-fits-all answer. Our linguistic training helps us here. That knowledge allows us to surmise what baby step should be next. When working with people without that background, we can observe the teacher modeling the story in the next iteration and see when the model's reach exceeds the student's grasp. Sometimes the evidence is clear from the responses of the student—they cannot assimilate changes they cannot understand. Other times, the answer is less clear. Is the step too far or does the student just need more time and more examples of that step in order for the "aha moment" to happen? Deciding which of these is the correct answer takes training, experience, and a willingness to backtrack to an earlier step to ensure that we don't discourage communication growth.

Use of Life Stories in One-on-One Work

When working one-on-one with an individual to increase communication effectiveness, we still use stories. Rather than being about topics external to the person, it is often easier to start with stories from their own lives. We typically start with stories that are the most important to them. The result is greater motivation by the student to successfully tell their story in a way that is more easily and completely understood by others. For instance, we met a deaf man while doing communication assessment in another state. He was clearly of Central American descent, and we could see he used familiar Central American gestures. He was introduced to us as Santi and he was eager to tell us his immigration story.

Santi was language deprived, having grown up in his native country without access to sign language and arriving in the United States too old to go to school. He was unable to tell us his life story, despite many attempts and some communication bridging by another deaf signer who was familiar with his signs and gestures. Santi could sign that he had been on a plane and came here (ME FLY-DOWN HERE), but he was unable to tell us more of the story. His coworkers, some deaf themselves, shared that he knew "signs" but he was not able to put together his signs into sentences that could be understood. The only exception were topics that were very familiar to all of them where the use of shared context such as work duties, lunch, soccer teams, and some gossip about coworkers allowed the other deaf to form inferences about what Santi might be saying. Every communication was a mix of object and action labels, as in WOMAN points to man LIE-TOGETHER BABY ("He was hanging out with that woman and she's pregnant") or THEY (waves hand at people) WHISTLE (looks at imaginary person) COME-HERE. TRUCK gestures BACK with thumb. ME (unidentified object) LIFT and PUT-SOMETHING-IN. ("So someone needs to tell the truck to back in so I can load the boxes").

One deaf coworker stated that he was teaching Santi signs and indicated he would be willing to help the man expand his communication abilities through helping him learn to elaborate his story. We began by a sleuthing expedition to his family, who were willing to show us pictures and fill in some gaps in his story. We sought pictures of different elements of the story to establish parts of the story we could confirm with Santi, making him the expert in selecting which "facts" were included and which pictures would be used to represent those facts. The story was then broken down into segments that could be worked on individually.

The segments of Santi's life story included his former life, plane ride, arrival here, and current life. Each segment had multiple pictures in it. His former life segment contained pictures for a house that resembled his former home, his family back in his home country (not all of whom immigrated with him), a car, and some suitcases. He could initially point to these pictures to explain that he used to live in this house with his family. He could use some gestures to lay out how one day when he awoke, his family told him to get dressed, and they loaded some family members in a car with some suitcases that didn't belong to them. Apparently, he thought they had stolen the suitcases and he was scared.

Other story segments tell of Santi's apprehension on the plane with its sudden sideways motion and its strange food, and his feeling of relief when the woman (flight attendant) gave him a familiar can of Coke. They tell of his amazement when the plane landed and he walked out to a different world that was cold and full of cars. They also tell of his pride in his current job in the clothing donation center where he sorts clothing and helps those with intellectual disability on related tasks.

Once we have this shared story of his arrival, we were able to begin by having the teacher (coworker) take his description (ME FLY-DOWN HERE) and tie the signs to the pictures in the segments. Unlike Nicaragua where the teacher can react to whatever segment the student chooses to sign or is asked to sign, it is often easier in one-on-one settings to establish a segment as the day's target for accountability. By selecting a target segment, the communication accountability can be focused primarily on that segment and then secondarily on other segments where vocabulary is still being mastered.

With the exception of focusing on life stories and the need for the teacher to provide the modeling and the accountability, the process is similar to that described previously. Using the example of the "Before" segment, the teacher modeled a basic message (e.g., BEFORE ME LIVE HOUSE, FAMILY [name family members]). Some words, such as "*live*," needed to be expanded on for Santi's understanding. When signing a segment, he seldom included a word that he did not understand at least in some limited way. Each day a coworker would ask him for his story and each day he would tell it. His teacher would then model the story segment by segment and Santi would retell it again.

During the second retelling, the teacher would be monitoring for understandability of Santi's signing, stopping him when he was not understood or cueing him if crucial information was left out by pointing to the picture in the segment. He may also repeat what Santi had signed and asking for clarifying details (e.g., who lived in the house?). As Santi progressed, modeling segments and communication expectations increased as appropriate, such as clearly indicating linking actions with people (Brother carry suitcase, or plane moved in this way). We expanded on the parts we had already taught, establishing more new locations (CAR) so they may be talked about and placed within the story (brother carried suitcases to car, put in trunk). Over time, there was clear progress in his ability to provide more details about his life story.

Santi could not learn all parts of language. His non-manual facial expressions were accurate for culturally-related gestures, such as the Central American "nose wrinkle" that signals "what's going on?" We were never able to train ASL non-manual markers for questions. Likewise, he used vigorous head-nodding consistently to mark key topics as we often see in some Central American countries, and we could teach him to recognize the ASL non-manual markers for topic, but they did not appear in his signing in any consistent way.

It may seem that being able to tell your life or immigration story is an insignificant accomplishment. By successively modeling parts of language that he still could learn, we have given him communication tools he could apply in other situations. His conceptual framework has expanded, and he is better able to understand the range of ideas that can be contained within one simple word like "house," "live," or "community." He learned the pieces of language that he must include in order for people to understand him. What he learns by *struggling* to tell his story allows him to generalize that communication strategy into his every day communication as long as the people around him establish expectations of communication accountability rather than accept minimal signs.

Teachers must require communication accountability when working one-on-one with language-deprived individuals. The teacher decides in advance what information needs to be included for a message to be complete. If the teacher decides that the response needs to include who performed the action and who was the recipient of that action (agent and patient) then MARY (give) BOOK (to) ME would be acceptable, while MARY BOOK or ME BOOK would not. What the teacher cannot do is immediately accept shortcuts or messages that do not meet the communication requirements. In this example, attempts that lack information concerning *who did what to whom* need to be summarily rejected even if understanding technically occurs. The teacher needs to send a signal that something is incomplete so that the person has the obligation and opportunity to repair the message to include the required information about who did what to whom. This requirement that the teacher set the expectation and holds the student accountable seems like a very simple step, but being able to apply this requirement consistently requires specialized training. Native signers have the skill in the language. That skill needs to be paired with the training to analyze the communication strategies of the student, identify key parts of language for training, and most of all, to identify when they accept versus not accept the student's signed message.

The process of learning in this method is not through acceptance of the teacher's modeling, but by establishing a dialogue that allows the student to create shared grammar rules in a collaborative way. The student sees the signal from the teacher that something was omitted, makes an attempt to repair the communication to include what is missing, and probes for the success of their attempt by looking at the feedback from the teacher.

In the MARY BOOK example earlier, when the student sees the confused signal from the teacher, they might pantomime someone giving something to someone else or use a prop, a physical book and then use actions that indicate physically moving the book from Mary to the recipient. If a prop is used, the teacher should prompt the student to make a sign that carries the equivalent information. The use of the prop creates a shared opportunity that allows the teacher to either elicit a gesture or sign from the student (BOOK-MOVE) or to offer a possible solution by offering the sign for "giving from one person to another." The goal is to continue the dialogue from that point on, always increasing the amount of communicative complexity expected. It is important to keep in mind that any time solutions are offered, such as showing the sign for GIVE moving from one person to another, they may be accepted or rejected by the student. The fate of the teacher's offering depends upon whether the proposed solution fits within the student's current communication strategy set. With this individualized technique, we gain a second benefit—the ability to systematically apply successive modeling techniques where we can choose the level of modeling that best matches the person's current strategy set.

What should not happen is traditional modeling by exhibiting the full, complex language-rich model at the outset and expecting the brain of the language-deprived person to figure out the salient and implicit features of the language on its own. This is not possible in a brain that has diminished neuroplasticity for language. It is important to meet the student where they are and develop their skills from there.

To get a sense of the benefits of following the language-deprived individual's lead and the individual inventiveness that can be stimulated when the situation demands communication accountability, let's consider a second example that involves the development of communication strategies around the concept of time. Through our work, we have developed some visual- and spatial-based strategies for communicating about time.

Maria Noname (a Nicaraguan deaf female gesturer in her 30s who lived alone and had no use of language) held down a job where she worked every day as a cook and housecleaner for a police officer. To keep that job, she had to be able to show up at his house on time every day to cook and serve breakfast, lunch, and dinner. Maria's walls were covered in calendars, none of which served to actually indicate time for her. She used them for the pictures. There was also a large wall clock. When the hands of that clock made a vertical line in the morning (6 a.m.), she would go to her employer's house to make him breakfast. When they both pointed up (12 p.m.), she went to make lunch. Finally, when they both pointed downward (6:30 p.m.), she went to make dinner. She could not tell time, but she had a work-around that allowed her to be places on time. She recognized three clock views. One meant "go make breakfast"; another meant "go make lunch"; and the last meant "go make dinner." None to her meant "it is X o'clock."

She could not use her clock strategy to allow her to show up at 6:15 a.m. or 12:20 p.m. Nonetheless, she could still "pass" the Turing test in the sense that her limited repertoire of behaviors mimicked the behaviors of someone who could indeed tell time. Maria's idiosyncratic solution to her time demands is innovatively simple. She cannot read the numbers the clock hand points to, and she cannot actually tell you what time it is. Instead, she has found a different solution for getting where she needs to be when she needs to be there (Figure 7.1).

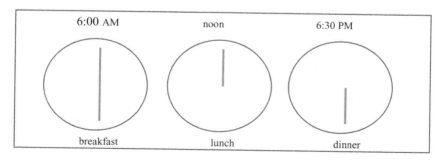

Figure 7.1 Maria's time pictures

Sign language and gesture both encode information primarily in terms of spatial information. Spatial reference (e.g., there, that person) and human action map directly onto human gesture. Time does not typically lend itself to the kind of direct encoding of information in gesture that spatial reference does. An individual relying solely upon gesture might capture time concepts through the repetition of events or reference to events located in time. To convey *three days*, for example, a gesturer might say SLEEP WAKE-UP, SLEEP WAKE-UP, SLEEP WAKE-UP. We can build upon this self-generated system of time reference to teach the concept of "week," using seven iterations. To convey a time of year, weather may be used (COLD, SNOW) or a shared event such as Christmas or a birthday can be referenced via gesture.

To communicate with and to expand the communication base of a gesturer without language, we need to accept their more direct visual and experiential way of encoding time rather than emphasizing the abstract way that sign languages represent time in terms of space. In our work, we use the gesturer's own experience of events to define points in time. It can take a long time to elicit gestures or pictures that can be used effectively. If the gesturer uses sleeping and waking to indicate a day, then we can attempt to use this to indicate more than one day. In the case of Maria, a picture of a clock face or an actual clock with the hands moved can be used to anchor times like morning, noon, and evening. More time references can be built from these, but only if they are built by or in collaboration with Maria. We could potentially build on such a visual strategy to represent 9:15, 9:45, and 3:15 just by rotating the circles 90 degrees to the left and associating specific events to them. We can give her experiences alongside communication accountability that lead her to create more references similar to the ones she has already invented herself.

Importantly, what works for Maria will not necessarily work for Santi. What works for Santi will not necessarily work for someone else, such as Harmon. In each case, we need to watch and discover the individual gesturer's own means of expressing a given concept and build from there. There is no systematic progression to follow—language-deprived adults do not follow a general pattern or developmental trajectory. Each one follows a unique path. The more gesture strategies teachers are exposed to, the more likely they can meet new gesturers where they are. Teachers need to build a bank of gestural strategies to allow for better understanding of the person's time concepts in order to identify those strategies that might lead to the discovery of a more elaborate time-referencing system.

Deaf interpreters and communication facilitators are likely to have the most experience establishing effective communication with language-deprived gesturers—not because they know what to do, but because they understand that the process requires flexibility. Over a lifetime, they build up a bank of strategies, often from trying to communicate with hearing people who don't know a signed language but also from bridging communication within a very heterogeneous community of deaf people. Communicating with language-deprived gesturers is a specialized skill that currently is developed through life experience more than formalized training. That reliance on life experience and "winging it" must be married to formalized training. Part of that training needs to be the ability to identify and clearly report what was understood versus what was inferred based on personal knowledge and context. We remember that we cannot do language or communication *for* a gesturer; they must be empowered to lead, while we follow, remaining flexible and patient.

Gramaticas: Use of Short Video Event Clips to Develop Language and Communication

In addition to life stories, we have developed a second technique to allow the teacher and student to engage in dialogue while developing new communication strategies. We use a series of short video clips describing simple events such as a man and a woman throwing a ball to each other (see sample that follows). This series of clips is called *Gramaticas* and is available at www.nicaraguan signlanguageprojects.org/. These clips provide just the kind of "shared" visual context needed to work on growing communication skills across a variety of learners. They illustrate events involving three people performing a number of actions (Figure 7.2).[1]

Figure 7.2 Grammaticas image: woman taps man

The clips were designed to systematically scaffold the learner into discovering more and more complex communication strategies. Examples of these forms include:

- Type 1: (The man cries) where the person does not need to resolve the issue of who did what because there is only one person involved.
- Type 2: (The man pushes the woman) where the problem of indicating who does what to whom (agent vs. patient) roles must be clearly distinguished and indicated.
- Type 3: (The man throws the ball to the woman) where problem of indicating who performs the action, what is acted upon, and who received the item acted upon must be solved.
- Type 4: Sentences requiring the use of locatives (The woman slides the piece of paper under the ball) where the problem of establishing figure-ground relationships must be solved in order to convey the meaning.
- Type 5: Sentences requiring successive spatial relations (The man puts the ball on the book that is on the table).

The clips are not organized sequentially in terms of complexity. We want students to be exposed to a slightly higher level of complexity while they are mastering simpler forms of grammar. Thus, the ordering of clips always includes some items that are easier to convey in terms of grammar combined with some slightly harder items. Students have the benefit of showing mastery while they are still trying to discover new communication strategies for more complex material. Since the teacher sets the expectation for communication accountability, the description of what happened in any clip can be altered to fit the student's current abilities.

The teacher and the student watching the video clip together provide the shared context. In that way, the clear action sequence described by the video clip is observed and understood similarly by both. As teacher and student progress through the Gramaticas, the teacher can identify the student's current communication strategies and move one baby step in setting the next goal. That step may be at the level of vocabulary, grammatical forms, or expanded detail. The Gramaticas give multiple opportunities to practice the same grammatical structure through video clips involving different people, actions, and objects. This aids in helping the student to generalize what they have discovered beyond the initial learning materials. Throughout, the highest priority must be set on grammatical growth through demanding communication accountability.

As a test of progress, it is often helpful to periodically bring in a foil (someone who did not see the video clip) in order for the student to try out his description of the clip "de novo." Success is measured by whether the new communication partner understands what was seen, not necessarily how grammatically correct the utterance is. It is also a way of imbuing a new inventiveness into the student as the imposition of interaction dependency now demands they modify their communication for a new (and possibly less tolerant) audience. Sending the clips home with the student is one more way of bringing new conversation partners into the learning process.

The topic of the Gramaticas is not fixed in stone. Following this protocol, any teacher could build their own version of Gramaticas tailored to match the interests of their own students. Current technology, such as smartphones, makes stimulus creation easy. The only requirement is that they create a series of clips describing situations that require a range of grammatical types of increasing complexity (as listed in the examples earlier).

Whether the situation is community-based or individual-based, the methodology for successful increasing communication remains the same. It involves these four teaching strategies: (1) Learning is centered upon a story of some kind which is clear to all parties. The stories are usually presented through pictures or other visual means. (2) The persons' current communication abilities are assessed based on their ability to describe the story. In this process, the teacher identifies what communication strategies they do and don't yet have. (3) The teacher, or other members, model new aspects of grammar and establish new and higher goals for communication. (4) Communication accountability is consistently required to move the process along.

Vertical versus Horizontal Learning

In the examples described thus far, we have focused on communication growth in terms of increasing grammatical complexity. That is a vertical kind of growth. We find that adults without language often can learn to some limit of that vertical growth and after that point, they stop growing vertically. That does not mean that learning is finished. The potential for learning to communicate more clearly within a given level of complexity (horizontal growth) is equally important. For example, the student who cannot grasp or express who did what to whom through grammar may not be able to grow past a particular vertical level. Yet they can learn to communicate more successfully at the level they are currently at by learning new vocabulary or learning to expand their use of detail. Sometimes instead of constructing a complex sentence, they may discover an alternative strategy such as breaking the action event into two pieces. For instance, in the example of Gramaticas provided earlier, the person might break the action into two statements—stating that the woman tapped the shoulder of the man (WOMAN TAP-shoulder), followed by a statement that the man reacted in some way (MAN LOOK-AT WOMAN). While this is not growth toward the grammar of ASL, it is still growth in terms of clear communication.

The goal is to continue expanding communication along any dimension possible. When one dimension, such as vertical growth, is blocked at least temporarily, the demand for communication accountability needs to remain, but the focus needs to shift to applying those same demands within horizontal growth. As with all teaching, patience and persistence are needed.

Communication Learners Reach Limits on Learning

Language-deprived individuals, who are beyond the critical period for acquiring language, tend to plateau at one of four end-states of communication growth. It is important to recognize and acknowledge the plateau so that the shift to horizontal growth can be implemented. From a students' performance perspective, we see the four end state groups as follows: static gesturers, expanded gesturers, blossomers, and grammar users. Remember, these are not sequences that people pass through. They are descriptions of end states where people reach their limit on vertical learning and where we need to shift toward increasing horizontal learning. A person does not begin as a static gesturer and many do not end up as grammar users.

Static gesturers are those individuals who exhibit no substantial increase in their gestural communication, even with training. From our experience, these are comparatively rare individuals and almost always come to us with a history of extreme isolation, socially and linguistically. We sometimes see deaf persons with additional disabilities, most notably autism spectrum disorders, who show this pattern; but, we also see deaf adults without additional disabilities who, after a lifetime of having family members do language for them, show no motivation to change their communication from one-way, preestablished requests or to seek new information through dialogue.

Expanded gesturers are people who have attained a sizeable collection of signs and may be quite good at using their sign/gesture symbols to communicate interests and needs in everyday contexts. They have words, but their utterances do not show any kind of true grammatical features. They may easily learn new labels for objects, actions, and descriptives (e.g., color, size, texture) and even locatives (in, under) and can have vocabularies in the hundreds of signs. They may combine their labels in to three to four sign phrases or use them to construct "sign lists" by producing signs one after another into long strings of fluidly produced signs. Yet, when you critically examine the "list" for indicators of structure, such as determiners for nouns or consistent regularities (the agent [person that does something] is consistently followed or preceded by the receiver [person it was done to] or the object [thing it was done with]), there is no overarching consistency or structure that can be traced from one utterance to another. It is as if they had learned that the use of multiple signs is needed to communicate, but remain unaware that our "sign strings" embody also the rules for combining signs in meaningful ways.

The lack of structure does not mean that the person cannot get their message across. Given a shared context or shared information, they can communicate a sometimes-surprising level of information. There is no grammar or structure, however, which makes the message decodable. An example would be TRAIN PULL-WHISTLE EAR PULL-WHISTLE YOU which is perfectly understandable in shared context; the person's brother has just let him know that he heard the train whistle blow (which marks the time for his father to come home), so I should collect my materials and leave because once the father arrives, it is time for dinner. As communication, it is very successful if the context is known, but without context, it is impossible to glean who is doing what to whom because it lacks any grammar.

Many people who come to exposure to signing, after the critical period for language, may remain as extended gesturers for years or for a lifetime. They may show tremendous horizontal growth—gaining more words or refining when they apply their words—yet it is not automatic that they will progress beyond this end state. Those who do are categorized as Blossomers or Grammar Users.

Blossomers are unique in that they exhibit a long plateau, sometimes a three- or four-year period, where there is no awareness that communication can be grammatically driven. Over this period, the only growth observed is horizontal growth at the level of sign lists. Yet, after this long plateau, blossomers begin to show evidence of grammar growth. These glimmers of grammar pop in and out of utterances in an inconsistent manner, suggesting that blossomers have not developed a true first language, but they did move from no grammar to some grammatical use.

Grammar users are individuals who, despite all odds, not only have grasped that languages have rules, but have been able to apply those rules in running conversation. As with second-language learners in general, the proficiency of these individuals can range from basic grammar use and conversational skills to near-native signing fluency, comprehension, and ability to make grammaticality judgments. This latter group is very unusual. We note that the handful of learners who fall into this exceptional category seem to have high levels of innate intelligence. The question of why some language deprived people do much better than others has not been researched because this whole topic is too new to even formulate the research questions.

Grammar users, while having very impressive capacities for learning, are not native users of a language. Unlike native users, for instance, they don't appear to have the ability to master a second language. Also, unlike native users, their language abilities will collapse when they are fatigued, ill, or under duress, as well as when the cognitive complexity of what they are asked to communicate becomes too great. At these times, they typically "lose" grammatical abilities and resort to a pattern more like that of expanded gesturers. Late-learning of communication and language will always have consequences for the learner. Even those who achieve the level of functional communicators and grammar users do not escape the impact of their earlier language-deprivation.

Conclusion

Our goal in writing this chapter was to begin a discussion that we do not see in the literature. How can we best approach the task of teaching communication and language to adults without language who are past the critical period for language acquisition? Nicaragua gave us the opportunity to explore ways to teach language both for children within the critical period for language acquisition and for adults beyond this critical period.

Language deprivation in deaf individuals exists anywhere there are deaf people, and natural sign language exposure opportunities are not abundant and easily accessible—that is to say, everywhere. It varies tremendously both in severity and impact. In Nicaragua, and much of the third world, profound levels of language deprivation in deaf people are common. In the developed world, we are also likely to encounter language deprivation, sometimes at moderate or milder levels. Most Deaf rehabilitation and mental health programs will encounter such people. Their existence raises many of the questions addressed in this book. Do they have unique mental health or developmental problems such as a "language deprivation syndrome?" How does one "interpret" for persons lacking language competency? How does one perform valid mental health and forensic assessments? What does a solid communication and language assessment look like? Can one do counseling or therapy with such people or should we be elaborating on the kind of "pre-therapy" work Glickman (2017) describes?

Nicaragua has given us the opportunity to formulate some initial strategies for habilitation. Direct habilitation efforts are new to this field. To do this work well, we need to have Deaf service programs in mental health, rehabilitation, and independent living that are designed to meet the needs of more than the fluently signing deaf population. Inside these programs, we need to have dedicated "communication specialists" who not only have exceptional communication awareness and abilities, but who can be trained in these specialized pedagogic techniques while building upon their intuitive skills.

Responding to language deprivation requires new skill sets in providers. Embracing an approach that emphasizes communication accountability expands the clinical specialty of Deaf mental health. We encounter these people on a daily basis in our work and the question of how best to teach them, and how far they can go, calls us to action.

Note

1   The different events represent a range of utterance types that occur within languages, but they are not a successively complex series of grammatical constructions.

References

Derry, R. (circa 1985). *Sign and shine: Pineland Center Signing Manual* (4th ed.). Manual available from authors by request.

Duggan, P. (2017). Deaf, mute and accused of murder, an undocumented immigrant has been in legal limbo for 12 years. *Washington Post*, March 13, 2017.

Glickman, N. S. (2007). Do you hear voices?: Problems in assessment of mental status in deaf persons with severe language deprivation. *Journal of Deaf Studies and Deaf Education*, *12*(2), 127–147.

Glickman, N. S. (2017). *Preparing deaf and hearing persons with language and learning challenges for CBT: A pre-therapy workbook*. New York, NY: Routledge.

Kegl, J., & Iwata, G. (1989). Lenguaje de Signos Nicaragüense: A Pidgin sheds light on the "Creole?" ASL. In R. Carlson, S. DeLancey, S. Gildea, D. Payne, & A. Saxena (Eds.), *Proceedings of the fourth meetings of the Pacific Linguistics Conference* (pp. 266–294). Eugene: Department of Linguistics, University of Oregon.

Kegl, J., & McWhorter, J. (1997). Perspectives on an emerging language. In E. Clark (Ed.), *Proceedings of the Stanford Child Language Research Forum* (pp. 15–36). Palo Alto, CA: Center for the Study of Language and Information.

Kegl, J., Senghas, A., & Coppola, M. (1999). Creation through contact: Sign language emergence and sign language change in Nicaragua. In M. DeGraff (Ed.), *Language contact and language change: The intersection of language acquisition, Creole genesis, and diachronic syntax* (pp. 179–237). Cambridge, MA: MIT Press.

Lenneberg, E. H. (1967). *Biologic foundations of language*. New York, NY: John Wiley.

Mayberry, Rachel. (2010). Early language acquisition and adult language ability: What sign language reveals about the critical period for language. *The Oxford Handbook of Deaf Studies, Language, and Education, 2*, 281–291. doi:10.1093/oxfordhb/9780195390032.013.0019

Newport, E. L. (2002). Critical periods in language development. In L. Nadel (Ed.), *The encyclopedia of cognitive science* (pp. 337–340). London, UK: Macmillan Publishers Ltd./Nature Publishing Group.

Pinker, S. (1994). *The language instinct*. New York, NY: Harper Perennial Modern Classics.

Polich, L. (2001). Education of the deaf in Nicaragua. *Journal of Deaf Studies and Deaf Education* 6(4), 315–326.

Senghas, A., & Coppola, M. (2001). Children creating language: How Nicaraguan Sign Language acquired a spatial grammar. *Psychological Science, 12*(4), 323–328.

Turing, A. (1952). Can automatic calculating machines be said to think? In B. J. Copeland (Ed.), *The essential turing: The ideas that gave birth to the computer age* (pp. 524–525). Oxford, UK: Oxford University Press.

Vernon, M., Steinberg, A. G., & Montoya, L. A. (1999). Deaf murderers: Clinical and forensic issues. *Behavioral Science Law, 17*(4), 495–516.

8
Interpreting for Deaf People with Dysfluent Language in Forensic Settings

Application of the Integrated Model of Interpreting

JOAN WATTMAN

To interpret one must first understand

—*Danica Seleskovitch, 1978*

Introduction: Interpreting Challenges with Dysfluent Signers

Interpreting for two people fully fluent in their respective languages is hard enough. But when one person presents with language dysfluency, the demands on the interpreter/s increase multifold.

In the last few decades, many models of interpreting have been introduced describing the relationship dynamic between the deaf client and the interpreter, the roles which the interpreter plays, the cognitive process of interpreting, and the sociolinguistic context in which interpreting occurs (Cokely, 1992; Colonomos (in preparation); Colonomos & Moccia, 2013; Llewellyn-Jones & Lee, 2013). The literature provides task analyses of interpreter functioning and analyses of interpreter decision-making (Cogen et al., 1986; Dean & Pollard, 2013). As difficult as interpreting can be between two standard languages, there are programs, workshops, and conferences all addressing the work. This has not, until very recently, been the case for interpreting with dysfluent deaf people. Although the literature has recognized the phenomenon, there are few guideposts in working with this population.

Each deaf person who experiences language deprivation has a unique level of competence in ASL. Production and comprehension are idiosyncratic and unpredictable. Each approach to interpreting for these clients therefore must necessarily be a process of accommodating to a wide range of communication styles, approximating meaning through a process of negotiation, mediation, and co-construction, and attempting through creative strategies to achieve message equivalence.

In this chapter, a specific case example will be used to illustrate how the Integrated Model of Interpreting (IMI) informed working with a deaf dysfluent signer in a legal setting. The team on this case was a certified Deaf interpreter, Janis Cole, and myself, a certified legal interpreter. Concepts from the IMI model will be introduced, and application and analysis of the model will be demonstrated by referring to issues within the case.

A colleague and I were assigned to interpret in court for a deaf defendant we'll call Jerome. He was an elderly man with a history of childhood language deprivation and adult-onset mental illness. He faced charges of indecent assault and battery. He was accused of aggressively touching a medical assistant on her hips and buttocks. My colleague and I knew we would be facing a difficult task for which there was no standard way of approaching our interpreting work, as each assignment working with a language dysfluent deaf person presents its own unique challenges. We knew we would be relying on our shared understanding of the Massachusetts criminal court system, including its specialized legal jargon, and our ability to navigate those in both English and ASL as a team.

As detailed elsewhere in this volume, some deaf people are dysfluent users of both signed and spoken languages. Some forms of syndromal deafness include cognitive deficits, which can present additional interpreting challenges, especially if the interpreting team doesn't know what those deficits are or how they will impact the deaf person's understanding of both language and *interpreted* language (Crump & Hamerdinger, 2017). Some deaf people have sustained injuries such as strokes which impede their expressive and/or receptive language use, causing aphasias. Severe forms of mental illness may also cause dysfluent language (Andreasen, 1986). The major reason for dysfluent language in deaf people, however, is the social cause of language deprivation. All these developments complicate interpreting. To make matters even tougher, in legal settings, the consequences of inadequate interpreting are potentially very serious.

Our job in this case was first to assist Jerome in speaking with his attorney who would review his police report, competency evaluations, and legal options. Jerome could then accept a plea deal from the prosecutor or proceed to a trial. Next, we would move to the courtroom to interpret his "plea colloquy," in which a judge seeks to ensure that the defendant's plea has been chosen "intelligently, knowingly and voluntarily" (Massachusetts Rules of Criminal Procedure, 2017). Any one of these concepts could present an insurmountable interpreting challenge, even for the most experienced, trained, and qualified interpreting team, when interpreting for a person with language dysfluency and lack of fund of knowledge (understanding of the legal system, right and wrong, laws, etc.)

Both members of the team had extensive training in legal interpreting and years of experience in the courtroom. Neither of us had previously worked with Jerome. Because of his unique linguistic, cognitive, and mental health needs, along with his attorney and the judge's incomplete understanding of his communication needs, we faced multiple challenges to fulfilling our responsibility to provide clear communication between the parties.

In this chapter, we will present a theoretical framework for interpreting which provides effective guidance for all interpreting situations, even those as challenging as this one. What we faced here is in some ways the "worst case scenario" for interpreters: a highly dysfluent client, very abstract, complex, and specialized legal terminology, and a high stakes outcome for our work. We will discuss how IMI guides interpreters generally as well as in team interpreting, how it applies to work with dysfluent consumers, and how it informs the use of a variety of interpreting strategies.

Interpreting is Challenging Even Under Ideal Circumstances

Interpreting is the process of conveying information between spoken or signed languages. This may at first seem a straightforward task. Naïve mono-lingual language users, for example, often request that a sign language interpreter, "just sign what I say, exactly as I say it." However, this simple request is impossible to obey, because there is no direct, word-for-word correspondence between any two languages, be they spoken or signed. Because language is born of culture and the two are inseparable, the task for the ASL-English interpreter working from English into ASL becomes taking American hearing culture-embedded information presented in spoken English, un-embedding it, and re-embedding into American Deaf Culture with an ASL interpretation, and vice versa.

Interpreting even a single word can be challenging. The English word "bread," for example, corresponds to some extent with the French "pain" but barely overlaps the meaning of "chapati" in Hindi. Sometimes there is no equivalent word or cultural concept between two languages. For example, the Spanish word *sobremesa* refers to the period of time after a meal when conversation still flows around the table. There is no English word that conveys this meaning. Instead, an entire English sentence is needed, and further cultural knowledge would be required to use it properly in context.

Even when close equivalences do exist between words from different languages, their grammatical use will often differ between languages. For example, the construction of time markers in ASL is quite different from English. In American Sign Language (ASL) the sign that means "tomorrow" actually means "one-day-future," so it can be used to mean literally tomorrow, as in English, or it can be used to mean "the next day." If an ASL speaker is talking about an event that happened two days ago, and then refers to something related that happened the next day, the speaker might use the sign TOMORROW to mean the next day. In that case, depending on the context, the best interpretation into English could be "yesterday," or it could be "the next day." But it would not be "tomorrow."

In ASL, the categorization of nouns has grammatical rules that don't exist in English, which means there is often no simple one-to-one correspondence between concepts expressed in ASL and English. In ASL, categories generally fall into one of three spheres: those where the title of the category is fingerspelled and all the things within it have ASL signs (e.g., SEASONS is fingerspelled and each season has a sign; or WEAPONS is fingerspelled and then each weapon has a sign), or the category title has a sign and all the things within it are fingerspelled (e.g., FLOWERS is signed and all the names of the flowers are fingerspelled), or the title of the category has a sign and all the things within it have ASL signs (e.g., CLOTHES is signed and each article of clothing has a sign). If the deaf person receiving the interpreted message doesn't understand fingerspelling, an appropriate interpretation of "what season is it now?" might be, "NOW WINTER, SPRING, SUMMER, FALL, WHAT?"[1]

Interpreting will proceed most smoothly when there is roughly corresponding vocabulary, grammar, and syntax in both languages, roughly similar cultural perspectives, and between language users who have roughly equivalent social status. The status of the language itself can affect interpretation, as when a language is recognized as dominant because of its affiliation with its country of origin, such as interpreting between speakers of Spain-based Spanish and Portugal-based Portuguese. Interpretation becomes much harder where one language is oppressed and one language is dominant, as between French and Haitian Creole (Kreyol) or between English and Puerto-Rican Spanish. Often in these situations a diglossic relationship occurs where the dominant language intrudes on the oppressed language, and a creole emerges such as Spanglish, Haitian Creole, and Pidgin Signed English. (Quinto-Pozos, 2007). Disentangling meaning in these instances presents an everyday challenge to the qualified interpreter.

Further, global languages such as Chinese or English have developed extensive scientific, medical, and legal vocabularies. Conversely, traditional cultures can have intricate vocabularies for such things as kinship structure, proper use of honorifics, gender categories, and even such things as local fish and wildlife. In these situations, specialized vocabulary existing in one language will often not exist in the other. As an oppressed language in the United States, ASL has historically lacked established vocabulary in technical areas (although this is changing as larger numbers of deaf people enter technical and medical fields, and as projects like the ASL Clear Initiative seek to standardize signs for technical vocabulary) (Reis, Solovey, Henner, Johnson, & Hoffmeister, 2015).

Interpreters must have fluency in both languages and cultures, the individual and collective cultural worldviews of both speakers, as well as a deep understanding of how oppression and the diglossic relationship between English and ASL affect both how a message is expressed and received. Consider the following cultural conflict that occurred between a mixed group of hearing and deaf people.

Generally speaking, the American Deaf community is more communal than American mainstream culture, which stresses individualism. Here, the cultural obstacle occurred in the drafting of a bill that a group of hearing and deaf people wanted to introduce to their state legislature. The hearing leader prepared a rough draft ahead of time, simply intending to give the group a starting point from which to work. Deaf members, however, had expected that the bill would be written during the meeting, an echo perhaps of the cultural tradition of the deep, open group conversations that occur when far-flung deaf people meet. The Deaf leader recognized this dynamic and named it, and the interpreters at the meeting, understanding how each perspective was rooted in social and cultural experience, could communicate to the hearing leader the nature of the cross-cultural misunderstanding while acknowledging her good intentions. This avoided causing her feelings of guilt or worry about being perceived as uncaring.

Idioms add another layer of complexity to interpreting. Misinterpreted idioms can be truly comical, as in this famous example: speaking in Poland, former President Jimmy Carter said he wanted to learn about the Polish people's "desires for the future." In an overly literal translation, his interpreter conveyed Carter as saying he had a sexual desire for the Polish people. When Carter added that he was happy to be in Poland, his interpreter also translated this too literally, presenting Carter as saying that he was "happy to grasp at Poland's private parts" (Macdonald, 2015).

Some wrongly or too literally interpreted idioms can lead to undesired consequences. For example, proverbs in English are often based in ancient popular cautionary tales which have a conventionalized metaphoric meaning. Most deaf people would not be familiar with these proverbs, having not been exposed to the stories as children nor to the way proverbs are used in conversational English. During psychiatric assessments, mental health professionals often ask patients what common proverbs mean, because certain forms of mental illness can affect a person's ability to appreciate the metaphorical meaning of the proverbs. ASL-English interpreters might be asked to interpret proverbs like, "a stitch in time saves nine," or "people who live in glass houses shouldn't throw stones," but these proverbs lose their metaphorical meaning in another language; and many deaf people would never have been exposed to them previously in any case. Thus, using these proverbs in an interpreted interaction as tools to assess mental status inevitably makes the deaf person look impaired. It also presents a near impossible challenge for the interpreters.

In sum, even when interpreting from fluent English to fluent ASL, it is naïve to hope that an interpreter might "just sign exactly what I say." One might as well ask a chef to prepare an Indian meal with Chinese ingredients. If this task is difficult when working with fully language fluent persons, how much more challenging does it become with non-fluent or cognitively impaired language users?

The Integrated Model of Interpreting

IMI began to be developed in the 1980s by interpreter educator Betty Colonomos, a fluent ASL/English bilingual, based on the groundbreaking work of the Parisian spoken-language interpreter Danica Seleskovitch (1978). Seleskovitch argued that interpretation involves far more than simply translating one set of words as accurately as possible to another. She shifted the emphasis in interpreting from finding word equivalencies to understanding the overall message and reconstructing it in the conceptual framework of the second language. Her key point is that "to interpret, one must first understand" (Seleskovitch, 1978).

In its most current version, the IMI describes the interpreter (or team) working between *source* (signer or speaker) and *target* (audience) (Colonomos, in preparation). Both parties in the interaction relate to the setting in which the exchange occurs and are situated within their own cultural and linguistic context. This is connected to and affected by age, gender, and ethnic background, among other factors, as well as any affiliated identities of the participants and power differentials between participants.

Interpreting between source and target proceeds through a part of IMI called Comprehension, Representation, and Preparation, or "CRP." As the message is received from the source (C), the interpreter analyzes for meaning, relying on general competence in the source language and culture, as well as more specific knowledge related to the situation. In a legal case, for example, the latter might include the client's case file or a standard legal text such as the "plea colloquy" mentioned earlier.

In the second phase of Representation (R), the interpreter's task is to "drop form," leaving behind the source's specific words, signs, sentence structure, and order of ideas to create a faithful mental representation of not only the information to be communicated, but also the source's goals, affect, and register. Register is linguistic variation related to the psychological distance between speaker and audience, ranging from formal to intimate (Joos, 1962; Shaw, 1987). Meaning now exists in the interpreter's mind, relatively stripped of the forms of signed or spoken language. The only lexical terms that will be transmitted in whole are proper nouns or, in some contexts, words or phrases purposefully retained from the source language for a specific reason.

In the Representation phase, each interpreter tags information in a unique way. Most describe a visual rendering, something like a movie. Others have a more kinesthetic experience, or even a multimodal experience. Tags are essential in organizing large chunks of information. The rights of a Massachusetts defendant pleading guilty, for example, are spelled out on a green sheet of paper. Having interpreted this information many times, it is tagged in my mind (and in the minds of others with whom I often work) simply as the "green sheet."

The interpreter's understanding of the message, as intended by the source, is referred to as the source representation (R1). In R1, the message remains within the source's frame of reference. This separates the process of understanding the source from the process of communicating to the target audience. Consciously remaining in the *source's* frame of reference, the interpreter can more readily identify which aspects of the speaker's meaning may need to be clarified and/or modified before moving forward.

The interpreter then constructs the target representation (R2), informed by competence in the *recipient's* language and culture. The interpreter envisions how the recipient will perceive the incoming information and evaluates her representation for potential difficulties. These include whether from the listener's point of view there will be cultural conflicts, issues in the way the message is structured that cause misunderstandings, and lexical items or phrases that trigger an emotional response that were not present in the original message. The interpreter must evaluate the speaker's goal and make decisions about formulating a representation that adequately encapsulates that goal without unintentionally including something that was not in the speaker's message or would generate a reaction that the speaker did not want. This is still before attaching any signs or words to the message, which occurs next, in the Preparation phase. A classic example of this on the lexical level is the sign INSTITUTION that Deaf people use to mean the residential school where they usually boarded as children. The word institution has a negative connotation for English speakers, whereas the ASL sign does not. When the interpreter sees the sign INSTITUTION, she must tag it so she conveys the positive experience of most Deaf people.

"Target switch" describes the interpreter's conscious reframing of the message from the speaker frame or schema (R1) to the audience frame or schema (R2). The interpreter needs to identify the issues with equivalence that will arise, holding these two representations in her head, and evaluate each issue to arrive at the most effective and equivalent interpretation. Even the order of events in the original text may cause difficulties. In the representation the interpreter now holds while she considers how the message will be perceived, she may need to purposefully restructure the message so that the flow of information matches real-world order of actions or to make implicit meaning explicit. She may, for example, reorganize the order of information to show cause and effect, or change the emphasis on certain items by placing them in the foreground or background.

It is important to "drop form" in R1 and R2 and get directly to the meaning of the message independent of the particular words used in order to avoid contamination from the source language or prematurely get into Preparation. Monolingual English speakers often wrongly assume that English words have inherent meaning for which ASL signs are simply visual representations. As we discussed before, overly literal adherence to the strict lexical meaning of words in a language often interferes with language interpretation, a process referred to as *source language intrusion*. In IMI, one does not prematurely pick a sign or word for the target language before fully exploring the meaning. Interpreters who jump ahead of this process will often use the wrong conceptual ASL sign (such as using FIX for repair, rather than FLAT if discussing fixed-rate mortgages), leaving the deaf person confused about why you would need to "repair" a mortgage. Finally, the interpreter prepares (P) to deliver the message. The preparation phase includes "process management"—an awareness of the overall efficacy of the interpreting process—along with a final check of coherence of content, affect, and register. The target message must accurately portray the context from which the original message issued. An example from court occurs when the deaf person signs to the judge "OK" and the interpreter conveys that as "Yes, your honor," which takes into account the power dynamics and formality of the interchange.

After delivering the message, the interpreter observes for feedback; both from team members (if any) and from the hearing and deaf clients. Determining meaning effectiveness is a dynamic process that responds to the degree of comprehension exhibited by the target audience. If a repair is needed, the interpreter revisits R2 and then reworks the target language output. In court, if the output was "on the record," process management might include asking to be recognized and requesting that the legal record be amended. If the repair requires a restatement in ASL, the interpreter might ask the judge for time to reinterpret, or request rephrasing to resolve a lack of clarity.

In addition to monitoring the effectiveness of communication between source and target, interpreters should monitor ourselves and one another, imagining an internal "supervisor" overseeing our work. When interpreters work alternately in teams, as is done for longer or more complex assignments, the interpreter who is not actively interpreting should monitor and "feed" corrections or clarifications to the "working" interpreter, enhancing the overall accuracy and efficiency of the process. This entire process is represented in Figure 8.1.

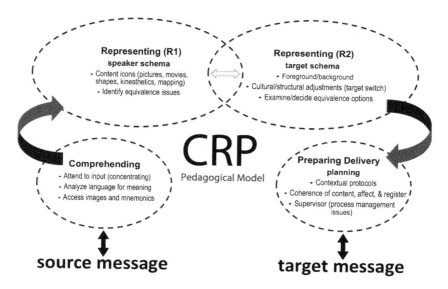

Figure 8.1 The CRP Pedagogical Model, a component of the Integrated Model of Interpreting

Source: Reprinted with permission. Copyright © 2007, 2013 by Betty M. Colonomos, Bilingual Mediation Center, Inc.

One item interpreters must check during both comprehension and preparation is what IMI calls "filters." Biases while interpreting can distort the message since they affect how we perceive people, situations, and meaning.

If an interpreter holds a strong belief about abortion rights and is called upon to interpret a contrary view, she may unconsciously telegraph her feelings as she signs, perhaps by a variation in speed or smoothness or via an unintentional facial expression. Another example is if one party insults the other, and the interpreter is not comfortable with open conflict, she might unconsciously tone down the attack. Awareness of personal biases helps the interpreter avoid these issues with message equivalence, as does openness to feedback from other members of the interpreter team.

In our case example, Jerome's victim made a statement about how the crime affected her. She spoke about the trauma of being assaulted at work and how it had impacted her functioning, well-being, and mental state. She told the judge what sentence she deemed appropriate and what conditions she wanted imposed (e.g., counseling). The team had been interpreting between Jerome and his attorney in a conference room and the defense was not prepared to go forward with the plea on the first appearance. The victim's schedule, however, did not allow her to return for the second hearing, so we were to interpret for her before Jerome had changed his plea to guilty. She was very emotional and described his actions as intentionally harmful. We had to correctly portray her affect as highly unsettled and angry. Jerome shook his head throughout and signed NO a few times. The team was cognizant that our earlier interactions with Jerome might color our work rendering the victim's message and had to be vigilant in accurately portraying her distress.

The Temptation and Danger of Not Dropping Form

Interpreters sometimes escape the difficulty of our work by skipping the step of fully understanding the message by developing the representation of the source message R1 or the target message R2. Many hearing interpreters are biased towards their primary spoken language and when working from English to ASL start with an English transliteration and work toward a more ASL version. Some interpreters worry that when using "grassroots"—indigenous, pure—ASL they may "insult the intelligence" of the deaf people. This represents an inner language bias, as if ASL is a "low" language and English a "high" language (Stokoe, 1969).

Interpreters may produce a signed rendition that matches the spoken message and can *appear* meaningful, but where form has not been released and R2 has *not* in fact been adequately constructed. For example, ASL does not use the passive voice found in an English sentence such as, "X was suspected of several prior indecent assaults." If the interpreter signed X SUSPECTS then "X" would incorrectly be made the subject of the verb rather than its object. This would be confusing to X. Instead, one might ask the attorney *who* suspected and then create an active sentence using the new subject: "POLICE SUSPECT X DID BREAK LAW."

There are also problems with not dropping ASL form when interpreting from ASL to English. Not dropping ASL form means that the interpreter provides the gloss for each ASL sign rather than actually interpreting what a deaf person signs. This process can make even an articulate ASL signer appear incoherent.

Applying the IMI to Interpreting for Dysfluent Persons

Because "to interpret one must first understand," interpreters who do not understand cannot proceed. Confronted with confusing input, the IMI encourages us to reflect, and our Code of Professional Conduct (RID, Inc. 2007) demands that we should not guess. We should not fill in missing pieces or alter ungrammatical language. Instead, we must pause to consider what we can do to achieve maximal understanding. If despite our best efforts, communication still cannot be established, we must disclose that interpreting cannot proceed.

When communication fails, interpreters using the IMI refer to the part of the model encompassing Comprehension, Representation, and Preparation to identify the root cause. The model relies on reflection and dialogue. When teams use a CRP analysis in preparation for and debriefing after assignments, they discover patterns in their work that may create obstacles to message equivalence and effective process management. Interpreters steeped in the model develop strategies to address these patterns. This rigorous practice informs their future work. Some of the questions the interpreter must ask herself are: Where or how did the breakdown occur? Did one or both of the interpreters misunderstand the source message? Did they reconstruct meaning in the target language incorrectly? Did they misperceive or misrepresent the type or degree of affect? Did the interpretation inadvertently shift an emphasis? Or did the team not make an implicit element in the source language explicit in the target rendition?

The CRP portion of IMI makes it uniquely suited to working with people who have suffered language deprivation. The IMI-practicing interpreter can stay in the Representation phase long enough to fully explore the message independent of words and signs. This frees us by allowing us the time to completely understand and the power to make decisions about rendering meaning as we move into Preparation. The IMI model affords an interpreter the ability to work with dysfluent deaf people in a substantively different way than many other models in that it resists the external pressure to sign or speak constrained by the form of the source language.

This means that the interpreting process should be consecutive, moving from source through interpreter to recipient and back again in sequence. *This process should be the norm for interpreting in any high stakes situation, especially when working with dysfluent people.* The interpreters thereby gain the time needed to complete and monitor the CRP process at the sentence, paragraph, or other informational "chunk" level. Simultaneous interpreting where comprehension, representation, and preparation all occur at the same time—typical of most sign language/spoken language interpreting—generally increases the risk of errors in court and legal interpreting (Russell, 2002; Russell 2003).

When process management demands more time than even consecutive interpreting permits, we must request it, regardless of external pressure to work less obtrusively or more quickly. This necessitates interrupting the conversational flow, and we must make sure to explain to the participants what we are doing and why. Hearing participants will typically ask, "Why is this taking so long?" Most dysfluent deaf clients, inured to being misunderstood, generally appreciate that the purpose of the interruption is to respect everyone's right to clear communication.

Application of IMI to Work with Deaf Interpreters and Dysfluent Signers

Deaf interpreters can add immeasurable value to the interpreting process with dysfluent signers. As native users of ASL steeped in Deaf culture, but also widely experienced in the hearing world, Deaf interpreters can often intuit what a deaf client is attempting to say and understand what obstacles are preventing clear receptive or expressive communication. ASL-English interpreters may lack this "gut sense" of the deaf client's worldview, frame of reference, and linguistic style.

Deaf interpreters can often construct a target message that is readily understandable by the deaf person. Because they navigate the world using a visual-spatial lens, they rely on extralinguistic knowledge that allows them to relate to the deaf client's experiences and perspectives. Simply by being in the room they provide reassurance and camaraderie for a deaf person who may feel isolated and overwhelmed. Yet even with Deaf interpreters, the basic rule of IMI interpreting remains true: to interpret, you must understand. Deaf interpreters make it more likely that understanding between all communication participants will occur, and IMI guides them in that task not just between languages, but between what are often very different thought worlds.

When there is an ASL-English interpreter and a Deaf interpreter both versed in IMI, the CRP model can be used to co-construct the Representation (R). The target message (output) of the ASL-English interpreter becomes the Deaf interpreter's source message. The Deaf interpreter can then clarify anything from the ASL interpreter's signing that is not readily understandable. This exchange within the team often highlights parts of the message that do not make sense and need to be reinterpreted, or questions that need to be checked with the speaker as further linguistic unpacking occurs. The hearing interpreter likewise can monitor the Deaf interpreter's output. When ASL interpreters are not native signers, they may not produce the target message as efficiently and effectively as native signing Deaf interpreters, but they usually can compare source and target messages for equivalency.

While this co-constructing process is happening, the deaf person can watch the output of the ASL interpreter when she is working from English to ASL and then observe the Deaf interpreter working in a visual-gestural mode. The first interpretation may not be completely understandable but can provide a frame or orientation that helps him comprehend the Deaf interpreter's message. When he replies, and the Deaf interpreter conveys his message in ASL to the ASL-English interpreter, he may understand enough that he can jump in to correct misunderstandings as well. He can observe any discussion between the team about the interpreting process that may highlight areas that need clarification. In this way, it is possible that the repeated iterations of the message between the two interpreters and his own active participation helps to reinforce the understanding of the deaf person. The experience of watching the two interpreters work can also be empowering.

In terms of workload balance, the Deaf interpreter ends up carrying much of the CRP process between the conceptual world of the deaf person and formal ASL. The ASL-English interpreter carries the weight of interpreting between English, including the highly technical legal language of a courtroom, and formal ASL. In our courtroom example with Jerome, the Deaf interpreter essentially became the cultural mediator between his worldview and that of the courtroom as she learned his idiosyncratic signs and sign names, going so far as to interact with Jerome's group home staff members to learn from them what idiosyncratic signs and sign phrasing meant. She initiated the role plays about "touching" and "sexual assault," creating several versions of each scenario until she and the ASL-English interpreter were confident that Jerome understood the concept.

In court, the question that had to be interpreted was, "did you assault the victim in an indecent manner?" The Deaf interpreter (Janis) had to act out all the elements of that criminal charge and satisfy herself that the client understood and could responsibly say he had done the accused acts. The Deaf interpreter created several scenarios that included touching in an appropriate manner, touching in an inappropriate manner, and not touching at all. She suggested what we would do and in what sequence, and for those scenarios in which she wasn't touching the hearing interpreter (me) she used her voice to cue me when and how to move. The defendant Jerome's version of the incident, as much as the interpreters understood it, was that somehow the woman moving away caused him to grab her. This version was contrasted with versions in which the Deaf interpreter touched the ASL interpreter, and the touching caused the hearing interpreter, as the role played "victim," to move away. When touch was included, each scenario also included forms of touching that would lead to simple assault (on a part of the body that is appropriate to touch but which the victim didn't want touched) and indecent assault (touching the hips and buttocks).

The relationship between team members is essential, especially as they are cocreating the target message. This connection could be based on prior experiences interpreting together or, if working with a new team member, on the recognition of a jointly shared process, through preparation and debriefing. There must be trust to try something that seems risky or embarrassing, as when the interpreting team role played different ways of touching and the meaning of "assault" and "indecent assault."

Role-playing aside, the demands of the challenging work described here are enhanced by the additional requirement in the legal realm of rigorous monitoring. The integrity of the record is paramount, as errors can have grave ramifications for the deaf person and, as described before, the team must disclose if errors are made or if interpreting accurately is not possible. The IMI stresses the inclusion of feedback and monitoring which helps ensure the integrity of the court record and can lead the interpreter to reexamine any part of the process—comprehension, representation, or preparation.

Specific Techniques for Working with Dysfluent Signers

Even given our general courtroom experience and training, we were imperfectly prepared to work with Jerome. A variety of special techniques, to be discussed next, are available to interpreters working with dysfluent clients like Jerome in high-stakes settings such as court. Ideally, we would have been able to read background information on Jerome and the charges against him prior to meeting him, and to have seen in advance any documents we would be asked to interpret. A pre-conference with the attorney would have familiarized us with the material, alerted us to potential problems with communication and strategies, and allowed us to establish cues for when we needed clarification. We might have video-recorded at our first appearance, to review our work in preparation for the client's next court appearance. In this case, we couldn't do any of this helpful preparation.

Strategies for working with dysfluent signers can extend well beyond purely linguistic communication. Each of the following techniques takes time, sometimes quite a bit of time, and all draw attention to the interpreters as active participants in the communication process. Consecutive, rather than simultaneous, interpreting is a minimum requirement for these approaches to be used. Further, the parties to the communication must grant the interpreters the latitude they need in their search for full understanding and linguistic equivalency. In many courtrooms, judges will simply not permit this latitude. Often there is more latitude in smaller settings such as a pre-conference meeting between attorney and defendant.

1. Clarifying Ambiguity in the Source Message by Asking Questions

Interpreter-initiated utterances, rare in many settings, are frequently required with dysfluent clients. These are statements that parties in the case have not spoken and that are not being interpreted by the team. They arise from the team itself. (Note that in court, permission must be asked before initiating clarification with the deaf party, to avoid the appearance of having a private conversation).

> Like many dysfluent clients, Jerome described place names and chronologies idiosyncratically. He referred to events out of chronological order, without dates, and compounded our confusion with phrases such as "the second time." He had a nonstandard sign name for his home area. He referred to medical appointments not by their purpose or timing, but instead by mode of transportation (e.g., by a staffed van) or visual features of the buildings where they took place. In each such case, we needed to pause our interpreting and explain to the court room audience that we needed to clarify referents. This is in direct contrast to the conference room setting where we had the advantage of being able to turn to residence staff who were often able to provide the context necessary to understand what the defendant meant.

When interpreting between a hearing and a deaf person in the courtroom, interpreters not only interpret what speakers say but also voice their own interpreting needs. For instance, interpreters might need to confer with each other during the assignment. They could make statements to the hearing and deaf participants for various purposes (including process management requests for repositioning, pausing, repeating), ask clarifying questions, or perform escort interpreting (explained below in number 9). Witter-Merithew and Mathers (2014) have researched interpreter-initiated utterances using videotaped mock legal assignments with teams involving a Deaf interpreter. In their preliminary findings, teams with a deaf member showed many more interpreter-initiated utterances than teams with two hearing ASL interpreters. The deaf members initiated these most often, especially when directed at the deaf participant, but also to the hearing participants, using the ASL interpreter to convey the message in English. When interpreters manage the process by speaking up in this way, they do become more obtrusive, but participants around them gain insight into the communication challenges they are handling, and communication becomes more successful overall.

2. Paraphrasing a Tentative or Partial Understanding to Check for Accuracy

Dysfluent clients' statements frequently leave interpreters with tentative or partial comprehension of the intended meaning. Often, the Deaf interpreter in a team will work to resolve unclear statements before the ASL-English interpreter renders the interpretation. Having achieved a partial Comprehension (C), we can reflect it back and check, "Is that right?" before proceeding further.

In order to interpret correctly, interpreters often need to seek a detailed understanding of a client's worldview and language use.

> Jerome did not seem to understand the ASL sign TOUCH when used in its most general English meaning of placing hands on a part of another person's body. Each time the team interpreted the question, "Did you touch the victim?" he answered NO. Even when the sign TOUCH was moved to the part of the body that was alleged to be touched, he still answered no. We had to act out various scenarios where touching occurred, having one team member using the hands in a natural way to touch the hips or waist of the other team member, instead of the handshape that is used in the sign TOUCH. After acting out several scenarios, we were able to successfully transmit the intended meaning and the defendant answered that YES he had, in fact, touched the victim in the way we were demonstrating.

3. Drawing, Using Photographs or Illustrations, Using Props, or Engaging in Role Play

> Jerome signed grammatically but ambiguously, WOMAN MOVE-FORWARD (ME) GRAB-WAIST. This could be understood two different ways: "Because the woman moved to escape me, I had to grab her waist" or the more neutral "the woman moved forward and then I grabbed her waist." Jerome was sufficiently dysfluent that determining which he meant required acting out each scenario via role play. A simple linguistic clarification would not have been possible.
>
> In this situation, an interpreter insufficiently attuned to the CRP process might have avoided these complexities and simply transliterated the client's unclear language, as in, "The woman moved and I grabbed at her," or even "Woman move grab." From an IMI perspective, this is not a successful interpreting outcome.

Incorporation of manipulatives can be used as substitutes for ASL grammatical features which the deaf person does not understand. For instance, it is common practice in ASL to refer to sequential events using the fingers of one hand in order (i.e., pointing to the thumb, forefinger, middle finger, etc.). This grounds the referent and is used very productively for many kinds of lists. The interpreter can point to one finger and then describe an event, such as YOU ARRIVE DOCTOR HIS OFFICE, then use the next finger for the next event to be described, DOCTOR EXAMINE YOU. Those fingers can represent a chronological series of events so the entire statement for each event does not need to be reiterated. Each finger becomes a depiction of an event, but naturally, this only works when the deaf person knows this aspect of ASL grammar.

Another type of grounding occurs when classifiers are used. ASL categorizes objects by size, shape, and instrument, among other classifications. One hand is used to show where a group of objects begins, such as a bookcase full of books, while the second hand moves to show how many shelves of books. Referring to the fingers of one hand and holding the space where a classifier begins to move are two examples of what is called anchoring. Dysfluent signers often have a difficulty with both methods of anchoring. Interpreters can address these difficulties by using manipulatives to make concrete and visible events or people that have been established and adding other events or people in relation to what is already established.

> Jerome's attorney had explained that the district attorney was offering a plea bargain with a "split sentence of thirty months with six months to serve and the balance suspended, and three years of probation." The team needed to clarify with the attorney when probation would begin—now or after the six months incarcerated? If the client were to violate probation, he would face the possibility of serving up to two years in jail. The Deaf interpreter's initial effort implied that there would be no further monitoring two years after being discharged from jail. The hearing interpreter, monitoring, noted and corrected the error. The team then repeated the interpretation, correcting the timeline and illustrating it with pens and eyeglass cases (objects that happened to be at hand). We represented the present time with one pen, and used others to show six months, two years, three years, and so forth. We also drew the timeline on paper, so we could refer back to a mark on the paper when speaking about the end of the jail sentence, the end of probation, and other important events in the timeline. With these techniques we were successfully able to explain the complex concept of the client facing a possibility of being re-incarcerated for up to whatever time had not yet been served (the remaining 24 months) even for a probation violation that occurred after he had been freed.

4. Remaining Alert for Common Errors with Dysfluent Language That May Skew the Message and Asking for Clarification

ASL uses non-manual markers such as facial movements (in particular, movements of the eyebrows and mouth) to establish adverbial meaning, such as in indicating that an action was done matter-of-factly or carelessly. Dysfluent signers, as well as second-language learners of ASL, often use these non-manual markers incorrectly. Dysfluent signers also frequently fail to use the spatial properties of ASL to indicate pronouns accurately (e.g., who did what to whom).

> When the defendant Jerome did not use spatial referencing for pronouns in his account of the alleged crime, the interpreters responded by acting out several scenarios until he agreed we had understood him by expressing, "YES. THAT!"

Often there is a weakness or rigidity rather than a complete lack of facility with spatialization and other grammatical features. ASL has an extremely complex and flexible system where one can set up a referent in one "scene" and assign it a temporary meaning. In another scene, the same point in space can be reassigned to another meaning.

> Jerome used the spatial field of ASL inflexibly. He used a spatial index to indicate where he had gone to a medical appointment and the treatment he had received there but was not able to use spatial indexing to show that the treatment had also occurred at other sites. He could not "clear the slate" to set up a new referent in a previously used location. This more concrete and inflexible rendering made it very difficult for the team to compare two different events.

Language dysfluency can be more complex than simply being illiterate in spoken language and non-fluent in sign language. The weakness and rigidity that affects syntax also can distort the semantics of signs. The person may use signs that have multiple meanings in a more narrow and limited way or he may use a sign incorrectly.

> Jerome used the sign GENERAL repeatedly. It seemed to function as an adjective or adverb but did not have the meaning it would carry for a fluent signer. The team was not able to discern any pattern to its use and could not interpret it with any confidence.

Dysfluent clients may be unable to generalize linguistic patterns, such as the ability to use sign inflection in a consistent way (e.g., the way signs like SICK, STAND, WAIT, and LOOK can be modulated to mean these actions occurred for a long time or repeatedly). When the deaf person does not use ASL grammar or vocabulary reliably and accurately, the interpreters can't be as confident as to what the person is intending to communicate. Instead, the interpreters need to actively check out their understanding of the intended message.

5. "Unpacking" Complex or Confusing Content into Smaller, More Concrete Parts

In American English, speakers often express statements without contextualization, assuming that the listener will ask questions if they do not have the background to understand a phrase or the entire proposition. This is especially true in more formal registers. American English users approach communication from the perspective of the linguistic and cultural majority. They enjoy a level of privilege in that they readily assume that if a message is unclear, the problem doesn't lie with them. They assume the other person needs to communicate better. Deaf signers may be more inclined to assume they don't understand because of their own limitations, and they may not feel empowered to ask clarifying questions, especially in an adversarial situation like the courtroom where the power dynamic is so imbalanced.

For example, an English statement such as "One of the employees had a car accident and will be delayed" does not necessarily elicit a need to know how the accident occurred, although in conversational (informal) register, an interchange about the accident might be expected. A question such as "What's your favorite color?" can be answered without the English speaker understanding whether the context refers to clothing, interior paint, or nail polish.

By contrast, the American Deaf community relies on implicit background underlying communication. Information needs to be more clearly embedded in its context to be understood. Communication in ASL is often more detailed, so that enough information is presented for the receiver to fully understand the message. For the ASL user, context grounds the meaning, and if an interpreter expresses only non-contextualized statements this may lead to intercultural misunderstanding. The interpreter develops linguistic and cultural expansion and contextualization with our own real-world knowledge and what we know of the deaf person's experience and understanding. In a non-legal setting, interpreters would be free to use examples that would illustrate the point. In legal settings, we are constrained by the legal interpreting protocol and cannot include additional information. We are limited therefore to expansions that have their base within the meaning of the concept.

An example of the need for interpreters to provide more detail than the original spoken language message occurs when the legal decision is made to release a defendant on personal recognizance with a condition of release being "no contact with the victim." A hearing defendant is likely to understand what "no contact" means. The dysfluent deaf defendant likely needs this spelled out. The interpreter could sign NO CONTACT. The sign CONTACT looks like TOUCH. A deaf defendant may assume they can't touch the victim, but all other contact is permissible. The interpretation must make it clear that NO CONTACT includes face-to-face interaction as well as Facebook, email, TTY, video phone, text, giving a note to a third party, or telling a third party to relay the message.

Many English phrases, like "indecent assault and battery," need to be clarified or "unpacked" by providing examples or context. These words or phrases are terms of art specific to the legal arena. We can develop an understanding of a term such as "assault and battery" via examples, working from ASL signs such as "touch" or "hurt." The sentences, "you've been charged with assault" or "you're charged with assault and battery," require the interpreter to express if the touch was with an open hand or a closed fist, whether it involved punching, slapping, or pushing, or whether the assault involved raising a fist and causing fear of imminent harm to the victim. In addition, the sentence must be expressed in ASL using active voice, so the act of charging the defendant would be attributed to the prosecutor.

A norm in American Deaf culture is to tap or touch a conversational partner to request attention and establish the eye contact needed for visual language. Tapping can also be used to hold the floor, to dictate turn-taking, or to emphasize points. Touch in Deaf culture has somewhat different norms than in the general American culture. Because Jerome faced charges related to inappropriate touch, it was important for the interpreters to attend to this cultural issue in constructing R2. We acted out a typical attention-getting touch. We contrasted this with persistently touching even when the recipient made clear she did not want to be touched (i.e., an illegal assault). Jerome was extremely surprised to learn that simply tapping someone on the shoulder in an ordinary way could be illegal if one had been asked to desist.

Having established that even "appropriate" touch when unwanted is not legal, the interpreters proceeded to act out touching in inappropriate places, such as the hips and the buttocks. We repeated each scenario several times, touching "appropriately" and "inappropriately."

Another example of unpacking occurred when the issue of disposition was raised. Would the defendant be sent to a psychiatric facility with Deaf services or to jail? The defendant's advocate urged the judge to send him to the hospital, but the judge ordered him to jail. The team interpreted the decision to the defendant, but he didn't seem to understand it. When the court officer approached him with handcuffs and started to lead him away, the defendant asked whether he was going to the hospital. Apparently, he had not understood the interpreted conversation between the advocate and judge. The interpreters asked for more time, and then replayed the conversation in more detail, making it more obvious that the judge had considered both options and decided on the latter.

6. Anchoring by Repeating Previously Established Context

In item 3 earlier, we discussed how ASL can create lists of sequential items by reference to fingers on one hand. We discussed how sometimes interpreters use manipulatives if the deaf person does not understand this ASL grammatical feature. In either case, however, interpreters often need to reestablish the facts before they can ask a question such as, "What did you do next?" Sometimes dysfluent signers will appear to contradict themselves in ways which require fully following their train of thought to disentangle. Sometimes the problem is that they do not understand the context for the question because it was not adequately reestablished in ASL. As in the aforementioned example concerning touch, a question answered by a seemingly clear yes or no may later be contradicted. It appears that the deaf person is confused or perhaps lying, but the problem may lie in a too literal interpretation from English to ASL, without the CRP process that could more accurately convey the linguistic and cultural equivalency of the source language.

7. Constructing Understanding of Abstract Concepts or Terms by Building a Foundation from Simpler Terms or Connecting Previously-Unrelated Ideas

This technique is related closely to item 5, unpacking, as some of the building blocks of the concept are not functionally present in the deaf client's frame of reference. Interpreters cannot rely on pulling out examples from the defendant's own experiences within the legal arena but must attempt to tag items that are within their sphere, such as building the idea of an illegal assault from conversational attention-getting behavior.

Courtroom interpreters are frequently expected to interpret abstract and technical legal vocabulary—terms such as "competence," "continued without a finding," "suspended sentence," or "beyond a reasonable doubt"—for deaf people who have never been exposed to these concepts. The legal arena also has many frozen texts, such as the colloquy and recitation of constitutional rights, parts of the charge to the jury, and even the daily call to order, that can tax the interpreting team, as they are usually read quickly and without affect. The interpreting challenge extends beyond there being no widely established signs for these concepts. The deeper problem for many dysfluent or poorly educated deaf clients is that understanding these concepts assumes at least a high school level of education, a fund of information about law, and well-developed linguistic reasoning skills. Many language-deprived deaf people lack the linguistic, educational, or conceptual foundation needed to understand such terms.

Within the Integrated Model of Interpreting, the task is to search for linguistic equivalence, as best we can. One can think of working off the scaffold of knowledge which the person already has and building out to the meaning that the attorney is trying to convey. The interpreters explain to the attorney or judge what they are attempting and ask for the time needed. They then build incrementally to the abstract concept by referencing terms, ideas, or experiences the person already has.

Legal interpreters working with language-deprived deaf people need to be prepared with strategies for conveying commonly used abstract legal terms such as "plea bargain." It can be challenging enough to do this when prepared in advance, but it can be extraordinarily difficult to do this live, in real time, without such prior preparation.

8. Ensuring That the Interpreting Process is Uncontaminated by the Denotations or Connotations of Any ASL Signs or English Words

In an example earlier, Jerome did not understand TOUCH in the general sense. He only understood the concept in relation to how the touching was done. Another issue was the term for "probation." Typical signs used for the concept would be WARN or MONITOR. When the interpreters signed WARN,

Jerome responded with stories indicating his interactions with police. The interpreters had to be creative in their search for true meaning equivalence. They should not think that because they have signed TOUCH or WARN, they have interpreted the meaning between these two very different conceptual worlds.

Another problematic term is the English word "access." In English, access is both a verb and a noun and has multiple sub-meanings, each of which would be interpreted differently into ASL. If the interpreter does not "drop form," and holds on to one of the signs used for "access," the interpretation will likely fail.

> Jerome's advocate argued that the defendant should be placed in a mental health facility where he would have communication "access." The correct interpretation was not related to the English meanings of ENTER or CONTACT, but rather required describing a place where deaf people and fluent non-deaf signers are interacting using ASL, so that the defendant would be understood. In the interpretation, the signs for ENTER or CONTACT, which could be interpreted to mean "access," were not used. Rather, the nature of an accessible program was described.

9. Taking an Escort Role

As efforts to establish communication proceed, the interpreter may take on an escort role (i.e., describing the progress of the interpretation process itself to the participants). Often, the hearing interpreter will describe what is being seen to hearing participants, while the Deaf interpreter describes what is being heard to the deaf participants. Although interpreters have been trained to use first person when working, taking the role of the person for whom we are interpreting, in the escort mode, interpreters adopt the third person: "My colleague is re-interpreting the part about 'time served'" or "Janis is introducing the various parties in the courtroom to the client."

> The police report was detailed and confusing. The interpreting team chose to read several sentences ahead to ensure full comprehension before beginning to interpret into ASL. Jerome also responded to the points the police made, denying statements and giving explanations of his actions, so the team repeatedly needed to contextualize the report by explicitly stating that it had been made at the time of the incident, relied on the statements of the victim, and was a written document and therefore static. We needed to deliver its meaning to him so he would know what the state intended to prove. Each time this occurred, the Deaf interpreter would reiterate the purpose of the police report and the ASL interpreter would inform the attorney that we were again giving context to the task.

Even given all the techniques presented here, it is sometimes the case that the interpreters cannot establish effective communication and must report this to the attorney and judge. In the example concerning Jerome's use of the sign GENERAL, the interpreters escort interpreted, advising the attorney that the defendant was using a sign in a nonstandard way and we could not adequately confirm its meaning. The transparency required therein is essential in forensic situations involving clinicians, as in the section that follows.

The IMI Trained Interpreter When "Keeping Form" is Important

How does IMI guide interpreters when it is important for examiners to see the dysfluent language, such as in a mental status exam or a determination of competency?

IMI-guided interpreting places great importance upon understanding the message in the source language and then reconceptualizing it in the target language. What we have described so far are techniques and strategies that interpreters can use when the message in one or both languages is unclear, perhaps because of dysfluent communication. In those cases, the interpreters can use these strategies to seek out clarification before interpreting.

The risk for this process is that dysfluent language and/or one person's lack of understanding can be masked by the interpreting process. In both a mental health and legal context, this masking of dysfluency can have negative unintended consequences. In a psychiatric interview, for instance, the clinician wants to know about dysfluent language because this can have clinical importance. A mental health clinician makes inferences about cognitive functioning based on how a person uses language. This process is certainly fraught with dangers when working through interpreters. It has layer upon layer of dangers when clinicians use interpreters to evaluate deaf individuals whose sign language dysfluency is chiefly related to the social problem of language deprivation, a phenomenon virtually unknown among hearing people, but common among a subset of deaf people. Nonetheless, if a mental health clinician is examining a deaf person whose language is atypical or dysfluent, they will normally want to know about it. If they cannot see the dysfluency themselves, they would usually want the interpreters to either expose or describe it, to the best of their abilities (Glickman, 2007; Glickman & Crump, 2017).

Similarly, in a legal context, such as evaluation of competence to stand trial, language dysfluency has great relevance (see Chapter 4 by Pollard and Fox). An interpreting process that inadvertently masks the language dysfluency can make a legally incompetent person appear competent; and this, of course, has huge relevance to what happens to them in court.

Since IMI informed interpreters put emphasis upon understanding, not preserving form, how would they handle the need of evaluators to see, as best possible, the language limitations of the deaf person or defendant?

The process used in IMI is completely under the interpreter's control and guided by her decisions. Context and goal affect the work substantially. The case discussed in this chapter concerned a legal situation in which the defendant had been deemed competent to stand trial. Interpreters working with dysfluent clients in clinical settings, including forensic evaluations, must be specially trained to recognize how mentally ill people might express themselves, and must work closely with the clinicians to develop cues so that the clinician is aware of any linguistic patterns that might have clinical significance.

Merely being dysfluent does not imply mental illness (indeed, milder forms of dysfluency are common in all people), but if the dysfluency is relevant to the evaluation, the interpreter and the clinician should discuss how it will be handled in a pre-conference, and they should discuss it further in a post-conference. If it is pertinent to the goals of the meeting, the interpreter can retain form and convey the source message more closely. She can also do escort interpreting, working in third person, and describing what she sees. Obviously, this needs to be handled with great sensitivity and skill, especially with clinicians who have little knowledge of Deaf mental health, or who think they sign better, or know more, than they actually do. The interpreters need to be well grounded in the specialty of mental health interpreting, not just the IMI framework.

Conclusion: The Visible Interpreter

Interpreters are often taught to become invisible, so that the process should proceed as if the interpreters were not present. As we hope this chapter has illustrated, invisibility is unlikely when working with dysfluent clients. Indeed, proceeding invisibly can contribute to social injustice, as it easily contributes to an unwarranted perception among the hearing people present that communication has been smooth and successful.

Interpreters working with IMI are active players in the interpretation process. Far from being invisible, they may inadvertently become the center of attention, as all eyes are drawn to the interpreting task. The model thus requires a special level of confidence and willingness to stand out in the service of optimizing communication.

Since the IMI approach is part of a reflective practice that operates at a high level of openness and activity, it is naturally important that interpreters who are teaming together be experienced with, and agree to use, the same approach. Interpreters working within the IMI have a common understanding of the Comprehension, Representation, and Preparation that assists them in correcting errors and process breakdowns. The solution for an issue in comprehension is different than an issue with representation. Repairs can be made given that both team members share a common understanding and a common reference point with which to go back and regroup.

As active participants in optimizing and clarifying the process of interpretation itself, the IMI-trained interpreters reduce the power differential so frequently present between a deaf client (in a medical or legal setting, say) and hearing authorities. The model embeds the interpreting act within the larger context of the interaction. If we ask a hearing person to move, or request a change in lighting, or openly work to ensure that a complex idea is successfully communicated, the respect that we show to both parties promotes mutual understanding.

"To interpret, one must first understand" is the creed that IMI practitioners never lose sight of. That means, as illustrated here, that they work tenaciously, using many interpreting and communication techniques, to ensure understanding and appropriate interpretation. They are creative in making interpretation happen, but if all this fails, they do not cover up the problem. They reveal to all parties that successful interpretation has not occurred.

Beyond seeking message equivalence, IMI guides interpreters towards making each party's worldview accessible to the other. If this visible interpreting process exposes the chasm of understanding between the legal system and the world of the dysfluent defendant, and just how much work it takes to bridge this chasm, this ultimately serves the interest of justice. We are a long way indeed from the misinformed statement that the interpreters should just "sign exactly what I say."

Note

1   Capitalization is conventionally used to identify specific ASL signs in English, because ASL does not have a written form. This shorthand used to notate ASL lexical items in the most basic way is called glossing. Such glosses do not represent the full meaning of the sign they merely label. Therefore, they may appear ungrammatical or awkward as English. The ASL that they imperfectly represent follows its own, complex and demanding, grammatical rules.

References

Andreasen, N. (1986). Scale for the assessment of thought, language and communication. *Schizophrenia Bulletin, 12*(3), 473–482.

Cogen, C., et al. (1986). Task analysis of interpretation and response. In M. L. McIntire (Ed.) *New dimensions in interpreter education: Task analysis – theory and application. Proceedings of the fifth national convention of the conference of interpreter trainers.* pp. 29–69. Retrieved from http://cit-asl.org/proceedings/index.html

Cokely, D. (1992). *Interpretation, a sociolinguistic model.* Burtonsville MD: Linstok Press.

Colonomos, B. M. (In preparation). *The integrated model of interpreting: A pedagogical approach to teaching interpreting.* College Park, MD.

Colonomos, B. M., & Moccia, L. (2013). Process mediation as mentoring. In E. Winston & R. Lee (Eds.), *Mentorship in sign language interpreting* (pp. 85–95). Alexandria, VA: RID, Inc.

Crump, C., & Hamerdinger, S. (2017). Understanding etiology of hearing loss as a contributor to language dysfluency and its impact on assessment and treatment of people who are deaf in mental health settings. *Community Mental Health Journal,* 1–7. doi:10:1007/s10597-017-0120.

Dean, R. K., & Pollard, R. Q. Jr. (2013). *The demand control schema: Interpreting as a practice profession.* USA: Robyn K. Dean and Robert Q. Pollard.

Glickman, N. (2007). Do you hear voices?: Problems in assessment of mental status in deaf person with severe language deprivation. *Journal of Deaf Studies and Deaf Education, 12*(2), 127–147.

Glickman, N., & Crump, C. (2017). Sign language dysfluency in some deaf persons: Implications for interpreters and clinicians working in mental health settings. In N. S. Glickman (Ed.), *Deaf mental health care* (pp. 138–180). New York, NY: Routledge.

Joos, M. (1962). *The five clocks*. Bloomington, IN: Indiana University Research Center in Anthropology, Folklore, and Linguistics. Reprinted in 1967 by Harcourt, Brace & World.

Llewellyn-Jones, P., & Lee, R. G. (2013). Getting to the core of role: Defining interpreters' rolespace. *International Journal of Interpreter Education, 5*(2), 54–72.

Macdonald, F. (February 2, 2015). The greatest mistranslation ever. Retrieved from BBC.com/culture/story/20150202-the-greatest-mistranslations-ever

Massachusetts Trial Court Law Libraries (2017). Massachusetts rules of criminal procedure, including amendments effective March 1, 2017. Retrieved from www.mass.gov/courts/docs/lawlib/docs/criminal-rules.pdf

Quinto-Pozos, D. (Ed.). (2007). *Sign languages in contact* (Sociolinguistics in Deaf Communities Series, vol. 13). Washington, DC: Gallaudet University Press. Retrieved from http://gupress.gallaudet.edu/excerpts/SLICintro2.html

Registry of Interpreters for the Deaf. (2007). Standard practice paper on interpreting in legal settings. Alexandria, VA.

Reis, J., Solovey, E., Henner, J., Johnson, K., & Hoffmeister, R. (2015). ASL clear: STEM education tools for deaf students. ASSETS 2015, 441–442.

Russell, D. L. (2002). *Interpreting in legal contexts: Consecutive and simultaneous interpretation*. Burtonsville, MD: Linstok Press.

Russell, D. (2003). A Comparison of simultaneous and consecutive interpretation in the courtroom, *International Journal of Disability, Community and Rehabilitation, 2*(1). Retrieved from www.ijdcr.ca/VOL02_01_CAN/articles/russell.shtml

Seleskovitch, D. (1978). *Interpreting for international conferences: Problems of language and communication*. Washington, DC: Pen and Booth.

Shaw, R. (1987). Determining register in sign to English interpreting. *Sign Language Studies* Winter, 295–322.

Stokoe, William C., Jr. (1969). Sign language diglossia. *Studies in Linguistics 21*, 27–41.

Witter-Merithew, A., & Mathers, C. (2014). The contribution of deaf interpreters to GATEKEEPING within the interpreting profession: Reconnecting with our roots. In D. I. J. Hunt & S. Hafer (Eds.) *Our roots: The essence of our future. Proceedings of the 2014 national convention of the conference of interpreter trainers* (pp. 158–173). Retrieved from www.cit-asl.org/new/past-conferences/proceedings/2014-proceedings/

9

Language Development in Children with Cochlear Implants

Possibilities and Challenges

AMY SZARKOWSKI

Introduction

Cochlear implants are uncontroversially helpful in restoring hearing to native spoken language users with later or progressive hearing loss. This chapter focuses not on this group, but rather on the more difficult issues in the cochlear implantation of children born deaf or with significant loss of hearing before fully acquiring their first language. The full constellation of factors involved in young children being "successful language users" is not entirely understood; this chapter will critically assess empirical research on those factors that are currently believed to contribute to a deaf child becoming a successful language user. I will emphasize *language fluency* in young deaf and hard of hearing children and make suggestions for the various professionals who work with children who receive cochlear implants and their families to foster linguistic competence. It must be emphasized that "language fluency" is independent of modality, and thus includes both signed and spoken language.

What are Cochlear Implants?

The cochlear implant (CI) is a biomechanical device, sometimes referred to as a neuroprosthetic device, used to promote audition in individuals with substantially reduced hearing (Yawn, Hunter, Sweeney, & Bennett, 2015). Surgically placed within the cochlea of the ear, the CI bypasses the hair cells that normally translate sound vibrations into electronic signals and provides direct stimulation to the auditory nerve. The first CI was implanted in 1961 (Mudry & Mills, 2013). CIs became available commercially—initially for adults who experienced adventitious hearing loss—in 1977. Children began to receive CIs in the late 1980s.

In the US, most CI recipients have had presurgical hearing levels in the severe-to-profound or profound range (i.e., not detecting sounds quieter than 90 dB) (ASHA, 2017; Smith, Shearer, Hildebrand, & Van Camp, 2014). In recent years, a broader range of patients have been considered for implantation, including individuals with moderate hearing loss (who detect sounds at 40 dB), those who receive inadequate benefit from hearing aids, and those with unilateral hearing loss (Yawn et al., 2015). Most CI programs have, in recent years, used a "12 month standard" – although this is changing nationally, and by program. Beyond the FDA guidelines, candidacy requirements vary by surgical setting.

Because cochlear implantation is a surgical intervention, it carries inherent risks, including those associated with use of anesthesia. The risk can be elevated for children with particular medical conditions, such as cardiac issues. For most children, the surgery requires an overnight stay. Typically, children recover from the surgery and anesthesia within 48 hours, and complications such as infection are rare.

Deaf Cultural Perspectives and Medical Perspectives

Historically, the Deaf cultural perspective on hearing assistive technologies has clashed with that of medical professionals (Lane & Bahan, 1998); indeed, many would argue that this divide continues (Blume, 2010; Humphries et al., 2014). Medical attempts to "cure deafness" are not appreciated by many members of Deaf culture or their allies within the wider Deaf community. From a cultural perspective, some argue that children with reduced hearing have the right to choose for or against this intervention when they are old enough to make a fully informed decision (Komesaroff, Komesaroff, & Hyde, 2015). Medical professionals point to the rapid development of the brain and argue that earlier implantation is better in order to increase the likelihood that a child can receive auditory benefit. Many members of the Deaf community support bimodal, bilingual access to language. Their primary resistance is less to spoken language acquisition, per se, than to the withholding of sign language from children whom it would benefit, which does occur in some settings where CIs are provided and promoted.

Some medical professionals have been accused of harboring prejudice against sign language and actively discouraging its use, despite both the lack of empirical evidence that signing interferes with spoken language acquisition and the significant evidence that it can benefit spoken language learning (Hall, 2017; Humphries et al., 2017). Many medical professionals and parents of deaf children do in fact assume—contrary to the actual feelings of many deaf people—that deaf individuals must want to be hearing (Blume, 2010). This cultural conflict remains evident, both in the extent to which deaf adults themselves seek CIs and in the commonly negative perception of medical professionals by members of the Deaf community.

In exploring the ethics pertaining to CIs, scholars highlight the lack of knowledge about Deaf culture on the part of many medical professionals (Pass & Graber, 2015). They argue for parents of deaf and hard of hearing children to meet and interact with members from the Deaf community in order to make informed and autonomous decisions regarding implantation. It does seem reasonable that medical professionals, particularly those working directly with deaf children, should seek a complete understanding of Deaf community perspectives when considering or recommending intervention options. After all, typical goals for the surgery include helping a deaf child to listen and speak, which may well affect a child's cultural identification.

Perspective of the Author

Everyone has biases. Here, I will attempt to describe mine. I am female, of European-American descent, cisgender, married to a Japanese man, and a mother of two who is raising her children to be bilingual in two spoken languages. I am also a hearing psychologist who has made a career of working with children who are deaf and hard of hearing, and their families.

I fell in love with the beauty and expressiveness of American Sign Language during my first ASL course and was fascinated by my early encounters with Deaf culture. I am a signer who values ASL as a full, complex language and someone who appreciates natural, visual-gestural means of communicating. I have taught my children signs and delight in watching them express themselves "through the air." I pursued graduate studies at Gallaudet University where there is a culturally Deaf majority within the campus population. At Gallaudet, I received specialized training in the cultural aspects of working with deaf and hard of hearing individuals and learned about the historical misapplication of psychology to deaf people.

In my present work at Boston Children's Hospital, I serve as a member of the Cochlear Implant Program team, composed of psychologists, speech-language pathologists, audiologists, otolaryngologists/surgeons, and administrative staff. Our program is rare in its inclusion of psychologists. My role varies depending on the needs of the child and family. At times, I might work with parents of babies, describing the importance of language for their infants' brains. At other times, I might help a child to prepare for CI surgery through play or explore issues of identity and the potential impact that a CI might have on an adolescent's self-concept. I have witnessed the full range of CI outcomes, from minimal detection of sound to sufficient audition for the child to readily acquire and use spoken language. I find that, to the extent one values the ability to hear, and to the extent risk factors are avoided, CIs can positively influence some children's lives.

I believe I bring to the topic a unique perspective—as someone who knows many deaf people, appreciates Deaf culture, can communicate directly with signing Deaf individuals, and as someone who works with implanted children while supporting families through that process. I have had the privilege of working with thriving young deaf children who communicate beautifully through ASL, and other deaf children who communicate beautifully through spoken English. I have also had the experience, all too often, of encountering older children and adults who did not have the benefit of early language exposure.

My work involves assessing neurocognitive abilities, giving appropriate diagnoses when necessary, and educating families and school teams about the implications of a child's insufficient early language exposure on cognitive, academic, and social functioning. Naturally, it can be devastating for families to feel that they could, or should, have done more early in their child's life. It can be tragic to see them realize the lasting impacts of insufficient language access on their child's brain development.

As a psychologist, I am driven by the need to prioritize neuropsychological and social-emotional health. Science strongly suggests that early access to language is important for later linguistic, cognitive, and psychological functioning. In general, it is my belief—both grounded in science and informed by my clinical work—that for most infants and toddlers exposure to a signed language fosters development of those later abilities. I do recognize some limitations to this approach. For example, some children with complex motor challenges are not able to expressively utilize signs efficiently, some children may have visual impairment in addition to reduced hearing that can make communication with signs more challenging, and some children have other conditions (such as Autism Spectrum Disorder) that limit their understanding of facial expressions, which convey essential grammatical information in signed languages. As such, I do not assume there is one answer for all children. I strive to help parents consider the many factors known to influence language development. As more research emerges over time, and through my natural growth as a clinician who strives to be both objective and culturally informed, my perspective and recommendations may well change.

In the remainder of the chapter, I present considerations that align with the subject of this book—the implications of reduced access to early language on lifelong functioning. Elsewhere in this book, the preferred term is "language deprivation." I prefer to use a softer phrase, "insufficient early language access." I personally reserve the term "language deprivation" to describe adults who experience the negative sequelae associated with having been deprived of the exposure to meaningful language. Others may certainly argue that any amount of time a child does not have access to language (signed or spoken) means that a child is being deprived of language. Indeed, I concur that children *need* exposure to language that is accessible to them from infancy. I believe that families should strongly be advised that the brain is constantly developing and will not wait for language to be present. When that exposure is not provided, a child's developmental trajectory will be negatively impacted. If language is akin to food for the brain, then certainly caregivers need to be informed about the importance of "language nutrition" and the need to feed their developing child. I recognize how language deprivation can foster a syndrome encompassing the constellation of negative sequelae outlined by Dr. Sanjay Gulati (see Chapter 1). The consequences of this in adults are real and devastating. In my clinical work and in my personal interactions within the Deaf community, I have certainly encountered individuals whom I would now conceptualize as having language deprivation syndrome. I believe that greater understanding of this phenomenon is immensely important.

These significant and lasting long-term effects of language deprivation, however, do not necessarily apply when discussing a newborn or young infant. Importantly, none of the families with whom I work sees themselves as denying a deaf child language. Quite the contrary, they believe they are intervening in the ways that best facilitate language acquisition. For them, the political term "language deprivation" can serve to shut down dialogue, sometimes even preventing them from considering the benefits of sign language for these children. Thus, for infants, toddlers, and very young children, I prefer to describe "reduced or insufficient early language access." With this terminology, for me, comes a more hopeful outlook that, with the appropriate supports and understanding of the need for language, caregivers and professionals working with these children can attempt to "right the course," increasing the child's language access, and avoid the devastating effects of long-term language deprivation.

Guiding a Family: The Story of Brock

Brock is a gorgeous baby boy, born at term and weighing a healthy 8 lbs. 3 oz. Shortly after birth, Brock's results on the universal newborn hearing screening suggested reduced hearing. He was referred for an appointment with a pediatric audiologist, who determined that Brock had bilateral sensorineural hearing loss in the severe-to-profound range. He had no other health complications.

There are many questions that professionals might consider as they guide Brock's loving caregivers through their journey as hearing parents raising a deaf child.

- What information will be most useful to the family at this early state? What information are they likely to find helpful later?
- What is the role that signed language could or should have in helping to foster Brock's ability to communicate? What is the role that spoken language could or should play? How can his caregivers critically evaluate the communication opportunities available to them and their son?
- What questions are Brock's parents, and others in similar situations to them, likely to have for Early Intervention professionals? For audiologists? For medical doctors? For facilitators of parent groups for families with deaf and hard of hearing children? For social workers, psychologists, or other helping professionals? For deaf adults?

- If the family wishes to consider a cochlear implant for Brock, what do they need to know about cochlear implant outcomes in order to make an informed and appropriate decision for their family?
- If Brock's parents were Deaf and communicated via American Sign Language (ASL), how might that change the questions they would have regarding cochlear implantation? Assuming that they could provide a language rich environment in ASL, what considerations/concerns might they have in deciding to proceed with a cochlear implant?

Early Language Exposure is Imperative

Collectively, studies support the argument that language input—*regardless of the modality in which it is presented*—is vital for cognitive and neuropsychological development. From a brain-based perspective, what matters is that infants are provided with meaningful, consistent exposure to fully accessible language from an early age in order to foster cognitive development, linguistic competence, and overall neuropsychological growth. Anatomical organization of the brain is influenced by linguistic input, with lack of early language experience having a particularly deleterious effect (Pénicaud et al., 2013). Different lines of investigation have pointed to the presence of critical periods for language development that are time-sensitive and likely cannot be fully remediated if missed (Newport, Bavelier, & Neville, 2001). Thus, it is imperative that children with reduced hearing are provided early and consistent access to high quality language input. Spitz and Kegl (Chapter 7) note that deaf individuals who were not exposed to accessible language during the critical period usually do not develop anything resembling native language abilities in any language, no matter the quantity or quality of language exposure later in life.

Deaf parents are typically able to provide rich linguistic environments for their deaf children, equivalent to the language rich environments produced by many hearing parents of hearing children. Deaf mothers, on average, demonstrate strong skills in obtaining their child's attention before providing information and facilitating joint attention to objects, which enhances learning (Lieberman, Hatrak, & Mayberry, 2014). Deaf toddlers interacting with deaf mothers tend to engage in frequent and appropriate shifting of their gaze to follow the mother's lead, to show interest, and to seek information.

Because most children with substantially reduced hearing are born into hearing families who do not know sign language (Mitchell & Karchmer, 2011), their risk for insufficient early language access is greater. This can occur for a variety of reasons. Understandably, hearing caregivers without extensive signing experience lack native fluency; they may be inconsistent in using signs or uncomfortable with signing in general. Additionally, they may not fully realize the limitations of hearing technologies and frequently assume that implanted children or children with hearing aids hear and understand more than they actually do.

It is extremely unfortunate, ill-informed, and perhaps unethical that many caregivers are advised **not** to use signs, gestures, or other visual "cues" to their child with reduced hearing on the mistaken assumption that this will limit later spoken language abilities. Parents are sometimes told that providing visual cues for information will be disadvantageous in attempting to "train the ear" of a child who is using a hearing aid or a CI. This continues to occur despite evidence that even hearing children rely heavily on visual information to aid their ability to comprehend what they hear (Teinonen, Aslin, Alku, & Csibra, 2008). Still other parents seem to believe that, if their child will receive a CI at approximately 12 months of age, there is no reason to learn to sign. Rather, these parents might consider the first year of life to be simply "waiting time" until the CI is provided and formal remediation for spoken language skills can begin.

Children born with substantially reduced hearing whose parents choose implantation too often experience a delay in the introduction of *any language*. It is not until the CI is implanted and activated that a child can begin to make some sense of the auditory information. Time is also required for a child to begin to develop the processing abilities in the brain that transform the incoming signals to meaningful input. "Learning to listen" takes time and targeted training. Even then, the CI may not prove sufficient to promote full language development. In other words, not introducing sign language to babies identified with reduced hearing and expecting their language development to catch up after several years of limited language exposure after implantation is a high-risk plan. Some deaf children with CIs will grow into deaf adults with experiences and developmental consequences of language deprivation.

Visual and/or Auditory Language Input and the Brain

Although some might argue, without the support of empirical evidence, that an individual can learn sign language fluently at any stage of life (e.g., Sugar, 2016), the timing of exposure to signed language has been shown to influence brain functioning (Mayberry, Del Giudice, & Lieberman, 2011). That is, the common approach of using sign language only as a "backup plan" in cases of a child failing to acquire spoken language is unlikely to succeed because cognitive and linguistic functioning is optimized when language exposure occurs early in the critical period.

The language used in the home, whether spoken or signed, significantly influences how the brain responds to visual and verbal input and how it organizes itself to use that input (Olulade, Koo, LaSasso, & Eden, 2014). In a study of prelingually deafened adults who had used ASL as their primary mode of communication for 18 years or longer, researchers found age of acquisition differences in the brain organization among those exposed to sign language in infancy, early childhood, and late childhood or adulthood (Pénicaud et al., 2013). The brains of late-signing adults, despite their reliance on ASL for communication and their many years of using ASL, were different from the brains of those who received early exposure to sign language in ways that correlate with reduced linguistic capabilities.

For children who rely on a CI for auditory access with the expectation of understanding and developing spoken language, the brain and auditory nerves also require early stimulation; thus, early implantation and activation is typically advised in order to optimize auditory access (Kral & Sharma, 2012; Sharma, Campbell, & Cardon, 2015). Neuroscience strongly suggests that spoken and sign languages share the same critical period of language acquisition; in essence, early and fully accessible exposure to sign and/or spoken *language* is necessary to optimize the brain's ability to comprehend and process linguistic information. Modality appears to be less important than the adequacy of exposure.

Communication Journeys

Many parents and caregivers cite the desire to talk to their children and to hear their child's voice as their reason for selecting oral communication methods. Yet often people do not realize that language (a systematic means of conveying ideas) is not synonymous with hearing and speech (the reception and production of sounds) (ASHA, 2017).

For many children with reduced hearing (perhaps, in particular, those with parents who have typical hearing), communication is not dichotomous; the child is neither "completely oral" nor "fully signing." Research based on a false dichotomy of spoken *versus* sign languages may miss the fact that modes of communication often change to meet the needs of the child in particular contexts. For example, a child might be exposed to one communication modality in the home and another modality in the day care or preschool setting. Additionally, the preferred mode of communication of a child may change or evolve. The child could use sign early in life and then later, after receiving a CI, shift to include more spoken words. The same child may later decide to embrace ASL as a teenager or as an adult. For example, categorizing that child at age five as "oral only" does not capture the fact that for the first two to three years of life, sign language was most accessible and served as the child's primary modality.

Children with reduced hearing are likely to undergo a "communication journey." Caregivers need not select just one means of communication. There seem to be benefits to espousing flexibility in one's approach to communication. Research suggests that flexibility fosters well-being (Kushalnagar et al., 2014). Flexibility of communication strategies has been associated in adolescents with improved cognitive and academic performance (Convertino, Marschark, Sapere, Sarchet, & Zupan, 2009; Knoor & Marschark, 2015).

Many deaf people and advocates for early sign exposure certainly appreciate the benefits of fluent use of the majority's spoken/written language. The recommendation on the part of some professionals that parents avoid exposing their children to sign and raise them "oral only" seems needlessly rigid and misguided.

Following a Child's Lead: The Story of Natalie

Natalie was in overall good health, but suffered from frequent, excruciating ear infections during infancy and toddlerhood. Identified with hearing loss in the severe-to-profound range when she was five months old, Natalie's parents choose to use hearing aids to optimize her access to spoken language. Natalie's parents attended a cochlear implant conference, where they were introduced to other families with children who used CIs, and were impressed with the spoken language abilities of those children.[1] Natalie's parents obtained a CI for her when she was 13 months of age. Shortly thereafter, Natalie began receiving services from specialists in developing spoken language skills. Those professionals urged her parents not to incorporate signs or gestures in their communication with Natalie. They were advised to "train her to listen" and told that visual cues would only make it harder for Natalie to "learn to hear" with her CI.

Natalie was just shy of two years old when her parents sought support from a clinic for deaf and hard of hearing children. Despite their commitment to regular speech therapy and her consistency in wearing the CI processor, Natalie was not meeting expectations for spoken language development for children her age. The psychologist who assessed Natalie's cognitive abilities incorporated some signs from American Sign Language (ASL) and noted that Natalie was fascinated with the signs. Likewise, her parents were fascinated with Natalie's level of engagement and interest when signs were used in communicating with her. During the course of the assessment, Natalie learned several signs that she then used spontaneously and correctly later in the session.

Acknowledging that their good intentions to help foster their daughter's language had been focused more on "an approach" than on monitoring Natalie's reactions to input and following her lead, her parents made substantial changes to her programming. They began to learn ASL and used signs to help communicate with Natalie. The family also found a speech-language therapist who incorporated signs, as well as other visual support, to foster Natalie's repertoire of vocabulary as well as her understanding of grammar, pragmatics, and more complex concepts both in spoken words and signs.

When Natalie returned for reassessment of her skills at the clinic after one year, she was using both signs and spoken English. At times, she would produce the signs when unsure of the correct English. Often, she spoke without sign. Sometimes, she would sign to indicate the topic of conversation and would follow this by asking in English, "What is this called?" Despite obtaining her cochlear implant "on time," Natalie's early complications with ear infections coupled with her reduced hearing meant that her auditory in-put during her first year had been inconsistent. Natalie had apparently been having difficulty making sense of the sound that she was receiving from the CI. Introducing her to signs was instrumental in helping Natalie to express herself. By allowing for flexibility in communication and following Natalie's lead, her parents reported that they began to understand her communicative attempts and could better appreciate their wonderful little girl.

Analysis of the Case

The story of Natalie's early life is all too common. Despite the necessity of pro-viding a rich language environment in infancy in order to optimize linguistic and cognitive abilities and overall brain development, Natalie's parents decided to wait to introduce language until the CI was placed. The emphasis by some of the treatment providers on reducing Natalie's access to visual "clues" was mis-guided, given the importance of visual information in processing and compre-hending information (even for children with typical hearing). Fortunately for Natalie, a professional involved in evaluating her abilities could communicate via signs and recognized Natalie's interest in visual language.[2] Appreciating their daughter's positive response to the visual-gestural and signed communi-cation with the clinician, the parents chose to "follow the lead" of their daugh-ter, who was showing them through her actions that she would benefit from more visual supports. Yet, given the delays in early access to language that oc-curred and the delayed introduction of sign language into Natalie's communi-cative repertoire, a lasting impact of early reduced access to language is likely to be seen. This might include difficulty comprehending higher level language (Yoshinaga-Itano, Sedey, Coulter, & Mehl, 1998), challenges in understanding more nuanced aspects of language such as reduced pragmatics skills or taking the perspective of others (Most, Shina-August, & Meilijson, 2010), and/or ex-hibiting behavioral challenges (Quittner et al., 2010).

Biological and Medical Factors Influencing Cochlear Implant Outcomes

It is important to remember that the cochlear implant is simply a technological tool; its use does not guarantee any specific outcome. It can be misleading to read the academic literature (as well as the literature published by the CI com-panies) that sometimes seems to suggest that a CI, in and of itself, results in particular developments in a child (often described in terms of spoken language skills). CI recipients who do not demonstrate the same outcomes (for example, those who have stopped using their implants or who never return for follow-up due to dissatisfaction with the results) may be excluded from CI outcomes stud-ies. In discussing the "successfulness" of CIs, it is important to consider a num-ber of factors known to have an influence on a child's ability to benefit from implantation. Understanding of the child characteristics that may influence the extent to which a CI might be beneficial can help to inform the decision-making process of the caregivers and professionals working with the child.

Age of Implantation

If a child is going to receive a cochlear implant and caregivers have opted for prioritizing spoken language, earlier implantation generally leads to better language-based outcomes (Kral & Sharma, 2012; Pénicaud et al., 2013; Peterson, Pisoni & Miyamoto, 2010). Younger age of implantation is associated with relatively increased comprehension, expression of oral language (Niparko et al., 2010), better oral vocabulary skills (Houston & Miyamoto, 2010), higher levels of spoken language competence and understanding (Nicholas & Geers, 2006), and heightened ability to expressively use spoken language (Ching et al., 2009)—particularly with respect to grammar and pragmatic use. While some children who are implanted later may "catch up" to the auditory detection and spoken language performance of their peers who received CIs earlier (Dunn et al., 2014), many others do not close that gap (Niparko et al., 2010).

Experience with Auditory Access/Residual Hearing

Spoken language development is better optimized when a child who has residual hearing, or who had hearing but experienced a progressive loss, uses hearing aids before implantation (Niparko et al., 2010). Children who have progressively reduced hearing and those with hearing in the severe range tend to have stronger spoken language development outcomes than those in the profound range (Yoshinaga-Itano, Baca & Sedey, 2010). Conversely, the longer the length of time a child experiences no access to language prior to implantation, the worse receptive and expressive language skill development tends to be (Niparko et al., 2010; Szagun & Stumper, 2012). When studies point to successful outcomes, it is fair to inquire whether the children in the samples had functional hearing for a period of time, as would be the case with progressive hearing loss, and whether their hearing loss was less than profound. The better outcome might be due to the fact that they were better "primed" by early auditory exposure for the development of later aural/oral language. The selective use of research subjects who have had spoken language exposure, either because they were functionally hard of hearing or because they had hearing and then lost, is a potential source of hidden bias in CI outcome studies.

Etiology

The etiology of the reduced hearing can also be associated with variable outcomes (Kammerer, Szarkowski, & Isquith, 2010). While it is beyond the scope of this chapter to detail the numerous possible causes of reduced hearing and outline their implications for CI outcomes, family members and professionals working with families in making decisions about cochlear implantation are advised to educate themselves about known CI outcomes for particular populations of children with reduced hearing, particularly where the underlying causes may create extra complications (Tharpe & Seewald, 2016).

Situational and Contextual Factors Influencing Language Outcomes in Children with CIs

Greater Parental Involvement and Engagement

Quality of parental involvement has been shown to have major impact on language development (Pressman, Pipp-Siegel, Yoshinaga-Itano, & Deas, 1999; Yoshinaga-Itano, Sedey, Wiggin, & Chung, 2017). When parents are more highly involved, implanted children show greater improvement in comprehension and higher levels of oral language expression (Niparko et al., 2010). Indeed, the magnitude of impact of maternal sensitivity on the growth of oral language skills in a group of children with CIs was found to be on par with the impact of age of implantation (Quittner et al., 2013).

Variation in spoken language skills is associated with quantity and quality of maternal linguistic input (DesJardin & Eisenberg, 2007). More highly engaged mothers tend to foster increased interactions with their children, which increases signed and/or spoken language skills (Hintermair, 2015; Niparko et al., 2010). Although studies often focus on mothers, they are not alone in influencing the language development of a child. The total number of different word types used by parents has been shown to significantly impact the child's oral receptive language skills (Cruz, Quittner, Marker, DesJardin, & the CDaCI Investigative team, 2013), and the extent to which children are exposed to rich vocabulary also influences their expressive use of spoken and/or signed language (Freel et al., 2012; Suskind et al., 2016).

Joint Attention

From very early in life, caregivers engage with infants in ways that facilitate shared attention. They might point to an object, direct their baby's attention toward it, share a facial expression related to the object—such as surprise or disgust—and then encourage the infant to respond in kind. This process of joint attention begins very early in life and contributes to attachment and positive relations between infants and caregivers (Brice, Plotkin, & Reesman, 2016). Recent work by Yoshinaga-Itano et al. (2017) has shown that children with reduced hearing, whether they have Deaf parents who use ASL or deaf parents who utilize spoken language, show stronger joint attention than their peers with hearing parents. Since the oral deaf parents were not using a signed language, this enhanced joint attention is not likely attributable solely to the use of a visual language, but may reflect the influence of deaf parents' own lived experiences leading to prioritizing attention to the communication process.

Parental Levels of Education and Family Socioeconomic Status

Higher levels of maternal education have been associated with faster "linguistic progress" in children with CIs (Pungello, Iruka, Dotterer, Mills-Koonce, & Reznick, 2009). Higher socioeconomic status (SES) has been linked to parental involvement and engagement in communication (Niparko et al., 2010), better receptive and expressive oral language skills in children who receive CIs (Geers, Moog, Biedenstein, Brenner, & Hayes, 2009; Holt & Svirsky, 2008), and to larger vocabularies and stronger communication abilities among deaf or hard of hearing children who sign (Freel et al., 2011).

In summary, language does not develop in isolation. Children learn to develop language through their interactions with others, and parents and caregivers are the most influential facilitators of their child's language. Parents who are highly involved and responsive to their child's communication needs tend to foster better language outcomes regardless of specific communication modalities. Higher levels of family income and education are linked with improved linguistic and cognitive outcomes as well, perhaps associated with increased engagement in parents with those advantages. Importantly, the responsibility for development of a child's language depends upon, and can be fostered by, others outside of the family. Professionals, appropriate language models for sign language and/or spoken language, and other loving adults around the deaf child who can foster development are all important and necessary to foster cognitive and linguistic growth.

Critical Analysis of Reported Cochlear Implant Outcomes

When considering the reported outcomes of children who utilize CIs, it is important to reflect critically on both the type of outcome being prioritized and how it was assessed. This is essential to gain a realistic understanding of the potential benefits and limitations of the CI as a tool. It is common that detection of auditory input, speech perception, and language development are conflated in outcome reports, when in fact they carry different and significant implications.

It should especially be cautioned that in much of the research, "better outcomes" are reported in one group over another. "Better outcomes" in a particular context can reflect an improvement of some abilities but may still be worse than the desired or expected development of those abilities in typical development. Certainly, much of the research on CI outcomes to date has largely been fraught with this issue, as children receiving earlier implantation perform "better" than those who implanted later in life yet remain well below age expectations on given measures. It is quite easy to read that one particular group demonstrated better outcomes than another group without realizing that both groups performed poorly. This is exemplified even in very recent publications such as Geers et al. (2017), where at least 49% of non-signing implanted children in elementary school were still not performing at expected levels.

Readers of the literature on CI outcomes should be aware of the situational and contextual factors that drive this work, the types of biases held by those conducting the research, the financial incentives that have played a role in the type and extent of research conducted in the field, and the significant limitations in what are reported as successful CI outcomes. **At this juncture, it is not possible to fully predict who will and will not succeed in developing and using spoken language with the support of a cochlear implant (Kral et al., 2012).** Given the wide variability in CI outcomes, it is important to consider the factors that are known or believed to contribute to more positive outcomes, and those that are likely to limit the ability to benefit from the CI.

Whereas many believe that the primary goal of cochlear implantation should be to allow "auditory-only speech understanding in every day listening environments" (Peterson et al., 2010, p. 2), that goal is not always appropriate. For example, for children with complex medical conditions, those who have motor limitations that would prohibit the development of speech, or those with neurological insults that limit overall cognitive abilities, the goals of implantation might simply be increased auditory awareness or appreciation of environmental noises rather than development of spoken language skills.

For a particular child, a CI might allow for greater participation in family life through increased awareness of communication partners, even if full speech perception and comprehension is not achieved. For that child, a "successful outcome" of a CI might be increased access to opportunities to interact with caregivers and siblings, as long as typical language milestones continue to be met through sign language. Clear and reasonable expectations about what the CI can and cannot do are critical. Recognition that "successful outcomes" can be unique to each child is important.

Discrete Listening Skills

CIs can provide access to auditory perception for individuals who could otherwise not hear specific sounds; when this is the outcome being measured, CIs often yield positive results. Speech perception, or the ability to detect when another is speaking, is another potential benefit. Yet, ability to *detect* speech and ability to *comprehend* what is being said are distinct functions. Many outcome studies assess a child's word recognition skills using either closed set word recognition (i.e., presenting a child a set of pictures, producing a word, and having the child indicate the word that was heard by pointing to the appropriate pictures) or open-set word recognition (saying a word and asking the CI recipient to repeat the word). Contextual knowledge (e.g., pertaining to the objects/actions in the pictures) and greater exposure to spoken English words can certainly improve a child's ability to perform well on many of the assessments used for perception and recognition tasks (e.g., using a CI, a child might actually hear "urt" but, recognizing that is not likely a word on a word list, might report hearing the word "hurt"). Word recognition skills, while important, should not be confused with the ability to use language competently.

The (Language) Whole is Greater Than the Sum of the (Word-Level) Parts

It is important to consider the limitations of drawing conclusions regarding broad outcomes on the basis of children's discrete listening skills or ability to demonstrate understanding of single-words and phrases. In real-world contexts, communication does not happen through single words. Instead, messages are conveyed by individuals with diverse skills who are communicating information in paragraph-length (or longer) chunks of information, in the presence of background noise and visual distractions. For instance, an implanted child, who can understand short phrases with contextual support and demonstrate knowledge of vocabulary terms at age expectation, may still struggle to understand a teacher's directions and the social exchanges of peers. By conflating these two outcomes, some advocates for cochlear implants give a misleading understanding of CI limitations and fail to acknowledge how implanted children may still develop significant language dysfluency. Understanding this reality can help parents appreciate why sign language exposure can be so beneficial for children who have implants.

Variability in Spoken Language Outcomes in Children with CIs

Even with CI technological improvements and decreasing ages of implantation, there remains significant variability among CI users in their ability to perceive speech and environmental sounds (Peterson et al., 2010; Niparko et al., 2010). Some children who appear to be good cochlear implant candidates do not develop spoken language skills (Peterson et al., 2010). For example, when accounting for child age and length of implant use, as many as 50% of deaf CI users out of a group of 70 showed severe delays in oral language abilities after two years of experience with the implant (Svirsky, Robbins, Kirk, Pisoni, & Miyamoto, 2000).

The significant variability in spoken language outcomes is an important concern even for the youngest children receiving implants (Boons et al., 2012; Levine, Strother-Garcia, Golinkoff, & Hirsh-Pasek, 2016). A study of children who were implanted between one to two years of age found only 29% scoring within normal limits of receptive and expressive language measures and word recognition tasks; furthermore, 71% of children implanted before their second birthday showed delays on at least one of the oral language measures (Holt & Svirsky, 2008). It has been previously mentioned, but is worth repeating, that the causes of variability are not fully understood and render predictions of any desired CI outcomes difficult.

In short, there are no "guarantees" that CIs will lead to strong spoken language; yet, exposure to sign language does seem to provide some "insurance" that a child will have better early language exposure. Hall, Caselli, and Hall (in preparation) have conducted a critical review of the CI literature, highlighting many limitations in how outcomes are measured and subsequent conclusions drawn—especially in the three largest CI outcome studies to date, the Childhood Development after Cochlear Implantation, the Dallas Cochlear Implant Program, and the Longitudinal Outcomes of Children with Hearing Impairment (LOCHI) study from Australia. They note that while some children with CIs do develop average spoken language skills, the distribution of language abilities of children with CIs in these studies is shifted downward. This means that a non-signing implanted child is more likely to not achieve average spoken language skills compared to their hearing peers. Even when the known "success with a CI" variables are accounted for, it is still not possible to determine which children will achieve successfully be able to acquire spoken language.

Differential Spoken and Signed Language Outcomes

Because most parents choose to foster only spoken language skills in their child, studies of signing implanted children are limited, and those that have been conducted have demonstrated variable results. For example, in a comparison of those who use only spoken English versus those whose families employed a total communication approach (using both sign and spoken languages), receptive language skills were equal (Peterson et al., 2010)—a trend also seen with speech perception (Ruffin, Kronenberger, Colson, Henning, & Pisoni, 2013).

Additionally, the expressive signed skills of children are often not assessed if a study is examining oral language outcomes only, which raises the possibility of a child's true language abilities not being accurately captured. For example, a child who has used any amount of signs might be placed in a "sign language" category—resulting in a widely mixed group that contains children with a few basic signs alongside fluent signing children. Indeed, a recent article by Geers et al. (2017), which claimed that non-signing implanted children had better spoken language outcomes than those with early exposure to sign language, suffered from this design flaw. Numerous deaf and hearing scientists have weighed in on this particular publication, pointing out problems with the premises of this work, the design of the research, the conclusions drawn by the research team, and the implications suggested as a result of the study. Interested readers are encouraged to explore the discussion on the *Pediatrics* journal website (http://pediatrics.aappublications.org/content/140/1/e20163489.full).

Generally, critical readers of outcome studies will often discover problems with the "signed vs. spoken" language groups in these comparisons of language modality. The amount of exposure to *any* and to *each* language does need to be considered. The number of caregivers who use particular communication methods with a child, the quality of their language modeling, and the extent to which the children are able to access the language input will all influence language-related outcomes. In practice, there is very little quality control over what constitutes a "signing" home or school environment and how these are described in the literature. Parents with a handful of individual signs, and no grammatical abilities in ASL, might be considered as offering a "signing" environment. Thus, the comparisons between "signing" and "oral" environments are frequently misleading.

There are new lines of research that are beginning to "tease out" the measurement of early language access provided to deaf and hard of hearing children (Hall, Bortfeld, Eigsti, & Lillo-Martin, in preparation; Hall & Szarkowski, in preparation). This work shows promise for helping researchers in the field to describe more objectively early language exposure and understand its implications for later language development and later cognitive and neuropsychological outcomes.

Bimodal and Bilingual

Results of research that has examined children with implants who use both spoken and signed languages has been mixed, likely in part due to the inconsistent application of definitions of language. Some research findings suggest that oral-only communication produces superior results (see Peterson et al., 2010), others show that total communication approaches for children with CIs yield the best outcomes (e.g., Jiménez, Pino, & Herruzo, 2009), while still others suggest that children with CIs who use sign language attain receptive and expressive language skills on par with peers who have typical hearing (Davidson, Lillo-Martin & Pichler, 2014). Critical readers will benefit from understanding how "sign language or sign use" is measured or defined, the types of language outcomes being assessed (i.e., comprehension of single words versus spoken paragraphs; ability to label objects versus ability to describe one's needs or desires), and whether those types of assessment were appropriate given the types of early language exposure experienced by the child.

Contradicting the notion that sign language use hinders development of spoken language skills, studies by Giezen, Baker, and Escudero (2013) showed that not only did sign language *not* have a deleterious impact on spoken word processing, it may have provided a benefit in perceiving spoken words. Knoors and Marschark (2012), on the basis of their extensive studies in education of deaf children, have argued for the use of sign-supported speech—particularly for children who utilize CIs and have relatively strong spoken language skills. Furthermore, in a study of bilingual native-signing implanted children, assessments of English scores were comparable to those of children with typical hearing (Davidson et al., 2014). Based on these findings, the researchers raised the possibility that early exposure to a natural signed language for children who later receive CIs may remediate some of the negative effects seen among many children who receive CIs without prior language exposure. Taking all the research presented as a whole, it seems likely that maximizing a child's access to language in **both** visual and auditory modalities is crucial for minimizing risk of delays in linguistic, cognitive, and other domains of development (Kushalnagar et al., 2014). In essence, natural sign language exposure from birth likely reduces the negative impacts of not having any access to spoken language before potential benefits of the CI may appear.

Clinically, many professionals would argue that the use of sign language prior to implantation is of value, as it lays the foundation for the brain to process *language* (e.g., ASL could be used as a first language foundation for second language acquisition of English). Essentially, it is proposed that when children have developed understanding of concepts through ASL and are later introduced to the spoken version of those concepts, ASL serves as a bridge to foster their understanding (Cummins, 2016). For example, because a child has already learned a sign such as MILK, they will be able to connect the spoken word "milk" with that sign while seeing and hearing it. Logically, this can significantly enhance their comprehension of specific spoken words from the first time they hear them.

Assisting a Family: The Story of Amanda

Amanda was born at 37 weeks. She had congenital cytomegalovirus (CMV), identified shortly after birth, and was followed by the Infectious Disease department at the hospital. There were no other medical complications. Amanda was referred for audiological testing on the basis of the Universal Newborn Hearing Screening (UNHS) and subsequently found to have reduced hearing bilaterally, in the profound range.

Amanda received extensive early intervention services including physical therapy for reduced tone and speech-language therapy that included visual-gestural support. A teacher of the deaf and a child specialist with knowledge about hearing met with the parents regularly. The family attended a parent infant program where they met other families who shared a similar journey. Amanda's parents worked with a Deaf mentor. Extended family members were included in the family-based sign language courses that they took.

Developmentally, Amanda was gaining language and communication skills at a rate that was on par with her hearing age-mates. At seven months, Amanda was receptively understanding at least eight signs. By ten months, she first expressively signed *mama* and *more*. A modified sign for *dog* soon followed. When she was 11 months old, prior to implantation, Amanda's developmental progress was assessed by a comprehensive team of professionals. She was found to be meeting developmental milestones across all domains (e.g., cognitive, linguistically through signs, motor, and behavior). At 12 months of age, Amanda received bilateral cochlear implants through a successful surgery. At 15 months, Amanda was expressively using many sign and word combinations. Finally, at 27 months, Amanda was experiencing a "language explosion" adding signs and spoken words to her vocabulary repertoire daily.

When she was approaching her third birthday, Amanda again had cognitive-developmental and speech-language-communication assessments to help inform her caregivers and team of professionals about her current functioning and to guide her programming as she prepared to transition out of early intervention into preschool. Cognitively, Amanda was on par with expectations for her age. Assessment of her receptive and expressive language skills, in both signed language and spoken language, showed that Amanda demonstrated age-appropriate competence in each. Increasingly, it was noted by her caregivers that Amanda was communicating via spoken language, although she frequently incorporated signs into her communication, especially if others did not understand her speech. Overall communication skills were found to be at the high end of the average range.

Analysis of the Case

In many ways, the case of Amanda demonstrates optimal interventions and supports. The parents received input from Deaf mentors and were made aware of Deaf cultural considerations in determining how best to raise their daughter. Identification of Amanda's hearing status occurred early, as did the introduction of early intervention support services. Professionals trained in working with children with reduced hearing were key members of her support team, and interventions were designed to promote Amanda's progress in *language* development, first in sign and later in spoken language—rather than simply to "address deficiencies" as intervention supports are commonly designed to do.

Her parents were not married to a particular methodology, but—very importantly—were able to see the "big picture" with respect to the importance of language input, and they incorporated both signed and spoken language when communicating with Amanda. The incorporation of a system for monitoring Amanda's progress, via formal assessments, helped to ensure that she was "on track" developmentally.

Factors Associated with Language Deprivation in the Presence of CIs

CIs can and do work as amazing tools of technology for some deaf children who do thrive with them. For others, however, the CI does not result in the desired spoken language outcomes the caregivers frequently want. The consequences of "CI failure" can feel devastating for families. It is possible to then witness insufficient early language access which, if not successfully remedied, can lead to language deprivation and its myriad negative consequences because these children were not proactively exposed to a signed language. Based on the author's *clinical experience*, the following seem to be associated with language deprivation in children who receive CIs:

1 *Focusing only on "the ear."* Given the strong desire on the part of many parents/caregivers to help their children learn to talk by "fixing their hearing," a great deal of emphasis tends to be placed on the ear. Focusing on what a child hears with a CI can lead to too much attention being paid to aspects of hearing and the ear, with insufficient attention given to other aspects of a child's development including their pragmatic skill development (how well the child can utilize language in social contexts), their social-emotional functioning, and their overall well-being.

2 *Emphasizing speech skills rather than language fluency.* Speech production by children with CIs is typically prioritized, often at the expense of language fluency. This may seem contradictory, but speech is not language itself per se; it is actually the expression of language. Examples include requiring a child to repeatedly say a given word until the child's articulation meets the expectations of the caregiver, which can limit the child's attempts to communicate ideas for fear of not being able to pronounce them correctly. This tendency to interrupt children to focus on speech production also interrupts the nature flow of communicative exchanges, with potential implications for how a child will interact in other social situations.

3 *Focusing on spoken language development rather than emphasizing cognitive development.* The ability to use language (regardless of modality, inclusive of receptive and expressive skills) helps to facilitate cognitive development. When the focus of intervention for children with CIs is on oral/aural language alone, the ability to conceptualize, understand relationships between constructs, and other cognitive skills can be overlooked. In other words, implanted deaf children sometimes learn to talk at the expense of not learning how to think.

4 *Not recognizing surgical/medical limitations.* Expectations of successful outcomes must be mediated by medical knowledge of a particular CI candidate. At times, caregivers are not fully aware that a given child's medical challenges may limit the ability to receive auditory benefit from the device. In such cases, they will often maintain high expectations for spoken language output from their child. When anatomical anomalies make optimal benefit from the CI unlikely, reliance on the device as the sole means of accessing information can result in insufficient language exposure. In these cases, the inclusion

of sign language exposure is even more important. Relying on a CI as one's only "tool in the tool box" for language acquisition is unnecessarily dangerous.

5 *Expecting that a CI makes a child "typically hearing."* There is a significant risk to assuming that because a child is wearing the cochlear implant processor, their access to auditory information is just like that of hearing peers. This is not the case; an implanted child is still deaf (especially when the CI processor is removed) and to some extent hard-of-hearing when it is on, remaining at risk for missing spoken language information—particularly in less than optimal listening environments, such as noisy classrooms. Adults need to monitor the comprehension of an implanted child and work to ensure that what is being said is both heard and *understood.* They especially need to remember that CI outcomes are highly variable, determined by many factors apart from the implant itself.

6 *Assuming that a CI will "fix the child's spoken language."* Insertion of a CI device does not automatically result in spoken language skills. Children with CIs must learn to make sense of the sounds that they hear, and intensive speech-language therapy is often required. Further, the presence of an internal device does nothing without the child also consistently wearing the external processor. Too often, it is wrongly assumed that once the surgery is performed, auditory/oral skills will "magically" develop.

7 *Withholding visual and contextual cues.* All children rely on visual input to learn language (Giezen et al., 2013). In order to differentiate noise from communication information, babies with typical hearing rely on visual cues from their environment. Learners of a second language, likewise, rely heavily on visual and contextual cues for understanding. "Supportive context" aids comprehension for young and old individuals, and for those with typical as well as reduced hearing (Pichora-Fuller, 2008). Intentionally not providing visual information to children who use CIs often creates an unnatural communication situation. While there may be times that training to improve listening is appropriate with reduced visual cues, in everyday communication, forced removal of visual, contextual information can result in interrupting the process of learning language. Anecdotally, excessive use of these training techniques can serve to normalize "avoiding eye contact" and other behaviors that may be socially inappropriate.

8 *Emphasizing discrete language skills over communication abilities.* Professionals working with children who use CIs, far too often, wait for "smaller skills" to develop before introducing more complex exposure to spoken language. This includes focusing on having a child repeat specific sounds before introducing words. Input needs to be meaningful, as a child is likely to learn what would typically be considered

"hard words" more readily than "easy words" if those terms are of interest (e.g., such as knowing all of the terms related to construction vehicles, or the solar system, or dinosaurs, or make-believe worlds presented through fairy tales or movies). In summary, it is important that children be exposed to advanced concepts and complex language, not limited to the "small pieces" that comprise language.

General Take Away Messages

Based on my professional training as a psychologist, my clinical experience working with deaf children and serving as a member of a cochlear implant team, a review of the current literature on brain development, language acquisition, and CI outcomes, and my interactions with deaf children and their families, I offer the following general take away messages:

1 *Early language is imperative for brain development.* Research shows that infants, from an early age, begin to make sense of the language in their environment. Lack of exposure to accessible language, as is the case in some children with reduced hearing, has documented impacts on the development of language centers in the brain, as well as on other cognitive functions. Withholding sign language from babies who are eventually implanted means at least one or more years of missing out on language exposure. Exposure to sign language in the pre-implantation period can foster infant brain ability to understand concepts and lays the foundation for acquiring a first language.

2 *Language is not "either/or."* Too many families are told that exposure to sign language will limit their baby's ability to develop spoken language skills. Families are often placed in a position where they believe that they must choose between sign language or spoken language and that they will have to stick with the choice they make in infancy.

   a. In practice, early exposure to signs serves as a bridge to foster understanding in implanted children who can go on to develop typical spoken language. Infants exposed to signs develop "symbolic representation" and understand that specific signs have meaning. Following CI activation, these signs can be paired with the spoken word, allowing for more rapid understanding of auditory input.

   b. Some implanted children will *not* develop spoken language or speech skills for a variety of reasons, many of which are not well understood. Early exposure to sign language can thus serve as "insurance" to facilitate linguistic input. Even if the family plans to use spoken language after implantation, sign language will help reduce the risk of the child becoming an adult who experiences the permanent consequences of language deprivation.

    c. The more language to which a child is exposed, the better. There are ample examples of deaf adults who are bilingual in a signed language and a spoken/written language. Many children with reduced hearing who communicate primarily in a signed language do develop fluent written (and, in some cases, spoken) language skills.

3   *Exposure to early language needs to be consistent.* Much of the variability in outcomes of signed or spoken language (beyond those described in the chapter related to research design and limitations of the measurements—e.g., considering only word-level understanding rather than more complex language) is related to the consistency of language exposure.

    a. It is imperative that infants and young children be provided consistent access to language. The use of "a few signs" by caregivers does not constitute a fully signing environment. Care must be taken to ensure access to information in their environment and to conversations.

    b. Naturally, families who are learning sign language will have difficulty "signing all of the time." Indeed, fear of not being "good enough signers" has deterred many well-meaning parents from using signs. There is an important role to be played by Deaf mentors and teachers of signed languages in helping families to prioritize their needs. Helping families to learn signs that they will use in everyday routines and prioritizing their needs to communicate with their baby needs to be an important goal for signing professionals.

4   Parent/caregiver involvement is key. The predictors of being a successful CI user are described previously—but, importantly, it cannot be determined with certainty. We do know that parental involvement and investment is vital. Deaf children with parents who are highly invested in their healthy development show better linguistic—as well as behavioral and social-emotional—outcomes than children with reduced hearing who do not have that same benefit. Sometimes, parents may believe that they do not know how to parent a child with reduced hearing. They should be assured that providing consistent love, engagement with the child, and responsiveness to the child's need will all help to foster their parent-child bond and foster the child's ability to develop a linguistic foundation.

5   There is often a role for sign language for deaf and hard of hearing individuals who are primarily oral communicators. Even when one can understand spoken language and use oral means to communicate with others, doing so requires substantial effort. For many oral communicators, there remains a role for sign language in their lives.

a. Many high achieving deaf individuals, who utilize CIs, report that, despite their success in taking in auditory information with the CI processor, doing so can be effortful. They appreciate the opportunity to be "off the air" at times and, in such situations, tend to rely more heavily on sign language.

b. Membership in Deaf culture has its privileges. Humans benefit from membership in groups and tend to seek opportunities to be with "like others." This is true for deaf people, who will often seek the company of others who are deaf or hard of hearing and share common experiences. Many children raised orally with or without CIs frequently find their way to Deaf communities as they reach adolescence and young adulthood.

In this chapter, I am not arguing for or against cochlear implantation. Cochlear implants exist, are here to stay, and have been widely adopted in many parts of the world. The debate seems to now center on the role of sign language in the lives of deaf children, with and without implants. There is real danger when cochlear implantation is used as a rationale for denying deaf children the richest sign language exposure possible for them. Given the highly variable results of cochlear implantation on language development in non-signing deaf children, preventing deaf children from having access to sign language before and after implantation remains a high-risk strategy. When it fails, it can have potentially lifelong, devastating consequences.

The complicated challenge of fostering language development in deaf children requires a complicated response. While deaf children, like hearing children, differ and no one strategy works for all deaf children, the inclusion of rich sign language exposure is far more likely to help than to hurt. Optimizing language access then, by including sign language as a "tool in the tool box," is likely the best insurance policy for promoting optimal linguistic, cognitive, and psychological functioning in children who use CIs.

Notes

1   It may be worthwhile to note that children, whose implant experience may be less "successful" or those who discontinue use of the device because it is not providing benefit, may be less likely to attend such conferences.

2   While it is "fortunate for Natalie" in this case, advocates for early language access would likely argue that it should not be left to chance or luck that a child receives the benefit of developing fluent language.

References

American Speech-Language-Hearing Association (ASHA). (2017). www.asha.org/Default.aspx

Blume, S. (2010). *The artificial ear. Cochlear implants and the culture of deafness*. Piscataway, NJ: Rutgers University Press.

Boons, T., Brokx, J. P., Dhooge, I., Frijns, J. H., Peeraer, L., Vermeulen, A., ... & Van Wieringen, A. (2012). Predictors of spoken language development following pediatric cochlear implantation. *Ear and Hearing, 33*(5), 617–639.

Brice, P. J., Plotkin, R. M., & Reesman, K. (2016). On the home front: Parents personality, support, and deaf children. *Diversity in Deaf Education,* 109–134.

Brice, P. J., & Strauss, G. (2016). Deaf adolescents in a hearing world: A review of factors affecting psychosocial adaptation. *Adolescent Health, Medicine and Therapeutics, 7,* 67–76.

Ching, T. Y., Dillon, H., Day, J., Crowe, K., Close, L., Chisholm, K., & Hopkins, T. (2009). Early language outcomes of children with cochlear implants: Interim findings of the NAL study on longitudinal outcomes of children. *Cochlear Implants International, 10*(1), 28–32.

Convertino, C. M., Marschark, M., Sapere, P., Sarchet, T., & Zupan, M. (2009). Predicting academic success among deaf college students. *Journal of Deaf Studies and Deaf Education, 14*(3), 324–343.

Cruz, I., Quittner, A. L., Marker, C., & DesJardin, J. L., & The CDaCI Investigative Team (2013). Identification of effective strategies to promote language in deaf children with cochlear implants. *Child Development, 84*(2), 543–559.

Cummins, J. (2016). The relationship between American Sign Language proficiency and English academic development: A review of the research. Retrieved December 16, 2017, from http://citeseerx.ist.psu.edu/viewdoc/download?doi=10.1.1.521.8612&rep=rep1&type=pdf

Davidson, K., Lillo-Martin, D., & Pichler, D.C. (2014). Spoken English language development among native signing children with cochlear implants. *The Journal of Deaf Studies and Deaf Education, 19*(2), 238–250.

DesJardin, J. L., & Eisenberg, L. S. (2007). Maternal contributions: Supporting language development in young children with cochlear implants. *Ear and Hearing, 28*(4), 456–469.

Dunn, C. C., Walker, E. A., Oleson, J., Kenworthy, M., Van Voorst, T., Tomblin, J. B.,... & Gantz, B. J. (2014). Longitudinal speech perception and language performance in pediatric cochlear implant users: The effect of age at implantation. *Ear and Hearing, 35*(2), 148.

Freel, B. L., Clark, M. D., Anderson, M. L., Gilbert, G. L., Musyoka, M. M., & Hauser, P. C. (2012). Deaf individuals' bilingual abilities: American Sign Language proficiency, reading skills, and family characteristics. *Psychology, 2*(1), 18.

Geers, A. E., Mitchell, C. M., Warner-Czyz, A., Wang, N. Y., Eisenberg, L. S., & CDaCI Investigative Team. (2017). Early sign language exposure and cochlear implantation benefits. *Pediatrics, 140*(1), e20163489.

Geers, A. E., Moog, J. S., Biedenstein, J., Brenner, C., & Hayes, H. (2009). Spoken language scores of children using cochlear implants compared to hearing age-mates at school entry. *The Journal of Deaf Studies and Deaf Education, 14*(3), 371–385.

Giezen, M. R., Baker, A. E., & Escudero, P. (2013). Relationships between spoken word and sign processing in children with cochlear implants. *Journal of Deaf Studies and Deaf Education, 19*(1), 107–125.

Hall, M. L., Bortfeld, H. B., Eigsti, I.-M., & Lillo-Martin, D. (In preparation). Auditory access, language access, and executive function in deaf children.

Hall, M., Caselli, N., & Hall, W. (In preparation). *Sign language for deaf children with or without cochlear implants: Nothing to lose and much to gain.* (Unpublished).

Hall, M. L. & Szarkowski, A. (In preparation). Impact of early language access on later cognitive outcomes.

Hall, W. C. (2017). What you don't know can hurt you: The risk of language deprivation by impairing sign language development in deaf children. *Maternal and Child Health Journal, 21*(5), 961–965.

Hintermair, M. (2015). The role of language in deaf and hard-of-hearing children's. In Marc Marshark & Patricia Spencer (Eds.), *The Oxford handbook of deaf studies in language* (pp. 62–78). New York, NY: Oxford University Press.

Holt, R. F., & Svirsky, M. A. (2008). An exploratory look at pediatric cochlear implantation: Is earliest always best? *Ear and Hearing, 29*(4), 492–511.

Houston, D. M., & Miyamoto, R. T. (2010). Effects of early auditory experience on word learning and speech perception in deaf children with cochlear implants: Implications for sensitive periods of language development. *Otology & Neurotology: Official Publication of the American Otological Society, American Neurotology Society [and] European Academy of Otology and Neurotology, 31*(8), 1248.

Humphries, T., Kushalnagar, P., Mathur, G., Napoli, D. J., Padden, C., & Rathmann, C. (2014). Ensuring language acquisition for deaf children: What linguists can do. *Language, 90*(2), e31–e52.

Humphries, T., Kushalnagar, P., Mathur, G., Napoli, D. J., Padden, C., Rathmann, C., & Smith, S. (2017). Discourses of prejudice in the professions: The case of sign languages. *Journal of Medical Ethics, 43*, 648–652.

Jiménez, M. S., Pino, M. J., & Herruzo, J. (2009). A comparative study of speech development between deaf children with cochlear implants who have been educated with spoken or spoken+sign language. *International Journal of Pediatric Otorhinolaryngology, 73*(1), 109–114.

Kammerer, B., Szarkowski, A., & Isquith, P. (2010). Hearing loss across the lifespan: Neuropsychological perspectives. In S. Donders & S. Hunter (Eds.), *Principles and practice of lifespan developmental neuropsychology* (pp. 257–275). Cambridge University Press: New York.

Knoors, H., & Marschark, M. (2012). Language planning for the 21st century: Revisiting bilingual language policy for deaf children. *The Journal of Deaf Studies and Deaf Education, 17*(3), 291–305.

Knoors, H., & Marschark, M. (Eds.). (2015). *Educating deaf learners: Creating a global evidence base.* New York, NY: Oxford University Press.

Komesaroff, L., Komesaroff, P. A., & Hyde M. (2015). Ethical issues in cochlear implantation. In J. Clausen & N. Levy (Eds.), *Handbook of neuroethics* (pp. 815–826). Dordrecht, Netherlands: Springer.

Kral, A., & Sharma, A. (2012). Developmental neuroplasticity after cochlear implantation. *Trends in Neurosciences, 35*(2), 111–122.

Kushalnagar, P., McKee, M., Smith, S. R., Hopper, M., Kavin, D., & Atcherson, S. R. (2014). Conceptual model for quality of life among adults with congenital or early deafness. *Disability and Health Journal, 7*(3), 350–355.

Lane, H., & Bahan, B. (1998). Article commentary: Ethics of cochlear implantation in young children: A review and reply from a Deaf-World perspective. *Otolaryngology—Head and Neck Surgery, 119*(4), 297–313.

Levine, D., Strother-Garcia, K., Golinkoff, R. M., & Hirsh-Pasek, K. (2016). Language development in the first year of life: What deaf children might be missing before cochlear implantation. *Otology & Neurotology, 37*(2), e56–e62.

Lieberman, A. M., Hatrak, M., & Mayberry, R. I. (2014). Learning to look for language: Development of joint attention in young deaf children. *Language Learning and Development, 10*(1), 19–35.

Marschark, M. & Knoors, H. (2015). Educating deaf learners in the 21st century: What we know and what we need to know. In H. Knoors & M. Marschark (Eds.), *Educating deaf learners: Creating a global evidence base.* New York, NY: Oxford University Press.

Mayberry, R. I., Del Giudice, A. A., & Lieberman, A. M. (2011). Reading achievement in relation to phonological coding and awareness in deaf readers: A meta-analysis. *The Journal of Deaf Studies and Deaf Education, 16*(2), 164–188.

Mitchell, R. E., & Karchmer, M. A. (2011). Demographic and achievement characteristics of deaf and hard-of-hearing students. In M. Marschark & P. E. Spencer (Eds.). *Oxford handbook of deaf studies, language, and education* (Vol. 1, pp. 18–31). New York, NY: Oxford University Press.

Most, T., Shina-August, E., & Meilijson, S. (2010). Pragmatic abilities of children with hearing loss using cochlear implants or hearing aids compared to hearing children. *Journal of Deaf Studies and Deaf Education, 15*(4), 422–437.

Mudry, A., & Mills, M. (2013). The early history of the cochlear implant: A retrospective. *JAMA Otolaryngology–Head & Neck Surgery, 139*(5), 446–453.

Newport, E. L., Bavelier, D., & Neville, H. J. (2001). Critical thinking about critical periods: Perspectives on a critical period for language acquisition. In E. Dupoux (Ed.) *Language, brain and cognitive development: Essays in honor of Jacques Mehler* (pp. 481–502). Cambridge, MA: The MIT Press.

Nicholas, J. G., & Geers, A. E. (2006). Effects of early auditory experience on the spoken language of deaf children at 3 years of age. *Ear and hearing, 27*(3), 286–298.

Niparko, J. K., Tobey, E. A., Thal, D. J., Eisenberg, L. S., Wang, N. Y., Quittner, A. L.,… & CDaCI Investigative Team. (2010). Spoken language development in children following cochlear implantation. *Jama, 303*(15), 1498–1506.

Olulade, O. A., Koo, D. S., LaSasso, C. J., & Eden, G. F. (2014). Neuroanatomical profiles of deafness in the context of native language experience. *Journal of Neuroscience, 34*(16), 5613–5620.

Pass, L., & Graber, A. D. (2015). Informed consent, deaf culture, and cochlear implants. *The Journal of Clinical Ethics, 26*(3), 219–230.

Pediatrics. Response to Geers et al. article http://pediatrics.aappublications.org/content/140/1/e20163489.comments#re-response-to-comments-on-ms2016-3489-early-sign-exposure-and-cochlear-implant-benefits-

Pénicaud, S., Klein, D., Zatorre, R. J., Chen, J. K., Witcher, P., Hyde, K., & Mayberry, R. I. (2013). Structural brain changes linked to delayed first language acquisition in congenitally deaf individuals. *Neuroimage, 66*, 42–49.

Peterson, N. R., Pisoni, D. B., & Miyamoto, R. T. (2010). Cochlear implants and spoken language processing abilities: Review and assessment of the literature. *Restorative Neurology and Neuroscience, 28*(2), 237–250.

Pichora-Fuller, K. M. (2008). Use of supportive context by younger and older adult listeners: Balancing bottom-up and top-down information processing. *International journal of audiology, 47*(sup2), S72–S82.

Pressman, L., Pipp-Siegel, S., Yoshinaga-Itano, C., & Deas, A. (1999). Maternal sensitivity predicts language gain in preschool children who are deaf and hard of hearing. *Journal of Deaf Studies and Deaf Education, 4*(4), 294–304.

Pungello, E. P., Iruka, I. U., Dotterer, A. M., Mills-Koonce, R., & Reznick, J. S. (2009). The effects of socioeconomic status, race, and parenting on language development in early childhood. *Developmental Psychology, 45*(2), 544.

Quittner, A. L., Barker, D. H., Cruz, I., Snell, C., Grimley, M. E., Botteri, M., & CDaCI Investigative Team. (2010). Parenting stress among parents of deaf and hearing children: Associations with language delays and behavior problems. *Parenting: Science and Practice, 10*(2), 136–155.

Quittner, A. L., Cruz, I., Barker, D. H., Tobey, E., Eisenberg, L. S., Niparko, J. K., & Childhood Development after Cochlear Implantation Investigative Team. (2013). Effects of maternal sensitivity and cognitive and linguistic stimulation on cochlear implant users' language development over four years. *The Journal of Pediatrics, 162*(2), 343–348.

Ruffin, C. V., Kronenberger, W. G., Colson, B. G., Henning, S. C., & Pisoni, D. B. (2013). Long-term speech and language outcomes in prelingually deaf children, adolescents and young adults who received cochlear implants in childhood. *Audiology and Neurotology, 18*(5), 289–296.

Sharma, A., Campbell, J., & Cardon, G. (2015). Developmental and cross-modal plasticity in deafness: Evidence from the P1 and N1 event related potentials in cochlear implanted children. *International Journal of Psychophysiology, 95*(2), 135–144.

Smith, R. J. H., Shearer, A. E., Hildebrand, M. S., & Van Camp, G. (2014). GeneReviews®[Internet]. Seattle, Washington: University of Seattle (WA).

Sugar, T. M. (2016). The Gallaudet Linguistics Department response to the AG Bell Association April 2016 statement. https://lingdept.wordpress.com/2016/04/15/the-gallaudet-linguistics-department-response-to-the-ag-bell-association-april-2016-statement/

Suskind, D. L., Leffel, K. R., Graf, E., Hernandez, M. W., Gunderson, E. A., Sapolich, S. G.,... & Levine, S. C. (2016). A parent-directed language intervention for children of low socio-economic status: A randomized controlled pilot study. *Journal of Child Language, 43*(2), 366–406.

Svirsky, M. A., Robbins, A. M., Kirk, K. I., Pisoni, D. B., & Miyamoto, R. T. (2000). Language development in profoundly deaf children with cochlear implants. *Psychological Science, 11*(2), 153–158.

Szagun, G., & Stumper, B. (2012). Age or experience? The influence of age at implantation and social and linguistic environment on language development in children with cochlear implants. *Journal of Speech, Language, and Hearing Research, 55*(6), 1640–1654.

Teinonen, T., Aslin, R. N., Alku, P., & Csibra, G. (2008). Visual speech contributes to phonetic learning in 6-month-old infants. *Cognition, 108*(3), 850–855.

Tharpe, A. M., & Seewald, R. (Eds.). (2016). *Comprehensive handbook of pediatric audiology.* Plural Publishing. United States Food and Drug Administration (FDA). www.fda.gov/

Yawn, R., Hunter, J. B., Sweeney, A. D., & Bennett, M. L. (2015). Cochlear implantation: A biomechanical prosthesis for hearing loss. *F1000prime reports, 7.*

Yoshinaga-Itano, C., Baca, R. L., & Sedey, A. L. (2010). Describing the trajectory of language development in the presence of severe to profound hearing loss: A closer look at children with cochlear implants versus hearing aids. *Otology & Neurotology: Official Publication of the American Otological Society, American Neurotology Society [and] European Academy of Otology and Neurotology, 31*(8), 1268.

Yoshinaga-Itano, C., Sedey, A. L., Coulter, D. K., & Mehl, A. L. (1998). Language of early-and later-identified children with hearing loss. *Pediatrics, 102*(5), 1161–1171.

Yoshinaga-Itano, C., Sedey, A. L., Wiggin, M., & Chung, W. (2017). Early hearing detection and vocabulary of children with hearing loss. *Pediatrics, 140*(2), e20162964.

10

Current Laws Related to the Language Development of Deaf Children and Recommended Advocacy Strategies

TAWNY HOLMES

Introduction

Stretching beyond the past century, educators, physicians, and other medical professionals have repeatedly advised families to exclude American Sign Language or any other sign language from their deaf children's language experience and education. When people (including Deaf community advocates) counter that the only way deaf children can be assured full and rich language development is through ASL, these professionals argue American laws and our society generally protects the right of parents to choose what to do with their children (i.e., parent choice). While the parents' choice is *generally* protected, American laws—along with international treaties—do recognize the right of deaf children to experience *effortless* language acquisition and fully accessible education.

This chapter will provide an overview of laws and research—while also pointing out visible legal violations that lead to language deprivation—and specific provisions that advocates for deaf children can utilize in their advocacy efforts. Successful legal strategies and arguments used by the National Association of the Deaf and other community advocates will also be shared.

Relevant National and International Laws and Treaties

Early Intervention Law

The concept of early intervention for deaf babies originated in 1989 when the Surgeon General, Dr. C. Everett Koop, "called for increased efforts to identify congenital hearing loss during the first few months of life" (White, 2017). The National Institutes of Health held a Consensus Development Conference in 1993, which then led to the passage of the Newborn and Infant Hearing Screening and Intervention Act of 1999 (now known as the Early Hearing Detection and Intervention Act, or EHDI), resulting in the current screening of all newborn babies' hearing before they leave the hospital (National Institutes of Health, 2013). In addition, the Joint Committee on Infant Hearing (JCIH) regularly provides recommendations on best practices for early intervention professionals (JCIH, 2007).

Civil Rights Laws in Education

In the United States, laws impacting deaf children's language acquisition and education are relatively young. While the youngest law is the Early Hearing Detection and Intervention Act that passed less than 20 years ago, the oldest is only 45 years old, Section 504 of the Rehabilitation Act. Section 504 is known as a precursor to the Americans with Disabilities Act (ADA) and provided protection from discrimination for people with disabilities at entities receiving federal funds. This second-oldest law (the Individuals with Disabilities Education Act, or IDEA, passed in its original form in 1975) set the bar for measuring communication access and established current regulations for determining educational environments for deaf students. The Americans with Disabilities Act was passed in July, 1990, and while it is hailed as the strongest disability rights law in the world, it does not specify language or cultural protection for the Deaf community. This is unlike the international treaty "Convention of Rights for Persons with Disabilities" (CRPD), described as follows. Both the 504 and ADA laws have made significant headway for providing interpreters and captioning access for students and teachers alike, and have raised the bar for measuring the communication access of deaf individuals in both federally funded and private schools (see Table 10.1 for a comparison).

Table 10.1 Comparison of Legislation

	IDEA	Section 504	ADA
Applicable age	Birth to 21 years	Any age	Any age
How to get the law's protection	Must "qualify"	Disability that substantially limits a major life activity	Identifiable disability or regarded as so
Applies to whom/what?	Local, state, and federal	Entities receiving federal funds	Public accommodations and private entities
Who decides?	IEP team	504 coordinator	Upon request or see need
Goal of law	Specialized education	FAPE and accommodations	Reasonable accommodations
Measure of law	"Educational benefit"	"Appropriate accommodations"	"Effective communication"
Can compare?	No comparison-individualized	Compares to other disabled students	Compares to hearing student

International Treaties

What does international law say about the educational and linguistic rights of deaf children? In 1989, the United Nations passed the Convention on the Rights of the Child treaty, which stated that children with disabilities must be protected from discrimination, including from society and *their parents* (United Nations, 1989). It also stated that the child's freedom of expression in all forms must be protected. This treaty has been ratified by over 140 countries, but, sadly, *not* by the United States.

Thanks to the hard work of the World Federation of the Deaf, which was among eight large organizations representing people with disabilities, there is another key international treaty with more specific language pertinent to deaf children. The United Nations Convention on the Rights of Persons with Disabilities (CRPD) has 50 articles covering education, employment, technology, and other topics. The document mentions sign language seven times and makes it clear that it is the human right of deaf children to acquire it along with knowledge of their culture (United Nations, 2006). Adopted in 2006, the CRPD provides benchmarks and framework to improve the human rights of people with disabilities all over the world. It came into force on May 3, 2008 and is now ratified by 175 countries, but unfortunately, again, not by the United States[1] (United Nations, 2017). Although international treaties traditionally do not have any enforcement measures in the eyes of the United States government, US ratification would provide grounds for the UN to express concern about the lack of support for sign language for our deaf children, especially when it comes to early intervention.

Early Intervention and Medical Ethics

Early intervention programs required by the Early Hearing Detection and Intervention Act (EHDI) vary from state to state and can be provided by a local district or state agency, school for the deaf, private schools, or a hospital. The early intervention team usually works off an Individualized Family Service plan, focusing on the family's requests and the child's identified needs, as required by Part C of the Individuals with Disabilities Education Act (2004). Despite the presence of such programs, and due to biases by professionals implementing these plans, there are still gaps in services to the families—particularly in the areas of family-to-family support, parent leadership, access to Deaf Mentor programs, and resources on language, literacy, and social-emotional development. For example, in the state of Georgia, only 5% of families are offered sign language acquisition services despite available Deaf mentors and school-based services and numerous professionals skilled in sign language (Dundon, 2017).

The first significant service gap occurs when parents learn their baby is deaf. When an audiologist provides confirmation of hearing loss, parents often are given limited information on sign language and/or are actively discouraged from using sign language with their children. The same is frequently true with family doctors, be they pediatricians, ENTs, or gynecologists. Deaf community advocates have often posed the question whether this constitutes a breach of legal ethics or, at the minimum, a violation of the Hippocratic Oath. Doctors who tell parents of deaf children not to send their child to a school for the deaf or expose their child to sign language are usually operating outside of their area of expertise and very likely causing harm. Yasmeen Alhasawi, a neuroethicist, has argued that such behaviors are unethical (Alhasawi, Sultan, & Giordano, 2016).

Families working with attorneys from the National Association of the Deaf have shared stories about having a representative from the cochlear implant company or a cochlear implant surgeon approach them almost immediately after they learned that their baby did not pass the hearing screening exam. Parents from four states (California, Delaware, Florida, and Indiana) have also told legal advocates that they were forced to sign a paper stating that they agree to not sign or take their child to a school for the deaf before the surgeons would agree to the implantation surgery.

The result of such practices is that approximately 85% of families decide on the speech-only method for their newly identified deaf baby (ASHA, 2012). These stories and statistics conflict with the fact that in recent years, experts' views have evolved to include the idea that parents don't need to make a choice between spoken or signed language but can incorporate both—some form of bilingualism—into a child's development (Napoli et al., 2015). Signing, speaking, and switching between both modalities are all viable options that can lead to success for deaf and hard of hearing children (DesGeorges, 2016).

The benefits and limitations of cochlear implantation are well discussed in Chapters 1 and 9, by Gulati and Szarkowski respectively. There is no question that some deaf children benefit from cochlear implantation, and there is also no question that others do not. Even when cochlear implantation is considered successful (and, as both Gulati and Szarkowski discuss, one must consider biases in the criteria used to judge success), this significant medical procedure is not normally undertaken before 11 months of age, and means that in the first critical year of life, the child may receive no language input. It can take up to one year after implantation to complete mapping of what sounds the child is able to identify, which means, potentially, yet another year lost before the child receives meaningful spoken language input, if, indeed, this is possible for them (Tomblin, 2005). This does not even consider the subsequent years of listening and speech training to reach some undetermined percent of effectiveness with the implant, during which time the child does not receive fully accessible language exposure. This is all time when, the child could be learning language through sign. Their brains can be forming the neural connections into which words and concepts from multiple languages can later attach.

Ironically, this first year of life is a time that many parents are encouraged to use sign language with their hearing children in order to promote their language development.

> My deaf son received a cochlear implant at age six. The cochlear implant team told me to stop signing with him and force him to speak English. That was two years ago. He has not learned any English since receiving his implant and I have started to sign with him again. His behaviors are getting out of control and I do not know what to do with him. He is angry and frustrated and refuses to behave in school. He is not learning anything and functions like a three-year-old. However, he is intelligent! He was just denied language.
>
> *–Key informant*

It is important to remember that cochlear implants require work and further commitment (financial, time, mental, and physical) not just for the child, but for the family. Many deaf children and/or their parents are unable to devote this kind of effort. This may be due to socioeconomic or personal stressors or physical failure of the implant. While private insurance companies and Medicaid are generally willing to pay for surgery, families often experience economic burden in paying for the follow-up sound mapping appointments and checkups that are essential to the use of the cochlear implant. Our argument, however, is not against implantation. It is in favor of quality sign language exposure. Being pro-sign language is not being anti-implant, despite the best efforts of anti-sign language activists to frame it this way.

In contrast to CI services, nearly all ASL classes/services/resources for families and deaf babies are provided free of charge by schools for the deaf, apps and websites, tele-intervention (ASL classes via videoconferencing), or directly from early intervention providers such as signing Deaf mentors (Poeppelmeyer & Reichert, 2015). Research shows that contact with deaf mentors helps families transition to acceptance of their child as a deaf person (Hintermair, 2006). Deaf mentors can provide the deaf child with something hearing parents and medical professionals cannot: rich and immediately accessible language exposure from birth (Chute & Nevins, 2002). One study found that with the support of Deaf mentors, parents were able to produce six times more signs than other parents and, as a result, create a language-rich environment at home (Watkins, Pittman, & Walden, 2008). Yet national statistics show that the majority of families choose not to utilize a Deaf mentor, and when their children reach school age, only 28% of parents know American Sign Language to some degree. This is a telling decline from 1995, when 60% of parents chose sign-language options (Brown, 2006). At the time of this writing (Fall of 2017), only 15 states promote families having access to Deaf sign language mentors (SKI-HI Institute). Thus, current practices are increasingly creating generations of deaf children at risk for significant language deprivation.

K-12 Education: Individuals with Disabilities Education Act

The Individuals with Disabilities Education Act (IDEA), which addresses services to deaf children from birth to age 21, has several components with great relevance to language acquisition in deaf children. These will be reviewed briefly here.

Least Restrictive Environment and a Continuum of Placements

The Individuals with Disabilities Education Act has four parts, A, B, C, and D. Part A introduces the law and its purpose. Part B describes the responsibilities of public schools in providing K-12 education and services to students with disabilities. Part C focuses on the definition and provision of early intervention services for children ages 0–4. Part D outlines the funding mechanisms for states. When children start full-time schooling, they depart the Part C services of the law and transition to the Part B services of the law, which includes the Least Restrictive (LRE) mandate. The purpose of this mandate is to encourage school districts to place students with disabilities in what are considered "less restrictive settings," with the use of supplementary aids and services, before they are placed in what are considered "more restrictive" settings such as separate special education classrooms or state schools (Yell, 2006). This generally results in ensuring that students with varying disabilities are provided education access and social interaction with nondisabled students. This was not the case before the IDEA was passed 40 plus years ago. Advocates and educational administrators have argued, however, that the LRE needs to be reversed for deaf students, increasing the percentage in state schools that have "language-rich" environments and therefore are the "real" least restrictive environment (CEASD, 2011; NAD, 2002).

The US Department of Education has conceded that mainstreaming does not always result in the least restrictive environment for deaf students (US Department of Education, 2016). However, state departments of education and local school districts often find this conflicts with the federal mandate to increase the percentage of students in regular education settings, something which much be reported in each state's yearly "State Performance Plan." School districts are supposed to provide a continuum of placement options (e.g., full inclusion in a regular classroom, use of a separate special education classroom, attendance in a deaf school, homeschooling), so that placements can be made based on the unique needs of each student. However, states face pressure to document "non-restrictive" placements (i.e., students with disabilities in mainstreamed environments), and this biases placement decisions to be against specialized placements (Individuals with Disabilities Education Act of 2004).

One national case study in 2007 stated that for deaf students in US, 47% are in regular education settings, 29.7% are in self-contained classrooms, 28.1% are in state schools, 14.1% are in resource room, and 2.6% are homeschooled (Cerney, 2007). The most recent national statistics from 2012 show the numbers are even lower—only 14% are being educated in schools for the deaf (Gallaudet Research Institute, 2013). In addition, it is estimated that nearly 50% of those in mainstream settings are the only deaf student in their public school (Oliva, 2004). These students risk not only language and educational delays but social isolation and traumatic experiences like bullying (Sullivan, 2006).[2] In this process, while not the main reason why deaf children need sign language, the Deaf community has also lost its "feeder system" or pipeline for the transmission of language and Deaf cultural information, and for the promotion of healthy Deaf identities (Gallaudet Research Institute, 2013). The full impact of these practices upon deaf people as a whole is just beginning to emerge.

Individualized Education Programs

To accomplish the goals of the IDEA law, schools are required to provide services to students with disabilities. For K-12 education, Part B of the IDEA expects schools to document services on an Individualized Education Plan (IEP). Each plan is supposed to be specifically tailored to the unique needs of each student, and not based on budgetary issues or school districts' predetermined preferred policy (Individuals with Disabilities Education Act of 2004). The IEP also requires schools to determine placements, such as a school where the services can be provided. Other placement option are resource rooms where deaf peers from various grade levels can interact and have access to a teacher more familiar with educational and language needs of deaf children. This is one good way that schools can satisfy the special factors for deaf students which the IDEA requires. The special factors include consideration of the child's language and communication needs, such as opportunities for direct communications with peers and professionals in the child's preferred language, and access to appropriate assistive technology (Centers for Parent Information & Resources, 2017; Individuals with Disabilities Education Act of 2004).

In recent years, however, resource rooms and large mainstreamed programs (defined generally as either having a critical mass of deaf students or being "anchor schools" in the school district/county) have been shut down. This is occurring at a more rapid pace than closures of schools for the deaf. Instead, deaf students might be placed on another type of plan mandated under a different law, the Section 504 of the Rehabilitation Act. Section 504 plans are limited to interpreters, FM access, or captioning. More often, 504 deaf students receive no services at all, which means they do not see or socialize with adult deaf teachers or deaf peers. Research has suggested that Deaf role models and fluent signers are key in ensuring native-like fluency in deaf children with hearing parents, no matter what signing level their hearing parents demonstrate (Humphries et al., 2012). While the closing of Deaf schools has been the more visible cause for community activism, the rapid decline of access to both sign language instruction and access to deaf peers in mainstream education is a serious contributing factor to the spread of language deprivation. The continuum of educational services for deaf students required under the IDEA is, in fact, disappearing.

Itinerant teachers are not specifically referenced in the IDEA but, with the shutting down of large mainstreamed programs, they are increasingly the strategy used by school districts to both cut down on cost of services and meet the federal requirements for individualized educational programs (Luckner & Ayantoye, 2013). Itinerant teachers, at minimum, meet individually with a deaf student in a public school. The meeting may be as short as 20 or 30 minutes, weekly or biweekly. If the itinerant teacher signs competently (something which cannot be assumed), this may be the only contact with a signing person that the deaf student receives.

Researching and documenting the impact of these practices upon deaf children is difficult because the US Department of Education does not require states to specify the nature of a child's disability. As a result, only 14 states have a specific count of deaf and hard of hearing students, and the data may not include information on placements and academic performance (Szymansky, 2013). The rapid decrease in enrollment in Deaf schools and mainstream programs with "critical masses" of deaf students means that increasing numbers of deaf students are more isolated from deaf peers and less exposed to quality sign language.

Supreme Court Cases

The current level of deaf students' isolation can be credited not only to federal law and policies, but also to Supreme Court decisions. The first-ever Supreme Court case concerning the IDEA and its regulations was the Board of Education of the Hendrick Hudson Central School District v. Rowley in 1982. This case determined that access to a sign language interpreter was not necessary for a bright deaf young girl who could "get by" (which means having good grades) without one. The Rowley standard of "the services being reasonably calculated to enable the child to receive educational benefits" is also known as the "de minimis" threshold of services provision. It was not until 2017 when another Supreme Court case, Endrew F. v. Douglas County School District, stated that this threshold was too low and that services should be calculated to provide progress appropriate to the child's circumstances (Endrew, 2017).

The impact of Endrew's case remains to be seen. Regardless, as seen from the history of regulations and court cases, the IDEA provides a low standard when it comes to measuring a deaf child's language and overall development.

The Americans with Disabilities Act

In contrast with the IDEA, the Americans with Disabilities Act mandates a much higher standard—"effective communication"—as measured by comparing the level of communication access of deaf students with those of hearing peers (US Department of Justice, 2014). In other words, deaf students are legally obligated to 100% of the information and communication that hearing students receive. The US Department of Education and the US Department of Justice recently reminded schools of their legal obligations under the ADA, which are separate from the IDEA (US Department of Education & US Department of Justice, 2014). This was due to four federal court cases occurring between 2011 and 2014, three of which concerned deaf students struggling with communication access (K. M. v. Tustin, 2013; US Department of Education & US Department of Justice, 2014). Indeed, the US Department of Education Secretary has affirmed in news reports that ADA likely offers greater protection for students with disabilities, even though it is more often used outside educational settings. The ripple effect of these interpretive guidelines has not yet been fully measured. Advocacy efforts are underway to educate parents that their deaf children have more rights under the ADA than they do under the IDEA.

Advocacy and Language Exposure Strategies

People who understand the importance for deaf children of having rich sign language exposure have many advocacy strategies available to them. Interventions can occur at the legislative level, through community-based education and resource development, and through early intervention programs. Utilizing knowledge of laws, proposing new laws, and helping implement systematic change are all examples of successful legal advocacy strategies. There are many other actions that one can take to combat language deprivation—be it as a community member, parent or family member, or teacher and administrator.

Community Action on the Local and State Level

Seeing that language deprivation is increasingly happening at both school and home, the Deaf community has mobilized to offer increased support to families. One way they have done this is by serving as education advocates. The National Association of the Deaf established the Education Advocates program in 2012 in direct response to the language deprivation crisis. The Education Advocates program recruits signing Deaf volunteers to work with each state association of the Deaf to provide resources for sign language exposure for deaf children and their families (www.nad.org/educationadvocates). Since its inception in 2012, the program has spread to all 50 states including the District of Columbia.

One example of such advocacy efforts is state-level Deaf mentor programs. The purpose of a Deaf mentor program is to have deaf and hard of hearing adults provide families support in language acquisition and Deaf cultural knowledge (SKI-HI Institute, 2017). This supports the development of self-esteem as a deaf or hard of hearing person in the family. It also sensitizes hearing family members to the communication and identity concerns of their deaf family member (Benedict & Sass-Lehrer, 2007; Leigh, 2009; Meadow-Orlans, Mertens, & Sass-Lehrer, 2003). Contact with the Deaf community also expands families' network of support. Interaction with Deaf professionals paves the way for a whole new world of information and experiences that would not otherwise be available to the family. The experience of such programs is that family members exposed to signing Deaf adults tend to become more motivated to learn sign language. Interested people can check to see whether their state has a Deaf mentor program and, if not, work with the state school or early intervention program to help establish one (National Center on Hearing Assessment and Management, 2017; SKI-HI Institute, 2017).[3]

One challenge in promoting the need for a Deaf Mentor program is the lack of data showing deaf children's language abilities once they arrive at school. In partial response, a recent nationwide mobilization campaign has been established focusing on establishing a state law requiring assessments of young deaf children in both ASL and/or English. This campaign is known as the Language Equality and Acquisition for Deaf Kids (LEAD-K) and calls for "kindergarten readiness" (2017). As of the spring legislative session in 2017, advocates in 30 states have been committed to bringing this bill to their state legislatures, following the success of four states, California, Hawaii, Kansas, and Oregon, in 2016 and 2017 (Holmes, 2017). The result of each bill has been to establish a taskforce composed of various stakeholders to discuss selection and implementation of mandatory language acquisition assessments for all deaf and hard of hearing children in the state. Implementation will start happening in the 2018–2019 school year.

Another potential state-level bill requires a higher level of qualifications for educational interpreters. Most states currently require scores of between 3.0 and 3.5 out of 5 on the Educational Interpreting Proficiency Assessment provided by Boys Town (Registry of Interpreters for the Deaf, 2017). The developer of this test has publicly stated that a score of 3.5 means that only 70% of the content is being interpreted accurately. This certainly results in academic inequality and does not fulfill the obligation of ensuring deaf students receive 100% of content that hearing students receive (Schick, 2006).

In 2016, the National Association of the Deaf's Education Strategy Team developed a new model bill template called the Bill of Rights for Deaf and Hard of Hearing Children (National Association of the Deaf, 2017b). It addresses many factors related to language deprivation for children. The Bill of Rights has been passed in 14 states since the 2000s and is an excellent resource for local, state, and federal advocacy. To promote successful legislation modeled on this Bill of Rights, advocates in each state are encouraged to develop relationships with their local district representatives and senators, educating them about the needs that deaf children have for rich sign language exposure, adequate skilled interpreters, and other matters specific to each situation. People are also encouraged to register and vote and to work on the campaigns of legislators who are or have the potential to become allies.

Other than proposing legislative bills, people can combat language deprivation directly by volunteering time as sign language models for deaf students at schools where they are not receiving sign language exposure. For example, public schools often welcome guest presenters or storytellers for the annual Deaf Awareness Week. Signing people can establish sign language classes or signing events for parents in their community, including providing it in native sign languages for Spanish-speaking parents and/or immigrants from other countries. State associations and Education Advocates have been doing this increasingly over the past three years with overwhelming positive response from parents and families.

Community members are also encouraged to get more involved with their states' early intervention services. For example, many states have an advisory board (known as a Part C advisory council, or Universal Newborn Hearing Screening council, or an Intra-Agency Early Intervention Stakeholders Council), and some are mandated to have a representative from the Deaf community. Deaf community members should find a way to join a council (National Center on Hearing Assessment and Management, 2017). People are also encouraged to review their state's early intervention website and materials to see if they provide accurate information on language acquisition that includes sign language acquisition, and if not, to send a letter requesting changes (National Center on Hearing Assessment and Management, 2017). To support those efforts, resources providing evidence for sign language acquisition that are user-friendly and easy to distribute are available (National Laurent Clerc Deaf Education Center, 2017; Visual Language and Visual Learning Research Center at Gallaudet University).

Community Action on the Federal Level

Other efforts by community members and advocacy organizations are focused on the federal level, such as the effort, spearheaded by the Conference of Educational Administrators Serving Schools and Programs for the Deaf (CEASD), National Association of the Deaf, and the American Federation of the Blind, to amend the Individuals with Disabilities Education Act through the Alice Cogswell and Anne Macy Sullivan Act bill. The purposes of the

Cogswell-Sullivan Act bill are to require professionals providing assessments to be qualified in the child's language, ensure there remains a critical mass of deaf children in school programs, and maintain the central role of state Deaf schools in the provision of centralized services and resources to deaf children and their families (National Association of the Deaf, 2017a). As of the time of this writing, this bill has not yet become law. Updates are available through the CEASD webpage (www.ceasd.org/child-first/child-first-campaign).

In the fall of 2017, during the 2017 US Congressional Session, the Early Hearing Detection and Intervention Act was up for reauthorization. The National Association of the Deaf and affiliates advocated for terminology changes, drawing less upon medical perspectives and more on linguistic and educational perspectives (National Association of the Deaf, 2016). While not all of the recommendations by the NAD were incorporated, there were still positive changes. As a result of the bill's passage, language acquisition assessments and services are now required for all families, in both oral and visual modalities, and states are expected to provide support for Deaf mentor programs (115th Congress, 2017). Interested people can keep an eye on the NAD's website to learning about new federal legislation (www.nad.org).

Actions by Parents and Family Members

Informed and empowered parents and family members can be powerful allies and advocates for their deaf children. Parents can, for instance, collaborate with Deaf community members and organizations on legislative advocacy, including providing testimonies about their personal experiences. Parents can benefit from being part of local and national parents' organizations and conferences such as those hosted by the American Society for Deaf Children or Hands & Voices. Parents are also encouraged to take advantage of the stipends provided to one parent in each state by the National Center on Hearing Assessment and Management to attend the annual Early Hearing Detection and Intervention (EHDI) meeting. Participation in such organizations and conferences helps parents learn about their rights and resources. For example, they learn they can request Deaf mentors or other services in sign language through their EHDI or Part C of IDEA services (including transportation to, and provision of, sign language classes specifically for them and their children) on their Individualized Family Service Plan.

As for K-12 education services, parents have successfully used independent evaluators to show the impact on their children of not having appropriate language access. These independent evaluations, along with the letters from the US Department of Education making it clear that the language needs of deaf children are to be addressed individually, has resulted in alternative educational placements and services (US Department of Education, 1992; US Department of Education, 2017.

Another successful strategy has been drawing upon the ADA's "effective communication" provision to request signing teachers or qualified interpreters.

The US Department of Justice and the US Department of Education have jointly released guidance emphasizing this point (US Department of Education & US Department of Justice, 2014). In doing so, parents effectively bypass the more complex Individualized Education Plan or the Section 504 procedures. An additional benefit of using the ADA in advocacy is that it requires the school to immediately provide the student's "preferred accommodation" until the school can prove this imposes "an undue burden" or "a fundamental alteration" of their program/services (Americans with Disabilities Act of 1990).

In navigating accommodations and services at school with the aim of preventing or treating language deprivation, parents are urged to consider several key factors derived from the National Association of the Deaf's position statement on inclusion (National Association of the Deaf, 2002).

> "We wanted to communicate as quickly as possible with Marissa, and for her to be able to do the same with us. We thought that if and when she was going to 'speak' she needed to have something to speak about. It made the most sense to begin with American Sign Language since she could not fully hear spoken language."
>
> –*Cheryl Cohen, Parent & Rabbi*

First, language access varies for every deaf child. Educators should always check on the deaf child's understanding by asking open-ended questions and determining that the responses are appropriate. Second, when raising a child to be bilingual, consistency is key both at home and school. Developing a language plan outlining which language is to be used when and with whom is recommended (Kite & Mitchner, 2015). Quality apps and videos, such as the Visual Language and Learning (VL2) Storybook Apps or the Clerc Center's Shared Reading Program, can also enhance the child's language development (http://vl2storybookapps.com/; www3.gallaudet.edu/clerc-center/our-resources/shared-reading-project.html). Parents who use these materials alongside of their children are actively participating in their child's language development.

Parents are also encouraged to check that their child has an opportunity to interact with other deaf children and adult deaf role models, in school and in the community. Parents should check on the qualifications and expertise of the personnel working with their child to ensure they establish high and age-appropriate expectations in both language and general education. For instance, at one IEP meeting, an eighth-grade student had third- and fourth-grade-level goals in math and reading, despite having language from birth at both home and school (She had a hearing mother who signed and attended a total communication program at school). The IEP team could not explain this discrepancy, except that they had boilerplate text describing low expectations for all the deaf children in their program.

Actions by Teachers

Teachers often hold unconscious biases about deaf children. Thousands of teachers interact with deaf children every year, and most of them do not have any background or training in working with deaf children. On average, a general education teacher sees a deaf student once every seven years. Yet teachers can be key players in combating or preventing language deprivation for deaf students in school. They can do this by seeking professional development and training in bilingual approaches. Good sources of professional training are the conferences offered by the newly established National Deaf Education Conference and the free in-person/online training provided by the Clerc Center (http://deafeducation.us; www3.gallaudet.edu/clerc-center/learning-opportunities.html).

There are pedagogical strategies that teachers can use to make a mainstream classroom more supportive of a deaf students' language development. For example, deaf students generally benefit from the use of visual aids like PowerPoint, handouts, or writing on the board. They can benefit from use of technology like iPad apps such as VL2 storybooks or real-time captioning. Teachers can include information about the Deaf community and history in their lectures, and they can give assignments that require all their students to learn some ASL. To measure students' language growth, they can use assessments designed for use with sign language and deaf children (http://vl2.gallaudet.edu/resources/asl-assessment-toolkits/). They can also make sure that language assessments are done by professionals specifically trained to work with deaf children. Strategies like these helps create real inclusion for deaf children and can lessen the risk of ongoing language deprivation.

Conclusions

The current state of educational services for deaf children is, indeed, dire. Specialized schools, programs, and services that ensured full language inclusion in the past are rapidly disappearing. The laws we depend upon for advocacy are nowhere near as strong as they need to be. Nonetheless, some laws are better than others and can be taken advantage of. The ADA, for instance, is generally a better tool than either the IDEA or the various rehabilitation acts. Similarly, some advocacy strategies, such as obtaining qualified independent evaluations of the language and educational needs of deaf children and drawing upon those aspects of the laws that mandate effective language access, have proven the most effective. The National Association of the Deaf is an important resource for advocacy efforts, but the NAD needs active collaboration from a "village" of contributors. For all of us in this village concerned with combating language deprivation in deaf children, there is still a mountain to climb. Whether we work to change the system through law or education policy, advocate for a deaf child, or contribute to a child's language development, all of us in this village have important roles to ensure that deaf children are provided rich exposure to fully accessible language they can learn effortlessly from birth.

Notes

1   President Barack Obama signed the Convention of Rights for Persons with Disabilities on July 24, 2009 but Congress has not yet approved official ratification.
2   Researchers found that children with disabilities are frequently targeted by bullies, and those with observable disabilities (such as deaf children) are twice as likely to be bullied as children with less noticeable disabilities.
3   The National Center on Hearing Assessment and Management provides information on funding and structures of Deaf Mentor programs. www.infanthearing.org/dhhadultinvolvement/.

References

115th U.S. Congress. (October 2017). Early hearing detection and intervention act of 2017. www.congress.gov/bill/115th-congress/senate-bill/652

Alhasawi, Y., Sultan, V., & Giordano, J. (2015). *Cochlear implant technology: Market forces and effects, and neuroethics:-Legal and social considerations.* Poster presentation presented at the International Neuroethics Society Conference, Chicago, IL.

Americans with Disabilities Act of 1990, Pub. L. 101–336, 104 Stat. 328.

American Speech-Hearing Association (ASHA). (2012). Pediatric statistics. Retrieved from www.hearsaylw.com/2013/10/ashas-facts-on-listening-and-spoken.html

Benedict, B., & Sass-Lehrer, M. (February 2007). Deaf and hearing partnerships: Ethical and communication considerations. *American Annals of the Deaf, 152*(3), 275–282. Retrieved from www.ncbi.nlm.nih.gov/pubmed/18018669

Board of Education of the Hendrick Hudson Central School District v. Rowley, 458 U.S. 176 (1982).

Brown, C. (2006). *Early intervention: Strategies for public and private sector collaboration.* Paper presented at the 2006 convention of the Alexander Graham Bell association for the deaf and hard of hearing. Pittsburgh, PA.

Centers for Parent Information & Resources. (July 31, 2017). Special factors in IEP development. *Center for parent information and resources.* Retrieved from www.parentcenterhub.org/special-factors/

Cerney, J. (2007). *Deaf education in America: Voices of children from inclusion settings.* Washington, DC: Gallaudet University Press.

Chute, P. & Nevins, M. E. (2002). *The parents' guide to cochlear implants.* Washington, DC: Gallaudet University Press.

Conference of Educational Administrators of Schools and Programs for the Deaf (CEASD). (2011). *Child first campaign.* Retrieved from www.ceasd.org/child-first/child-first-campaign

DesGeorges, J. (April, 2016). Avoiding assumptions: Communication decisions made by hearing parents of deaf children, *AMA Journal of Ethics, 18*(4), 442–446.

Dundon, K. (2017). *100 babies project: Identifying outcome barriers for deaf and hard of hearing children in Georgia.* Paper presented at the early hearing detection and intervention meeting in Atlanta, GA.

Endrew, F. v. Douglas County School District 580 U.S. (2017).

Gallaudet Research Institute (GRI). (2013). *Regional and national summary report of data from the 2011–2012. Annual survey of deaf and hard of hearing children and youth.* Washington, DC: Gallaudet Research Institute.

Hintermair, M. (October 2006). Parental resources, parental stress, and socioemotional development of deaf and hard of hearing children. *Journal of Deaf Studies and Deaf Education, 11*(4), 493–513. Retrieved from https://academic.oup.com/jdsde/article/11/4/493/409057

Holmes, T. (November 2017). Personal knowledge from LEAD-K core team meetings.

Humphries, T., Kushalnagar, P., Mather, G., Napoli, D. J., Padden, C., Rathmann, C., & Smith, S. R. (2012). Language acquisition for deaf children: Reducing the harms of zero tolerance to the use of alternative approaches. *Harm Reduction Journal, 9*(16). doi: 10.1186/1477-7517-9-16

Individuals with Disabilities Education Act of 2004, § 1400-300.115 *et seq.*

Joint Committee on Infant Hearing (JCIH). (2007). *Position statements from the joint committee on infant hearing.* Retrieved from www.jcih.org/posstatemts.htm

Kite, B. J., & Mitchner, J. (2015). *Family language policy and planning.* [Powerpoint Slides]. Retrieved from http://ehdimeeting.org/archive/2015/System/Uploads/pdfs/Monday_Nunn_1105_JulieMitchiner_1492.pdfK.M. v. Tustin Unified School District, 725 F.3d 1088 (9th Cir. 2013), cert. denied, 134 S. Ct. 1493 (2014).

Leigh, I. (2009). *A lens on deaf identities (perspectives on deafness).* Oxford: Oxford University Press.

Luckner, J. L., & Ayantoye, C. (July 2013). Itinerant teachers of students who are deaf or hard of hearing: Practices and preparation. *The Journal of Deaf Studies and Deaf Education, 18*(3), 409–423. doi: 10.1093/deafed/ent015

Meadow-Orlans, K. P., Mertens, D. M., & Sass-Lehrer, M. A. (2003). *Parents and their deaf children: The early years.* Chicago, IL: University of Chicago Press.

Napoli, D. J., Mellon, N. K, Niparko, J. K, Rathmann, C., Mathur, G., Humphries, T. Landos, J.D. (2015). Should all deaf children learn sign language? *Pediatrics, 136*(1), 170–176. Retrieved from www.ncbi.nlm.nih.gov/pubmed/26077481

National Association of the Deaf. (2002). *Position statement on inclusion.* Retrieved from www.nad.org/about-us/position-statements/position-statement-on-inclusion/

National Association of the Deaf. (2016). *Amendments recommended for the early hearing detection and intervention act of 2015.* Retrieved from www.nad.org/2016/03/14/amendments-recommended-early-hearing-detection-intervention-act-2015/

National Association of the Deaf. (2017a). *Cogswell bill history and update.* Retrieved from www.nad.org/resources/education/cogswell-bill-history-and-update/

National Association of the Deaf. (2017b). *Bill of rights for deaf and hard of hearing children.* Retrieved from www.nad.org/resources/education/bill-of-rights-for-deaf-and-hard-of-hearing-children/

National Center on Hearing Assessment and Management Center (NCHAM). (June 21, 2017) *EDHI/UNHS program guidelines and websites by state.* Retrieved from http://infanthearing.org/stateguidelines/index.php

National Center on Hearing Assessment and Management Center (NCHAM). (n.d.). *State parent information about EDHI programs.* Retrieved from http://infanthearing.org/statematerials/index.html

National Center on Hearing Assessment and Management (NCHAM). (n.d.). *Deaf/hard of hearing adult involvement learning community.* Retrieved from www.infanthearing.org/dhhadultinvolvement/index.html

National Institutes of Health (2013). *Newborn hearing screening.* (Research portfolio online reporting tools). Retrieved from https://report.nih.gov/nihfactsheets/ViewFactSheet.aspx?csid=104&key=N

National Laurent Clerc Deaf Education Center. (2015). *Schools and programs for deaf and hard of hearing students in the U.S.* Retrieved from www3.gallaudet.edu/clerc-center/info-to-go/national-resources-and-directories/schools-and-programs.html

National Laurent Clerc Deaf Education Center. (2016). *Early intervention network: Supporting linguistic competence for children who are deaf or hard of hearing: Visual language.* Retrieved from www.gallaudet.edu/clerc-center-sites/early-intervention-network-supporting-linguistic-competence-for-children-who-are-deaf-or-hard-of-hearing/early-intervention-factors/factor-1.html

National Laurent Clerc Deaf Education Center. (2017). *Sign language use for deaf, hard of hearing and hearing babies: The evidence supports it.* Retrieved from www3.gallaudet.edu/clerc-center/our-resources/publications/the-evidence-supports-it.html

National Laurent Clerc Deaf Education Center. (n.d.). Learning opportunities. *Clerc center on-site training.* Retrieved from www3.gallaudet.edu/clerc-center/learning-opportunities/on-site-training.html

Oliva, G. A. (2004). *Alone in the mainstream: A deaf woman remembers public school.* Washington, DC: Gallaudet University Press.

Poeppelmeyer, D., & Reichert, L. (2015). Pioneering program teaches families sign language through tele-intervention. *Odyssey: New Directions in Deaf Education, 16,* pp. 46–50. Retrieved from https://eric.ed.gov/?id=EJ1064221

Registry of Interpreters for the Deaf. (2017). *State-by-state regulations for interpreters and transliterators.* Retrieved from www.rid.org/advocacy-overview/state-information-and-advocacy/

Schick, B. (January 2006). Look who's being left behind: Educational interpreters and access to education for deaf and hard-of-hearing students. *The Journal of Deaf Studies and Deaf Education, 11*(1), 3–20. doi:10.1093/deafed/enj007

SKI-HI Institute. (2017). Section 504 of the Rehabilitation Act of 1973, 34 C.F.R. Part 104. *Deaf mentor.* Retrieved from www.skihi.org/DeafMentor.html

Sullivan, P. (2006). Children with disabilities exposed to violence: Legal and public policy issues. In M. Feerick & G. Silverman (Eds.), *Children exposed to violence* (pp. 213–237). Baltimore, MA: Paul Brookes.

Szymansky, C. (2013). Critical needs of students who are deaf or hard of hearing: A public input summary. *Laurent Clerc National Deaf Education Center.* Retrieved from www3.gallaudet.edu/clerc-center/our-resources/publications/pi-summary.html

Tomblin, J. B., Barker, B. A., Spencer, L. J, Zhang, X., Gantz, B. J. (2005). The effect of age at cochlear implant initial stimulation on expressive language growth in infants and toddlers. *Journal of Speech, Language, Hearing Research, 48*(4):853–867.

United Nations. (2017). Convention on the rights of persons with disabilities. Article 24. Retrieved from www.un.org/development/desa/disabilities/convention-on-the-rights-of-persons-with-disabilities.html

United Nations, Convention on the Rights of the Child. (1989). Retrieved from https://treaties.un.org/Pages/ViewDetails.aspx?src=TREATY&mtdsg_no=IV-11&chapter=4&lang=en

U.S. Department of Education: Office for Civil Rights. (October 26, 1992). *Deaf students education services.* Retrieved from www2.ed.gov/about/offices/list/ocr/docs/hq9806.html

U.S. Department of Education. (2016). Part B State Performance Plan (SPP) and Annual Performance Report (APR) Part B indicator measurement table. *OMB, 1820-0624,* 4, question 5(c). Retrieved from www2.ed.gov/policy/speced/guid/idea/bapr/2014/2014-part-b-measurement-table.pdf

U.S. Department of Education: Office of Special Education and Rehabilitative Services. (January 9, 2017). *Dear colleague letter related to preschool least restrictive environment.* Retrieved from www2.ed.gov/policy/speced/guid/idea/memosdcltrs/preschool-lre-dcl-1-10-17.pdf

U.S. Department of Education and U.S. Department of Justice. (2014). *Frequently asked questions on effective communication for students with hearing, vision, or speech disabilities in public elementary and secondary schools.* Retrieved from www2.ed.gov/policy/speced/guid/idea/memosdcltrs/doe-doj-eff-comm-faqs.pdf

U.S. Department of Justice and Department of Education: Office for Civil Rights. (November 2014). *Guidelines and frequently asked questions on effective communication.* Retrieved from www.ada.gov/doe_doj_eff_comm/doe_doj_eff_comm_faqs.htm

U.S. Department of Justice: Civil Rights Division: Disability Rights Section. (January 2014). *Effective communication*. Retrieved from www.ada.gov/effective-comm.htm

Watkins, S., Pittman, P., & Walden, B. (2008). The deaf mentor experimental project for young children who are deaf and their families. *American Annals of the Deaf, 143*(1).

White, K. (2017). The evolution of EHDI: From concept to standard of care. In L. Schmeltz (Ed.), *NCHAM eBook: A guide for early hearing detection and intervention* (Chapter 1). Retrieved from http://infanthearing.org/ehdi-ebook/

Yell, M.L. (2006). Least restrictive environment, mainstreaming, and inclusion. In *The law and special education* (pp. 310–314). London, U.K.: Pearson Education, Inc. Retrieved from www.education.com/reference/article/mainstreaming-inclusion/

Index

Note: Page numbers in **bold** and *italics* indicate tables and figures, respectively.